D0138659

Make 'em Laugh!

Make 'em Laugh!

American Humorists of the 20th and 21st Centuries

ZEKE JARVIS, EDITOR

An Imprint of ABC-CLIO, LLC
Santa Barbara, California • Denver, Colorado

Library of Congress Cataloging-in-Publication Data

Make 'em laugh! : American humorists of the 20th and 21st centuries / Zeke Jarvis, editor.
pages cm
Includes bibliographical references and index.
ISBN 978–1–4408–2994–9 (cloth : alk. paper) — ISBN 978–1–4408–2995–6 (ebook)
1. Humorists, American—20th century—Biography—Dictionaries. 2. Humorists, American—21st century—Biography—Dictionaries. 3. Authors, American—20th century—Biography—Dictionaries. 4. Authors, American—21st century—Biography—Dictionaries. 5. Comedians—United States—Biography—Dictionaries. I. Jarvis, Zeke, editor.
PS430.M36 2015
817′.509—dc23 [B] 2014040154

ISBN: 978–1–4408–2994–9
EISBN: 978–1–4408–2995–6

19 18 17 16 15 1 2 3 4 5

This book is also available on the World Wide Web as an eBook.
Visit www.abc-clio.com for details.

Greenwood
An Imprint of ABC-CLIO, LLC

ABC-CLIO, LLC
130 Cremona Drive, P.O. Box 1911
Santa Barbara, California 93116-1911

This book is printed on acid-free paper ∞

Manufactured in the United States of America

Contents

Preface

This work represents the culmination of decades of careful study and practice of humor. Special thanks go to the contributors: Dr. Stephen Powers, Brian Davis, and Kristen Franz. While this text represents a thorough study of American humorists, an exhaustive study would be impossible because of the pace with which the canon of American humor expands. As such, this book should serve as an effective launching point for future studies into an exciting and growing field.

Introduction

Humor has not received the amount of scholarly attention that other forms of art such as tragedy or horror have. Indeed, it might be assumed that scholars are afraid of analyzing humor. The terms "serious" and "humorous" are often seen as opposites, which might feed into the lack of "serious" investigation of humor. When they do approach humor, many scholars might discuss how humor is unstable or unpredictable, or might give a description of why a pun was clever (often in a footnote that explains a reference that today's readers do not understand). Other scholars simply skip talking about humor at all, focusing instead on more traditionally investigated literary topics, even when the piece that they are discussing is genuinely funny.

Of course, scholars might also have good reasons for not spending time talking about humor. E. B. White might have put it best when he compared humor to a frog, saying that when someone tries to dissect it, "it dies on the table, and you don't learn much from it"—meaning that trying to analyze humor does more to make it stop being fun than it does to teach us anything. But that does not automatically mean that we should not think about humor. Instead, it might tell us that the best way to learn about humor is to be exposed to it—that is, to read funny things, to hear funny people talk, and to watch funny movies and skits in the same way that a biologist might study a frog by observing it its habitat and watching it move instead of trying to look at it when it is already dead. Unlike some forms of learning that are laid out with clear rules (it might be tempting to say "algebra" would be an example, but many readers might feel as if this subject lacks clear rules), the lack of hard-and-fast rules in comedy might very well make the most effective training a careful observation of humor.

That said, to get a full view of the subject of humor, this text tries to take a very broad view of humor so as to see as many different aspects of humor as possible. While this text does not necessarily include the complete humorous pieces themselves (although it provides some summaries of books and selected quotations from stand-up routines, movies, and television shows), it does give readers a good sense of where to turn for some of the best and most noteworthy humor produced in the United States in the last century.In fact, this book's focus is not simply "humor" as an entire body of work. Instead, it addresses American humor, which is often different in nature and execution from British, Eastern European, or Latin American forms of humor, which might often be characterized as subtle, dark, or offbeat, respectively. While American humor can be all of these things (America's cultural diversity can be seen in many of its cultural forms, and humor is definitely one of those forms), it also has some unique characteristics. Thus this book is an encyclopedia of both the forms of humor and the history and culture of 20th- and early 21st-century America. From the shock and horror expressed by Edna St. Vincent Millay and Dorothy Parker over the coming of World War II to the celebration of absurdity that can be found in present-day satirists like Stephen Colbert and *The Onion*, the concerns of various eras of U.S. history can easily be tracked through the style and content of America's prominent humorists. Looking at the times and places that helped shape these works should add to the appreciation of each humorist's significance and imagination. Indeed, one of humor's strengths is its sense of playfulness, which can make humor the perfect vehicle for artistic innovation, because it is not limited by the seriousness of some other art forms.

With this focus on artistic breakthroughs in mind, although this text will definitely examine humor and it certainly values humor, this encyclopedia largely examines the issues of craft and technique found in each artist's work as well as the social significance of these artists and their work. That said, its primary focus remains humor, so every entry will balance honoring the humor of a given artist with recognizing the overall historical significance of the artist's cultural contribution.

The Dawn of the Century

New technology will always affect the way people communicate, and with each new form of communication, humorists find a way to play with the way that we have communicated in previous generations. Still, even as they push us away with one kind of strangeness or playfulness, they often try to pull readers in with something more familiar. In the early decades of the 20th century, humorists such as Damon Runyon and Anita Loos observed and wrote about the worlds they saw, bringing the underworld (in the case of Runyon) and the seedy underbelly of fame (in the case of Loos) to a larger, mainstream audience. While these two writers introduced new experiences and new types of characters to pop culture, they held onto familiar kinds of humor like puns, buffoons, and ridiculous plots.

Beyond new types or classes of characters and situations, American humorists found places to be a good source of comedy. At the beginning of the 20th century, there was still a strong focus on regionalism in literature—an influence stemming from Mark Twain and other humorists of earlier generations. This regionalism would continue with writers like Eudora Welty and Flannery O'Connor, two Southern writers, but it was also seen in the work of Dorothy Parker and other members of the Algonquin Roundtable, whose quick wit and high-class references were clearly shaped by their time on the East Coast, particularly in the New York City area. As people became more mobile and magazines were more easily delivered across the country, the portrayal of specific groups or places became popular with both readers who had once lived in those places and the many people who liked to see those places poked fun of in print.

Of course, humor was not just found in print. Even before the turn of the century, vaudeville (the set of traveling theater, humor, and musical acts appealing to working-class audiences) was going strong. Although technology would affect vaudeville's performers when movies gained a larger audience, around the turn of the century one-liners, wacky characters, and dirty jokes were being perfected in ways that would later be used by performers ranging from Sid Caesar to the cast of *The Simpsons*. Vaudeville also served as a training ground for many performers, including the likes of George Burns, the Marx Brothers, Buster Keaton, and W. C. Fields.

The Great Wars

Although little attention is often paid to the link between war and humor, the impact of World War I and World War II on American culture was so deep and so broad that it clearly influenced humor. Some of these effects can be seen directly, as in the antiwar poems "Apostrophe to Man" and "I Sing of Olaf Glad and Big" by Edna St. Vincent Millay and e. e. cummings, respectively. Other works, such as Gertrude Stein's playful writing, sought to challenge the sense of certainty and authority that some artists believed could lead to wars and hatred. War also had an impact on some humorists. For example, Dorothy Parker and Robert Benchley, who voiced outspoken criticism of the wars, were blackballed or had other negative reactions to their work. Still, Parker and others kept to their beliefs, not caving into the pressure of mainstream, patriotic American culture.Reactions to the world wars went in the other direction as well, often with humorists portraying the people of other nations in very stereotypical ways. This was similar to the stereotypes or caricatures used by vaudeville performers, but a bit different in that it took place on a larger scale and had a more clearly political purpose. There were also appeals to simpler or more pure, innocent approaches to humor during the time of the wars and the Great Depression. Child star Shirley Temple rose to stardom during the Depression and continued to provide cute and funny performances for many years. Whether it led to breaking boundaries or a longing to return to innocence and simplicity, the impact of the wars upon the American humor landscape was significant and lasting.

Humor and Social Class: The Attack on Authority

The challenges to American safety and the country's problematic isolation were not the only sources of discomfort and anxiety in American culture. In the era of *Father Knows Best* and *Leave It to Beaver*, families were portrayed as stable and happy, and fathers were depicted as professionals who were supported by satisfied, nurturing wives and idolized by mostly well-behaved children. With the rise of shows like *The Honeymooners*, however, men were not necessarily financially successful, and they were certainly not considered moral or intellectual authorities. Outspoken wives would make fun of their buffoonish husbands, and the husbands were often caught flatfooted, to the delight of some audience members and the discomfort of others. If the father was no longer seen as the clear and justified leader of the family, and the mother was no longer the demure, purely nurturing figure in the family, then the family—one of the core concepts of American culture—was no longer a stable source of comfort. This evolving environment was met with equal parts of humor and genuine frustration.For men on television, the first line of targets usually comprised blue-collar workers. While humor was eventually directed toward professionals, as on *The Cosby Show* or *Empty Nest*, the early challenges to the husband or father of a family were made acceptable to mass audiences by focusing the attacks on less educated members of the working class, such as a bus driver in the case of Ralph Kramden, a manual laborer in the case of *The Flintstones*, and an ethnic minority on *I Love Lucy*. In addition to not taking on more educated and wealthy males, this perspective also fit the mold of vaudevillian humor, which used oversized, buffoonish characters and appealed to working-class audiences.

The influence of this development also can be seen in the self-deprecating humor later demonstrated by talk show hosts like David Letterman and Conan O'Brien. While Letterman has consistently denied that he was trying to create a parody or satire of late night talk shows, his approach of using crew members instead of professional performers to do bits instead and to ridicule his own jokes in the midst of telling them is very similar in both spirit and structure to the post-World War II humor. Of course, these more contemporary hosts had their own influences—comics like Bob Hope, Jack Benny, and Phyllis Diller, all of whom often joked about themselves—but the satirical approach to hosting itself exhibited by Letterman in particular can be traced back to the slow but significant shift in the sense of authority imbued in prominent television personalities.

War and Scandal

During Vietnam War and the Watergate scandal, the U.S. public's confidence in its government and its leaders faltered, and the rage and anxiety felt from these crises brought about another shift in humor. Rebellious shows and humorists like the Smothers Brothers gave voice to the anger and disappointment with politicians. This approach was particularly evident with figures like Pat Paulsen, who spoofed politicians with his ridiculous claims and total lack of charm and personality. The Smothers Brothers also undercut the sense of moral superiority claimed by authority figures with their frequent barbs directed at network censors. The pair also gave voice to the counterculture with their references to drugs and refusal to support the war. Other performers and writers were likewise outspoken about their disagreement with the government and the status quo. Humorists such as Harlan Ellison, Norman Lear, and Kurt Vonnegut provided a voice for Americans uncertain about the nation's future with their satirical portrayals of various authority figures or their outright disdain for the ruling class.These challenges were not always aggressive, however. During the 1970s, a number of important breakthroughs occurred in American comedy that were more about opening doors than breaking down walls. Many sitcoms (situation comedies) in particular broke through in that decade. *Taxi*, *Soap*, and *The Mary Tyler Moore Show* all challenged boundaries and had a sense of experimentation. Whether the shows featured a homosexual character, as happened with Billy Crystal in *Soap*, or let a female character be strong and independent, the performances of 1970s humorists both mirrored and (in some ways) led the shifts in cultural norms during that decade. Likewise, print humorists like Hunter S. Thompson, Donald Barthelme, and Mike Royko challenged the status quo in terms of both literary and political expectations. While much of 1970s culture is sometimes seen as lacking in weight, the groundbreaking approaches of these writers and shows often helped shine a light on the rights and interests of oppressed or overlooked groups. Many of the established taboos, such as drugs, sexual promiscuity, and embracing the lower class's perspective, were taken down by the daring but fascinating work of humorists writing and performing in this decade, and many of their efforts are still being explored by humorists today.

Riding High

If the 1970s were a time of challenges and changes, then the 1980s—the "Me Decade"—might be seen as an ironic return to tradition and stability. Rather than focusing on personal freedoms, many pieces of pop culture addressed fitting in and getting ahead in the financial world. While earlier generations had challenged the father and other authority figures, the conservative optimism of President Ronald Reagan was rooted in the idea that an emphasis on traditional values and structures like church and family would help return America to greatness, particularly against the perceived threat of communism that many associated with the Soviet Union. Even so, comedy remained one of the few arenas that allowed people to explore the boundaries and anxieties of the nation's social pressures. John Hughes's screenplay *Mr. Mom* flipped the typical family, but it made the flip in a way that was funny while still understanding the root of this change. *The Cosby Show* held up a model of a family of African Americans with professional parents and a stable home life. Edgy comics like George Carlin and Sam Kinison found large audiences despite (or perhaps because of) their obscene language and challenging views.

That said, not all comedy during the 1980s was edgy or challenging. Performers like Jay Leno, who often served as guest host on *The Tonight Show*, generally catered to older and more conservative audiences, playing for safe and predictable laughs to achieve commercial success. Even edgy humorists like Sam Kinison mined prejudices that were usually associated with conservative viewpoints, such as a lack of respect for women in Kinison's case, in their comedy. The influence of these approaches can be seen in later comedians like Andrew Dice Clay and Dane Cook. Other forms of comedy also emerged in addition to conservative and cutting humor. More oddball comics like Judy Tenuta and Emo Phillips kept audiences on their toes, and Robert Townsend, with his move *The Hollywood Shuffle*, gave a voice to the frustration that African Americans felt with their still limited portrayals in pop culture.

Indeed, while the United States has been known as a melting pot—that is, thought of as a country that accepts all races, creeds, and religions so long as they all become "American"—the idea of a single and homogenous culture started to break down as the 1980s blurred into the 1990s. In its humor perhaps as much as anywhere, America shows how different and unpredictable its culture can be.

While strong representations of liberal or progressive political beliefs in humor can certainly be cited, as with performers like Mort Sahl and Lenny Bruce and writers like Harlan Ellison and Kurt Vonnegut, there has also consistently been a representation of conservative humor, with humorists like P. J. O'Rourke and Andrew Dice Clay. In addition, a wide variety of humorists have been interpreted as holding all manner of positions on the political spectrum. Flannery O'Connor, for instance, has been seen as both close-minded and conservative in her allegedly unthinking defense of Catholicism, yet also perceived as potentially challenging Catholicism and, more clearly, undercutting only certain aspects of organized religion. Owing to her irony and satire, O'Connor's success as a humorist is precisely what makes it so difficult to clearly determine what her viewpoint is. What *is* clear, however, is that America's humor and its responses to its humorists are difficult to pin down.

Beyond the large spectrum of political views held by different American humorists, some humorists have evinced opinions that might seem contradictory. Figures like Hunter S. Thompson, whose comments are both blunt and bizarre, challenge readers and critics with their distinctive positions. Simultaneously promoting gun rights (generally seen as a conservative cause) and the legalization of any number of drugs (generally seen as a liberal cause), Thompson's positions have such a complex and distinctive tension among them that some of the humor of his work comes simply from readers trying to tease a coherent point of view out of the wildly divergent opinions he articulates and trying to determine what his true views and experiences are. In an odd way, Thompson's freewheeling attitudes can be seen as a perfect representation of humor and culture during the 1980s.

New Media, New Critical Approaches: Television and Cinema

As critics and casual viewers or readers have become more sophisticated in their analysis and enjoyment of humorous texts, humorists have begun to incorporate the techniques of many critics into their works so as to upset the total separation found in the reader/writer dynamic. Techniques like the self-referentiality of *Family Guy* and *The Simpsons* (among many others),the breaking of the fourth wall (usually by having one of the characters turn directly to the camera and address the audience) found in Kevin Smith movies, and the boundary breaking of the expectations and even understanding of what a performance is in Andy Kauffman's life and art have demonstrated that American humor always finds ways to push critics, forcing them to find new ways to talk about what is surprising and meaningful. One other reason why humor can embrace an experimental approach is that a moment of quiet or a sharp failure can often lead to laughs if the performer knows how to react. This flexible principle has made some major figures in American humor (David Letterman, in particular, with his seeming satirical approach to talk shows) almost failure proof, because good humor succeeds and poor humor, paradoxically, opens the door for success (as Letterman jokes about his own failures). Of course, not all critics and fans agree with this approach or analysis, but even some of the more challenging figures like Letterman (who is now generally seen as mainstream, owing to his role as a mainstay of late-night television) have garnered popular and critical success. At the same time, this strangeness has been picked up and pushed even further by more challenging programs and movies like the shows on *Adult Swim* or offbeat comic strips like *Bizarro*.

New Beginnings: Shifts in Acting Careers

Another innovation that came into mainstream culture was the rise of "serious" actors and respected figures like Christopher Walken and Robert De Niro taking roles in funny films. Conversely, many comedic actors like Will Ferrell and Jim Carrey began to take on more dramatic work, often to critical acclaim. Of course, many actors did succeed in this transition. Adam Sandler's striking but largely forgotten turn in *Punch Drunk Love*, Leslie Nielsen's work in his later movies and Mike Myers's role in *Studio 54* were largely met with unfavorable responses by critics, popular audiences, or both. Nevertheless, with James Woods having a semiregular role on *Family Guy*, James Spader's and William Shatner's well-received turns on *Boston Legal*, and many other examples, the crossing of dramatic and comedic boundaries has been easier than ever.

Arguably, the boundaries started to crumble once shows like *Saturday Night Live* and, much later, *Mad TV* began to rise in popularity. Dramatic actors and respected musicians often were featured in comedic performances as they strove to promote their more serious projects through their appearances on these shows. As national audiences began to see these actors participate and succeed in humorous projects, departing from their typical work became less risky and more rewarding. Indeed, actors like Alec Baldwin, who performed successfully on *Saturday Night Live*, have gone on to have prominent roles on sitcoms; indeed, Baldwin's comedic turn on *30 Rock* may now be more well known than any of his serious work.

Just as the border between serious acting and comedic acting has eroded, so the balance between literary writing and genre or comedic writing has also deteriorated. Writers like Joe Queenan, who is best known for his nonliterary writing, including both humorous sketches and reviews of movies or other forms of pop culture, have also written literary memoirs or have published works in literary magazines, as Queenan did with *ELM* and other small, literary magazines. Likewise, well-respected literary writers such as Michael Chabon, Jonathan Lethem, and Sherman Alexie have begun to work in genres outside the literary mainstream, such as science fiction or magical realism. In turn, this flexibility has allowed them to inject a greater degree of humor into their work.

The Internet Age

As new forms of social media have made their way into mainstream culture, the nature of popularity and the way America interacts with popular culture have changed. This evolution has had a clear impact on both the critical reception and commercial success of various forms of comedy. One of the most striking examples is *Family Guy*, which was canceled by the Fox Network, only to be brought back after DVD sales indicated significant fan support for the show. Other shows have also been brought back, albeit sometimes by a different network. *Futurama*, for example, was also canceled by Fox. After strong DVD sales of the television show and the subsequent straight-to-DVD movies (along with the strength of syndicated episodes), the Cartoon Network began to produce new original episodes of the show. Likewise, *Arrested Development*, also canceled by Fox and supported by various petitions and fan clubs, was brought back by Netflix, though not to the same critical acclaim that its original run received.Even if a number of these consumer-originated efforts have not been answered with unmitigated success, the influence of social media and DVD sales on network support for television humorists is undeniable. Of course, this development has not been solely limited to television. As with the TV shows mentioned previously, a number of movies have found a second life on DVD. In particular, cult favorites like *Army of Darkness*, *Big Trouble in Little China*, and *Caddyshack* have enjoyed an even greater presence on VHS and DVD than they did in their original theatrical releases. This factor, along with the rising practice of quoting individual lines that seems to be inherent to the nature of condensed, brief communications that fit Twitter, Facebook, and other social media outlets, helps to give support to cult or marginalized humorists in a way that simply would not have been possible in a previous era.

Beyond the cult aspect of some forms of humor, comedy has, like many other forms of culture, have become increasingly specialized.*Foxtrot*, a popular newspaper comic strip, regularly employs math humor, as do shows like *Futurama*, whose writing staff has people holding degrees in mathematics and physics. In a different area of specialization, *Dilbert*, while not enjoyed exclusively by businesspeople, clearly is geared toward people who can access the experiences and discourse of the office workplace. In addition, an entire field of humor, the Internet meme, typically focuses upon shared marginal references and experiences. Often found on Facebook, memes can be quickly and easily passed from person to person. Given the specialized nature of much Internet communication, memes have gained in popularity. Moreover, they have helped shape the nature of humor, often relying upon puns and putting images from pop culture near each other. Examples include comparing political figures to symbols of evil like Darth Vader or Sauron from the *Lord of the Rings* trilogy. This cross-referential approach to satirical humor has, in turn, influenced a number of humorous forms outside of the meme. For example, *The Daily Show* so regularly played the imperial march music associated with Darth Vader whenever the show's participants talked about former Vice President Dick Cheney that when Cheney's wife, Lynne, went on the show, she brought a Darth Vader doll onto the show.

Although specialized humor is certainly apparent in contemporary comedy, broader forms of comedy persist. Humorists like Jay Leno and the cast and crew of *Saturday Night Live* continue to take on major, common cultural figures like Paris Hilton or Donald Trump, playing humor for safe and sometimes predictable comedy rather than engaging in specialized work that might leave broader audiences scratching their heads instead of laughing. America's comedic landscape is, therefore, likely to remain as diverse and varied as its population, encompassing both humor that is built for small and specific audiences and broader jokes that anyone can get. Given the wide variety of media and large number of outlets in American pop culture, there seems to be few limits to the volume and types of humor that can be produced and consumed.

Section I: Literature

While literature is often discussed as an entirely serious pursuit, much of America's greatest literature is wonderfully humorous, whether the comedy is the driving force in it or not. In the first half of the 20th century, humorists like Dorothy Parker and Anita Loos made fun of the wealthy by showing the hypocrisy of their high society behaviors as contrasted with some of their more basic drives, such as drinking and the desire for sex. But these portrayals were not simply intended to attack polite society; they also often served as a forum for groups without a voice to express their anxiety or frustration. Parker's short piece, "The Waltz," shows that not all women enjoyed the attention of men. This social satire, with its exaggerated characters and scathing observations, was clearly indebted to earlier writers like Mark Twain, as were regional writers like Flannery O'Connor and Eudora Welty. Many Southern writers put on display the problems that arise out of slavery and the unequal distribution of wealth. Of course, this type of hypocrisy was not unique to the South. Writers like John Cheever often mined the upper class as a source of humor, particularly focusing on the eccentric behavior and ridiculous expectations of wealthy families.

As the century progressed, other groups followed suit as they began to be accepted into the literary canon. From Philip Roth's sometimes harsh portrayal of Jewish American culture to Sherman Alexie's brutal examination of addiction on Native American reservations, ethnic minority writers began to find their own brands of humor, which have added a striking and lively voice to the literary conversation. While some critics feel that these dark brands of humor are too blistering in their attacks, many readers appreciate the fact that these humorists take on potentially touchy subject matter (such as race relations and substance abuse) in a frank and blunt way that makes it difficult for critics to avoid discussing the real issue. Unlike the stereotypical portrayals of members of the upper class found in the work of Cheever or Parker, the caricaturing of minorities in these schools of literature has been the topic of a great deal of debate. Some scholars and readers feel that portrayals that totally ignore stereotypes would be unrealistic, whereas others suggest that the use of any stereotypes allows readers to oversimplify a text, seeing it just as "funny" instead of carefully examining the work. As with writers not primarily known for their humor, the pressure to either emphasize their culture with their work or try to move away from the limits of only showing their culture is clearly felt by many ethnic writers in a way that many white writers have not been forced to consider. While many critics appreciate bringing new writers and cultures into the conversation, there has been some pushback within some of the cultures to the expectation that all writers of color write about characters of color.

As ethnic writers worked to gain more mainstream acceptance, many white literary writers began to turn their attention to experimental approaches to writing and genres that had once been seen as being beneath literary work. From David Eggers breaking the fourth wall in his works of creative nonfiction to Michael Chabon and Jonathan Lethem writing sci-fi (science fiction) and fantasy, many literary writers have challenged literary expectations without sacrificing a sense of depth and complexity in their work. In fact, both Eggers and Chabon have also written scripts for large-budget movies, which had sometimes been looked down upon by previous generations of literary writers. It is worth noting, however, that not all contemporary writers clearly or aggressively break boundaries. Nevertheless, even some of the less literary writers employ unconventional narrative strategies that demonstrate the influence of postmodernism. Chuck Palahniuk, for instance, echoes Kurt Vonnegut's repetition of phrases (compare "So it goes" in Vonnegut's *Slaughterhouse V* and "I'm counting one, I'm counting two" in Palahniuk's *Lullaby*) and use of characters who are less noble than conventional heroes, clearly rejecting many traditional aspects of the novel. Indeed, both Vonnegut and Palahniuk challenge the traditional approach to first-person narration. Several other authors, including Chabon and Ellis, use first-person narrators in a way that is in some ways traditional and in other ways on the cutting edge.

Like the ethnic writers who struggled with their roles in the literary canon in the 20th century, many female writers began to break out of restrictive roles in their writing and portrayal of female characters. Whether it was the very abstract and challenging work of writers like Gertrude Stein or the skewering of traditional expectations seen in the work of Eudora Welty and Anita Loos, female writers employed a wide variety of approaches to humor. Of course, as with ethnic minority writers, this spectrum of approaches to writing and humor makes it impossible to put a singular stamp on women writers or humorists. Some critics argue that the difficult position to which women are often relegated to can give the best women writers a perspective that lends itself to the complexity and subtlety of literary writing. Of course, this view is difficult to test and is certainly no justification for the oppression of women.

To move beyond the issue of subcategories of writers, the impact of the two world wars was felt across all races, genders, and classes. As Adorno has said, "It is barbaric to write poetry after Auschwitz," meaning that it can seem challenging, if not intimidating, to put humorous words on the page after the horrors of the world wars and the terrorist attacks of September 11, 2001. That said, the pressures of war, economic hardships, and intercultural tensions often led people to seek humor as a positive outlet. Likewise, the Vietnam War's impact on the United States' sense of patriotism and trust in traditional sources of authority has been felt in contemporary humor. Writers like Palahniuk have directly confronted the changes in U.S. attitudes toward war and coming of age with works that see men frustrated but unable to find a positive outlet for those frustrations. Other writers, including Don DeLillo, have examined changes in gender roles and the family unit in more subtle but still surprising wars. Vietnam itself figures prominently in the work of many writers, including Alexie, who looks at what it means for Native Americans to serve in the military for a country that often oppresses or alienates them. A similar concern features in Kurt Vonnegut's masterwork, *Slaughterhouse V*, marking how dramatically the American attitude toward Vietnam War differed from how Americans viewed World War II.

Finally, while all of the writers included in the literary section publish primarily in print, the rise of digital media has impacted a number of the more recent writers. Writers like Lethem and Chabon have picked up on DeLillo's sense of pop and junk culture in America, particularly the way that academics incorporate low culture into their works. Both writers examine the absurdity of the emphasis people place upon childhood and childish topics, discussing fandoms and other trends that have become more common in the digital age. Also, many of the contemporary writers, such as Alexie, maintain blogs as a way to promote their writing and to voice their stance on a variety of issues, ranging from literature to politics. This form of communication is more immediate and has a broader audience than many conventional methods for achieving prominence, such as touring in support of the writer's work. The reliance upon touring (often focusing on readings done at college campuses) and the rising popularity of YouTube videos have led many more writers to incorporate a sense of humor and playful performance into many of their pieces. This can be seen not only in the printed pieces that comedic literary writers have published, but also in the rise of practices like slam poetry, which, although not always humorous, incorporate playful and performative elements. The latter events also feature the keen sense of rhythm that is often present in comedic writing.

In addition to creating their own literature, many literary writers have consistently served as literary critics or editors. Writers like Dorothy Parker have wielded tremendous power in their reviews of other writers, and often for good reason. Parker's reviews of Hemingway's work not only helped that author break into national prominence, but also put him above writers who have since been largely forgotten, demonstrating the accuracy of her critical views. In addition, writers like Dave Eggers have helped to bring many writers into print, which has in turn shaped cultural tastes. This assistance has taken the form of book-length publications put out by *McSweeney's* as well as literary magazine issues and anthologies that link established humorists and writers like Sherman Alexie and Harlan Ellison with up-and-coming writers like Chris Offutt and Kelly Link. Offutt and Link had been very successful in literary magazines and publications from small presses, but had not broken through into mainstream or national prominence. Although not all of the writers included in this volume have broken through into a mainstream readership, collectively they have consistently published in noteworthy magazines and books from well-respected presses. As creative writing programs and literary magazines have developed within colleges and universities, the link between critics and writers has become very strong. That has not yet meant, though, that the humor of literary writing has become too difficult or obscure for common readers.

While some writers like Donald Barthelme seem to gear their work toward more purely academic audiences, many—like Robert Olen Butler in his work *Tabloid Dreams* and Richard Russo with his effective but more plain narrative style—use ideas and approaches that welcome a wide audience. With this point in mind, it may be helpful to think of humorous literary writing as filling a spectrum that runs from the more straightforward, open style to the more niche approaches to playfulness. This diversity shows the depth and richness of humor in the American literary canon.

ALEXIE, SHERMAN (1966–)

Sherman Alexie was born on the Spokane Indian Reservation in Wellpinit, Washington. When he was born, he had fluid on his brain, leading to serious concerns for his health. Doctors did not expect him to live without severe mental disabilities. Nevertheless, Alexie survived and demonstrated a good deal of intelligence. He grew up on the reservation, and much of his work is heavily informed by what he witnessed there as well as by his father's struggles with alcoholism, along with his own struggles with the same issue.

As a child, Alexie excelled academically and eventually left the reservation to further his education. When he moved off the reservation, he spent time as one of the only Native American students in a primarily white school. This experience enhanced his awareness of the impact of culture and the disturbing consequences of ignorance and prejudice from multiple sides of racial inequality. After graduating from high school, Alexie went to Gonzaga University, where he studied medicine and law, but eventually dropped out. He returned to college at Washington State University, where he began to study writing in a formal program. It was then that he wrote and published *The Business of Fancydancing*, which helped to launch his success.

Sherman Alexie is well known for his daring portrayal of life on Native American reservations. He also has made waves for his frank discussions of sexual desire in his young adult work. (Getty Images)

Alexie's early publications, such as *The Business of Fancydancing*, quickly set the tone for his work. His writing combines a sense of sadness with a sense of humor, giving it layers of depth and allowing Alexie to alternate between brutal honesty and comic relief in his examination of contemporary life. Arguably, this sort of approach is not found in more strictly earnest works by other writers focusing on similar struggles. This trend has continued in Alexie's prose works, such as *The Lone Ranger and Tonto Fistfight in Heaven,* which is arguably his most well-known and critically acclaimed work of fiction. While much of his work involves mythical or magical elements, such as "A Good Story" or the anthropomorphism in "Do Not Go Gentle," where "Mr. Grief" is a living entity that controls Alexie and his wife at times, it is in his later work that he fully engages in genre fiction. Specifically, he writes in the young adult mode in the novel *The Absolutely True Diary of a Part-Time Indian*. Critics and readers have generally been receptive to both his more literary and more genre-based work.

An important feature of Alexie's work that enhances his humor is the juxtaposition of various traditions of storytelling found in his works. His creative nonfiction piece, "Do Not Go Gentle," incorporates pieces of Native American culture, including the power of song and ritual; details taken from his son's medical issues; and conflicts and controversies from contemporary American life, such as his use of the sex toy shop near his son's hospital. This weaving together of seemingly disparate contexts is both humorous and in keeping with a Native American trickster sense of disruption of stable categories. Alexie's willingness to step over boundaries and intermix images and modes of storytelling from various cultures and traditions makes him a leader in contemporary literary writing and a favorite of many critics and readers, who appreciate his thoughtful playfulness. This characteristic also runs through his short fiction, screenplays, and poetry, helping him to break through into mainstream culture while still maintaining a clear understanding and valuing of Native American culture.

Because of this complexity, his strong use of humor, and his clear reverence for literature from many traditions, critical reception of Alexie's work has generally been favorable, citing his humor and bravery in confronting very troubling material. Still, there are detractors. The two core complaints against Alexie's work are that he employs stereotypes and that he gives a sense of darkness without tempering it with a genuine sense of hope. The first complaint is often lodged by scholars such as Louis Owens and more experimental Native American authors such as Gerald Vizenor. Alexie has responded by stating that an honest appraisal of reservation life is more helpful to younger Native Americans than a work that deconstructs stereotypes but is largely inaccessible to most audiences. Different critics engage the second complaint in different fashions. While the vast majority of critics recognize the darkness of Alexie's work, some feel that his darkness accurately reflects the reality he has experienced and continues to examine. Others suggest that the humor within his work is meant to allow him to confront the dark subject matter in a more palatable way so that readers can also confront, discuss, and move past or examine issues concerning his characters.

Alexie straddles both the literary and nonliterary brands of humor, having his work published in respected literary venues like *The New Yorker* and *McSweeney's* but also regularly posting short humorous messages on his blog, winning poetry slam competitions, and going on speaking tours. He has also appeared in one of the movies produced from his screenplay, *The Business of Fancydancing*. In that film, he played a minor role as a Native American on the reservation to which a successful poet returns, providing an interesting dynamic as a more stereotypical counterpart to the poet, who represents the "actual" Alexie. This film was noteworthy in that it shared the title of his collection of poetry, but was more of an examination of Alexie's post-book success than an adaptation of any single poem from the book.

The movie *Smoke Signals* also took an unconventional approach, incorporating elements from a number of stories from *The Lone Ranger and Tonto Fistfight in Heaven* rather than expanding a single story.

Alexie serves as an important writer, humorist, and representative of Native American culture. Scholars continue to examine his work, and he has enjoyed tremendous success as an author and performer. While Alexie has definite and vociferous critics, his defenders are numerous, and he often directly engages his critics, publishing columns and speaking in response to what he perceives as attackers. Alexie has taught and studied in academia and his work is enjoyed by a large body of readers.

Further Reading

Alexie, Sherman. *The Lone Ranger and Tonto Fistfight in Heaven*. New York: Grove Press, 1993.

Bergland, Jeff, and Roush, Jan, eds. *Sherman Alexie: A Collection of Critical Essays*. Salt Lake City: University of Utah Press, 2010.

Lewis, Leon. *Sherman Alexie: Critical Insights*. Ipswich, MA: Salem Press, 2011.

Owens, Louis. *Mixedblood Messages*. Norman: University of Oklahoma Press, 2001.

Zeke Jarvis

BARTHELME, DONALD (1931–1989)

Donald Barthelme was born in 1931 in Philadelphia, although his family lived in Texas for much of his childhood. Barthelme served in the army in 1953, fighting in the Korean War. He went to the University of Houston both before and after his time in the army. Barthelme's brothers, Frederick and Steven, are also acclaimed fiction writers. Donald Barthelme was married a total of four times and had two daughters, one from his second marriage and one from his fourth. In addition to his work as a writer, Barthelme worked as an editor, editing *Location* and cofounding *Fiction*. Barthelme died in 1989 after suffering from throat cancer. A significant amount of his work was published posthumously.

Barthelme is well known for his incorporation of philosophical ideas in his writing. Barthelme has a particular knack for examining complex and sophisticated ideas while still employing a vibrant sense of absurdity. His work often takes a fearless approach to life and death, the human body, and sexual relations. Works like "The School" and "Miss Mandible and Me" take approaches to serious issues that are ridiculous, insightful, and daring. Generally writing short pieces of fiction, Barthelme explodes conventional narrative by having earnest characters work through madcap situations and esoteric conversations. This eschewing of plot helps Barthelme's transgressive approach to writing focus on ideas rather than on character or conflict. Much of Barthelme's work was published in *The New Yorker*, whose well-read audience would be able to access Barthelme's obscure or challenging examinations of philosophical concepts.

Although Barthelme consistently includes highly sophisticated philosophical questions and debates as undercurrents in his writing, he clearly is unafraid of incorporating base or vulgar elements, discussing sexual desire and sex acts as well as acts of incredible violence. This gives his work an even greater complexity, balancing both high and low forms of art, as even some of the characters in his works do. Peterson in "A Shower of Gold," for instance, struggles to achieve prominence as a sculptor while also appearing on a television game show. The breadth of properties and details included in an incredibly short space gives Barthelme's writing a complexity and unpredictability that enhances the humor, much like the similarly offbeat and short work of Russell Edson.

Perhaps even more challenging and striking are Barthelme's novels. Like his shorter work, they often leave behind traditional notions of plot to explore a long strand of references over the course of the book. In the same way that he explores philosophical ideas in his short work, Barthelme plays with well-known tales. For example, his *Snow White* is not so much a retelling as a reshaping of the classic story to dazzling comic effect.

Critical reception to Barthelme's work has been mixed. Many critics feel that his work is playful for the sake of tearing down conventional language, but indicate that its refusal to suggest any positive model for language and ideology leaves readers with nothing to work with and with a distinct feeling of despair. While his critics are numerous and vociferous, Barthelme has also received widespread critical acclaim from astute scholars who see influences from Franz Kafka and Jorge Luis Borges in his consistent use of absurd settings and conceits to reflect upon the challenging and seemingly foolish aspects of culture and society. While Barthelme's work is not likely to ever achieve a large mainstream readership, his daring and sophisticated pieces have assured him his place in the literary canon.

See also: Edson, Russell

Further Reading

Barthelme, Donald. *Sixty Stories*. New York: Penguin Classics, 2003.

Daughtery, Tracy. *The Hiding Man: A Biography of Donald Barthelme*. New York: St. Martin's Press, 2009.

Hudgens, Michael Thomas. *Donald Barthelme, Postmodernist American Writer*. New York: Edwin Mellen Press, 2001.

McCaffery, Larry. *The Metafictional Muse: The Works of Robert Coover, Donald Barthelme, and William H. Gass*. Pittsburgh: University of Pittsburgh Press, 1982.

Zeke Jarvis

BUTLER, ROBERT OLEN (1945–)

Born January 20, 1945 in Granite City, Illinois, Robert Olen Butler, Jr., is the child of an actor and theater professor and an executive secretary. His early exposure to performance and theatricality has had a clear and lasting impact on Butler's writing and view of the world, as has the balance of academia and the more working-class surroundings of his hometown. With wild experiments like *Tabloid Dreams* and his experiment of allowing readers to watch him compose a story, Butler has been very invested in the idea of the writer's persona, which, much like his writing, has had a very polarizing effect upon critics.

Butler served in the army during the Vietnam War from 1969 to 1971, working in counter-intelligence and as a translator. He held a number of odd jobs before finding work with Fairchild publications and eventually in academia, teaching at Florida State University.

Butler folds his interest in the public persona and perception very naturally into his more transgressive writing, such as *Tabloid Dreams*, which examines stock characters literally drawn from tabloid headlines and examined without nuance or complexity. Of course, not all Butler characters are built to deliver such simplistic, albeit funny, reactions. A number of his works draw from less experimental sources of inspiration. In addition, Butler dabbles in genre fiction, as many contemporary literary humorists do, with a focus on magical realism, one of the early genres to gain acceptance within academic and literary circles.

Other forms of experiments are also found in Butler's body of work. In addition to his work like *Tabloid Dreams,* Butler finds outlets for his playful sensibilities through the promotion of his work and craft. For example, he put online the writing of one of his stories so that people could track his revisions as he wrote "This Is Earl Sandt." This sort of literary playfulness is in keeping with Butler's willingness to challenge expectations and reinvent himself. Some critics react negatively to this activity, feeling that his behavior does calls more attention to his creative efforts as an object than as a genuine work of art, but many others find his work to be courageous, inventive, and innovative. Both sides can find support for their argument in the "This Is Earl Sandt" event, given the amount of discussion that its writing received relative to the amount of discussion given to the story as a piece of literature.

That said, even Butler's experimental work has received significant and sustained critical acclaim. His surprisingly understated humor and discipline have earned him a number of awards, including a Guggenheim Fellowship, a PEN/Faulkner Award, and a National Endowment for the Arts Fellowship. He has also published in many of the top literary journals, including *The New Yorker*, *Atlantic Monthly*, and *GQ*, among many others. His strange, conceit-driven stories and deadpan delivery recall the work of earlier *New Yorker* writers like Robert Benchley.

Although Butler has generally enjoyed literary success, his personal life has sometimes overshadowed his work, as it did when one of his wives, Elizabeth Dewberry, left him for Ted Turner. The e-mail Butler sent in response to this event has been widely circulated, and has been, like his work, met with equal parts fascination, adulation, and derision. Still, in Butler's writing and professional career, he has had a major impact on both literary writing and humor contained in the written word. While support for Butler's work has never been unanimous, all readers and critics recognize him as a major force in literary humor.

Butler's influence has been felt not only in his writing, but also in his role as an academic. As a professor in the Florida State University creative writing program, which has produced a number of prominent humorists and writers. Butler's daring style and interest in pop and low culture can be seen in the students whom he has taught. In both his teaching and his writing, Butler has been and continues to be a major in the field of literary humor.

Further Reading

Butler, Robert Olen. *Tabloid Dreams*. New York: Henry Holt, 1996.

Clark-Whinger, Alice. "Introduction to Robert Olen Butler." *Journal of the Short Story in English* 59 (Autumn 2012): 19–20.

Moffett, Joe. "The Cultural Divide and Robert Olen Butler's *Tabloid Dreams*." *Genre: Forms of Discourse and Culture* 42, nos. 3–4 (Fall-Winter 2009): 41–60.

Nagel, James. "Robert Olen and the Very Short Story." *Short Story* 18, no. 2 (Fall 2010): 71–79.

Zeke Jarvis

CHABON, MICHAEL (1963–)

Michael Chabon was born in Washington, D.C. His father, a lawyer and physician, and his mother, also a lawyer, divorced when Chabon was young, so Chabon split his coming-of-age years between Columbia, Maryland, and Pittsburgh, Pennsylvania. Chabon has written of his mother's marijuana use, and the role of drugs comes up fairly regularly in a number of his prominent works. While Chabon was growing up, he often heard Yiddish in his home, another facet of his life that would become a key part of his work.

Chabon studied at Carnegie Mellon University and the University of Pittsburgh, and earned a master of fine arts degree from the University of California, Irvine. In 1987, Chabon married poet Lollie Groth—a notable event in his life, given that Chabon would later be mistakenly included in a *Newsweek* article discussing up-and-coming homosexual authors (although Chabon has indicated that he had a sexual relationship with another man prior to his marriage). One year after marrying, Chabon published his first novel, *The Mysteries of Pittsburgh*, which was also his master's thesis. It became a bestseller upon its publication, and it immediately put Chabon on the map of literary stars. In 1994 and 1997, Chabon and his wife had a daughter, Sophie, and a son, Ezekiel, respectively.

For several years after the success of *The Mysteries of Pittsburgh*, Chabon worked on a follow-up entitled *Fountain City* that remained unpublished until *McSweeney's* printed a four-chapter sample in 2010. Chabon's real-life troubles finishing this novel about a baseball park in Florida—at one point a draft totaled more than 1,500 pages—eventually became the premise for his second published novel, *Wonder Boys*. While the novel was a commercial success, the film adaptation (directed by Curtis Hanson and released in 2000 by Paramount Pictures) was not, though it did receive positive reviews from critics.

The Amazing Adventures of Kavalier & Clay, published in 2000, was inspired by Chabon's childhood love of comic books. Chabon was awarded the Pulitzer Prize for Fiction for this book.

In 2001 and 2003, Chabon and his wife had another daughter, Ida-Rose, and a son, Abraham, respectively. Chabon has continued to publish fiction as well as nonfiction and even an original draft of the screenplay for *Spiderman 2*. He has received numerous awards from both the literary and fantasy and science fiction industries. Chabon lives with his family in California.

Michael Chabon has managed to achieve both literary and mainstream success. His dabbling in film and science fiction help to set him apart from many other literary authors. (AP Photo/Marcio Jose Sanchez)

Chabon's work often incorporates themes of fatherhood, divorce, and Jewish identity. Noted for its treatment of gay love and bisexuality, *The Mysteries of Pittsburgh* focuses on the son of a mobster who falls closer to organized crime himself. *Wonder Boys* is a tale about an aging novelist and English professor named Grady Tripp, who has trouble finishing his follow-up to a novel that was published to great success and acclaim seven years before. Tripp also struggles with the fact that his wife has recently left him. When Tripp's editor comes to town, both Tripp and the editor get involved in a strange web of misadventures with one of Tripp's students, who is a promising writer, but also a pathological liar and with whom Tripp's agent has an affair.

Both *The Amazing Adventures of Kavalier & Clay* and *The Yiddish Policeman's Union* explore issues of Jewish identity. Also noteworthy about *Kavalier & Clay* is the fact that it was featured in *The Amazing Adventures of the Escapist*, a 2004 Dark Horse Comics series intended to be an homage to the Golden Age of Comic Books, which saw the introduction and popularity of such icons as Superman, Batman, and Captain America from the late 1930s until the early 1950s. *The Amazing Adventures of the Escapist* treats the history of the character, the Escapist, and his fictional creators as being a part of the real history of comic books. Chabon has similarly played with real publication history through his invention of a fictitious literature critic who discusses the work of August Van Zorn, a horror writer who appears as a character in some of Chabon's works.

Chabon is widely known for his embrace of genre writing, which many members of the literary community frown upon. In addition to writing for comic books and movies, Chabon has gladly accepted the Nebula Award, a prize for science fiction, for his book *The Yiddish Policeman's Union*, and he regularly incorporates discussions of science fiction and horror in his writing. He also has edited a collection of genre writing for Dave Eggers's *McSweeney's* imprint. Chabon is a rare and in some ways cutting-edge figure who has helped push the value of genre writing into the mainstream without losing his own positive critical reception. In fact, one of the strategies that has led to Chabon's success as a writer and humorist is his use of both high and low culture to create funny and surprising turns.

See also: Eggers, Dave; Lethem, Jonathan

Further Reading

Chabon, Michael. *Wonder Boys*. New York: Villard Books, 1995.

Dewey, Joseph. *Understanding Michael Chabon*. Columbia, SC: University of South Carolina Press, 2014.

Meyers, Helene. *Reading Michael Chabon*. Santa Barbara, CA: Greenwood, 2010.

Wang, Huei ju. "'Dr. Fredric Wertham Was an Idiot': Reclaiming Batman and Robin in Michael Chabon's *Kavalier and Clay*." *NTU Studies in Language and Literature*, 28 (December 2012): 59–86.

Stephen Powers

CHEEVER, JOHN (1912–1982)

Born May 27, 1912, in Quincy Massachusetts, John Cheever was part of and knew the world that he would eventually write so much about: the privileged life of the suburbs. His father spent much of his life as a wealthy shoe salesman, and Cheever went to a private school for a time. Unfortunately for the Cheever family, John's father fell victim to alcoholism, eventually losing his job. To support the family, John's mother opened a gift shop, which John felt was humiliating to her and to the family. This tension between the desire to keep up a reputation and appearance of respectability and the inner realization of one's personal turmoil often surfaced in Cheever's work. Just as his father lost his social standing, Cheever left his private school, although it is not entirely clear whether he was asked to leave or if he left of his own volition.

Cheever served in the military during World War II. He worked as an editor after the war until his writing career was successful enough to support him. Cheever died of cancer in June 1982.

Cheever's disdain for and fascination with the wealthy society of New England featured prominently in his writing. In the early going, his work could be more broadly drawn, looking for absurd characters more than the more disciplined and nuanced humor that would come in the later portions of his career. Still, his work was very popular, landing in top-notch publications like *Harper's* and *The New Yorker*. Given his influences like Charles Dickens, F. Scott Fitzgerald, and Anton Chekhov, it is clear that Cheever was interested in nuance and class conflict. As his career progressed, Cheever became better able to incorporate the subtlety of Chekhov and the richness of Dickens. At the same time, an examination of the nosiness of neighbors and the competitiveness of the suburbs are both present in much of Cheever's work. With works like *The Wapshot Chronicles*, Cheever examines a well-to-do New England family, satirizing the sense of corruption and desperation to avoid discovery of their inner secrets. This sense of competition and the burden of public anxiety are particularly American, and they mark the duality that allowed Cheever to employ the sense of complexity and play that gave his work both its humor and its literary merit.

While Cheever's work has generally been received with genuine critical acclaim, both his early work and his final work drew criticism from both critics and from Cheever himself. Cheever, in retrospect, often spoke poorly of his early work, and he also gave hints that he expected his final work to not measure up to his best work. That said, his final work, *Oh What a Paradise It Seems*, was generally met with critical acclaim, although many feel that the reason for this was that Cheever was known to be ill at the time of the book's publication. Cheever was diagnosed with cancer of the kidney in 1982, and, in follow-up examinations, it was found that the tumors had spread to his femur, pelvis, and bladder. Shortly before his death, Cheever was awarded the National Medal for Literature.

After his death, as part of an agreement to publish some stories posthumously, Cheever's personal letters were published, making public Cheever's bisexuality. While this factor has not had an impact on his literary reputation, it has shaped his place in the nation's cultural consciousness, as his affair was referenced in a *Seinfeld* episode. Overall, Cheever is remembered for his lasting and widespread impact on American literature and humor.

Further Reading

Bailey, Blake. *Cheever: A Life*. New York: Knopf, 2009.

Cheever, John. *The Stories of John Cheever*. New York: Alfred A. Knopf, 1978.

Cheever, John. *The Wapshot Chronicle*. New York: Harper Brothers, 1957.

Shivani, Anis. "John Cheever's *Bullet Park*: The Suburbs Were Never More Unreal." *Antigonish Review* 154 (Summer 2008): 123–135.

Zeke Jarvis

COOVER, ROBERT (1932–)

Robert Coover was born in Charles City, Iowa. After graduating from high school, he attended Southern Illinois University before transferring to Indiana University. After his college graduation in 1953, Coover served in the Navy. He later earned his master's degree from the University of Illinois, Chicago. In 1959, Coover married; he and his wife have three children.

Coover's first novel was *The Origin of Brunists*, which established his unorthodox material and approach. He has continued to write novels and short stories, earning awards such as the William Faulkner Foundation Award and the Rea Award for the Short Story.

Coover is known for his edgy and experimental material. He often pushes boundaries in terms of both story structure and politeness. Never afraid to incorporate sexually or politically charged material, Coover has been a consistent and successful social satirist. Although he has not broken through into the mainstream cultural consciousness, his sustained and artistically diverse successes have made him an important figure in American humor and literature.

Further Reading

Coover, Robert. *The Public Burning*. New York: Viking, 1977.

McCaffery, Larry. *The Metafictional Muse: The Works of Robert Coover, Donald Barthelme, and William H. Gass*. Pittsburgh: University of Pittsburgh Press, 1982.

Vanderhaeghe, Stéphane. *Robert Coover and the Generosity of the Page*. Champaign, IL: Dalkey Archive, 2013.

Vayo, Brandon K. "A Trinity of Iconoclasms in Robert Coover's *The Public Burning*." *Critique* 54, no. 4 (2013): 478–488.

Zeke Jarvis

EDSON, RUSSELL (1935–2014)

Russell Edson was born in Connecticut. His father, Gus Edson, was a famous cartoonist known for his work on *The Gumps*, a popular, long-running comic strip about an ordinary middle-class family created by Sidney Smith, and *Dondi*, a comic strip about a war orphan that Gus Edson co-created and that ran from 1955 to 1986. Russell Edson, like his father, studied art at the Art Students League, a school based in New York City, with campuses elsewhere, that offers an informal setting for amateurs and professionals to study art without earning degrees or grades.

Edson's first book, *Ceremonies in Bachelor Space*, was published in 1951. He began to more regularly publish his poetry in the 1960s, starting with *Appearances: Fables and Drawings* in 1961. His next full-length collection of prose poetry, *The Childhood of an Equestrian*, was published in 1973 and followed several short collections of stories and fables published in the 1960s. A volume of selected poems, *The Tunnel: Selected Poems of Russell Edson*, appeared in 1994. Edson has also written a few plays, and published two novels, *Gulping's Recital* (1984) and *The Song of Percival Peacock: A Novel* (1992). His poem, "Let Us Consider," was animated for the Poetry Foundation's Poetry Everywhere project. He has won a Guggenheim Fellowship and three National Endowment for the Arts Creative Writing Fellowships.

Edson was reclusive, living in Connecticut with his wife, Frances. Nevertheless, he sometimes traveled, accompanied by his wife, to give readings of his work at colleges and universities around the country. Edson died in 2014.

Edson has earned a reputation for his work with the prose poem—a form of poetry in which there are no line breaks. This form maintains other elements of poetry, however, such as repetition, rhyme, distinctive imagery, and compressed language. At the same time, it can be argued to associate more with prose, because of its reliance upon narrative. Because prose poems are neither poetry nor prose, but rather a hybrid of the two, they have been said to be subversive in their departure from strict poetic conventions. This blending lends itself to the strange and offbeat topics and images found within Edson's poetry. The prose poem has drawn its share of criticism, and interest in the prose poem had waned by the middle of the 20th century prior to its revitalization by writers like Edson, Allen Ginsberg, and Bob Dylan. Edson is often referred to as "the godfather of the prose poem," because he was working in this form long before other contemporary American poets. Edson even referred to himself as "Little Mr. Prose Poem."

Edson's humor has been described as having the zaniness of a cartoon, but his body of work also interposes a sense of discomfort under the humor, as with other short-form writers such as Donald Barthelme. A typical Edson prose poem might feature an ordinary man who finds himself lost in an alternate reality. For example, in "The Wounded Breakfast," the speaker of the poem is sitting down to breakfast when he finds himself in the shadow of an enormous shoe that has appeared from over the horizon. In "The Automobile," the speaker playfully instructs his son to compare to his mother the car that his son has married. This female/automobile comparison appears again in "The Wounded Daughter," in which the speaker takes his daughter in for repairs as if she were a car. Edson continues the Cinderella story in "Cinderella's Life at the Castle" by portraying Cinderella as having little interest in her marriage to the prince.

See also: Barthelme, Donald

Further Reading

Chandran, K. Narayana. "Russell Edson's 'Piano Lessons' in an Indian Classroom." *Notes on American Literature* 21 (Spring 2012): 34–42.

Edson, Russell. *The Rooster's Wife*. Rochester: BOA Editions, 2005.

Hardy, Donald. "Russell Edson's Humor: Absurdity in a Surreal World." *Studies in American Humor* 6 (1988): 93–100.

Upton, Lee. *Structural Politics: The Prose Poetry of Russell Edson. South Atlantic Review* 58, no. 4 (November 1993): 101–115.

Stephen Powers

EGGERS, DAVE (1970–)

Dave Eggers was born in Boston, Massachusetts. While he was still a child, his family moved to Lake Forest, a city near Chicago, Illinois. One of his high school classmates was future actor Vince Vaughan. After graduating, Eggers attended the University of Illinois at Champaign, majoring in journalism. Partway through his studies, both of his parents passed away from cancer. When his parents died, they left behind an eight-year-old son. Although Eggers had two older siblings, neither felt able to take care of their much younger brother, leaving Eggers to be his caretaker. After dropping out of college, Eggers moved to Berkeley, California, with his brother and girlfriend. All of these events were later recounted in his book, *A Heartbreaking Work of Staggering Genius*.

To help pay for his brother's care and schooling, Eggers worked as a graphic designer, then ran a paper and a satirical magazine, *Might*. In addition to continuing to write, Eggers went on to found and edit *McSweeney's Quarterly Concern*, a prominent literary magazine. He has worked in a variety of other media, including creating comic strips and writing the screenplay for the film adaptation of *Where the Wild Things Are*. In addition to his creative work, Eggers has done significant activist work for impoverished families and children in the San Francisco Bay Area. He has received various honors and awards for this work. Interestingly, his older brother has worked with a number of conservative think tanks. Currently, Eggers lives with his wife in San Francisco. The couple has two children.

Eggers most first, groundbreaking book, *A Heartbreaking Work of Staggering Genius*, is known for its playfulness and technical innovation, with characters breaking the fourth wall and having a general sense of self-reference not always seen in the memoir genre. He also fictionalized some aspects of his life, stretching the boundaries of memoir. This sort of boundary breaking continued in his work on *McSweeney's*, which has put out anthologies of prominent authors writing in nonliterary genres (edited by Michael Chabon) and has played with the format of literary magazines, once sending out an issue as a stack of postcards rather than as a magazine proper. Individual issues often feature humorous stories or stories that take on abstract, absurd premises, ranging from a series of plagues (including carnivorous butterflies) to a woman with a frozen vagina. These examples give a sense of both the lack of fear and the comedic style of the magazine. Even with his sense of playfulness, Eggers has been able to take on issues of depth and genuine social significance, as he did with the fictionalized autobiography of a Sudanese boy in the book, *What Is the What*.

Although Eggers has had a clear and lasting impact on contemporary literary writing with his own creative work, he may well have exerted an even deeper influence through his editorial efforts. In addition to breaking down barriers among genres, Eggers emphasized the importance of incorporating social merit into a writer's creative work—a consideration that was sometimes left behind by writers taking a playful, postmodern approach as Eggers does with his work. For both his creative vision and his keen interest in social issues, Eggers is a prominent figure in literary and comic circles.

See also: Chabon, Michael

Further Reading

D'Amore, Jonathan. *American Authorship and Autobiographical Narrative: Mailer, Wildeman, Eggers*. New York: Palgrave Macmillan, 2012.

Eggers, Dave. *A Heartbreaking Work of Staggering Genius*. New York: Simon and Schuster, 2000.

Eggers, Dave. *What Is the What: The Autobiography of Valentino Achak Deng*. San Francisco: McSweeney's, 2006.

Leonard, Devin. "Dave Eggers: Novelist, Publisher, Education Non-profit Co-founder." *Bloomberg Businessweek* 4292 (August 13, 2012): 70.

Zeke Jarvis

ELLIS, BRET EASTON (1964–)

Born March 7, 1964 in Los Angeles, California, Bret Easton Ellis has consistently worked to turn on its head the idea of progress that is so often associated with heading west. Ellis's account of his father was one of an abusive parent. After graduating from high school, the young Ellis attended Bennington College in Vermont, entirely across the country from his family. There, he met a number of writers, including Donna Tartt and Jonathan Lethem.

With *Less Than Zero* in 1985, Ellis achieved a high degree of fame and notoriety, which only intensified with the subsequent publication of his book *American Psycho*. In 1992, the year after *American Psycho* was published, his father died. Although Ellis had engaged in physical relationships with other men, it was after his father's death that he began to be more open about his sexuality. Ellis examines these themes in his semi-autobiographical work, *Lunar Park*. In addition to his controversial works, Ellis has garnered negative attention for his surprising tweets criticizing other artists, most notably Kathryn Bigelow and David Foster Wallace. Ellis continues to work in both literary fiction and screenplays, and he lives in Los Angeles.

Examining the wealthy, pampered lifestyle that he witnessed and was part of growing up, Ellis's writing often portrays privileged children as naïve and weak at best and totally immoral at worst. From the drug-addled, directionless characters in *Less Than Zero* to the outright psychotic killer in *American Psycho*, Ellis has consistently satirized America's upper class in books that incorporate elements of autobiography, wild satire, and close and deep examinations of American popular culture.

While Ellis has a clear fan base, he has also drawn significant criticism from a number of groups. His book *American Psycho*, has been a particular lightning rod, being denounced by groups as far apart on the political spectrum as feminists and conservative political commentators. While many critics suggest that his stark and unflinching portrayals of American culture are not a far cry from the sort of harsh satire found in Mark Twain's *A Connecticut Yankee in King Arthur's Court*, others feel that the misogyny and violence in the book rendered it lacking in real literary merit. Still, the book has had a significant impact on popular culture, even being made into a movie starring Christian Bale and directed by Mary Harron.

Beyond the shock value of his work, Ellis is notable for his ability to incorporate a strikingly postmodern approach to considering symbols and incorporating real people into his writing. The consistent use of landscapes and lifestyles (including his geographical interests, his privileged background, and his open examination of his sexuality) with which Ellis has a clear and significant familiarity draws many critics in as they begin to decode his writing. Also giving his body of work a postmodern feel is the sense of the world he creates edging beyond the boundaries of any single work. The self-references between his works give a sense of Ellis working on one large, single work instead of writing stand-alone novels.

In terms of Ellis's comedic style, many critics note a certain deadpan expression that keeps his satiric approach to social commentary particularly vibrant. While his characters are often exaggerated and ridiculous to fit the absurdist situations that they inhabit, the narration often proceeds in a simple, disarming fashion that can make readers accept what they are reading at face value until they are struck by a particularly vicious act or observation. This gives Ellis's most biting satire a level of surprise and punch that can be devastatingly effective, though it can also leave many readers uncertain of his position. Clearly, this unpredictability is part of what keeps many scholars reading his work and writing about him. Still active in both books and screenplays, Ellis is both an inspiration and a lightning rod for many.

See also: Loos, Anita

Further Reading

Blazer, Alex E. "Chasms of Reality, Aberrations of Identity: Defining the Postmodern Through Bret Easton Ellis's *American Psycho*." *Americana: The Journal of American Popular Culture (1900–Present)* 1, no. 2 (Fall 2002).

Colby, Georgina. *Bret Easton Ellis: Underwriting the Contemporary*. New York: Palgrave Macmillan, 2011.

Ellis, Bret Easton. *American Psycho*. New York: Vintage Books, 1991.

Mandel, Naomi. *Bret Easton Ellis: American Psycho, Glamorama, Lunar Park*. New York: Continuum, 2011.

Zeke Jarvis

ELLISON, HARLAN (1934–)

Harlan Ellison was born in Cleveland, Ohio. Although his family moved away briefly, Ellison returned to the city after his father's death. He frequently ran away from home, taking a variety of odd jobs. He eventually attended Ohio State University for a brief time before being expelled. Shortly after his expulsion, he moved to New York City to pursue writing. He was generally successful, publishing more than 100 short stories and articles over a two-year span.

Towards the end of the 1950s, Ellison decided to write a book about youth gangs. To research the culture, he joined a gang in New York for a brief time. Although he left the gang shortly after joining, he did draw from his experience in a novel, a prose collection, and his memoir, *Memos from Purgatory*.

In 1957, Ellison was drafted into the army, serving until 1959. Upon his return, he moved to Chicago to continue work as a writer and editor. During this period, he strayed from his general focus on science fiction to explore erotica. Even in this genre, Ellison's iconoclastic social views and fast-paced style were clearly present. Indeed, Ellison has been noted as being influenced not only by early science fiction writers, but also by Beat writers, which can be seen in both his style and in many of his social stances. In 1962, Ellison moved to California, where he regularly sold scripts to shows such as *Star Trek*, *The Outer Limits*, and even *The Flying Nun*.

In his personal life, Ellison's eccentric behavior and quick temper have made him a lightning rod for controversy. His appearances on Bill Maher's *Politically Incorrect* have often been noted for his memorable and controversial statements, as has some of his behavior, such as touching fellow science fiction writer Connie Willis's breast while onstage at the 2006 Hugo Awards Ceremony. At first, Ellison's reaction to the latter event was conciliatory, but, after receiving extended criticism, Ellison bridled publicly. In addition to this controversy, Ellison has been involved in a number of lawsuits over intellectual property rights. Nevertheless, he has consistently produced work in a number of media for an extended period of time, thereby cementing his cultural prominence.

Beyond his success in publishing, Ellison was active and outspoken in social and political causes, participating in the 1965 March from Selma to Montgomery, led by Martin Luther King, Jr. He also wrote a number of stories during this period that featured overt social commentary or direct antagonism of public figures such as Roy O. Disney and Frank Sinatra. Although Ellison has received mixed critical reactions, he has attained both commercial and critical success with a number of pieces. Notably, "The Man Who Rowed Christopher Columbus Ashore" was selected for the 1992 edition of *Best American Short Stories*. He also has teamed with well-respected writers such as Neil Gaiman. Ellison's writing has been included in major anthologies, including *McSweeney's Tales to Astonish*, along with other literary writers who dabble in genre fiction, such as Sherman Alexie and Michael Chabon.

Further Reading

De Los Santos, Oscar. "Clogging up the (In)Human Works: Harlan Ellison's Apocalyptic Postmodernism." *Extrapolation: A Journal of Science Fiction and Fantasy* 40, no. 1 (Spring 1999): 5–20.

Ellison, Harlan. *I Have No Mouth, and I Must Scream*. New York: Galaxy, 1967.

Harris-Fain, Darren. *Understanding Contemporary American Science Fiction: The Age of Maturity, 1970–2000*. Columbia: University of South Carolina Press, 2005.

Lerner, Fredrick Andrew. *Modern Science Fiction and the American Literary Community*. Lanham, MD: Scarecrow Press, 1985.

Zeke Jarvis

LETHEM, JONATHAN (1964–)

Jonathan Lethem was born in Brooklyn, New York. His mother was a political activist and his father was an avant-garde painter, and this valuing of art and politics influenced both Lethem and his siblings, Blake (who became an artist) and Mara (who became a photographer and writer). In addition to exploring his parents' bohemian lifestyle, Jonathan Lethem frequently incorporates the setting of Brooklyn into much of his work. He also includes many of the cultural influences from his childhood, including *Star Wars*, comic books, and Philip K. Dick. An even greater influence was his mother's death (she died of a brain tumor), which has informed his portrayal of relationships and families.

Lethem's first novel, *Guns, with Occasional Music*, sets the tone for much of his later work by combining elements of science fiction and detective novels with the discipline and complexity found in literary works. This novel was very well received by critics. Its film rights were also optioned, giving Lethem the opportunity to focus exclusively on writing. After two other novels and a short story collection,

Lethem wrote *Motherless Brooklyn*, a detective novel with a protagonist who suffers from Tourette's syndrome. While Lethem hardly made fun of the character (in fact, Lethem has said that he more strongly identifies with this character than with any others in his writing), the awkwardness and difficulty of the character are indicative of the absurdity and exploration of social anxiety that run through much of Lethem's work.

After more short stories and two edited anthologies, Lethem published the semi-autobiographical novel *The Fortress of Solitude*, which was critically acclaimed and translated into 14 languages. In addition to his success in novels and short stories, Lethem has written a number of creative nonfiction pieces, including "The Genius of Bob Dylan," which mixed an interview with Dylan and reflections on his work from Lethem. He explored publishing in comic books with his run on *Omega the Unknown*. His interest in comic books also features in *The Fortress of Solitude* and multiple stories in *Men and Cartoons*. The most prominent example from that collection is "Super Goat Man," which explores an original, unpopular comic book character who comes to life and meets a young character who has a bohemian background very similar to Lethem's. Both eventually enter into academia, in what becomes an interrogation of both scholarly pursuits and the inability to let go of childhood interests and concerns. In this respect, many of Lethem's conflicts and characters have a Seinfeldian feel, which is not surprising given the generation and geographical area that both men represent and explore.

Because of Lethem's interest in popular culture and genres outside of psychological realism, he is often compared with Michael Chabon. In addition to these sorts of contextual concerns, both Lethem and Chabon often examine Jewish culture and contemporary urban landscapes. Lethem has also been associated with Chabon in his connection to major literary figures or publishers, such as *McSweeney's*, which published his novella *This Shape We're in*, which was also later included in his short story collection *Men and Cartoons*. These sorts of ties, combined with the regular appearance of his work in *Best American Short Stories* and *Best American Essays*, have kept Lethem at the foreground of contemporary literary writing.

See also: Chabon, Michael

Further Reading

Coughlan, David. "Jonathan Lethem's *The Fortress of Solitude* and *Omega: The Unknown*, A Comic Book Series." *College Literature* 38, no. 3 (Summer 2011): 194–218.

Lethem, Jonathan. *Men and Cartoons*. New York: Vintage, 2005.

Peacock, James. "Jonathan Lethem's Genre Evolutions." *Journal of American Studies* 43, no. 3 (December 2009): 425–440.

Salerno, Alexandra. " 'Pop Wrote the Boy': The Personal Critical Essayist and Hybrid-Critical Memoir." *Fourth Genre: Explorations in Nonfiction* 15, no. 1 (Spring 2013): 167–174.

Zeke Jarvis

LOOS, ANITA (1889–1981)

Anita Loos was born Corinne Anita Loos, daughter to the founder and a core writer for a tabloid newspaper. When she was four, Loos's family moved from Sisson,

California, to San Francisco. Her father, an alcoholic, often would take Anita to the pier to fish. They would regularly talk to locals. Loos has indicated that this practice triggered her interest in the seedy underbelly of society. Loos also followed her father when he began managing a theater company in San Diego, where she acted while also acting in another company and publishing her writing. This level of work was necessary to help support her family. In addition to her publishing printed work, Loos had plays produced and sold a one-real screenplay, *The New York Hat*. Much of her work incorporated reports of Manhattan social life or rich vacationers from the San Diego resorts and even some of her father's associates. This sort of skewering would set the tone for much of Loos's work, which frequently incorporated thinly veiled portrayals of real public figures.

Loos wrote prodigiously in her early career, selling more than 100 scripts between 1912 and 1915. While working as a writer for Triangle Film Corporation, Loos traveled to New York for the first time for a premiere. It was there that she met Frank Crowinshield and began her career as a contributor for *Vanity Fair*. Loos continued to write screenplays, garnering as much attention and acclaim for her work as many of the actors and actresses who appeared in the films. In addition to bringing attention to writers, Loos sought to make strides for women writers, joining Ruth Hale's Lucy Stone League, an organization that encouraged professional women keep their maiden names after marriage.

Loos married three times, with her final marriage being to John Emerson. Emerson and Loos enjoyed success both in the theater and in film, and they traveled to Europe, exposing Loos to many of the places and pieces of culture that she would bring into her most famous work, *Gentleman Prefer Blondes*. This script was also partly inspired by her disappointing interactions with H. L. Mencken, whom she admired, but whom she thought too often surrounded himself with attractive but vapid women. Loos admitted that a number of other characters in the book were based on real people. In particular, the eponymous character was based on a real showgirl. Loos's husband sought to suppress publication of the book, possibly recognizing that its success would put him permanently in Loos's shadow. Emerson often claimed a variety of illnesses during this period. Loos responded by stating that she would retire after the release of *Blondes*'s follow-up, *Gentleman Marry Brunettes*. Ultimately, Loos and her brother checked her husband into a mental institution, where he was diagnosed with schizophrenia.

Although Loos was in some ways a rival of Dorothy Parker, her humor was similar to Parker's in that she would often undercut the pretensions and sense of moral superiority of the upper class in her writing. Unlike Parker, Loos employed a light touch, using a naïve character to unintentionally demonstrate the hypocrisy and idiocy of different people in power. Loos also incorporated thinly veiled versions of prominent public figures as well as made direct references to public figures like Sigmund Freud to make observations about figures and cultural trends. In this sense, Loos is a precursor to Bret Easton Ellis, albeit with a generally less aggressive feel. Loos's work has been both imitated and adapted many times, most notably in the movie version of *Gentleman Prefer Blondes*, starring Marilyn Monroe.

Owing to both her legacy and the work itself, Loos has reached a significant and lasting level of literary acclaim.

See also: Mencken, H.L.; Parker, Dorothy

Further Reading

Carey, Gary. *Anita Loos*. New York: Knopf, 1988.

Frost, Laura. "Blondes Have More Fun: Anita Loos and the Language of Silent Cinema." *Modernism/Modernity* 17, no. 2 (April 2010): 291–311.

Hefner, Brooks E. " 'Any Chance to Be Unrefined': Film Narrative Modes in Anita Loos's Fiction." *PMLA: Publications of the Modern Language Association of America* 125, no. 1 (January 2010): 107–120, 264.

Loos, Anita. *Gentleman Prefer Blondes*. New York: Boni and Liveright, 1925.

Zeke Jarvis

O'CONNOR, FLANNERY (1925–1964)

Mary Flannery O'Connor was born on March 25, 1925, in Savannah, Georgia. O'Connor spent her childhood on Lafayette Square in Savannah, a block from St. John the Baptist Cathedral, where she was baptized. She achieved exposure to fame early as a child when she taught a pet chicken to walk backward in the backyard of her home. The British newsreel company Pathé documented this feat in footage that was shown before films in theaters around the United States. Her father, Edward F. O'Connor, a real estate agent, was diagnosed at a young age with lupus, an autoimmune disease in which the body attacks its own tissues. Flannery O'Connor herself would become a victim of the disease in early adulthood.

After her father's death from lupus, O'Connor attended Georgia State College for Women, where she contributed cartoons to the school newspaper. She enrolled in the Iowa Writers' Workshop at the University of Iowa, and completed a master of fine arts degree. After spending some time living in Connecticut in the home of friends Robert and Sally Fitzgerald, and following her own diagnosis with lupus, she moved with her mother, Regina Cline O'Connor, to Andalusia, a dairy farm in Milledgeville, Georgia, where she wrote her best-known short stories. O'Connor attended church with her mother every morning at Sacred Heart Catholic Church in Milledgeville, raised a plethora of exotic birds at Andalusia (namely peacocks), consistently kept up a writing regimen for several hours each day, composed letters and entertained visitors in the afternoons, and dabbled in painting. Her best-known painting is a self-portrait entitled *Self-Portrait with Pheasant Cock*. It shows a young, spinster-looking O'Connor in a wide hat with one of her signature peacocks. O'Connor was also known to be a voracious reader.

In 1952, O'Connor published her first novel, *Wise Blood*, and, just a few years later, she published a collection of short stories, *A Good Man Is Hard to Find*. Both works attracted significant attention.

In terms of her reading, studies of Catholicism occupied much of O'Connor's interest, and she showed a preference for the writings of St. Thomas Aquinas.

She traveled on occasion—when her health allowed—to give lectures and readings of her work. In 1958, O'Connor traveled with her mother to Lourdes, France, to visit a grotto considered by Catholics to be an important pilgrimage site with healing effects. This trip to Europe included an audience with Pope Pius XII.

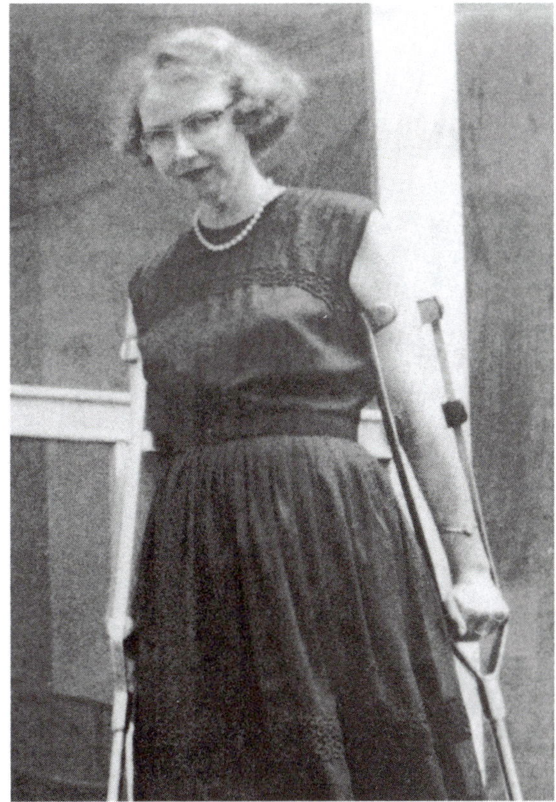

Despite the brevity of her career, Flannery O'Connor became known as one of the finest short-story writers of the 20th century. Her willingness to take on religion, social class, and other dicey issues garnered her significant critical success. (Library of Congress)

O'Connor's mother was known to express embarrassment about her daughter's writing. She remarked on numerous occasions that she wished her daughter would write something more befitting a lady.

With her mother, O'Connor lived out the rest of her life on Andalusia Farm, unmarried, on crutches, enduring flair-ups of her disease, and tending to her dozens of exotic birds that quickly gained a formidable reputation in town. O'Connor died in a hospital in Milledgeville on August 3, 1964, from complications related to lupus. She was buried in Memory Hill Cemetery in Milledgeville. Today, her childhood home in Savannah and Andalusia Farm are open to the public. Georgia College & State University (formerly Georgia State College for Women) maintains a museum dedicated to O'Connor.

O'Connor's second novel, *The Violent Bear It Away*; a second collection of stories, *Everything That Rises Must Converge*; and a compilation of her letters, *The Habit of Being: The Letters of Flannery O'Connor*, were published after her death. *Mysteries and Manners: Occasional Prose* appeared in 1969. *The Complete Stories*, also published posthumously in 1971, compiles all of the stories from her first two story collections, *A Good Man Is Hard to Find* and *Everything That Rises Must Converge*, along with several unpublished stories. *The Complete Stories* won the National Book Award for Fiction in 1972.

O'Connor's fiction is classified as Southern Gothic, a subgenre of American literature that takes place in and focuses on issues related to the South. Inspired by the English Gothic genre from more than a century earlier, Southern Gothic writers utilize a literary device known as the grotesque to instill in characters a physical deformity or mental deficiency that evokes both laughter and disgust. The grotesque can be said to undercut the value of beauty for a dark comic effect.

Violence, poverty, rural isolation, decay, and racism are topics generally addressed in Southern Gothic fiction. Influenced by her devout Catholicism in a predominantly Protestant South, O'Connor's fiction often puts her characters in situations where they are forced by circumstances to confront their own moral flaws. Almost always disturbing, and portraying the decay evident in rural areas, Southern Gothic fiction such as O'Connor's writings makes use of the grotesque in Southern settings to bring out both empathy and revulsion regarding its characters, who typically fail to see their own shortcomings. For example, in "A Good Man Is Hard to Find," the titular short story in O'Connor's first collection, the grandmother, who considers herself a devout Christian, never realizes that she holds responsibility for the death of her family at the hands of the Misfit. Julian's mother in "Everything That Rises Must Converge," the titular short story in O'Connor's second collection, dies without dignity after a racist confrontation on a bus. In "Good Country People," Hulga, an intellectual who considers herself superior to her uneducated, simple mother, is left behind in the loft of the barn by Manley Pointer, a phony Bible salesman, after he tricks her into taking off her prosthetic leg. Physical deformities such as this are a hallmark of characters in Southern Gothic fiction. O'Connor's short story, "The Life You Save May Be Your Own" portrays the antagonist, Mr. Shiftlet, as having only half an arm. The balance of interest in physical weakness, Southern morality, and social class conflict make these stories very representative of O'Connor's work.

See also: Welty, Eudora

Further Reading

Cofer, Jordan. *The Gospel According to Flannery O'Connor: Examining the Role of the Bible in Flannery O'Connor's Fiction*. New York: Bloomsbury, 2014.

Nisly, L. Lama. "Idolizing O'Connor: Tim Gautreaux's Tribute to Flannery O'Connor." *Southern Quarterly: A Journal of the Arts in the South* 50, no. 2 (Winter 2013): 31–48.

O'Connor, Flannery. *A Good Man Is Hard to Find*. New York: Harcourt, Brace, 1955.

O'Connor, Flannery, and W. A. Sessions, ed. *A Prayer Journal*. New York: Farrar, Straus and Giroux, 2013.

Stephen Powers

PALAHNIUK, CHUCK (1962–)

Charles Michael (Chuck) Palahniuk was born in Pasco, Washington, in 1962. He grew up in a mobile home. After his parents divorced when he was 14, Palahniuk lived on a cattle ranch with his grandparents. Palahniuk graduated from the University of Oregon's School of Journalism in 1986. During college, he interned at a National Public Radio station in Eugene, Oregon. After college he worked briefly for a newspaper in Portland, and then he worked as a diesel mechanic. He also volunteered for a hospice and a homeless shelter. Palahniuk eventually became a member of the Cacophony Society, which was founded in 1986 for the purpose of encouraging its members to have experiences that would not be considered part of the mainstream. Pranks are a common hallmark of the club, which would play a role in Palahniuk's fiction.

During this time, Palahniuk began writing fiction and participating in workshops for writers. His workshop teacher, Tom Spanbauer, is credited with influencing what became known as Palahniuk's minimalist style. Palahniuk's first written novel, *Insomnia: If You Lived Here, You'd Be Home Already*, was not published. His second novel, *Invisible Monsters*, was rejected numerous times. His next novel, *Fight Club*, for which Palahniuk is most well known, was published in 1996 by W. W. Norton. It received largely positive reviews, but it was not originally a bestseller. In 1999, a film adaptation of *Fight Club,* directed by David Fincher, was released to generally modest and somewhat negative reviews from a large number of film critics. Starring Edward Norton and Brad Pitt, the movie failed to generate successful returns for the studio at the box office, but it did gain a large cult following. In 2008, *Fight Club* landed at number 10 on *Empire* magazine's list of the 500 greatest movies of all time. Since its first DVD release, the film has gone on to achieve the commercial success that first eluded it theaters, and it has only grown in cult status.

Chuck Palahniuk is the author of such cult favorites as *Choke*, *Invisible Monsters*, and *Fight Club*. His edgy style has had such an impact that some audience members have even fainted during his readings. (AP Photo/Greg Wahl-Stephens)

Invisible Monsters, Palahniuk's second published novel, came out in 1999. *Survivor*, a novel about the last surviving member of a death cult who becomes a celebrity, was also published in 1999. Even so, Palahniuk did not land on the New York Times Bestseller list until his novel *Choke* was published in 2001. Palahniuk's next novel, *Lullaby*, published in 2002, was written partly in effort to cope with his father's 1999 murder and the subsequent sentencing of Dale Shackleford, the man convicted of this crime. Palahniuk was asked to help make the decision regarding whether Shackleford would receive the death penalty;

a month after Palahniuk finished *Lullaby*, Shackleford did, in fact, receive the death sentence.

Palahniuk has continued to publish both fiction and nonfiction, frequently commenting that the money paid for rights to adapt his works to the screen help give him time to write. While on tours to promote various books, Palahniuk would begin public readings of "Guts," one of the stories in *Haunted*, by instructing everyone in the audience to hold their breath and not breathe again until he finished reading the story; this mandate has reportedly caused dozens of spectators at various events to faint. Palahniuk consistently publishes a novel every year or every other year. Never married (but believed by many to have been), Palahniuk currently lives in Oregon and Washington with a long-term same-sex partner.

Palahniuk has stated that he does not like many of his characters, because they hold values that he does not agree with. In fact, many readers have been shocked by the actions portrayed in Palahniuk's works, which include brutal violence, sexual promiscuity, and even acts of sacrifice. Palahniuk's male characters often make troubling statements about women, leading many critics to compare Palahniuk with Ernest Hemingway (although that comparison stems in part from Palahniuk's use of a minimalist style). In fact, some of Palahniuk's struggles to achieve publication of his early writings reflected the darkness of his subject matter rather than the quality of his writing. Nevertheless, his lasting success has turned him into a significant figure in American literature and humor. Indeed, Palahniuk's dark humor meshes in spirit with the work of other humorists (both literary and performance based) who confront dark truths and the fragility of the human body in a disturbing but humorous way. Palahniuk's significance is demonstrated by the fact that he remains in demand for readings and public appearances, and has appeared on television to discuss issues related to his work.

See also: Vonnegut, Kurt.

Further Reading

Aparicio, Jose Antonio. " 'Your Heart Is My Pinata': Chuck Palahniuk's Unconventional Love Stories." *ANQ: A Quarterly Journal of Short Articles, Notes, and Reviews* 26, no. (2013): 210–215.

Burgess, Olivia. "Revolutionary Bodies in Chuck Palahniuk's *Fight Club*." *Utopian Studies: Journal of the Society for Utopian Studies* 23, no. 1 (2012): 263–280.

Collado Rodríguez, Francisco. "Textual Unreliability, Trauma and the Fantastic in Chuck Palahniuk's *Lullaby*." *Studies in the Novel* 45, no. 4 (Winter 2013): 620–637.

Palahniuk, Chuck. *Fight Club*. New York: W. W. Norton, 1996.

Stephen Powers

PARKER, DOROTHY (1893–1967)

Dorothy Parker was born Dorothy Rothschild in Long Branch, New Jersey. Her father was Jewish and her mother was Protestant. Shortly before Parker turned five, her mother died. When her father remarried, Parker became incredibly

Ten Great Political or Social Literary Satires

Tom Wolfe, *Bonfire of the Vanities* (New York: Farrar Straus, Giroux, 1987).
This biting satire ridicules the upper class in a daring way.

Dorothy Parker, "The Waltz" (1933) and "You Were Perfectly Fine" (1929).
These clever pieces joke about gender politics and power in ways that are decades ahead of their time.

Christopher Buckley, *Thank You for Smoking* (New York: Random House, 2006).
This novel skewers marketing and capitalism in a striking way.

Bret Easton Ellis, *American Psycho* (New York: Vintage Books, 1991).
This very daring and obscene novel plays with the expectations of young members of the upper class in the 1980s.

William Faulkner, "A Rose for Miss Emily," *Forum*, April 30, 1930.
The Southern upper class runs amok in this disturbing but funny short story.

Flannery O'Connor, "Good Country People," appearing in *A Good Man Is Hard to Find* (New York: Harcourt, Brace, 1955).
Dark comedy reaches new heights of bleakness in this striking short story about faith, trust, and family.

John Cheever, "The Swimmer," *The New Yorker*, July 18, 1964.
Cheever shows the shallowness (pun intended) of upper-class life in this memorable short story.

Kurt Vonnegut, *Slaughterhouse-Five* (New York: Laurel/Dell, 1969).
War may never look the same after this incredible novel.

Joseph Heller, *Catch-22* (New York: Simon and Schuster, 1961).
There is no topping the absurdity of this daring and satirical novel.

Anita Loos, *Gentleman Prefer Blondes* (New York: Boni and Liveright, 1925).
Loos uses the narrator as a filter to critique thinkers, stars, and political figures in this stunning novel.

unhappy, openly criticizing her stepmother. In an early display of her acerbic wit, Parker opted to call her stepmother "the housekeeper" rather than "Mother" or even "Stepmother." Despite her parents' religious background, Parker spent some time in a Catholic school, though she was asked to leave, after which she attended a finishing school.

Shortly after Parker graduated, her father died. She supported herself by playing piano, but also began writing poetry. She published her first poem in *Vanity Fair*, where she would later work on the magazine's staff. It was while she was working at *Vanity Fair* that she met Robert Benchley, Robert E. Sherwood, and other writers who would become members of the famed Algonquin Round Table, so named because they would have lunch at the Algonquin Hotel. The group became nationally famous when their quips were published by newspaper columnists Franklin Pierce Adams and Alexander Woollcott, among others. One of Parker's most famous one-liners came in response to hearing the news that Calvin Coolidge had died: "How they could tell?" This demonstrated her dark strain of humor.

Parker had success in both publishing and cinema, but she struggled in her personal life, having three marriages and making multiple suicide attempts. She died in 1967. She left her money to the Dr. Martin Luther King, Jr., fund; after King died, her bequest went to the National Association for the Advancement of Colored People (NAACP). In recognition of her work toward racial harmony and equality, the NAACP put up a memorial garden for her outside of its Baltimore headquarters. Parker was also honored with an appearance on a U.S. postage stamp. Her name, along with Benchley's, is also part of Parkbench Productions, the company responsible for *Gilmore Girls* and other television shows.

While many readers appreciated her cutting wit, Parker's quips offended some of the powerful producers of *Vanity Fair*, which led to her termination from her job at the magazine. When she was let go, Robert Benchley and Robert E. Sherwood resigned in a show of solidarity. Parker and Benchley were subsequently included on the board of editors for the newly founded *New Yorker*. Parker's work appeared in the second issue of the magazine. She regularly wrote for *New Yorker*, along with Benchley, James Thurber, and many other notable writers, and eventually putt out her first book of poetry, *Enough Rope*. The title referred in part to her suicide attempts, which she wrote about publicly, most notably in the poem "Resumé," which listed the problems with various methods of suicide, ending with the line, "You might as well live." In addition to her verse, Parker was well known for her reviews. She was often scathing, as in her blistering critique of A. A. Milne's work, which she called overly sweet and lacking in any kind of nuance, concluding that the reader nearly "fwowed up" after encountering it, putting her response of nausea into the register of a child to further drive home her point. But Parker's work was not always so harsh. She used a review of Hemingway's work to make a claim that he would be talked about well after some of the popular writers of the day were forgotten, and her claim has been validated by Hemingway's lasting popularity and critical acclaim.

In addition to her work as a critic, Parker was politically outspoken. She and Benchley often demonstrated in favor of unions, which was particularly striking given their position as well-read and urbane writers. In addition to this tension, Parker felt backlash from the Hollywood community, being blacklisted after being listed as a communist. Along with her commitment to worker's rights and racial equality, Parker had ties to European nations, which some of the more conservative members of Hollywood saw as being disloyal to America. Parker and her associates did not recant her commitment to the causes that she championed. Her disillusionment with her fellow writers is often seen as one of her major sources of bitterness. Another was her struggles with marriage and having a child. Her twice-husband Alan Campbell eventually committed suicide, and Parker drank heavily, such that her work became inconsistent toward the end of her life.

Parker's work often contains a strong vein of cynicism and dark humor. Her work typically ridicules politeness codes and the strict expectations of gender and class roles. One of her famous pieces, "The Waltz," is narrated from the perspective of a woman waltzing with a suitor. The external dialogue of the narrator indicates politeness, but stands in stark contrast to the interior monologue, which belittles the man dancing. A similar piece, "You Were Perfectly Fine," examines an alcoholic boyfriend and a fiancée who forgives and even supports his excesses. By the end of the piece, the man has proposed and the woman is fixing him a drink. These sorts of pieces emphasized that high society was not always admirable. In this sense, Parker's approach to fiction pieces was in keeping with her one-liners from the Algonquin. Also like her quips, her poetry often employed clever references and wordplay.

See also: Benchley, Robert; Loos, Anita; Mencken, H. L

Further Reading

Cerasulo, Tom. *Authors out Here: Fitzgerald, West, Parker and Schulberg in Hollywood.* Columbia: University of South Carolina Press, 2010.

Keats, John. *You Might as Well Live: The Life and Times of Dorothy Parker*. New York: Simon and Schuster, 1970.

Meade, Marion. *Dorothy Parker: What Fresh Hell Is This?* New York: Penguin, 1989.

Parker, Dorothy. *Enough Rope*. New York: Horace Liveright, 1926.

Zeke Jarvis

ROTH, PHILIP (1933–)

Philip Roth was born to first-generation American parents, and he grew up in Newark, New Jersey. After graduating from Weequahic High School in Newark, Roth attended Bucknell University, earning a degree in English. He then earned his master's degree in English from the University of Chicago, where he also taught writing as an instructor. After finishing his studies, Roth served in the U.S. Army. Upon returning from his military service, he taught at the University of Iowa and Princeton University before going to the University of Pennsylvania, where he finished his teaching career.

Roth has had multiple marriages. His first wife, Maureen Tarnopol, separated from him and later died in a car crash. Roth also was married to actress Claire Bloom, before the two went through a bitter divorce with numerous public statements being fired from both sides and many interviewers and critics discussing the exchanges. In general, it is difficult to separate Roth's life from his work because of the heavily autobiographical components of his writing. Roth has increased his output with age rather than diminishing it. He continues to publish books on a regular basis, maintaining a strong presence in the literary world.

Roth's work is characterized by a few recurrent themes. He has focused on the meaning and practice of Judaism in a number of books, playing on different stereotypes and images associated with Jewish life, such as striking mother figures, along

Author Philip Roth is shown in 1960. Roth was known for his frank portrayals of male sexual desire as well as for his keen examination of Jewish culture. (AP Photo)

with tensions within his characters toward their cultural and religious background. In works like the story "Defender of the Faith" and the novel *Portnoy's Complaint*, Roth presents a very complex, conflicted examination of his religion, which includes people misusing their religious positions, leaving behind religion, and gaining striking insights into the nature of contemporary religion. This has led some critics to read him as being a self-hating Jew, but Roth has responded that he is simply presenting the tangled and difficult relationship many Jews have to their place in contemporary culture.

In addition to religion, Roth consistently examines sexuality and relationships, never shying away from frank portrayals and discussions of sex and sexual desire. While this has led some readers to pull away from Roth, his writing is generally more complex than a simple display of graphic content. With issues such as interfaith relationships and Freudian imagery, Roth uses sex to challenge moral strictures and to present weaknesses of his characters as well as desires for personal freedom. These examinations are one of the core sources of humor in Roth's work. He often uses his characters' desires to demonstrate their selfishness or shallowness, helping the reader feel comfortable in laughing at their struggles or misfortunes. In addition, Roth uses the interactions in his stories to satirize many social expectations and politeness codes, demonstrating their absurdity in a humorous, surprising way.

A final core source of humor comes from the strangeness of seeing Roth present his own anxieties, frailties, and interior life in a strikingly honest and direct way in much of his work. The postmodern, unstable nature of much of his work keeps his readers off guard, allowing the door for humor to be opened as he takes surprising turns.

Owing to his use of unstable texts, transgressive material, and heavy focus on faith, Roth has drawn comparisons to Don DeLillo and Saul Bellow. Roth has received numerous awards for his writing, including the Pen/Faulkner Award (Roth is the only writer to have won this award three times), two National Book

Awards, and two National Book Critics Circle Awards, among numerous other prestigious awards. As Roth has aged, his protagonists have often been older men, giving him the chance to further examine and present his ruminations on aging and mortality.

Further Reading

Cooper, Alan. *Philip Roth and the Jews*. Albany: State University of New York Press, 2010.

Ivanova, Velichka. "Philip Roth's *Professor of Desire* in the Light of Its French Translation." *Partial Answers: Journal of Literature and the History of Ideas* 11, no. 2 (June 2013): 293–304.

Philip Roth Studies. West Lafayette, IN: Purdue University Press, various years.

Roth, Philip. *Portnoy's Complaint*. New York: Random House, 1969.

Zeke Jarvis

RUNYON, DAMON (1880–1946)

Born Alfred Damon Runyan in Manhattan, Kansas, Runyon grew up in a newspaper family. His grandfather was a newspaper printer in New Jersey, and his father ran a newspaper in Kansas until he was forced to sell it. The family then moved to Colorado, where he learned to work in print under his father. Runyon worked for various outlets until 1898, when he enlisted in the army during the Spanish-American War. After the war, Runyon moved to New York, where he covered the New York Giants along with professional boxing. Both the city and sports would continue to feature prominently in Runyon's future writing. He also frequently wrote about gambling and was a gambler himself. As Runyon began to cover baseball, he started to incorporate not just facts and statistics, but also the unusual details that made up the experience of the game. This trait led him to be seen as a major influence on how baseball was covered and, often, continues to be covered.

During his time in New York, Runyon married his first wife and had two children. The two later divorced, and Runyon pursued a woman whom he met in Mexico while covering the Pancho Villa raids. They married for a time, though his second wife eventually left Runyon. Runyon died of throat cancer at the age of 66.

Runyon's work is distinctive and consistent enough to establish the term "Runyonesque," with his writing being characterized by a focus on the days of Prohibition, often incorporating characters from the underworld, who are presented less as threatening or even distasteful and more as either bumbling or glamorous. His heavy use of slang and dialect helps to establish the era, geography, and atmosphere of the setting that he examines. Runyon also often tells stories from the perspective from a side character or observer rather than the primary actor or protagonist of the story. This trait also enhances the sense of the reader getting a glimpse into the Runyonesque world of bootlegging and gambling. Runyon's work influence can still be felt in the work of humorists exploiting dialect for puns and other bits of humor as well as in the lively portrayals of underworld figures.

See also: Royko, Mike

Further Reading

Clark, Tom. *The World of Damon Runyon*. New York: Harper and Row, 1978.
Mosedale, John. *The Men Who Invented Broadway: Damon Runyon, Walter Winchell and Their World*. New York: R. Marek, 1981.
Runyon, Damon. *Guys and Dolls: The Stories of Damon Runyon*. New York: Penguin Books, 1992.
Schwarz, Daniel R. *Broadway Boogie Woogie: Damon Runyon and the Making of New York City Culture*. New York: Palgrave Macmillan, 2003.

Zeke Jarvis

SAUNDERS, GEORGE (1958–)

Although Saunders was born in Amarillo, Texas, he grew up on the south side of Chicago. He attended Oak Forest High School in a suburb of Chicago, then went to the Colorado School of Mines in Golden, Colorado, where he received a degree in geophysical engineering. Although he did not go directly from his undergraduate program into a graduate creative writing program, Saunders did eventually attend Syracuse University, where he received a master's degree in creative writing. In between these studies, he worked as a technical writer and with an oil exploration crew.

For a time, Saunders dabbled in the political school of thought known as Objectivism, though he went on to renounce those views, equating them with neoconservatist thought, meaning that he found people embracing the works of Ayn Rand to do more to uphold unequal distribution of wealth than to protect an individual's freedom. Even so, the spirit of disenchantment with much of mainstream society can be seen in much of his writing. Saunders has received a number of prestigious awards, including the MacArthur Fellowship and the Guggenheim Fellowship, both awarded in 2006. Currently, Saunders lives in Syracuse, New York, with his wife and two daughters.

Beyond its satirical nature, Saunders's work often stretches the boundaries of realism. In his story "Pastoralia," a worker at a historical theme park acts the part of a caveman along with a female coworker. The protagonist is pressured by the park's management to file a complaint against his coworker, because she allows anachronisms (her cigarettes, for example) to be seen by tourists visiting the park. While this conflict might be realistic, the comical backdrop of cavemen and the exaggerated seriousness of the protagonist and the management give the story an absurd feel that leads the reader to see the characters as symbolic figures representing the shortcomings of consumer culture rather than being pulled into the story in a purely emotional way.

While some of Saunders's work may fall into the category of slipstream, he has also been recognized for his work in the fantasy genre. This aligns Saunders with other contemporary writers, such as Jonathan Lethem and Michael Chabon, who explore genres outside of the strict boundaries of psychological realism. Not surprisingly, Saunders has been compared to Kurt Vonnegut, and Saunders himself has recognized the debt he owes to Vonnegut.

In addition to his work in short stories and novels, Saunders has written children's books and a column in *The Guardian*. He has also written a feature-length screenplay, and the rights to his book, *CivilWarLand in Bad Decline*, have been purchased by Ben Stiller.

Further Reading

Moore, Fernanda. "George Saunders, Anti-minimalist." *Commentary* 135, no. 5 (2013): 50–52.

Pogell, Sarah. " 'The Verisimilitude Inspector': George Saunders as the New Baudrillard." *Critique* 52, no. 4 (2011): 460–478.

Rando, David. "George Saunders and the Postmodern Working Class." *Contemporary Literature* 53, no. 3 (Fall 2012): 437–460.

Saunders, George. *Pastoralia*. New York: Riverhead Books, 2001.

Zeke Jarvis

THURBER, JAMES (1894–1961)

James Thurber was born in Columbus, Ohio. His father dreamed of being an actor or lawyer, but struggled to find regular employment. His mother was a regular practical joker, sometimes even going so far as pretending to be disabled and attending faith healings where she would claim to have been healed. Thurber regularly acknowledged his mother's skill as a humorist, though she did not pursue publication or professional performance. Thurber had two brothers, one of whom accidentally shot Thurber in the eye while attempting to re-enact William Tell's feat of shooting an apple off of his son's head. As a result, Thurber lost sight in one eye; he would eventually lose his vision completely.

Because of his injury, Thurber was unable to participate in sports like other children, so he began to focus on creative outlets. After graduating from high school, he attended Ohio State University, though his vision problems prevented him from fulfilling all of the requirements for graduation. From 1918 to 1920, Thurber served his war-time country in a variety of capacities, unable to serve in the military. In 1921, Thurber began to work as his reporter. One year later, he married for the first time. The marriage, which was generally an unhappy one, ended in 1935.

In 1925, Thurber moved to New York to write first for the *New York Evening Post* and then for *The New Yorker*. E. B. White, an editor for the latter, encouraged Thurber to pursue his cartooning. In 1935, Thurber married for the second time; this marriage lasted until the time of his death.

Thurber wrote and drew cartoons, achieving and maintaining both commercial and critical success into the 1950s. Eventually, Thurber had to end his career due to health issues. In 1961, Thurber died after experiencing complications from a stroke.

Thurber is known for his playful but dark take on life. Examples include his short story "The Greatest Man in the World," which portrays a man who has accomplished greatness in his field (flying) but is horrible on a personal level. Thurber often employed laughable characters—sometimes still admirable, but often more purely laughable. In his cartooning work, Thurber's vision problems led him to adopt an often simplistic style that fit his comedic views. Thurber was also able to playfully interrogate cultural trends, as he did in his lampooning of radio soap operas and his examination of the hen-pecked husband, Walter Mitty. Thurber was very well respected by writers of his generation, and his work continues to inspire humorists, even having spawned an adaption of "The Secret Life of Walter Mitty" into a film directed by Ben Stiller. Thurber was also a prototypical *New Yorker* writer, combining playfulness, well-observed humor, and a witty, urbane delivery. Given the significant amount of work he completed in his relatively brief career, Thurber is a significant American literary humorist.

See also: Benchley, Robert; Parker, Dorothy

Further Reading

Bodi, Russ. "James Thurber, Midwestern 'Innocent Abroad.' " *Midwestern Miscellany*, 25 (1997): 38–47.

Tanner, Stephen J. "James Thurber and the Midwest." *American Studies* 33, no. 2 (Fall 1992): 61–72.

Thurber, James. *My Life and Hard Times*. New York: Harper Brothers, 1933.

Ward, L. E. "Thurber on Film." *Lost Generation Journal* 10, no. 24 (1990): 17.

Zeke Jarvis

TOOLE, JOHN KENNEDY (1937–1969)

John Kennedy Toole was born in New Orleans to John Dewey Toole, Jr., and Thelma Ducoing Toole. He was taught from a young age to appreciate culture. His mother was the driving force in his affairs, choosing everything from her son's friends to appropriate associations. At her urging, Toole became a stage performer at 10 years old. At age 16, Toole wrote his first novel, *The Neon Bible*, which he later dismissed as "adolescent;" the book was not published until after his death.

Toole attended Tulane University on an academic scholarship, where he wrote for the college newspaper and pursued a degree in engineering. After only a few weeks of studying engineering, he changed his collegiate focus to English. In 1958, after receiving his English degree from Tulane, Toole enrolled in Columbia University in New York. He received a Woodrow Wilson Fellowship to study English literature at the university and took on such a heavy workload that he was able to complete his master's degree in a year. Toole returned to his home in 1959 and spent a year there as an assistant professor of English at the University of Southwestern Louisiana (since renamed the University of Louisiana at Lafayette). In May 1960, Toole was to move to Seattle to teach Renaissance literature at the University of Washington on a three-year fellowship. Instead, he jumped at the chance to teach at Hunter College in New York, where he became the youngest professor in the history of the college.

While working at Hunter College, Toole pursued his doctorate degree at Columbia University. His work was interrupted when he was drafted into the U.S. Army in 1961. Because he spoke Spanish, Toole was stationed in Fort Buchanan in San Juan, Puerto Rico, for two years. At Fort Buchanan, he taught English to the Spanish-speaking recruits. Toole received a hardship discharge, as his parents had fallen on economically hard times. He turned down the offer to return to his position at Hunter College and went home to his family. In New Orleans, he accepted a teaching position at Dominican College, a Catholic all-girls school.

While living at his parents' home, Toole completed the manuscript for his novel *A Confederacy of Dunces*. He submitted the manuscript to multiple publication agencies, but only met with disappointment. Eventually, Toole gave up entirely on getting the novel published. He began writing a new novel, *The Conqueror Worm*, and focused on his job at Dominican College. Toole fell into a deep depression following his rejections. His depression manifested in him being drunk and unkempt, which ultimately resulted in him losing his job. Shortly thereafter, Toole left home and committed suicide.

Upon Toole's death, his mother took it upon herself to see *A Confederacy of Dunces* published. After numerous rejections, she finally succeeded in her quest. The book caused waves in the literary world, being awarded the Pulitzer Prize for Fiction. Since its publication, the book has sold more than 1.5 million copies in 18 languages.

Although he did publish *The Neon Bible*, Toole is known primarily for *A Confederacy of Dunces*. This book is characterized by ridiculous characters, clear social commentary, and a bleak view of humanity. Characters like the Levys show a rich family that is too removed from most people to care about anything meaningful, even each other. Likewise, the main character, Ignatius, is a well-educated but immature character, never connecting to anyone in a meaningful way or holding down even a modest job. Ignatius lies and cheats his way through life, misapplying religious and philosophical teachings, and always dreaming of a book that he plans on writing without ever coming close to actually writing it. In the novel, Toole shows a skepticism toward social movements, higher education, and pop culture. Although this leaves very little for readers to cling to, many readers appreciate the broad satire and bizarre behaviors found in the book.

Further Reading

Gletcher, Joel. *Ken and Thelma: The Story of* A Confederacy of Dunces. New Orleans: Pelican, 2005.

MacLauchlin, Cory. *Butterfly in the Typewriter: The Tragic Life of John Kennedy Toole and the Remarkable Story of* A Confederacy of Dunces. Boston: Decapo Press, 2012.

Nevils, Rene Pol, and Deborah George Hardy. *Ignatius Rising: The Life of John Kennedy Toole*. Baton Rouge: Louisiana State University Press, 2001.

Toole, John Kennedy. *A Confederacy of Dunces*. Baton Rouge: Louisiana State University Press, 1980.

Kristen Franz

VONNEGUT, KURT (1922–2007)

Kurt Vonnegut, Jr., was born in Indianapolis, Indiana, on November 11, 1922. He studied chemistry at Cornell University and worked on the campus newspaper, *The Cornell Daily Sun*. While at Cornell, Vonnegut enlisted in the army, which transferred him to the Carnegie Institute of Technology and the University of Tennessee to finish his studies. He went to Europe to fight in World War II, where he was captured as a prisoner of war at the Battle of the Bulge in 1944. Vonnegut witnessed the firebombing of Dresden while in prison there, surviving the aerial assault in an underground meat locker that was used by the Germans as a prison. His experiences as a prisoner of war influenced his later fiction, especially *Slaughterhouse-Five*.

When he returned to the United States after the war, Vonnegut pursued graduate studies in anthropology at the University of Chicago. After his master's thesis was rejected, he went to Schenectady, New York, to begin a career with General Electric as a technical writer. Around this time, Vonnegut married his first wife, Jane Cox. The pair had three children together, but would ultimately divorce after a long separation. During this time, Vonnegut lived with Jill Krementz, who became his second wife and with whom Vonnegut adopted four children, including three children of Vonnegut's sister after her death.

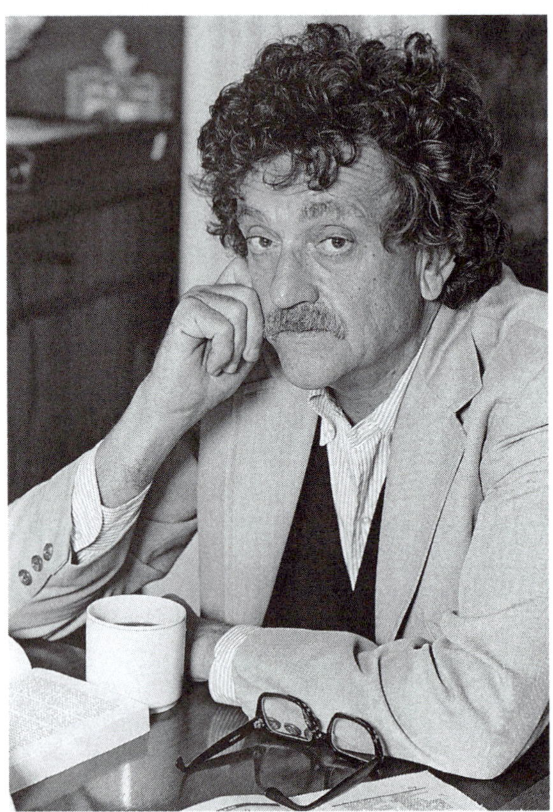

Kurt Vonnegut is best known for his novels, which include *Slaughterhouse-Five* and *Breakfast of Champions*. Vonnegut's work is both brilliant and vulgar, capturing the chaotic and complex nature of life. (AP Photo)

Vonnegut's first novel, *Player Piano*, was published in 1952. *Sirens of Titan* followed in 1959. *Mother Night* appeared in 1961. Published in 1963, his fourth novel, *Cat's Cradle*, was accepted by the University of Chicago as Vonnegut's master's thesis in 1971. The university then awarded him his master's degree in anthropology. *God Bless You, Mr. Rosewater, or Pearls Before Swine*, was published in 1965. *Slaughterhouse-Five, or The Children's Crusade: A Duty-Dance with Death*, which was published in 1969 and nominated for a Nebula Award and Hugo Award, is Vonnegut's best-known novel. Vonnegut continued publishing novels, with *Breakfast of Champions, or Goodbye Blue Monday* appearing in 1973. His last novel, *Timequake*, was published in 1997.

Afflicted with depression, Vonnegut attempted suicide in 1984. A collection of short fictional interviews with Dr. Jack Kevorkian, a physician who attracted controversy for assisting his patients in committing suicide, was published in 1999 and broadcast on National Public Radio. Later in his life, Vonnegut focused on his art, which he had begun earlier in his writing career with illustrations for *Slaughterhouse-Five* and *Breakfast of Champions*. He continued addressing political issues, offering cynical commentary on the Iraq War and the George W. Bush administration. Vonnegut died in 2007 after falling down the stairs at his home in Manhattan.

Vonnegut is best known for his humorous science fiction work. Inspired by his experiences as a prisoner of war in Dresden, *Slaughterhouse-Five* is an account of an optometrist who was once a soldier captured by the Germans during the Battle of the Bulge. The optometrist believes he was also once an exhibit in an alien zoo. The novel's examinations of free will and fate are apparent in the film adaptation, which won the Jury Prize at the Cannes Film Festival, in addition to a Hugo Award and a Saturn Award. Like later writers such as Michael Chabon and Chuck Palahniuk, Vonnegut often incorporated lofty ideas and themes, such as Christianity and anthropology, into his work, along with more vulgar practices, like pornography and war. For this reason, Vonnegut's body of work is distinctly postmodern in that it experiments with form and narration and explores themes relevant to the post-World War II nuclear age. Much of his work, such as his short story "Harrison Bergeron," can be considered science fiction, but there is also a clear sense of social commentary and satire. This has led to many comparisons of Vonnegut and Mark Twain. Vonnegut certainly acknowledged the influence of Twain and even named his first-born son after Twain. Even so, the use of genre fiction and the minimalist style coming out of his experience as a technical writer and journalist are all Vonnegut's own.

See also: Palahniuk, Chuck

Further Reading

Freese, Peter. "The Critical Reception of Kurt Vonnegut." *Literature Compass* 9, no. 1 (January 2012): 1–14.

Shields, Charles J. *And So It Goes: Kurt Vonnegut: A Life*. New York: St. Martin's Griffin, 2012.

Vonnegut, Kurt. *Slaughterhouse-Five*. New York: Delacorte, 1969.

Ward, Joseph J. "Following in the Footsteps of Sisyphus: Camus, Vonnegut and Rational Emotive Behavior Therapy." *Interdisciplinary Literary Studies: A Journal of Criticism and Theory* 14, no. 1 (2012): 79–94.

Stephen Powers

WELTY, EUDORA (1909–2001)

Born in Jackson, Mississippi, in 1909, novelist and short fiction writer Eudora Welty became a voracious reader at a young age. She studied at Mississippi State College for Women, the University of Wisconsin, and Columbia University, where she learned to type at the Graduate School of Business. Welty lived briefly in New York, but, unable to secure a job during the Great Depression, returned home to Jackson. At this time, she worked for a radio station, a newspaper, and the Works

The 20th-century writer Eudora Welty is best known for her short stories and for novels such as *Delta Wedding* and *The Optimist's Daughter*. Welty's work skewers Southern culture for its absurd and disingenuous sense of politeness. (Library of Congress)

Progress Administration. Her work with the Works Progress Administration would give her experiences to draw on when she began writing and publishing her fiction. Welty also took a series of celebrated photographs while working for the Works Progress Administration. These photographs are known for their documentation of the effects of the Great Depression on the rural poor living in the South.

Welty published her first short story, "The Death of a Traveling Salesman," in 1936. She then went on to publish a string of stories in several respected magazines and journals, including *The New Yorker*, *Harper's Bazaar*, *Atlantic Monthly*, and *The Southern Review*. In 1941, Welty received a second-place O. Henry Award for her story "A Worn Path," which is about a character named Phoenix who has many traits similar to the mythological bird. Welty also published her first book-length collection of stories, *A Curtain of Green*, with an introduction by Katherine Anne Porter, a Pulitzer Prize-winning American writer. *A Curtain of Green* contains 17 stories, including "Petrified Man" and "Why I Live at the P.O."—two of Welty's best-known works that continue to be reprinted in anthologies. "Petrified Man," which was first rejected by *The Southern Review* before the editors relented and agreed to publish it after all, was rewritten from memory after Welty burned the only copy she had of the version that was rejected. *A Curtain of Green* established Welty's reputation as a Southern writer.

Welty received a first-place O. Henry Award in 1942 for her short story "A Wide Net." Also in 1942, she published her first novel, *The Robber Bridegroom*. In 1963, Welty wrote "Where Is the Voice Coming from?," a short story inspired by the assassination of civil rights leader Medgar Evers, who was shot outside his home in Jackson, Mississippi. The story was an attempt to enter the mind of Evers's assassin, Byron De La Beckwith, a white supremacist who belonged to the Ku Klux Klan. Welty stated that the story was an exercise in understanding De La Beckwith's motivations. "Where Is the Voice Coming from?" was published in *The New Yorker* shortly after De La Beckwith was arrested and charged with the murder of Evers.

Welty continued writing throughout the 1960s and won another first-prize O. Henry Award in 1968 for her story, "The Demonstrators." It focuses on the civil rights movement, including the way it was treated in the press as well as the way it was seen by Southerners. The story appeared in *The New Yorker* in 1966.

Welty's novel *The Optimist's Daughter* was published in 1972. Considered by many to be her best work, *The Optimist's Daughter* is her last novel. It won the Pulitzer Prize for Fiction in 1973.

Throughout her lifetime, Welty gave numerous lectures, including at Harvard University. She held the William Allan Neilson professorship at Smith College and the Lucy Donnelly Fellowship at Bryn Mawr College. She also held a lecturer post at Cambridge University. She received grants from the Rockefeller Foundation and held a Guggenheim Fellowship.

Welty continued her streak of winning awards throughout the 1980s, including the Presidential Medal of Freedom in 1980, the National Book Award in 1983 for *The Collected Works of Eudora Welty*, and a National Medal of Arts in 1986. In 1998, Welty became the first living author to have her works compiled in the Library of America series, which publishes volumes collecting major writings by important U.S. literary figures in an effort to keep their work in print. The Library of America series devoted two volumes to Welty: one for her stories and essays, and one for her five novels.

Welty died in 2001 at the age of 92. Her home in Jackson, Mississippi, is listed on the National Register of Historic Places and is open to the public. A portrait of Welty also hangs in the National Portrait Gallery in Washington, D.C.

Welty's body of work is known for its emphasis on place. Welty stated numerous times that she felt place made fiction seem real and that the job of the fiction writer is to give place importance by connecting it to memory. In particular, Welty was well known for satirizing the Southern sense of politeness by showing the appearance of politeness along with prejudices and pettiness on the part of the characters, much like other Southern writers—most notably, Flannery O'Connor. Citing Mark Twain and Henry James as her influences, Welty portrays in her stories the South and its people as both tragic and comic, as well as mundane. The stories in *A Curtain of Green* present the racial tensions of the South with a frank realism not seen in many other literary works written during Welty's time. Welty does not make racial tensions the central focus, however; the South—more specifically, Mississippi—becomes a place of beauty and reverence in many of her stories.

See also: O'Connor, Flannery

Further Reading

Brown, Carolyn J. *A Daring Life: A Biography of Eudora Welty*. Jackson: University of Mississippi Press, 2012.

Marrs, Suzanne. *Eudora Welty: A Biography*. New York: Mariner Books, 2006.

Welty, Eudora. *The Optimist's Daughter*. New York: Random House, 1972.

White, Elizabeth. "Observations: Eudora Welty at Home in the World." *Southern Quarterly* 51, nos. 1/2 (Fall 2013/Winter 2014): 106–116.

Stephen Powers

Section II: Popular Writing

What makes it into the literary canon is hard to state in a way that is both clear and consistent. Some writers, such as genre writers like Kurt Vonnegut, have often derided scholars for their attempts to keep them out of the literary canon. Vonnegut's eventual inclusion in the literary canon via the *Norton Anthology of American Literature* validated his skepticism. But if his skepticism was validated, then the canon that includes him through examinations in scholarly journals and presentations and other outlets could still be suspect. At the same time, the inclusion of Vonnegut could show that the literary canon is dynamic in a way that demonstrates its relevance. That said, some writers have consistently turned their back on literary validation, focusing instead on a popular readership. While Robert Benchley did have a major impact on literary tastes through his role in the Algonquin Round Table and on the staff of *The New Yorker*, he also wrote popular humorous shorts and had a clear presence in Hollywood in both comedic short films and regular side roles in feature-length movies. The overlap of literary, popular, and performance work has helped a number of writers support themselves and gain lasting fame.

Other humorists have straddled genre boundaries in another way—that is, by creating work that has the complexity of a literary text, yet also immediacy and popular appeal. Cartoonists fall into this category. These artists have found the detail- and image-driven nature of comic strips and political cartoons the perfect venues in which to deliver short but memorable bits of humor. From the benign, uncontroversial humor of *Garfield* and *Peanuts* to the blistering critiques of race, politics, and pop culture concerns found in *The Boondocks*, the sometimes belittled "funny pages" were regarded very much like the science fiction and horror genres were in literary circles. While many comic strips have fallen in or out of favor on the pages of nationally syndicated newspapers, others, although well read, have not broken through into the national consciousness (strips like *Arlo and Janis* or *Frank and Enrest* are long running and widely published but have not published stand-alone books, unlike their more popular counterparts *Garfield* and *Calvin & Hobbes*). Still, cartoon strips and comic books exploded in their cultural relevance in the 20th century. Although political cartoons have had a significant impact on American culture, the rise in popularity of comics like *Batman* and *The Uncanny X-Men* as well as television cartoons ranging from *The Flintstones* to *The Simpsons* to *Family Guy* has also brought animation and cartoons into cultural prominence, and humor in both comic books and comic strips have benefited from this new level of attention. Cartoon strips have also expanded beyond the confines of newspapers, spilling over into television, page-a-day calendars, T-shirts, and more. With the rise of the Internet, comic strips are now even easier to publish, market, and distribute. Moreover, the advent of publishing and layout software and the easy access to resources like clipart have greatly simplified the task of assembling cartoons. Strips like *Get Your War On* and forms like the memes on Facebook and other social media outlets have put the recycling of established images to comedic use. While these efforts are often directed toward belittling celebrities, they also have been used for clear political messages. This sort of work has helped increase the cultural relevance of image-based humor, which in turn has increased both popular interest and scholarly attention in these media.

In fact, while many scholars value literary writing above "popular" writing, others see the printed work with the larger readership to be more worthy of study, because it has the broadest impact upon American culture. Whether it was *The Boondocks* discussing Jesse Jackson or Brian K. Vaughan's complex but focused skewering of both unthinkingly and overly simplistic political views in *Y: The Last Man* and *Ex Machina*, writers have found outlets through these media to articulate views and scenarios that are both realistic and fantastic to get at the key and pervasive issues of the day—and scholars have taken notice. In fact, because it is often younger scholars examining these sorts of texts, they often receive some of the most novel and innovative analysis.

ADAMS, SCOTT (1957–)

Scott Adams was born in Windham, New York. By age six, he was already beginning to draw comics, using *Peanuts* and *Mad* for inspiration. After failing to gain entrance into an art school, Adams decided to pursue a more mainstream career. During his time working in banks, he often would rely upon his humor to help make a positive impression during presentations. It was during this time that Adams created Dilbert, his signature character. Having worked at a number of positions and levels in management, Adams found a good deal of business-oriented material to infuse into his comic-strip work.

In 1989, Adams first began publishing *Dilbert* with United Media, although he continued working in the business world on a full-time basis. Adams's success built up steadily, gaining a wider base of publication, which led to a book *The Dilbert Principle*, a television adaptation of *Dilbert*, and the Reuben Award for Outstanding Cartoonist (the top annual honor for cartoonists) in 1997. Adams has shown interests outside of his humor pursuits, becoming a member of MENSA, being an advocate for vegetarian cuisine, and often commenting on politics outside of his strips. Adams has been married since 2006, and he currently lives with his wife in California.

Adams's work is characterized by pompous and stereotypically incompetent authority figures behaving in an idiotic manner. Dilbert, the title character, generally serves as the voice of reason to the absurd boss and the tyrannical Dogbert. There is often a strong sense of sarcasm behind much of the dialogue. Adams also satirizes corporate modes of speaking, highlighting the emptiness of certain ways of phrasing policies or philosophies to demonstrate the essential selfishness and laziness of many high-level corporate workers. This has led him to be a hero for many middle- and lower-level managerial workers who appreciate seeing their superiors taken down in a comedic way. While Adams has had some written and performance work outside of his cartoon strip, *Dilbert* remains the core of his body of work.

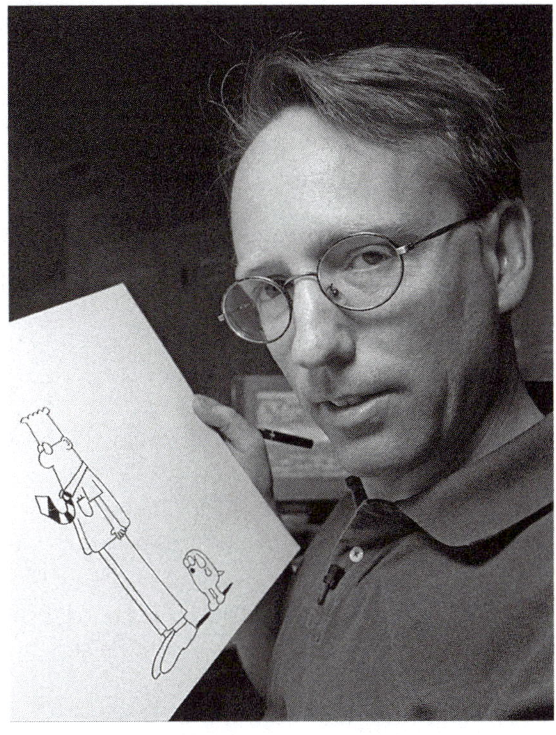

Scott Adams is the creator of the popular comic strip, *Dilbert*. His irreverent take on office work has pleased fans for years. (AP Photo/Ben Margot)

Further Reading

Adams, Scott. *The Dilbert Principle*. New York: HarperBusiness, 1997.

Lindborg, Henry J. "The Dilbert Syndrome." *Quality Progress* 46, no. 10 (October 2013): 46–47.

Locker, Melissa. "Watch Scott Adams and Paul Rudd Recreate *Bosom Buddies*." *Time.com*, January 27, 2014, p. 1-1.
McGinn, Daniel. "Scott Adams." *Harvard Business Review* 91, no. 11 (November 2013): 144.

Zeke Jarvis

BARRY, DAVE (1947–)

Dave Barry was born in Armonk, New York. At Pleasantville High School, he was elected "class clown." After graduating from high school, Barry went on to Haverford College, where he graduated with a degree in English. Barry avoided service in the Vietnam War by declaring himself a religious conscientious objector, being the son of a minister and a graduate of a Quaker college. Ironically, Barry would later describe himself as an atheist, despite the fact that he attended a synagogue with his wife.

In 1971, Barry began working as a journalist, writing for the *Daily Local News* in West Chester, Pennsylvania. In addition to covering local civic events, Barry began writing a humor column. It was around this time that Barry married his first wife, although he divorced her not long after their wedding. He moved on to work at other papers and also taught professional writing to businesspeople, an effort that he would later belittle. In 1976, he married his second wife, Beth, with whom he had one child.

In 1981, Barry wrote a guest column for *The Philadelphia Inquirer*, which garnered him the attention that would allow him to get a position regularly writing a humor column for the *Miami Herald*. Barry's column became nationally syndicated, and he won a Pulitzer Prize for his work. In addition, Barry worked in other media, writing the novel *Big Trouble*, which was later adapted into a film, and having a television show, *Dave's World*, based up his work. The character based on Barry was played by actor Harry Anderson, although Barry did appear in the show. After four seasons and a time-slot change, the show was canceled.

In 1996, Barry married his current wife Michelle, with whom he has a child. Barry and his wife live in Miami, where they both work on the *Miami Herald*—Barry as a columnist and his wife as a sports reporter.

In addition to his work as a writer, Barry is the member of a musical group whose members have included fellow writers and humorists such as Matt Groening, Stephen King, Roy Blount, Jr., Mitch Albom, and Amy Tan, among others. The group's name, The Rock Bottom Remainders, is a reference to the term for unsold books, with such "remainders" often being sold at heavily discounted prices.

Barry's style is often absurd, highlighting the failures of logic in human behavior. Not surprisingly, he has listed Robert Benchley as an influence. Although Barry often takes on other figures, he does not shy away from critiquing his own behavior. For example, he laughed at his "guy" qualities in the introduction to his book *Dave Barry's Complete Guide to Guys*, such as taking on a bet to perform a physical act that he is not in good enough shape to complete, only to injure himself in the process.

See also: Benchley, Robert; Groening, Matt

Further Reading

Barry, Dave. *Dave Barry's Complete Guide to Guys*. New York: Ballantine Books, 1996.

Sheffield, Katherine E. "Dave Barry's Serious Political Satire: An Analysis of *Dave Barry Hits below the Beltway*." *Studies in American Humor* 3, no. 18 (2008): 39–58.

Stein, Joel. "Dave Barry." *Time International (Canada Edition)* 154, no. 15 (October 10, 1999): 66.

Whitehouse, Beth. "Talking with Dave Barry." *Newsday (Melville, NY)*, March 17, 2014.

Zeke Jarvis

BENCHLEY, ROBERT (1889–1945)

Robert Benchley was born in Worcester, Massachusetts. His grandfather, a Texan, had been arrested for his role in helping slaves escape along the Underground Railroad. Like his grandfather, Benchley was committed to causes of equality and the rights of the oppressed. Benchley's older brother fought in the Spanish-American War. When he was killed, Benchley's mother was said to have responded to the news by saying, "Why couldn't it have been Robert?" The fiancée of Benchley's brother would go on to help pay for Robert's education at Phillips Exeter Academy and, later, at Harvard College. Benchley was involved in academic and traveling theater productions during his time at Phillips Exeter, so much so that his grades suffered toward the end of his schooling. During his time at Harvard, Benchley gained a good deal of experience entertaining audiences, both in performances and at the *Harvard Lampoon*, on whose board of directors he served during his junior year.

Benchley worked a number of writing jobs after graduating from Harvard and honed his approach to humor with a variety of public practical jokes (some more successful than others) until he eventually got regular freelance work reviewing plays and writing satirical and absurd pieces. This led to his staff position at *Vanity Fair*, where he met Dorothy Parker, with whom he would regularly collaborate. The two of them, along with other writers such as Robert Emmet Sherwood, would form the Algonquin Round Table; the group was named for the Algonquin Hotel, where they would have lunch and trade quips. Many of these quips would be published by journalists attending these lunches.

After Parker was let go by *Vanity Fair*, Benchley and fellow Algonquin Round Table member Sherwood resigned in a show of solidarity. Benchley continued to get freelance work, often publishing humorous pieces in *Life*. After an adaptation of his short piece "The Treasurer's Report" achieved critical and financial success, Benchley wrote and starred in a number of films, both short and feature length, making him part of the group of writers who turned to Hollywood to make a living (this group included James Thurber as well). Benchley's work in film eventually began to dominate his time, which left his writing unattended. While he continued to appear regularly on film and radio, Benchley eventually succumbed to cirrhosis from his heavy drinking.

Benchley's writing often employed a deadpan style that came from a seemingly serious or pompous man failing to effectively explain or defend a principle. In pieces like "The Treasurer's Report" and his *How To . . .* series, Benchley drew laughs by feigning a desire for seriousness and confidence in the face of increasingly absurd developments. This sort of combination of sacrificed dignity, madcap turns, and comic wordplay has been acknowledged as influential by both Steve Martin and Dave Barry in their comments on Benchley's work. Benchley also regularly lampooned bits of culture held dear by the upper class. In his short piece "Opera Synopses," for instance, Benchley creates fictitious operas whose plots are filled with non-sequiturs and obscure references to ridicule the tendency of opera goers to attend such events without having any notion of the performance's plot or story. While Benchley is not as well remembered as some of his contemporaries, like James Thurber, he has had tremendous influence on some contemporary humorists, and his children and grandchildren (Nathaniel Benchley and Peter Benchley, in particular) have gone on to be prominent authors in their own right.

See also: Barry, Dave; Parker, Dorothy; Thurber, James

Further Reading

Altman, Billy. *Laughter's Gentle Soul: The Life of Robert Benchley*. New York: W. W. Norton, 1997.

Benchley, Nathaniel. *Robert Benchley: A Biography*. New York: Cassell, 1956.

Benchley, Robert, and Nathaniel Benchley, eds. *The Benchley Roundup*. Chicago: University of Chicago Press, 2001.

Goldsworthy, Kim. *Lunch at the Algonquin*. New York: CreateSpace Independent Publishing Platform, 2011.

Zeke Jarvis

BOMBECK, ERMA (1927–1996)

Erma Bombeck was born in Bellbrook, Ohio, and raised in Dayton. She started elementary school a year younger than the typical age and was quite successful in her studies. Before Bombeck turned 10, her father died, and her family moved in with her grandparents. Just two years after her father's death, Bombeck's mother remarried. Around the same time, Bombeck began performing, focusing on singing and dancing. In middle school, she began writing a column for the school newspaper.

After graduating from high school, Bombeck took a year to work as a typist to save money for college. She enrolled in Ohio University, but dropped out after one semester when she ran out of money. She later enrolled in Dayton University, working at a department store to help pay for her tuition. While working there, she wrote humorous pieces for the company newsletter.

In 1949, Bombeck graduated from Dayton University with a degree in English. That same year, she converted to Catholicism and married Bill Bombeck. In 1953, the two adopted a daughter, because doctors had claimed that the two would not be likely to have a child. Erma Bombeck continued to write humorous pieces while staying home to raise their daughter. In 1955, the pair had a son, with a second son following in 1958.

In 1964, Bombeck began publishing columns in the local newspaper. In 1967, her first collection of columns was published under the title *At Wits End*. By 1969, Bombeck's column was nationally syndicated. Bombeck continued to write her column and publish books. By 1975, she even began to have pieces on the television show *Good Morning America*. In 1992, Bombeck was diagnosed with breast cancer. Although she survived the cancer, she died of long-term kidney disease in 1996.

Bombeck was highly regarded for her clever sarcasm and ability to laugh at herself. Like other female humorists, she often dealt with family issues, particularly the frustrations of having to focus on others while trying to maintain a sense of self. Although Bombeck generally had a broad appeal, she did experience some backlash from conservative figures when she worked for effective and efficient implementation of the Equal Rights Amendment, in hopes that she could serve to bring more protection to women. Nevertheless, Bombeck is primarily known for her observational humor and her ability to find the humor in everyday struggles and subjects that gave her a broad appeal.

Further Reading

Bombeck, Erma. *Aunt Erma's Cope Book*. New York: McGraw-Hill, 1979.

Edwards, Susan. *Erma Bombeck: A Life in Humor*. New York: Avon Books, 1997.

Foster, David William. "Erma Bombeck: The Phoenix Suburban Underbelly." *Journal of Popular Culture* 45, no. 1 (February 2012): 27–40.

King, Norman. *Here's Erma: The Bombecking of America*. New York: Caroline House, 1982.

Zeke Jarvis

CRUMB, ROBERT (1943–)

Robert Crumb was born in Philadelphia, Pennsylvania; he was one of five children born to Charles and Beatrice Crumb. The couple's marriage was unhappy and was further complicated by their two other sons' (Charles and Maxon) struggles with mental illness. Crumb's love of illustrating comics came about when he and his brothers began creating their own and selling them door to door in his early teen years. Shortly after, he began collecting blue and jazz records.

Crumb's first job came in 1962, where he drew greeting cards for American Greetings in Cleveland, Ohio. Through one of his coworkers, he met his future wife, Dana Morgan. The two married in 1964. It was around this time that Crumb began submitting his cartoons to comic book companies, though his work drew little interest from them. Crumb got some of his work printed in the humor magazine, *Help!*, but the magazine stopped publication soon after his pieces appeared, which kept him from staying in New York.

Shortly after marrying Morgan, Crumb began experimenting with LSD. This experimentation had a large effect on the work he was doing. Many of his more famous characters—Mr. Natural, The Snoid, Shuman the Human, the men from "Keep on Truckin"—came out of this period. He moved to San Francisco in 1967 to be at the center of the counterculture movement. The first issue of *Zap Comix* appeared the following year, featuring some of Crumb's work. Robert and Dana welcomed their only child, Jesse, the same year.

The late 1960s and early 1970s found Crumb at his most prolific. In 1978, he and Dana divorced. Soon thereafter, Crumb married cartoonist Aline Kominsky, who became a long-time collaborator. He began a comic magazine (*Weirdo*) in 1981 and had his only daughter, Sophie, in 1981. Robert and Aline moved the family to southern France around this time and collaborated on *Dirty Laundry Comics*.

Apart from his cartoons, Crumb has been an active musician with various bands and has illustrated many album covers. Between 1994 and 2009, he was the subject of a documentary (*Crumb*), created *The Crumb Family Comics* (with pieces written by members of his family), and published *Self-Loathing Comics*. In 2009, Crumb published *The Book of Genesis*, a graphic novel of the biblical book of Genesis.

Despite starting out reserved and fairly typical, Crumb's work after his LSD exposure evolved into a uniquely surrealistic style. Over the years, he has been lauded for his satire and detail-oriented work, but has generated tremendous controversy owing to his depiction of graphic sexuality, drugs, violence, and abnormal psychology. The success of the *Zap Comix* series is viewed as the (unofficial) beginning of the underground comix era (1968–1975). Much of Crumb's work is satirical, taking on major American systems and structures like capitalism. Crumb has cited Carl Banks (Donald Duck) and John Stanley (Little Lulu) as major influences on his development and narrative style. He was nominated for the Harvey Special Award for Humor in 1990 and the Angouleme Grand Prix in 1999. He was also among those honored by the Jewish Museum in New York City in 2006–2007 in its exhibition "Masters of American Comics."

Further Reading

Alleva, Richard. "Comic Erudition: R. Crumb Meets Kafka." *Commonweal* 129, no. 13 (July 12, 2002): 18–19.

Crumb, Robert. *R. Crumb's Fritz the Cat*. New York: Ballantine, 1967.

Jolly, Don. "Interpretive Treatments of Genesis in Comics: R. Crumb and Dave Sim." *Journal of Religion and Popular Culture* 25, no. 3 (Fall 2013): 333–343.

Widmer, Ted. "The Art of Comics I." *Paris Review* 193 (Summer 2010): 19–57.

Brian Davis

DAVIS, JIM (1945–)

Jim Davis was born in Marion, Indiana, where he grew up on the family farm. The family had a variety of animals, including 25 cats. Davis stayed in Indiana for his college years, attending Ball State University. After graduating from college, he worked at an advertising agency. He also helped fellow cartoonist Tom Ryan on the strip *Tumbleweeds*, a satirical take on the old west. After assisting Ryan, Davis created his own strip *Gnorm Gnat*. While his editor complimented Davis on his art and jokes, he also recommended that Davis try a different, more relatable animal.

In 1978, Davis created his most famous comic strip, *Garfield*. *Garfield* was syndicated in 41 strips and had a steady readership. The readership's loyalty became clear when the *Chicago Sun-Times* canceled the strip and the outcry from readers was so great that the newspaper quickly began publishing it again. In the 1980s, Davis created *US Acres*, which is where his character Orson the Pig began. Orson and some of the other characters from *US Acres* showed up in the cartoon series *Garfield and Friends*, which debuted in 1988, 10 years after *Garfield* began running as a comic strip. Davis has been married twice. He has one child with his first wife and two children with his second wife, whom he married in 2000.

Davis is clearly best known for *Garfield*, which employs sarcastic digs at the various characters, including the lazy, constantly eating titular cat; the cat's owner Jon Arbuckle, who, like Davis, grew up on a farm and is a cartoonist; and the owner's good-natured but dim-witted dog Odie. Other characters serve as love interests and foils for the other characters. *Garfield* is typical of many nationally syndicated comic strips in that it finds its readership partially by eschewing politically or socially complicated topics, focusing instead on the characters' idiosyncrasies. While Davis's work does not push boundaries or experiment with form, his relatively simple style serves the straightforward, conventional approach to joke making. Davis has established his work as a competent and consistent cartoonist who is greatly respected by a large and sustained readership, with *Garfield* becoming the most financially successful comic strip in U.S. history.

Further Reading

Davis, Jim. *30 Years of Laughs and Lasagna: The Life and Times of a Fat, Furry Legend.* New York: Ballantine Books, 2008.

Gonzalez, Matt. "Comic Relief." *Indianapolis Monthly* 32, no. 7 (February 2009): 30.

Raugust, Karen. "A Big, Fat, Hairy Anniversary." *Publishers Weekly* 250, no. 25 (June 23, 2003): 26.

Rees, David. "Why Did Garfield Jump?" *American Letters & Commentary* 15 (2003): 70–72.

Zeke Jarvis

LARSON, GARY (1950–)

Gary Larson was born in University Place, Washington, to Verner and Doris Larson. Larson had taken an interest in music during high school, playing guitar and banjo. He graduated from Washington State University with a degree in communications.

Larson began experimenting with cartooning while taking a few days off from his job at a music store, which he says he hated. In 1976, he submitted six cartoons to *Pacific Search*, a Seattle-based magazine. A few years later in 1979, Larson published work in the *Seattle Times* under the title *Nature's Way*. As he continued to try to support himself, while on vacation in San Francisco, Larson approached the *San Francisco Chronicle* with his work. The newspaper accepted and syndicated it, renaming the strip *The Far Side*. It became Larson's major success. He continued writing *The Far Side* until January 1995, with distribution to more than 1,900 newspapers.

Larson married anthropologist Toni Carmichael in 1987; shortly thereafter, she became his manager. In addition to his comic work and interest in music,

Twenty Great Comic Strips

BC by Johnny Hart, 1958–2007
Caveman humor abounds in this great strip.

Bizarro by Dan Piraro, 1985–
This off-the-wall strip has a unique vision.

Bloom County by Berkeley Breathed, 1980–1989
Odd animals rule the day in this inventive comic.

The Boondocks by Aaron McGruder, 1999–2006
Racial boundaries are broken by this comic.

Calvin and Hobbes by Bill Waterson, 1985–1995
This strip balances goofiness with depth.

Dennis the Menace by Hank Ketcham, 1951–
This is a classic naughty child with a heart of gold.

Dilbert by Scott Adams, 1989–
This strip plays on office politics.

Doonesbury by Gary Trudeau, 1970–
Real politics are the core of this strip.

The Far Side by Gary Larson, 1980–1995
This odd strip plays on human behavior.

Foxtrot by Bill Amend, 1988–
Math jokes and silly humor abound in this comic.

Garfield by Jim Davis, 1978–
This fat cat looms large.

Krazy Kat by George Herriman, 1913–1944
Here is the original oddball animal.

Life in Hell by Matt Groening, 1977–2012
This strip is where *The Simpsons* creator got his start.

L'il Abner by Al Capp, 1934–1977
Hillbillies get the laughs here.

This Modern World by Tom Tomorrow, 1988–
Conservatives beware in this strip.

Mother Goose and Grimm by Mike Peters, 1984–
This is a nice, mild but strongly funny strip.

Non Sequitur by Wiley Miller, 1992–
Odd observations rule this strip.

Peanuts by Charles Schulz, 1950–2000
Generations have fallen in love with this gang.

Pogo by Walt Kelly, 1948–1975
The bayou gets a voice in this comic strip.

Red Meat by Max Cannon, 1989–
Blistering absurdity runs through this strip.

Wizard of Id by Jeff Parker, 1964–
Weirdness rules the day in this strip.

Larson has consistently demonstrated his commitment as a staunch environmentalist—a theme that often informs his work. He retired from *The Far Side* because of his fear that the cartoon was becoming repetitive. Although not as prolific as he was during *The Far Side* years, Larson continues to work in the field. His more than 20 books of cartoon collections have collectively sold more than 45 million copies. *The Far Side* was merchandised into popular greeting cards until 2009 and was made into two animated features in 1994 and 1997—*Tales from the Far Side* and *Tales from the Far Side II.*

Larson's style is often referred to as surreal. Specifically, in *The Far Side*, he often uses anthropomorphism among his animal characters, comparing the "superior" humans to animals by putting them in dense housing neighborhoods and surrounding them with fences. His surrealist topics include material like "How Cows Behave When No Human Watches." Larson has been the recipient of many awards for his work. He was awarded the Newspaper Panel Cartoon Award in 1985 and 1988, the Reuben Award in 1990 and 1994, and has had an insect species (*Strigiphilus garylarsoni*), a species of butterfly (*Serratoterga larsoni*), and a beetle (*Garylarsonus*) named after him. He was also honored by the National Cartoonist Society for individual comic strips in 1989, 1990, 1991, 1993, and 1995.

Larson created a minor bit of controversy when he wrote a comic in which a female gorilla refers to Jane Goodall (who became famous for her studies of gorillas and their societal structures) as "that Jane Goodall tramp" after finding a human hair on her mate. Although the Jane Goodall Institute wrote an angry letter to Larson, Goodall herself rose to Larson's defense, indicating that she thought the comic was funny. Subsequently, all money raised as a result of the marketing of the comic has been donated to the Jane Goodall Institute.

Larson has become and remained a cultural touchstone, with his work appearing on T-shirts, calendars, and other items across the globe.

Further Reading

Higdon, David Leon. "Frankenstein as Founding Myth in Gary Larson's *Far Side*." *Journal of Popular Culture* 28, no. 1 (Summer 1994): 49–60.

Larson, Gary. *The Complete Far Side*. Riverside: Andrews McMeel, 2003.

Stein, ML. "*Seattle Times* Readers Do Panels Paying Tribute to *Far Side*." *Editor & Publisher* 127, no. 52 (December 24, 1994): 27.

Brian Davis

MCGRUDER, AARON (1974–)

Aaron McGruder was born in Chicago, Illinois. When he was six years old, he moved to the predominantly white suburb of Columbia, Maryland, due to his father's new job with the National Transportation Safety Board. While in Columbia, McGruder attended a Jesuit school from seventh through ninth grade; he then attended Oakland Hills High School and the University of Maryland, where he graduated with a degree in African American Studies. At the University of Maryland, McGruder worked on the campus newspaper, *The Diamondback*, where he created and debuted his comic *The Boondocks*. When *The Boondocks* transitioned from a campus phenomenon to a national newspaper comic strip, it debuted in more than 160 newspapers, which was a record-setting circulation of the comic. At the end of its first year, *Boondocks* was printed in over 200 newspapers and is currently carried by over 300 today.

McGruder resides in Los Angeles, California, where he works on numerous projects, including the *Boondocks* animated series. He has written five *Boondocks* collections: *All the Rage, Public Enemy #2, A Right to Be Hostile, Fresh for '01: You Suckaz,* and *Boondocks: Because I Know You Don't Read the Newspaper*. He also cowrote the 2004 graphic novel, *Birth of a Nation: A Comic Novel*. Aside from his work on comics and graphic novels, McGruder has worked as a screenwriter on the final treatment of the film *Red Tails*.

The Boondocks **comic strip creator Aaron McGruder pauses in his studio on June 21, 1999, in Columbia, Maryland. McGruder covers a lot of territory in his work, devoting time to both significant social issues and lighter fare like *Star Wars*. (AP Photo/Gail Burton)**

McGruder has been the center of numerous controversies for opinions expressed in the *Boondocks* comics and cartoons. He continuously targets prominent figures such as Condoleezza Rice, Whitney Houston, Bill Cosby, and political commentator Larry Elder. His numerous jabs at Elder led Elder to create the "McGruder," which is an award for statements made by black public figures that Elder considers "dumb," "vulgar," and/or "offensive." Despite the controversial outcry, McGruder has garnered a following within the African American community. His satire and criticism is not limited to social issues, however. He was one of a chorus of voices taking George Lucas to task for his second set of *Star Wars* movies, and the characters in *The Boondocks* regularly comment on various films, songs, or other pop cultural topics. His fan base caused many papers to struggle with whether to drop the strip because the positive outcry seemed as strong as the negative feedback. Even through polarized reactions to the comic, McGruder has consistently had a well-read output.

Further Reading

McGruder, Aaron. *A Right to Be Hostile: The Boondocks Treasury*. New York: Three Rivers Press, 2003.

Stein, Daniel. "The Black Politics of Newspaper Comic Strips: Teaching Aaron McGruder's *The Boondocks* and Keith Knight's *The K 26 Chronicles*." *Teaching Comics and Graphic Narratives: Essays on Theory, Strategy and Practice*. Edited by Lan Dong. Jefferson, NC: McFarland, 2012.

Swanigan, Pamela. "Much the Same on the Other Side: *The Boondocks* and the Symbolic Frontier." *Children's Literature: Annual of the Modern Language Association Division on Children's Literature and the Children's Literature Association* 40 (2012): 28–48.

Tyree, Tia C. M., and Adrian Krishnasamy. "Bringing Afrocentricity to the Funnies: An Analysis of Afrocentricity within Aaron McGruder's *The Boondocks*." *Journal of Black Studies* 42, no. 1 (January 2011): 23–42.

Brian Davis

MENCKEN, H. L. (1880–1956)

Born Henry Louis Mencken in Baltimore, Maryland, this author moved into what is now the H. L. Mencken House in the Union Square neighborhood of west Baltimore at age three and lived there for all but five years of his life. After reading Mark Twain's *The Adventures of Huckleberry Finn* at age nine, Mencken became focused on becoming a writer. While he worked at his father's cigar factory, he took one class in writing at the Cosmopolitan University, which ended up being the extent of his formal education.

Following the death of his father, Mencken applied to the *Morning Herald* and received a part-time position in February 1899. He obtained a full-time position the following June. He began writing editorials that garnered him attention. His side projects included short stories, a novel, and poetry. Mencken also worked as a literary critic for *The Smart Set* magazine, and cofounded *The American Mercury* in 1924.

In 1930, Mencken married Sara Haardt, an English professor at Goucher College. Due to tuberculosis, she was in poor health throughout their marriage; she died just five years later. Mencken continued to contribute to various newspapers until he suffered a stroke in 1948. Due to the effects of the stroke, Mencken was almost incapable of reading or writing. He referred to himself in past tense and became obsessive with organizing his writings to secure his legacy. He died in his sleep on January 29, 1956.

Mencken's satire and humor were driven largely by his major influences—Joseph Conrad, Ambrose Bierce, and Mark Twain. Using his syndicated columns and books

H. L. Mencken was respected for both his humor and his political commentary. His biting satire made him a favorite of fans and a pain to many authority figures. (A. Aubrey Bodine/Keystone/Getty Images)

as a stage, Mencken often spoke out against religious belief and the notion of God, creationism, and the "Booboisie," Mencken's term for the ignorant middle class. One of his seminal works was *The American Language*, published in 1919. It attempted to bring together American expressions and idioms. It garnered attention immediately and continued to grow with each reissue.

His opposition to creationism led Mencken to take an interest in, and attend, the Scopes trial in 1925. His columns were critical of the case and routinely mocked those in favor of antievolutionism. The reporter E. K. Hornbeck from the fictionalized play of the trial, *Inherit the Wind,* is based on Mencken.

Mencken was often critical of public officials he disliked as well as the American political system. His harsh and public criticism of Arkansas as the "apex of moronia" led the Arkansas legislature, in 1931, to pass a motion to pray for his soul, a move that he clearly thought was absurd. He wrote 33 books throughout his life and had 10 additional books published posthumously. While Mencken may not occupy a major role in contemporary US humor, he has had a lasting impact, being cited as an influence on many humorists. He also, like Dorothy Parker, is known for his quips, such as "No one has ever gone broke underestimating the intelligence of the American public." His scathing cynicism and careful observation of human behavior have made him a favorite among readers of humor.

See also: Benchley, Robert; Parker, Dorothy

Further Reading

Mencken, H. L. *A Mencken Chrestomathy: His Own Selections of His Own Choicest Writings.* New York: Vintage, 1982.

Poitros, J. M. "Fabula Menckeniana." *Maryland State Medical Journal* 29, no. 9 (September 1980): 30–32.

Rodgers, Mary Elizabeth. *Mencken: The American Iconoclast*. New York: Oxford University Press, 2005.

Teachout, Terry. *The Skeptic: A Life of HL Mencken*. New York: Harper Perennial, 2003.

Kristen Franz

O'ROURKE, P. J. (1947–)

Patrick Jake O'Rourke was born in Toledo, Ohio. After graduating from high school, he went to the University of Miami-Ohio for his undergraduate work. In the 1970s, O'Rourke began writing for *National Lampoon* as well as for a number of underground newspapers. While he had Republican leanings early in life, he claimed to have explored communism during his young adulthood before returning to conservative thought, albeit with a more libertarian streak.

In the 1980s, O'Rourke left *National Lampoon* to become a freelance writer, publishing his work in various magazines from *Playboy* to *Vanity Fair* to *Car and Driver*. He also regularly appeared on television talk shows and National Public Radio's program, *Wait, Wait, Don't Tell Me*. O'Rourke has been married twice, and he has two daughters and one son with his second wife. He currently splits time between residences in New Hampshire and Washington, D.C.

While O'Rourke is a self-described libertarian, his work often ridicules politicians of all philosophies. This proclivity can come to the fore with his observations that the American political system has many built-in problems stemming from the dominance of the two-party system. That said, O'Rourke does have a consistent and conservative political view of his own that he directly refers to in his writing.

Great Print Humor

While many great print magazines have sections with humor (*The New Yorker*, for instance), two popular print magazines have had a profound impact upon American culture.

The Onion, originally published in Madison, Wisconsin, has satirized newspapers and politics for years. With its outrageous headlines and well-observed send-ups, *The Onion* has helped a generation of readers to become more savvy readers and observers of politics. Its approach to humor often allows this magazine to make more biting and truthful observations about societal problems than the mainstream print publications can.

Equally important is *Harvard Lampoon* magazine. While this magazine might have a smaller readership than *The Onion* did at its peak, it launched the careers of many comedic writers and performers. From Conan O'Brien to Al Jean (one of the most consistent and significant writers on the staff of *The Simpsons*), writers from the *Lampoon* have gone on to write for some of the most widely viewed shows in the United States, including *Saturday Night Live*, *Seinfeld*, and many others.

While there are a host of other humorous publications, these two magazines might well be the ones that have had the broadest and deepest impact upon American humor.

This separates him from both many journalists and from many political humorists. While many journalists want to appear objective, O'Rourke has been a champion of Gonzo journalism from early on, believing that the most incisive and clear way to make effective political and social observations is to be direct and honest in his writing. Likewise, while many political humorists tend more toward the progressive or liberal views, O'Rourke has not only spent most of his career espousing conservative views, but has also done so in venues that typically tend toward liberal views. His regular appearances in *Rolling Stone*, the magazine closely associated with Hunter S. Thompson (whose work is also libertarian, albeit of a different sort), are unusual for someone with his general brand of politics. This cross-spectrum popularity likely comes from both O'Rourke's willingness to take on systems in general and his balance of crass humor and erudite references and delivery.

See also: Thompson, Hunter S.

Further Reading

Lee, Hoon, and Nojin Kwak. "The Affect Effect of Political Satire: Sarcastic Humor, Negative Emotions and Political Participation." *Mass Communication & Society* 17, no. 3 (2014): 307–328.

O'Rourke, P. J. *Parliament of Whores*. New York: Atlantic Monthly Press, 1991.

Tylee, John. "PJ O'Rourke Takes a Quizzical Look at British Eccentricity in BA Film." *Campaign (UK)* 27 (July 9, 1999): 7.

Wood, James. "MSM S&M." *New Republic* 234, no. 19 (May 22, 2006): 42.

Zeke Jarvis

PIRARO, DAN (1958–)

Dan Piraro is a painter, cartoonist and illustrator who is best known for his highly successful strip *Bizarro*. Piraro was born in St. Louis, Missouri, but his family moved to Tulsa, Oklahoma, early in his life. In Tulsa, Piraro graduated from Booker T. Washington High School. He then went to Washington University in St. Louis, where he eventually dropped out. Piraro married once, to Ashley Lou Smith, but has since separated from her, moving to Los Angeles after their split.

While most of his humor is focused on nonpolitical observations, often taking the form of absurd and odd wordplay, Piraro has demonstrated a sympathy for more progressive or liberal political leanings. Beyond his politics, Piraro's style is rough, giving a strange, striking look to match his off-the-wall concepts.

In addition to his progressive politics, Piraro has been very outspoken about his veganism both on his website and within his syndicated material. While much of Piraro's work is silly and playful, his work on veganism depicts the absurdly tragic treatment of animals used for food. His anthropomorphism demonstrates an interesting balance of being very traditional in its approach to comics, yet surprisingly distinctive in its particular views that are articulated, clearly parting ways with the anthropomorphism of cartoonists such as Gary Larson or Bill Watterson. In fact, Piraro has indicated that his cartoon has consistently had a commitment to animal rights. Beyond the confines of his cartoons, Piraro has toured the United States with his one-man comedy show, *The Bizarro Baloney Show*

Although Piraro has enjoyed success in a number of media, his central commitment remains to his cartoons. His style is quite distinctive, often employing single-panel cartoons, which is a rarity rather than the norm for Piraro's time. The simplicity of Piraro's visual presentation often helps to counterbalance the offbeat and absurdist style of his humor, which frequently revolves around wordplay and surprising juxtapositions. Nevertheless, Piraro has garnered a great level of commercial and critical acclaim. In 2010, he won the National Cartoonists Society's Reuben Award for Outstanding Cartoonist of the Year. This came after he had been nominated for the award in every year since 2002.

Further Reading

Caws, Mary Ann. "Surrealism from Outside and In." *L'Esprit Createur* 10 (1970): 150–156.

Haynes, Doug. "The Persistence of Irony: Interfering with Surrealist Black Humor." *Textual Practice* 20, no. 1 (March 2006): 25–47.

Piraro, Dan. *Bizarro*. San Francisco: Chronicle Books, 1986.

Vorhees, Deborah. " 'Bizarro' Cartoonist Dan Piraro Explores Life's Absurdities." *Dallas Morning News*, March 29, 2002.

Zeke Jarvis

QUEENAN, JOE (1950–)

Joe Queenan was born in Philadelphia, where he grew up within an abusive, alcoholic family. He graduated from St. Joseph's University. Queenan went on to edit and write for a number of well-known publications, including *TV Guide*, *Forbes*, *Rolling Stone*, and a host of other magazines. In addition, Queenan is a regular guest on shows like *Politically Incorrect* and *The Daily Show*. He lives in Tarrytown, New York, with his wife and two children.

Queenan is well known for his acerbic wit and blunt, aggressive critiques of pop culture. In his book *Red Lobster, White Trash and the Blue Lagoon*, Queenan targets prominent figures of "low culture," belittling them. One of his well-known essays about bad movies suggests that, to be in the running for the title of "worst movie ever," the makers of a movie had to believe that it would be artistically successful. From this premise, he explains why the movie *House of Wax*, featuring Paris Hilton, is not a fair candidate for the title. This is followed by an extended discussion of why *Heaven's Gate*, by comparison, has the correct balance of good intentions and artistic failure to achieve the title. Queenan applies this sort of no-holds-barred delivery to more mainstream forms of culture as well.

Not all of Queenan's writing focuses on popular culture. His book *Imperial Caddy: The Rise of Dan Quayle in America and the Decline and Fall of Practically Everything Else* focuses on politics, giving his writing a more substantive feel without sacrificing his characteristic cynicism. His memoir *Closing Time* also opens up the scope of his writing, giving a much greater focus on his personal life and childhood than previously seen in his work.

Queenan has delved into his love of sports in a number of pieces, writing for *Golf Digest* and publishing the book *True Believers: The Tragic Inner Life of Sports Fans*. His examination of his own interest in sports also employs his cutting wit while turning his attention to his own eccentricities. In his focus on sports, Queenan in part marks his generational affiliation. Although it is not fair to characterize him as conservative, his views do offer a sense of traditionalism and disenchantment with the deterioration of American culture. This is particularly ironic given the relationship that Queenan had with his father. In addition, Queenan writes about his love of books, including both canonical works like Shakespeare's oeuvre and *The Razor's Edge* and less literary writing.

Further Reading

Carrigan, Harry. "The Legacy of an Irish Father." *Publishers Weekly* 256, no. 7 (February 16, 2009): 120.

McClinton-Temple, Jennifer. "Expressing 'Irishness' in Three Irish-American Autobiographies." *New Hibernia Review/Iris Éireannach Nua: A Quarterly Record of Irish Studies* 17, no. 2 (Summer 2013): 103–118.

Queenan, Joe. *Closing Time: A Memoir*. New York: Penguin Group, 2010.

Queenan, Joe. *Red Lobster, White Trash and the Blue Lagoon: Joe Queenan's America*. New York: Hyperion, 1999.

Zeke Jarvis

ROYKO, MIKE (1932–1997)

Mike Royko was born September 19, 1932. He grew up in Chicago, living in apartment above a bar. This early exposure to working-class life was something that impacted Royko and was often seen in the values underlying much of his work. After high school, Royko briefly attended Wright Junior College before joining the Air Force in 1952. It was while in the military that he first began working as a columnist. Upon returning to civilian life, Royko wrote for a variety of papers before settling on the *Chicago Daily News*, where he developed the column that would be nationally syndicated. In this column, he was known for his sharp criticism of some of the powerful politicians in Chicago, for which he received significant pushback. Royko died of a brain aneurysm in 1997.

In his column, while Royko often stated his views directly, he sometimes employed comedic mouthpieces to make points while entertaining his audience. Slats Grobnik was a stereotypical Polish Chicagoan who would regularly speak with Royko at a predominantly Polish bar. This character was one of the figures that allowed Royko to both satirize and appreciate his working-class, Eastern European roots. Another such fictitious character was the imagined psychologist, Dr. I. M. Kookie. Kookie helped Royko to examine a working-class perspective as well, albeit from a different direction than Grobnik. Kookie often represented the absurdity and impracticality of thinkers most interested in more esoteric ideas. While these and other fictitious characters were created largely to get laughs, they allowed Royko to make social commentary in subtle ways. This practice was very much akin to

Damon Runyon's use of jokey names and working-class references to flesh out the world of questionable characters and loveable oafs. Of course, many of Royko's columns were written directly from his perspective, not filtering his points through anyone else, fictitious or real.

In addition to his column, Royko wrote a number of books. His best-known book was *Boss*, an examination of Richard Daley's control of Chicago. Published in 1971, *Boss* takes a long examination of Daley's career as mayor. Royko regularly skewers the effects of Daley's harsh conservative views, noting the racism and exclusion that were natural consequences of his corrupt political machine. That said, Royko also acknowledges Daley's political shrewdness. In one famous column, Royko referred to Daley as demonstrating the success of democracy, because, although Daley's government was incredibly corrupt, he provided jobs for many people, so Chicagoans were generally satisfied with his performance—that is, the people, although in some ways oppressed, were generally happy. Royko also wrote a surprisingly complimentary column eulogizing Daley after his death. This sort of honest, sometimes brutal, and often surprising approach to political commentary is similar to the work of Hunter S. Thompson and P. J. O'Rourke, though it is neither as shocking as Thompson's screeds nor as urbane as O'Rourke's dry wit.

In terms of style, Royko's sometimes understated delivery helped to build the humor of what could easily become a humorless, aggressive, and simplistic rant. His willingness to concede Daley's strengths and to playfully ridicule himself and much of his core readership helped Royko craft surprising and complex columns that often used not only one-liners, but also the structure of his pieces to achieve memorable comedic triumphs.

See also: Runyon, Damon

Further Reading

Blei, Norbert. "Hearing Chicago Voices: Studs Terkel, Mike Royko, Nelson Algren." *Rosebud* 16 (1999): 99–103.

Ciccone, Richard F. *Royko: A Life in Print*. Jackson: Public Affairs, 2001.

Moe, Doug. *The World of Mike Royko*. Madison: University of Wisconsin Press, 1999.

Royko, Mike. *Boss*. New York: Plume, 1988.

Zeke Jarvis

SCHULZ, CHARLES (1922–2000)

Charles Schulz was born in Minneapolis, Minnesota, as the only child of Carl Schulz and Dena Halverson. He first showed his interest in art by drawing the family dog, Spike, and sent one of those drawings to *Ripley's Believe It or Not!*, where it was published in Robert Ripley's syndicated panel. Schulz skipped two half-grades in elementary school, which resulted in him becoming shy among older classmates. In a now-famous event, Schulz's drawings were rejected by his high school yearbook—the same high school that would honor Schulz with a five-foot-tall statue of Snoopy 60 years later. In 1943, Schulz's mother died, which was both a shock

Cartoonist Charles Schulz draws a picture of his cartoon character Charlie Brown in his Sebastopol, California, home in this 1966 file photo. Schulz may be one of the most influential and successful comic artists in American history. (AP Photo)

and a blow to Schulz, who had not been told that she had cancer. Around the same time, he was drafted into the army, where he served as a staff sergeant. He was discharged in 1945.

In July 1946, Schulz got a job at Art Instruction Inc., where he graded lessons of students. He worked at the school for several years while he developed his comic strips; he remained there until the money from his comics allowed him to pursue them full time. His first cartoon to be published regularly was a series called *Li'l Folks* (1947–1950) in the *St. Paul Pioneer Press*. In 1948, his work was published in *The Saturday Evening Post*.

In 1951, Schulz moved to Colorado Springs, Colorado, and married Joyce Halverson, with whom he had four children. Following the end of *Li'l Folks* in the *Pioneer Press*, he went to United Feature Syndicate with it. While it garnered interest from the company, United Feature preferred the four-panel cartoon that Schulz was working on—*Peanuts*. It debuted on October 2, 1950. While he created a few other minor comic strips throughout the years, the highly demanding *Peanuts* encompassed much of Schulz's time. At its peak, *Peanuts* was syndicated in 2,600 papers in 75 countries and published in 21 languages.

In 1972, Schulz and his wife divorced. The following year, Schulz married his second wife, this time remaining married until his death. Throughout *Peanuts*' almost 50-year run, Schulz took just one vacation—to celebrate his 75th birthday in 1997. This five-week hiatus was the only time during the *Peanuts* run that rerun strips were printed.

Schulz announced his retirement on December 14, 1999, following several small strokes, revealing that he was suffering from colon cancer. He died from complications from the cancer on February 12, 2000. Ironically, and not by design, the final *Peanuts* strip ran the very next day, on February 13, 2000.

Schulz's work—*Peanuts*, specifically—was known for recurring gags like Lucy's repeated ploy of pulling out a football from under Charlie Brown as he attempted to kick it. A request was made to Schulz that he allow Charlie Brown to finally kick the football in the *Peanuts* final strip. He declined, but expressed sadness in a 1999 interview that "he (Charlie Brown) never had a chance to kick the football."

Schulz was widely recognized for his work. He received the National Cartoonists Society's Humor Comic Strip Award in 1962 (*Peanuts*), received the Elzie Segar Award in 1980, was a two-time winner of the Reuben Award in 1955 and 1964, and received the society's Milton Caniff Lifetime Achievement Award in 1999. He is in the U.S. Hockey Hall of Fame for his contributions to the sport of hockey and was awarded a star on the Hollywood Walk of Fame in 1996. For his service to the youth of America, he was awarded the Silver Buffalo Award, the highest award given by the Boy Scouts of America. The U.S. Congress honored Schulz posthumously by awarding him the Congressional Gold Medal in 2000.

Although there was often an innocence to many of Schulz's characters, commentators have observed that there is also a darkness in many *Peanuts* strips as well as in the many television specials with Charlie Brown. Charlie Brown's lack of success in connecting with "the little red-haired girl," the frustration he experiences at the hands of Lucy and his other tormentors, and the pitiful tree he selects in the *Peanuts* Christmas special all suggest the sadness that permeates much of Schulz's work, even if it exists mainly in the background. Still, many fans of Schulz remember him primarily for his whimsical and entertaining characters and conflicts.

Further Reading

Johnson, Rheta Grimsley. *Good Grief! The Story of Charles M. Schulz*. New York: Pharos Books, 1989.

Lind, Stephen J. "Christmas in the 1960s: *A Charlie Brown Christmas*, Religion, and the Conventions of the Television Genre." *Journal of Religion and Popular Culture* 26, no. 1 (Spring 2014): 1–22.

Michaelis, David. *Schulz and Peanuts: A Biography*. New York: Harper Perennial, 2008.

Schulz, Charles. *The Complete Peanuts Box Set*. Seattle: Fantagraphics, 2014.

Brian Davis

SEDARIS, DAVID (1956–)

David Sedaris was born in Binghamton, New York. His family subsequently moved to Raleigh, North Carolina, where Sedaris spent most of his childhood. Sedaris is the second of six children. After graduating from high school, he attended West Carolina University for a time before transferring to Kent State University. Sedaris did not graduate from either school, eventually dropping out and moving to Chicago, where he graduated from the School of the Art Institute of Chicago.

Sedaris also began reading in clubs from a diary that he had kept for years. During one such performance, local radio host Ira Glass was in attendance; he invited Sedaris to read on the air. This led to national exposure on National Public Radio (NPR), which helped Sedaris gain a new level of success. Sedaris continued his rise by not only reading on NPR's *This American Life* but also publishing regularly in *Esquire* and *The New Yorker*. While most of Sedaris's work has been and continues to be personal essays, he has also written a collection of fables, titled *Squirrel Seeks Chipmunk*. In addition, Sedaris has written a number of plays with his sister, Amy. Sedaris continues to work, and he and his long-time partner split their time between Europe and New York.

Sedaris is best known for his keen wit and self-deprecating humor. In pieces like "Remembering My Childhood on the Continent of Africa," Sedaris makes himself the comic foil to a host of other, more reasonable characters. He often incorporates a sense of self-ridicule or not belonging in pieces like "Six to Eight Black Men," in which Sedaris satirizes American culture by claiming to support the idiosyncrasies of his own culture as compared with the idiosyncrasies of other cultures. Critics regularly laud Sedaris's ability to find the strangeness in everyday actions and habits that others fail to notice. Also, like Sarah Vowell and other regular artists on NPR, Sedaris creates relatively brief and imaginative pieces that combine odd observations with genuine insight. While his fictional work has not been as well received as his memoir work (and even his memoir work has been questioned for its veracity), Sedaris remains an active and successful humorist, often touring and publishing.

See also: Sedaris, Amy

Further Reading

Cardell, Kylie. "The Ethics of Laughter: David Sedaris and the Humour Memoir." *Mosaic: A Journal for the Interdisciplinary Study of Literature* 45, no. 3 (September 2012): 99–114.

Gana, Myrsini. "Is David Sedaris Funny in Greek?" *World Literature Today* 88, no. 2 (March/April 2014): 41–44.

Kozlowski, Carl. "David Sedaris." *Progressive* 75, no. 4 (April 2011): 31–34.

Sedaris, David. *Naked*. New York: Back Bay Books, 1998.

Zeke Jarvis

SHEPHERD, JEAN (1921–1999)

Jean Shepherd was born in Chicago, Illinois, and grew up in nearby Hammond, Indiana. He began his radio career in Cincinnati before moving to a station in Philadelphia for a short time, only to later return to Cincinnati. In 1956, he moved to a radio station in New York City, where he soon became popular for his humorous stories and anecdotes about growing up in the Midwest. He also attracted controversy for a stunt in which he claimed to have written a book that did not exist. The objective of the stunt was to show how easily the best-seller lists could be influenced by demand rather than sales, and his point was effectively made. Also, Shepherd made a commercial for a soap company that was not a sponsor for his show, which resulted in him being fired, much to the ire of his fans. Shepherd was reinstated soon thereafter. In 1963, Shepherd participated in the March on Washington; he subsequently discussed his involvement with the March on his radio program. In addition to his stories about growing up, Shepherd's show offered witty commentary on life in New York. Ironically, even though radio launched him into the limelight, Shepherd later went on record as saying his days in radio were not important in the overall arc of his career, even though he was known for miraculously performing long monologues with no script and little preparation.

Shepherd wrote numerous short stories for *Playboy* about growing up in Indiana. These stories, which often grew out of the stories he told on his radio program, were later compiled into a book, *In God We Trust, All Others Pay Cash*, published in 1966. During development of the book, humorist Shel Silverstein recorded Shepherd telling his stories and transcribed them. He and Shepherd both worked on editing the transcriptions into book form. The book became a best seller and is considered Shepherd's most influential work. Three other books of stories based on Shepherd's youth in northwest Indiana soon followed.

At this time Shepherd also worked in television and film, as both an on-camera personality and a behind-the-scenes writer. The stories that were collected his books often became the basis of his television and film work. Shepherd wrote and hosted a series for Boston Public Television called *Jean Shepherd's America* and created a show called *Shepherd's Pie* for a network of public television broadcasters in New Jersey. Both shows featured people and locales of local interest.

In 1983, Shepherd narrated the role of the adult Ralphie Parker in the holiday classic film, *A Christmas Story*. Shepherd also appears on screen in a brief cameo. *A Christmas Story*, based on *In God We Trust, All Others Pay Cash* and a handful of stories in Shepherd's other books, was only a mild box office success upon its initial release, but it became a favorite after repeated television airings. In 1994, Shepherd was involved in the film's sequel, *It Runs in the Family*, which utilized a different cast. The sequel failed to achieve the recognition and affection felt for the original.

Shepherd was married a total of four times, with the longest marriage being that to his fourth wife, who died in 1998. He had both a son and a daughter with his second wife. Shepherd died in 1999 on Sanibel Island, Florida.

Shepherd is known for a number of things, but especially for his playful discussions of his childhood and especially the pop cultural artifacts from his childhood. For this reason, Jerry Seinfeld cites Shepherd as being a significant influence. Given the childish subject matter of much of Seinfeld's work (including baseball, Superman, and other topics primarily of interest to young boys), this is not surprising. Shepherd is also known for being able to appeal to audiences both on the East Coast and in the Midwest, where many of his childhood stories are rooted. Shepherd's ability to laugh at his childhood while not alienating people with similar backgrounds is a mark of the care and precision of his humor. In particular, his ability to ground his humor in specific details helps to bring in Midwestern readers. Finally, Shepherd is highly regarded for his ability to speak extemporaneously, narrating stories from memory and imagination, which has impressed generations of audiences and other humorists.

See also: Seinfeld, Jerry

Further Reading

Bergmann, Eugene. *Excelsior, You Fathead! The Art and Enigma of Jean Shepherd*. New York: Applause Theatre & Cinema Books, 2004.

Shepherd, Jean. *In God We Trust, All Others Pay Cash*. New York: Doubleday, 1966.
Smith, James F. "Humor, Cultural History and Jean Shepherd." *Journal of Popular Culture* 16, no. 1 (Summer 1982): 1–12.
Trimmer, Joseph F. "Memoryscape: Jean Shepherd's Midwest." *Old Northwest: A Journal of Regional Life and Letters* 2 (1976): 357–369.

Stephen Powers

STEIN, JOEL (1971–)

Joel Stein grew up in Edison, New Jersey. His father was a salesman; his family was Jewish. During high school, Stein wrote for his school's newspaper and edited the entertainment section. After graduating, he went to Stanford University, where he majored in English. While there, he wrote a weekly column for *The Stanford Daily*, the university's student newspaper. After getting his degree from Stanford, Stein moved first to New York, and then to Los Angeles. He began his professional writing career with *Martha Stewart Living*. After being fired from that job, he worked as a fact checker and in other capacities for a variety of publications.

In 1997, Stein began writing for *Time*. He has also appeared on television programs such as VH1's *I Love the 80's* and has been a writer and producer for the sitcom *Crumbs*.

Stein has received some minor backlash for his work. On one occasion, his comments about not supporting the troops received significant complaints about his perceived lack of empathy for the American troops in Iraq. In another column, Stein indicated that he was uncomfortable with the impact that Indian immigrants had had upon his hometown. After the minor uproar, Stein apologized for the latter column. Stein indicated that, in fact, he meant to portray his discomfort as surprising and unfounded, not as reasonable or justified. Stein still lives in Los Angeles and his work continues to appear in print and on television.

Stein's work often focuses on issues in popular culture. In his television work, he regularly discusses minor celebrities and cultural trends with pithy, sarcastic lines; his column often does likewise. Although he sometimes takes on weightier issues, as indicated by the controversies mentioned previously, Stein's work generally does not aspire to be complex or deep in its scope or execution. Still, his writing has a large audience, particularly garnering the attention of younger readers and viewers who appreciate his focus on contemporary culture and clever wordplay.

Further Reading

LaRocque, Paula. "Humorous Touch Can Be Natural in Media Writing." *Quill* 85, no. 8 (October 1997): 37.
Stein, Joel. *Man Made: A Stupid Quest for Masculinity*. New York: Grand Central Publishing, 2012.

Zeke Jarvis

THOMPSON, HUNTER S. (1937–2005)

Dr. Hunter Stockton Thompson was an American journalist and author born in 1937 in Louisville, Kentucky. His father's death when Thompson was 14 years old forced Thompson's middle-class family into poverty. The young Thompson

Journalist Hunter S. Thompson sits at his typewriter, circa 1976, at his ranch near Aspen, Colorado. Thompson was a foundational figure in the transgressive "Gonzo" journalism movement. (Michael Ochs Archives/Getty Images)

attended Louisville Male High School, but was unable to graduate after he was convicted of aiding in a robbery and was sent to prison for 60 days. Thompson joined the Air Force, then became a journalist after he took a position as sports editor for a Pennsylvania newspaper. Numerous other newspaper assignments, including one in San Juan, Puerto Rico, and another in South America, followed. After difficulties with a variety of parties in Puerto Rico, Thompson returned to the United States, where he continued to write.

An article Thompson wrote in 1965 for *The Nation*, "Motorcycle Gangs: Losers and Outsiders," evolved into his first book, *Hell's Angels: The Strange and Terrible Saga of the Outlaw Motorcycle Gangs*. Thompson spent a year embedded with the San Francisco and Oakland chapters of the Hells Angels, an outlaw gang of bikers feared for their crimes and reputation for violence. Even though they mistrusted reporters, the Angels grew accustomed to Thompson's presence and voluntarily contributed information and interviews. Thompson documented these stories and their activities for the book, including an alleged gang rape, which drew controversy from feminist circles. He ended his association with the Hells Angels after several members beat him when Thompson made an offensive remark to one of them. *Hell's Angels* was well received by critics, and it established Thompson's status as a prominent counterculture figure of the 1960s.

Thompson used royalties he received for this book as a down payment for his mountain home in Woody Creek, Colorado, which he fortified with a large collection of firearms and explosives. While in Colorado, Thompson also ran for office, forming the Freak Party to support his unsuccessful bid for the position of sheriff of Aspen. During this time, he married his first wife, with whom he had one child.

In 1970, Thompson wrote the article "The Kentucky Derby Is Decadent and Depraved," which was published in *Scanlan's Monthly*. Thompson often worked with Ralph Steadman, who illustrated a number of Thompson's works, including *Fear and Loathing in Las Vegas: A Savage Journey to the Heart of the America Dream* (published in 1972) and *Fear and Loathing on the Campaign Trail '72* (published in book form in 1973 after most of it had been serialized in *Rolling Stone* in 1972). Thompson followed up *Campaign Trail* with a four-volume collection of essays, *The Gonzo Papers* series.

In 1979, Thompson divorced his first wife, Sondi. A novel he wrote in the 1960s based on his experiences in Puerto Rico, *The Rum Diary*, was published in 1998 after actor Johnny Depp discovered the manuscript among Thompson's papers. Near the end of his life, Thompson was primarily writing about sports for ESPN. In 2003, Thompson married his second wife, Anita, to whom he remained married until his death. Thompson committed suicide by self-inflicted gunshot wound at his cabin in Woody Creek in 2005.

Hunter S. Thompson is generally regarded as the father of Gonzo journalism, which rejects typical journalistic objectivity in favor of making the reporter a central part of the story, often including the reporter's subjective interpretation of the events being reported on. While other writers like P. J. O'Rourke and Tom Wolfe have also been connected to Gonzo journalism, Thompson is generally seen as the core figure in its development. In many cases, the reporter becomes the central figure in the story. Thompson's style in particular is characterized by mania and incomprehensible use of language, often a result of the use of drugs and alcohol while reporting, combined with the desperation Thompson would feel in working against a deadline.

Thompson was known for his particular dislike of Richard Nixon, comparing him to everything from Hitler to reptiles. He was also known for his flamboyant personal appearances, where he could be combative with hosts, appear with a drink in his hand, and show general disregard for the expectations of other celebrities. This sort of aggressive approach to humor was later emulated by writers like Chuck Palahniuk and challenging performers like Andy Kaufman. It also made Thompson into a celebrity; he was even featured as a character (Uncle Duke) in the comic strip *Doonesbury*, written by Garry Trudeau. Nevertheless, Thompson will always be primarily known for his wild approach to covering politics and his abrasive and often vulgar writing style.

See also: O'Rourke, P. J; Trudeau, Garry

Further Reading

Hale, Michael. "Outlaw Blues." *Sight and Sound* 19, no. 1 (January 2009): 12.

Rak, Julie. "Memoir, Truthiness and the Power of Oprah: The James Frey Controversy Reconsidered." *Prose Studies: History, Theory, Criticism* 34, no. 3 (December 2012): 224–242.

Thompson, Hunter S. *Fear and Loathing in Las Vegas*. New York: Vintage, 1998.

Vredenburg, Jason. "What Happens in Vegas: Hunter S. Thompson's Political Philosophy." *Journal of American Studies* 47, no. 1 (February 2013): 149–170.

Stephen Powers

TOLES, TOM (1951–)

Tom Toles was born in Buffalo, New York. After high school, he attended the State University of New York at Buffalo, where he graduated magna cum laude. Toles then began writing for the *Buffalo Courier-Express*. He has been nominated for the Pulitzer Prize a number of times, winning this award in 1990. He has also been named Cartoonist of the Year by *Editor and Publisher* magazine.

Toles often incorporates autobiographical elements into his work, with the strip *Randolph Itch 2 AM* being based on his own struggles with insomnia. He also includes doodles of himself at his desk in the margins of many of his strips. Toles is married with two children. In his spare time, he is part of a band, Suspicious Package, along with a number of other writers and government officials.

While Toles has been successful in terms of both critical reception and commercial success, his work has sometimes met with resistance. The most prominent example came from a cartoon in which Toles represented the army as an amputee veteran who resembled Donald Rumsfeld and who bore the phrase "battle hardened." The response from the Pentagon was both vocal and swift, with a letter from the Joint Chiefs of Staff claiming that the cartoon was offensive because the use of an amputee veteran was tasteless and manipulative. Toles replied that the Joint Chiefs of Staff's interpretation of the cartoon was off base and unfair. Fellow cartoonist Tom Tomorrow came to Toles's aid in this controversy, comparing the response from the Joint Chiefs to the Islamist condemnation of a cartoon featuring an image of the prophet Muhammad and indicating that the defense of that strip in the name of the freedom of speech and the condemnation of Toles's strip were hypocritical.

Toles's strips often feature a simple, cartoonish style that emphasizes the sometimes childish behavior of characters and can serve to counterbalance the sharp political critiques. Of course, not all of Toles's strips have a clear political stance. Many simply play with the humor of illogical conclusions or mild forms of hypocrisy. Nevertheless, it is often his more political cartoons that get the most attention from readers and critics.

Further Reading

Mihlrad, Leigh. "The Art of Ill Will: The Story of American Political Cartoons." *Library Journal* 132, no. 15 (September 15, 2007): 67.

Niedowski, Erika. "No Laughing Matter, Cartoons Shape Our Political History." *Hill* 18, no. 17 (February 11, 2011): 20.

Shaw, Matthew. "Drawing on the Collections." *Journalism Studies* 8, no. 5 (October 2007): 742–754.

Toles, Tom. *At Least Our Bombs Are Getting Smarter*. New York: Prometheus Books, 1991.

Zeke Jarvis

TOMORROW, TOM (1961–)

Dan Perkins, who was born on April 5, 1961, in Wichita, Kansas, writes under the pen name "Tom Tomorrow." While best known for his comic strip *This Modern World,* his work has also appeared in *The New York Times, The New Yorker, Spin, Esquire, The American Prospect,* and other venues. Tomorrow is also the author of 10 books and anthologies. *This Modern World* debuted in 1990 in *San Francisco Weekly.*

Apart from his published work, Tomorrow has had several projects that have either gone unfinished or have been canceled. In 1998, he was asked to do a biweekly cartoon for *U.S. News and World Report,* but was fired six months later. In 1999, he produced three animated shorts for *Saturday Night Live* that never aired. Tomorrow also collaborated with director Michael Moore on a post-September 11 animated film that never went into production beyond the script. In 2009, Village Voice Media removed all syndicated cartoons from its publications; as part of this move, Tomorrow lost 12 papers in Los Angeles, Minneapolis, New York, and Seattle that had carried his comic strip. Eddie Vedder, the front man of the band Pearl Jam and a friend of Tomorrow, published an open letter on the band's website in support of Tomorrow. Subsequently, Tomorrow was commissioned to do the artwork for Pearl Jam's album *Backspacer.*

While often critical of those in power, Tomorrow's strip also criticizes the media and Americans' support for those leaders. Due to his attacks on those in power—specifically, the past administration of President George W. Bush and the conservative right—Tomorrow is a polarizing figure in American culture. Even so, he has received numerous awards, including the Media Alliance Meritorious Achievement Award in 1993, the Robert F. Kennedy Journalism Award in 1998 and 2003 for *This Modern World,* the 2001 James Aronson Award for Social Justice Journalism, the Altweekly Award in 2004 (second place) and 2006 (third place), and the 2013 Herblock Prize for editorial cartooning.

Further Reading

Kinsella, Bridget. "Independents Get Comic Relief." *Publishers Weekly* 241, no. 10 (March 7, 1994): 20.

Mihlrad, Leigh. "The Art of Ill Will: The Story of American Political Cartoons." *Library Journal* 132, no. 15 (September 15, 2007): 67.

Niedowski, Erika. "No Laughing Matter, Cartoons Shape Our Political History." *Hill* 18, no. 17 (February 11, 2011): 20.

Tomorrow, Tom. *Too Much Crazy*. New York: Soft Skull Press, 2011.

Brian Davis

TRUDEAU, GARRY (1948–)

Born Garretson Beekman Trudeau to Jean Douglas and Francis Burger Trudeau in New York City, Trudeau was raised in Saranac Lake, New York. In 1966, he enrolled at Yale University. While initially planning to major in theater, Trudeau found that he was interested in art design. This newfound interest led him to spend a large portion of his time contributing cartoons and writings to *The Yale Record,*

Yale's humor magazine. He eventually became the editor-in-chief. Concurrently, he began writing for the *Yale Daily News* in the form of editorial cartoons. A drawing of Yale quarterback Brian Dowling was the starting point for his strip *Bull Tales*. It was out of *Bull Tales* that Trudeau's most celebrated work, *Doonesbury*, originated. *Doonesbury* was syndicated in 1970 and is now published in almost 1,400 newspapers internationally.

In 1973, Trudeau graduated with a master of fine arts degree from the Yale School of Art. In 1980, he married Jane Pauley, a journalist. They have three children. Trudeau has maintained a low personal profile for much of his career, but has done occasional interviews and been the subject of a profile in *Wired* (2000), *Rolling Stone* (2004, 2010), *The Washington Post* (2006), *The Colbert Report* (2010, 2013), and others.

In 1975, Trudeau was awarded the Pulitzer Prize—the first comic strip artist to receive this honor. He would be a finalist for the award again in 1990. An animated short film of his work, *The Doonesbury Special*, was nominated for an Academy Award in 1977 and won the Cannes Film Festival Jury Special Prize the following year. Trudeau was the recipient of the National Cartoonist Society Newspaper Comic Strip Award in 1994 as well as the Reuben Award in 1995.

Wiley Miller, creator of *Non Sequitur*, has called Trudeau "far and away the most influential editorial cartoonist in the last 25 years." Conversely, in 1985, *Saturday Review* voted Trudeau as one of the country's "Most Overrated People in American Arts and Letters," claiming that his strip was "predictable, mean-spirited, and not as funny as before."

Trudeau is known for having a clear political bent, albeit not always with a specific party affiliation. Typically, Trudeau leans slightly more libertarian than either Democratic or Republican, but his general approach is to criticize the figures in power. However, the character of Uncle Duke (a play on Hunter S. Thompson's pseudonym, Raul Duke) serves as a figure who can undercut the value of simply complaining or working outside the system. Trudeau also comments on issues of social merit even if they are not directly political. Issues such as changes in higher education and funding for the military have been featured in long runs on *Doonesbury*'s panels. Still, his clever political commentary is clearly the core of what fans most like about *Doonesbury*. Whether they find him funny or not, many political figures recognize Trudeau's commentary as both incisive and influential.

See also: Thompson, Hunter S.

Further Reading

Lamb, Christopher. "Changing with the Times: The World According to *Doonesbury*." *Journal of Popular Culture* 23, no. 4 (Spring 1990): 113–129.

Soper, Kerry D. *Garry Trudeau: Doonesbury and the Aesthetics of Satire*. Jackson: University of Mississippi Press, 2008.

Trudeau, Garry. *The Doonesbury Chronicles*. New York: Henry Holt, 1975.

Walker, Brian. *Doonesbury and the Art of GB Trudeau*. New Haven, CT: Yale University Press, 2010.

Brian Davis

VAUGHAN, BRIAN K. (1976–)

Brian K. Vaughan was born in Cleveland, Ohio. In high school, he decided that he wanted to pursue writing. To do so, he went to New York University, where he studied film. While he was still a student there, he took part in Marvel Comics' Stan-hattan Project, beginning his work on comic books. Currently, Vaughan and his wife, a playwright, live in Los Angeles with their two daughters.

Vaughan has worked on high-profile projects in both comic books and television, with some work in film as well. His work is often characterized by large plots with intricate stories. This bent is evidenced in both his comic book work, such as *Y: The Last Man* and *Ex Machina*, and the television shows with which he has been involved, such as *Lost*. In terms of the humor seen in his work, Vaughan has two clear approaches. First, his dialogue employs many puns and a high degree of referential humor that spans from low culture to canonical literature. Second, he employs a sense of irony and political satire, often having characters who are artists or storytellers who also discuss art and storytelling within his works. In one plotline in *Y: The Last Man,* two of the surviving women begin a comic book about a woman surviving a great plague, clearly paralleling the series itself, in which a male character, Yorick, is believed to be the only man to survive a "gendercide," in which the rest of the men on the planet die out. These sorts of philosophical discussions about the topics beyond the strict boundaries of the plot add a level of depth to Vaughn's work that is not always found in graphic novels.

In both his comic book and television work, Vaughan incorporates elements of science fiction or fantasy, often with a particular political issue in mind. In *Ex Machina*, he examines the separation between governmental justice and popular notions of justice, the role of politics in art, and many other issues that extend out of the basic premise of a bionic-hero-turned-mayor.

Further Reading

Brown, Lyndsay. "Yorick, Don't Be a Hero: Productive Motion in *Y: The Last Man*." *ImageTexT: Interdisciplinary Comics Studies* 3, no. 1 (Summer 2006): 33.

McCloud, Scott. *Understanding Comics: The Invisible Art*. New York: William Morrow, 1994.

Vaughan, Brian K. *Y. The Last Man*. Illustrated by Pia Guerra. New York: Vertigo Comics, 2003.

Wolk, Douglas. "Masters of the Universe." *Time* 182, no. 6 (August 5, 2013): 54.

Zeke Jarvis

Section III: Television and Film

In many ways, the United States can be considered the major producer of television and film in the world. Although countries from France to India to Israel all have significant film industries, Hollywood and New York are still seen as the greatest source of commercial production in film and television. It should not be surprising, then, that these media have been a significant source of America's work in humor. Early humorous television shows often had ensemble casts playing a variety of characters—a format and group of performers similar to radio programs that were, in turn, influenced by the traveling troupes of vaudeville performers. Early film humorists were also clearly influenced by vaudevillian performers (some of them had even gotten their start in vaudeville), using slapstick or physical comedy with exaggerated movements. Such was the case with figures like Buster Keaton and Charlie Chaplin in silent films and, later, rapid-fire exchange groups and duos like Abbot and Costello and the Three Stooges. The latter often wound up in ridiculous and complicated situations that let them give big and silly performances that could be enhanced by sound effects, make-up, and other effects that were not available to live performances. The characters in these films and shows were often oversized to match their comic situations. Some figures, Milton Berle and Sid Caesar, ultimately found work as hosts of television shows, where they often portrayed goofball characters as they might have on traveling circuits.

That said, while some aspects of the vaudevillian approach to comedy stayed in common practice (the use of rapid exchanges, for instance, would be a staple of cinematic dialogue for generations), many humorous films and shows began to explore more realistic situations. Shows like *Leave It to Beaver* and *Father Knows Best* featured more realistic situations (although the characters were still not quite realistic because they were more idealized and well behaved than typical families) that were measured for character-driven humor as much as plot-driven situational humor. Some critics have theorized that part of the reason for this evolution was that longer-running characters with half-hour stories required a greater emotional investment to keep audiences returning to their stories. Later sitcoms (situation comedies) like *Seinfeld* and *Modern Family*, however, have used characters as ridiculous and laughable as the Three Stooges.

In the 1960s and 1970s, the variety show format made a return, with shows like *Laugh-In* and *The Smothers Brothers Comedy Hour* taking the old setup and injecting it with more daring and experimental humor, poking fun at authority figures (though Richard Nixon, a figure of traditional authority who would be the butt of many jokes from more liberal comics, did appear on *Laugh-In*). Likewise, cinema's widening landscape allowed more experimental approaches and more off-the-wall characters to make it back into the mainstream cinema. More progressive films like *Harold and Maude* and *Blazing Saddles* used strange characters and unusual situations to achieve maximum comedic effect. The 1970s also had a number of humorous films with strong political messages, such as *Network*, which predicted developments like the reality television trend by looking at figures who became more famous for their public behavior than for any type of talent or skill and who were exploited by television networks. Other films of the era, such as *Being There* and *The Graduate*, seemed to demonstrate general disenchantment with society without necessarily having a clear or stable social message.

In the 1980s, the sitcom rose to prominence once again. While situation comedies had been around for decades, the 1980s had a number of successful examples. *Cheers*, *Night Court*, *ALF*, and other shows strayed from the short sketch format of variety shows. Nevertheless, *Saturday Night Live* was also a mainstay of the era, launching several of its stars into other areas of film and television fame. Indeed, in the mid-1980s, *Saturday Night Live* had what is often considered to be its greatest season ever, with an all-star cast including Billy Crystal, Martin Short, Christopher Guest, and other luminaries on both the writing and performing staffs.

The television landscape also had talk shows as a mainstay form of entertainment, although they began to demonstrate a slightly different feel than they had during the days of Milton Berle and Steve Allen. Whether on daytime or late-night shows, celebrities made appearances to help raise their visibility and promote current projects, with the hosts serving to help the celebrities be likable, funny, and effective in doing so. This type of venue helped stand-up performers become regular fixtures on the television landscape. Performers such as David Letterman and writers such as Conan O'Brien found stable work and national prominence through their hosting duties. Just as a previous generation's hosts, such as Ed Sullivan and Johnny Carson, had often served as gatekeepers for comedians, determining who received national attention by both who they had on to perform and who they allowed to sit down and talk with them, so Letterman and Jay Leno often could help to launch (or stifle) pop stars' careers.

In later formats, hosts would give performers even greater opportunities to exhibit their work and discuss their personal lives. Indeed, many shows, such as *The Daily Show*, supplement their broadcast material with online-exclusive content, extending the interviews or bits done for their TV broadcasts or showing behind-the-scenes material (sometimes real and sometimes staged) that invites loyal viewers to continue engaging with the show beyond the boundaries of usual television programs. Less than 15 years into the new millennium, the use of Twitter accounts and Facebook promotion is almost mandatory for comedic performers and programs. While this use of technology might seem to be cutting edge or entirely different from earlier generations of humorists, the pithy nature of Twitter recalls the quips of Johnny Carson and one-liners of the Algonquin Roundtable, showing that while some forms of humor are contextual, some forms are timeless.

But not all humor has a traditional feel. With adult-themed animated shows and movies like *Family Guy* and *South Park*, along with shows that are simultaneously humorous, dramatic, and scary like *Buffy the Vampire Slayer*, there continues to be genuine innovation in American comedy forms. While critical work has addressed the emergence of these forms of humor, much work remains to be done to track and understand the practice of humor in television and cinema.

AYKROYD, DAN (1952–)

Dan Aykroyd was born in Ottawa, Canada. During his early years, he intended to be a Catholic priest. After graduating from high school, Aykroyd briefly attended Carleton College in Ottawa, but he dropped out to focus on his comedy career. He worked in a number of stand-up comedy clubs and also began to perform as a musician.

By 1975, Aykroyd's comic work had earned him a spot as a writer and original cast member for *Saturday Night Live*. He portrayed many memorable characters and did a wide variety of impressions, from Bob Dole to Jimmy Carter to Tom Snyder. He also began to perform as Elwood Blues along with fellow *SNL* cast member John Belushi. The two recorded an album together and co-starred in the film *The Blues Brothers* to great critical and commercial acclaim. During and after his tenure on *SNL*, Aykroyd both wrote (or cowrote) and starred in a number of comedic films, perhaps most notably *Spies Like Us* and *Ghostbusters*, both of which had roles intended for John Belushi, but which were not filmed until after Belushi's death. Aykroyd was also part of the Blues Brothers revival, along with John Goodman and John Belushi's brother Jim. In 1983, Aykroyd married actress Donna Dixon. The two have three children.

Aykroyd has been prolific as both a writer and an actor. However, as is the case with many humorists with a large output, he has experienced mixed success with his various projects. Still, Aykroyd had a significant hand in some of the most significant comedic films and television shows of the 1980s. He can play a broad range of characters, including uptight characters, as in *Spies Like Us* and the *Ghostbusters* movies; the imbecile, as in the plumber he frequently played on *Saturday Night Live*; and the mentally unbalanced, as in *Nothing But Trouble*. His mix of writing and acting talent and his ability to play a wide variety of characters have given Aykroyd the staying power that has made him a true comic success.

See also: Belushi, John

Further Reading

Bellafante, Ginia. "Burgers and Blues." *Time* 140, no. 23 (December 7, 1992): 85.

Day, Amber, and Ethan Thompson. "Live from New York, It's the Fake News! *Saturday Night Live* and the (Non)Politics of Parody." *Popular Communication* 10, nos. 1/2 (January–March 2012): 170–182.

Hill, Doug. *Saturday Night Live: A Backstage History*. New York: Untreed Reads, 2011.

Machosky, Michael. "Cinematic Ghosts Scare up Laughs." *Pittsburgh Tribune Review*, September 19, 2008.

Zeke Jarvis

ALLEN, TIM (1953–)

Tim Alan Dick was born in Denver. When he was only 11, his father died in a car accident with a drunken driver. When he was 13, his mother remarried, moving the family to a suburb of Michigan. After graduating from high school, Dick, who would change his name to Tim Allen for his stage career, attended Central Michigan University and then Western Michigan University, where he earned a degree in communications and worked at the college radio station.

In 1975, Allen performed at a stand-up comedy night on a dare. Allen found that he thrived doing stand-up, so he continued to perform, eventually moving to Los Angeles to further pursue his career. In 1978, Allen was arrested for drug possession and spent two years in prison. In 1984, he married his first wife, with whom he has one child. The couple divorced in 2003.

Allen continued to perform and began work on a sitcom, *Home Improvement*, in 1991. His character on the show was rooted in his stand-up act, being a likable oaf interested in tools and home improvement, but not being particularly good at the work. As his television career took off, Allen also began to act in films, though not to widespread success. In 1999, *Home Improvement* ended, and Allen began to focus on his film career. He enjoyed major commercial success as the voice of Buzz Lightyear in the *Toy Story* movies and as the star of *The Santa Clause* films. In 2006, Allen married for the second time, this time having two children with his wife. Allen continues to work in both film and television.

Allen is known for portraying an everyman, often immature or in some other way flawed, but essentially likable. His stand-up career often referenced stereotypically manly interests like manual labor and sports, though he was willing to laugh at these pursuits. Allen was also one of a number of performers to make a successful transition from stand-up comedy to a sitcom rooted in that stand-up work. This trend was particularly evident in the 1990s, with Allen, Jerry Seinfeld, and others achieving sustained commercial success. Although Allen is not a particularly groundbreaking figure, his lasting success makes him an important performer in both comedy and American pop culture more generally.

Further Reading

Allen, Tim. *Don't Stand Too Close to a Naked Man*. New York: Hyperion, 1994.

De Moreas, Lisa. "Tim Allen's 'Last Man' Gets Last Laugh on Critics." *The Washington Post*, October 13, 2011.

Jones, Chris. "The Triumph of Tim Allen." *Esquire* 155, no. 8 (September 2011): 56.

Rovin, Jeff. "Tim Allen's Merry Christmas." *Ladies' Home Journal* 109, no. 12 (December 1992): 44.

Zeke Jarvis

ALLEN, WOODY (1935–)

Allan Stewart Konigsberg was born in the Bronx, but primarily grew up in Brooklyn. His grandparents were Jewish immigrants; growing up, the young Allen heard not only English, but also Yiddish, German, and Hebrew in his home. His parents had a difficult relationship, so Konigsberg sought out sports, magic, and comedy to find enjoyable distractions from his home. While still in high school, he began writing and selling jokes. By the time he was 17, he had changed his name to Heywood Allen and had begun to out-earn his parents. After graduating from high school, Allen attended New York University, where he studied film, though he eventually left college behind.

Woody Allen is known for both his art and his controversial personal life. He is multitalented, having achieved success as a writer, a director, and a musician. (AP Photo)

After earning money for writing individual jokes, Allen began getting work writing scripts for *The Ed Sullivan Show* and *The Tonight Show*. At the suggestion of his agent, he began performing his own stand-up material, which is when he formed the neurotic persona that would be evident among most of his characters in his films. In 1956, Allen married his first wife; they divorced in 1962. In addition to his stage work, Allen wrote pieces for *The New Yorker* and plays.

In 1965, Allen was asked to write the screenplay for a Warren Beatty film, *What's New Pussycat?* Allen had a small part in the film, but was disappointed with the final project when he saw that he did not have the level of control he had expected. This led him to take on directorial duties for later films.

In 1966, Allen married for the second time, this time divorcing in 1970. His first solo film was *What's Up, Tiger Lily?* The film involved voices dubbed over an existing film. This sort of playfulness and absurdity would continue to appear throughout much of Allen's early work. Allen continued to write, star in, and direct films, though his first major success came in 1977 with *Annie Hall*, which won four Academy Awards. In 1979, Allen put out another of his major successes, *Manhattan*.

In 1980, Allen began a long-term relationship with Mia Farrow, with whom he would have one son and adopt other children. Allen continued to regularly put out films, once again getting Academy Awards recognition in 1995 with *The Mighty Aphrodite*. In 1997, Allen married Soon-Yi Previn, who had been Mia Farrow's stepdaughter. This relationship would create a continuing controversy surrounding Allen, including accusations of his engaging in sexual relations with underage women, splitting his family between those who sided with Allen and those who sided with Mia Farrow. Despite his sometimes tumultuous personal life, Allen has continued to regularly put out films, often receiving great critical acclaim for his work.

Allen is known for appearing in many of his films, generally playing a slightly exaggerated version of himself. He has attributed his nervous, fidgety delivery to having watched Bob Newhart succeed with a similar persona. In addition, Allen often incorporates ideas from both philosophy and psychoanalysis in his writing and performance. This gives his characters a tortured sense of searching, which brings in both emotion and a silliness that many audiences have come to love. He also places a heavy emphasis on dialogue and miscommunication, a characteristic that has been emulated by many writers and directors. Although some critics find the work of Allen to be either self-indulgent or redundant, his massive output and consistent success make him a significant fixture in film in general and in comedy in particular. Allen also comes from a tradition of comics looking at the Jewish experience in America, with common themes like sexual desire, baseball, and a tension about family relations. Many of his works are set in New York, and many of his most dedicated fans appreciate his East Coast sensibilities. This comes through in both Allen's very educated, erudite delivery and his incorporation of conversational but strong voices in his dialogue.

In addition to his sustained excellence in film, Allen has achieved success in a wide variety of endeavors, including printed work, the theater, and even music. Although there have been questions about Allen's personal life, as a humorist, his importance and success cannot be denied.

See also: Newhart, Bob

Further Reading

Allen, Woody. *The Insanity Defense*. New York: Random House, 2007.

Epstein, Lawrence. *The Haunted Smile: The Story of Jewish Comedians in America*. Jackson: Public Affairs, 2002.

Morreal, John. *Comic Relief: A Comprehensive Philosophy of Humor*. Hoboken, NJ: Wiley-Blackwell, 2009.

Schwanebeck, Wieland. "Oscar's Unrecognized Adaptations: Woody Allen and the Myth of the Original Screenplay." *Literature Film Quarterly* 42, no. 1 (2014): 359–372.

Zeke Jarvis

APATOW, JUDD (1967–)

Judd Apatow was born in Flushing, New York. When Apatow was 12, his parents divorced. Thereafter, he lived mainly with his father, seeing his mother on the weekends. His mother worked for a record label, a backdrop that Apatow would use in his films. She also worked one summer at a comedy club, where Apatow gained first-hand experience to augment his existing interest in stand-up comedy. During his high school days, Apatow hosted a radio program where he would call established stand-up comics; he managed to interview a mix of established comedians, such as Steve Allen and Howard Stern, and then up-and-coming talents, such as Steven Wright and Jerry Seinfeld. Toward the end of his high school career, Apatow began to apply the lessons that he learned from these comics as he started his own stand-up career.

After graduating from high school, Apatow attended the University of Southern California, studying screenwriting. He dropped out during his sophomore year, focusing on gaining first-hand experience in comedy. He also moved in with Adam Sandler at that time. Apatow began to meet and work with a number of prominent comics, including Garry Shandling and Ben Stiller; Stiller and Apatow, for example, co-created *The Ben Stiller Show*. Apatow worked a combination of sitcom writing positions and film script rewriting jobs for a time. He met his wife, Leslie Mann, while working on a draft of a Ben Stiller film, *The Cable Guy*. The two married in 1997 and have two children, both of whom have appeared in Apatow's films.

Judd Apatow is well known for letting his actors improvise lines. This open approach led to great success in films like *The 40-Year-Old Virgin* and *Knocked Up*. (AP Photo/Kevork Djansezian)

In 2001, Apatow created the television pilot *North Hollywood*, which featured Seth Rogen and Jason Segel, both of whom would go on to be regulars in Apatow's films. Apatow also helped develop a number of shows that have gone on to achieve cult status, including *Undeclared* and *Freaks and Geeks*. In 2005, Apatow's first film as a director was released. *The 40-Year-Old Virgin* starred Steve Carell, with whom Apatow had worked on *Anchorman: The Legend of Ron Burgundy*, as well as Seth Rogen and Paul Rudd. Since that film's success, Apatow has produced and directed a number of well-received films, including *Knocked Up* and *Superbad*. In 2009, he wrote and directed the film *Funny People*, which reunited him with Adam Sandler and allowed Apatow to explore the stand-up comedy business and lifestyle.

Apatow continues to write, direct, and produce films. He and his family live in California.

Apatow's films have a number of overlapping elements. Like the Coen Brothers, Apatow uses a steady company of actors, including his wife, Seth Rogen, Paul Rudd, and Jason Segel. They sometimes repeat roles, as Rudd and Mann did in *Knocked Up* and *This Is 40*, though they may play similar but not necessarily the same characters. In addition, many critics have noted the realistic and improvised style of the films' dialogue. This is often mirrored by the loose plot of many of Apatow's films, which rely more on the humor of individual scenes and particular lines of dialogue instead of an overarching plot. This approach has sometimes led to the criticism that the films are too long and unwieldy, although some audiences find the more meandering style of film to be realistic in a way that many comedies are not. Apatow has characterized his family as more culturally than religiously Jewish, which is another link between his work and the Coen Brothers. Apatow's films also often examine the theme of growing up or failing to grow up, particularly in the male figures in his films. From exploring sexuality in *The 40-Year-Old Virgin* to coming to terms with parenthood in *This Is 40*, the characters in his films often explore their own sense of responsibility and maturity over the course of the film. This has led Apatow to be held as a humorist clearly marked by his generation.

See also: Carell, Steve; Sandler, Adam

Further Reading

Alberti, John. " 'I Love You Man': Bromances and the Construction of Masculinity, and the Continuing Evolution of the Bromantic Comedy." *Quarterly Review of Film and Video* 30, no. 2 (March 2013): 159–172.

Lagambina, Gregg. "Interview: Judd Apatow." A.V. Club. *The Onion*, July 30, 2009. Web. Accessed August 25, 2013, http://www.avclub.com/article/judd-apatow-31045.

Rodrick, Stephen. "Judd Apatow's Family Values." *New York Times Magazine* (May 27, 2007): 36–43, 58, 64–66.

Stein, Joel. "Judd Apatow, Seriously." *Time* 174, no. 5 (August 10, 2009): 46–52.

Zeke Jarvis

ARNOLD, TOM (1959–)

Tom Arnold was one of six children born in Ottumwa, Iowa. Early in his life, Arnold's mother left the family, leaving his father to raise the children. As a youth, Arnold worked in a meat factory to help the single-parent family make ends meet. Arnold attended Indian Hills Community College and then the University of Iowa, graduating with a degree in business administration and writing.

At the age of 23, Arnold began working as a stand-up comedian. After some success, he got a position on the writing staff for Roseanne Barr's show, *Roseanne*. From this position, Arnold began appearing on the show and began a romantic relationship with Barr. The two married in 1990, but had a tempestuous relationship that suffered from a number of problems stemming from drug and alcohol abuse. They often appeared on tabloid covers and, after their divorce in 1994, the pair would belittle each other in the media. In 1994, Arnold appeared in *True Lies*, playing the sidekick to Arnold Schwarzenegger. He received a good deal of attention for his performance, escaping from the shadow of Barr, with whom he had been almost exclusively associated prior to the role.

In 1995, Arnold married for a second time, this time to Julie Armstrong. The two divorced in 1999. Arnold remarried in 2002, divorcing in 2008 and marrying again in 2009. Arnold continues to work, hosting the Fox Sports Net show *The Best Damn Sports Show Period* and appearing in films, like the minor but successful independent film *Happy Endings*.

Arnold is noted for his high-energy, outrageous persona. He frequently references his personal life, laughing at his own misfortune and referring to aspects of his life that other performers might avoid. He allows himself to be the butt of his own jokes, discussing his status as "a jerk" while hosting *Saturday Night Live* and appearing as part of a group of unwanted celebrities being shot into the sun on *The Simpsons*. This willingness to appear ridiculous has also served Arnold as he has taken on projects of questionable quality, such as the movie version of *McHale's Navy* and *The Stupids*. He has performed in a large number of small parts in a wide variety of films, from *Austin Powers* to *Coneheads*. During his time with Roseanne Barr, Arnold had his own sitcom, *The Jackie Thomas Show*. While his recent work has allowed him to show more range and subtlety than the work done earlier in his career, he is still best known for his rapid-fire delivery and intense, sometimes obnoxious persona.

See also: Barr, Roseanne

Further Reading

Johnson, Steven. *Everything Bad Is Good for You: How Today's Popular Culture Is Actually Making Us Smarter.* New York: Riverhead Trade, 2006.

Moritz, Robert. "The Days and Nights of Tom Arnold, Hollywood Fat Guy." *GQ: Gentlemen's Quarterly* 70, no. 3 (March 2000): 244.

Schwarzbaum, Lisa. "Tom in the Eye of the Storm." *Entertainment Weekly* 234 (August 5, 1994): 32.

Zeke Jarvis

BALL, LUCILLE (1911–1989)

Lucille Ball was born in Jamestown, New York. When Ball was three years old, her family moved to Montana and Michigan, relocating for her father's work. After her father's death, Ball, her mother, and her brother moved back to New York to live with her maternal grandparents. Her grandfather enjoyed vaudeville and took the family to shows. Ball's mother eventually remarried and, while her mother and stepfather worked, Ball was left to be raised by her stepfather's parents, who were quite strict. Even so, her stepfather encouraged her to pursue entertaining. Ball's mother encouraged this interest as well, sending her to the John Murray Anderson School for the Dramatic Arts, although this move was also partly intended to get Lucille away from a bad relationship with an older man. Bette Davis was also at the school at the time; she received significantly more adulation than Ball, who was told that she was too shy.

Although Ball did not value her time at the school, she did return to New York in 1928, finding work as a model. Unfortunately, she had to leave after coming down with a serious illness. In 1932, Ball returned to New York once more, this time achieving success as a model and in films, where she obtained a number of small roles and, eventually, leading roles. She then moved to Hollywood to pursue a career in movies.

Lucille Ball broke many barriers for female comics. She won numerous awards and has had a lasting impact on situation comedies. (Library of Congress)

While filming *Too Many Girls* in 1940, Ball met her future husband, Desi Arnaz. The two married later that year. Interestingly, after some concern was voiced over the difference in their ages, Ball and Arnaz began to give false birth dates to seem closer in age than they actually were. The two had two children, one in 1951 and another in 1953. Ball and Arnaz continued to perform together and, after a successful role on radio, Ball was asked to develop a domestic comedy for television. The resulting show was *I Love Lucy*, which revolved around Arnaz's character being a performer and Ball's character trying to be part of his act. Not only did the show succeed, but Ball also broke new ground, becoming the first female head of a production company, Desilu Productions (Desilu combined her name with Arnaz's). Ball also achieved a first in that her second pregnancy was written into her show—pregnancy had not been discussed directly on mainstream television up to that point. The show was a tremendous success, not only in terms of its ratings, but also in that the network gave rebroadcast rights to Desilu Productions. In the early days of television, the value of reruns was not clear, but this seemingly small advantage ended up providing Ball and Arnaz with tremendous financial gain. Another major innovation that came out of *I Love Lucy* was the use of a three-camera setup for shooting the show. This would become the standard approach for sitcoms, but until that time it had never been used.

Although *I Love Lucy* was a major success, running from 1951 until 1957, with specials and other shows running until 1960, Ball encountered some hardships. Her marriage to Arnaz was troubled and ended in divorce in 1960. Following the divorce, Ball began appearing in a stage production of *Wildcat*, where she met Paula Stewart. Stewart and Ball quickly became friends, and Stewart introduced to Ball to Gary Morton. The two married, with the union lasting until Ball's death. In addition, Ball made Morton part of the Desilu Productions company. Unfortunately, Ball had to end the run of *Wildcat* due to health issues. After some rest, Ball returned with two successful shows, *The Lucy Show* and *Here's Lucy*.

Although Ball's career slowed in the late 1970s, she remained a well-respected figure in American comedy and television, receiving a wide variety of awards and honors both prior to and after her death in 1989.

Ball was known for her high-energy performances and her willingness to put herself at the center of the joke. She was a gifted physical comedian, with one of her most famous bits from *I Love Lucy* involving her trying to wrap candies on a conveyor belt, eventually stuffing many in her mouth and dropping others on the floor. She also broke down a variety of television barriers, as mentioned previously. After her divorce from Arnaz, her characters were single women—a role that other, less recognizable actresses might have had more trouble performing. Ball was also a champion for the women's movement, providing an on-screen portrayal of a woman who both valued and provided comic relief in relation to many developments in gender issues. Her show brought a variety of debates on gender into the cultural mainstream in a relatively uncontroversial way.

Further Reading

Ball, Lucille. *Love, Lucy*. New York: Berkley Publishing, 1997.

Karol, Michael. *Lucille A to Z: The Lucy Encyclopedia.* New York: Universe Star, 2008.

Sanders, Coyne, and Tom Gilbert. *Desilu: The Story of Lucille Ball and Desi Arnaz*. New York: It Books, 2011.

Vineberg, Steve. *High Comedy in American Movies: Class and Humor from the 1920s to the Present*. New York: Rowman and Little, 2005.

Zeke Jarvis

BEE, SAMANTHA (1969–)

Samantha Bee was born in Toronto, Ontario. She was raised in an unconventional family. In Bee's book, she recalls being introduced to human sexuality by having her elders show her pornography. She also discusses her time at Catholic school in Toronto, often in a way that demonstrates a clear antagonism toward the nuns who taught her. Bee lived with her father and stepmother, though as she discusses this time and part of her life, Bee generally focuses more on the awkwardness of the situation than on any sense of tenderness. Bee studied at the University of Ottawa and then at McGill University in Montreal, Quebec. In 2001, Bee met her husband, Jason Jones. The two have two children together.

Bee's major break came when she landed a regular role on *The Daily Show*. Her use of deadpan fit in well with many of the other correspondents and the show's approach to humor as a whole.

Bee is best known for her ability to maintain her façade through truly absurd situations. In an exchange with Bill O'Reilly in which O'Reilly played a clip of Bee's work on *The Daily Show* without acknowledging that she was being satirical, Bee made a joke of her pregnancy rather than directly attack O'Reilly for his gaffe. Bee's work is also characterized by a lack of embarrassment. This comes through both in her willingness to discuss awkward issues such as bodily functions and sexual issues and in her surprisingly frank discussions of her life in her book. While some figures shy away from discussing private issues in their lives, Bee describes her unconventional upbringing without cringing or appearing bitter. Moreover, she explores both her work on *The Daily Show* and the portion of career where she struggled. Although she demonstrates the same sense of absurdity in the book and in her work on *The Daily Show*, Bee's cracking of the façade in her memoir marks a clear departure from her on-screen work, establishing her versatility as a humorist. Like many of the other correspondents on *The Daily Show*, Bee balances both political humor and simple weirdness in her work. After a wave of other actors left, Bee became the longest-running correspondent on *The Daily Show*, keeping her status rather than leaving for more film work as many of her peers have. Mainly for this reason, even though Bee has received positive reviews for her book, she is still best known for her work on *The Daily Show*.

See also: Stewart, Jon

Further Reading

Bee, Samantha. *I Know I Am, But What Are You*. New York: Gallery, 2011.

Evans, Rory. "Rocking the Vote with Samantha Bee." *Women's Health* 5, no. 9 (November 2008): 60–64.

Riss, Suzanne. "Samantha Bee." *Working Mother* 34, no. 1 (December/January 2011): 28–32.

Tannenbaum, Rob. "Samantha Bee's Fake News Triumph." *Rolling Stone* 1202 (February 13, 2014): 24–25.

Zeke Jarvis

BELUSHI, JOHN (1949–1982)

John Belushi was born in Chicago. His father and maternal grandparents were all Albanian immigrants. While Belushi and his three siblings were growing up, the family moved to Wheaton, a city near Chicago. Belushi exhibited some behavior problems in grade school, but by high school he had demonstrated a greater level of discipline and was even co-captain of the football team. He also began to develop an interest in performance while in high school. After graduating from high school, Belushi attended the University of Wisconsin at Whitewater, but he dropped out after failure to attend classes. He then attended the College of DuPage, closer to his home.

At DuPage, Belushi began performing with an improvisational group. This led to his entry into Chicago's chapter of the Second City comedy theater in 1971. Belushi thrived while there, but eventually moved to New York to further pursue his comedy career. In 1973, he began work on *The National Lampoon Radio Hour*, where he met future collaborators like Gilda Radner and Bill Murray. In 1975, Belushi became one of the original cast members of *Saturday Night Live*. Around this time, he also starred in *Animal House*. He married his wife in 1976.

In 1979, Belushi decided to leave *Saturday Night Live* to pursue a film career. His films were met with mixed success; his most notable film was a spin-off of the

Saturday Night Live characters, the Blues Brothers; Belushi co-starred in this film with friend and former *SNL* cast member Dan Aykroyd.

In 1982, Belushi died of a drug overdose. At the time of his death, he was slated to appear with Aykroyd in two films, *Spies Like Us* and *Ghostbusters*. His roles went to Chevy Chase and Bill Murray, respectively.

Belushi is best remembered for his over-the-top, extreme characters. These characters included the samurai he played on *SNL* as well as John Blutarsky from *Animal House*. Partly because of these roles, Belushi was very well respected for his mastery of physical comedy. His eyebrows were particularly expressive, and he often got his biggest laughs without any dialogue. That same sense of the extreme, however, is often what people discuss regarding his eventual death. In an interview discussing drug use, Robin Williams pointed out that many people saw Belushi as such a force of nature that it was hard to believe that drugs could kill him. As such, his overdose served as a wake-up call for many comics and actors. Although Belushi is still highly respected, not all critics welcomed his work. Some saw his performances as being either too vulgar or too juvenile. Still, for such a brief career, his output is impressive and his high points will always be remembered.

See also: Aykroyd, Dan

Further Reading

Belushi, Judith Jacklin. New York: Carroll & Graf, 1990.

Schultz, Barbara. "The Blues Brothers Ride Again." *Mix* 37, no. 7 (July 2013): 24.

Woodward, Bob. *Wired: The Short Life and Fast Times of John Belushi*. New York: Simon and Schuster, 2012.

Zeke Jarvis

BENNY, JACK (1894–1974)

Jack Benny was born Benjamin Kubelsky in Chicago, Illinois, and grew up in nearby Waukegan. His parents were both Jewish immigrants from Eastern Europe. Benny was not successful in school or his early work, getting expelled from high school and struggling in business school and in his work at his father's saloon. He excelled at performance, however, having been trained in the violin from the age of six. Benny performed first as a musician. It was during his time working as part of a musical duo that Benny adopted his stage name to avoid a dispute with an established violinist, Jan Kubelik. While performing at the same theater as the Marx Brothers, Benny's work impressed them, and he developed a friendship with the Brothers that would help Benny gain prominence first in radio and later in television.

After struggling with some musical performances, Benny left vaudevillian work to join the Navy during World War I. It was in the Navy that he began to add comedy to his repertoire. After receiving boos for a violin performance, Benny joked his way back into the audience's favor, finding that his off-the-cuff remarks were better received than his practiced work. When he returned to performance after his

Jack Benny achieved success both on television and in nightclubs. He had tremendous staying power, hosting *The Jack Benny Show* on the radio for 33 years. (Library of Congress)

war-time service, Benny's career began to take off as he was featured on radio programs where he could play characters and deliver humorous quips and responses to other performers. This work soon developed into television work, where he continued to succeed with a number of shows under a number of sponsors. In those performances, he often relied not just on funny lines but also on pauses and awkward silences for humor.

In many ways, Benny was a predecessor to later hosts like David Letterman and Conan O'Brien, in that he employed self-effacing humor and an everyman character to comic effect. The jokes Benny made about himself often focused on his cheapness and his lying about his age, and he frequently played a perplexed or confused character trying to retain a sense of dignity in the face of an absurd exchange or situation. Benny's willingness to feign an attempt at dignity helped him to play the straight man to other characters who would play buffoons.

Beyond the willingness to appear absurd or confounded within the context of a skit or exchange, Benny's joking extended outside of the boundaries of his own show, particularly when he engaged in a mock feud with Fred Allen. The two would regularly trade barbs on their own shows and include skits that would parody the other's show. Many viewers believed that the two men generally disliked each other, but the pair were actually friends and admired each other's work. This sort of careful understanding of how to fully use the media in which they appeared is one of the reasons for Benny's success.

Beyond the self-effacing nature of Benny's work, the impact of his longevity and multifaceted approach to entertainment—he mastered multiple forms of entertainment and appeared in a wide variety of media—can still be felt. Many humorists now use multiple media outlets, as with Marc Maron's podcasts, Conan O'Brien's Twitter posts, and Sherman Alexie's blog, to support their core projects and media.

See also: Carson, Johnny; Letterman, David; O'Brien, Conan

Further Reading

Baughman, James L. "Nice Guys Last 15 Seasons: Jack Benny on Television, 1950–1965." *Film & History (03603695)* 30, no. 2 (September 2000): 29–40.
Fein, Irving. *Jack Benny: An Intimate Biography*. New York: Putnam, 1976.
Livingstone, Mary. *Jack Benny*. New York: Doubleday, 1978.
Wilson, James Graham. "Jack Benny and America's Mission after World War II: Openness, Pluralism, Internationalism, and Supreme Confidence." *Journal of American Studies* 45, no. 2 (May 2011): 337–353.

Zeke Jarvis

BERLE, MILTON (1908–2002)

Milton Berlinger was born in Harlem to Jewish parents. Berlinger, who would be known professionally as Milton Berle, began performing at the age of five, when he won an amateur talent contest, which led to his appearances in silent films. Berle claimed to have appeared in a number of films as a child, but his claims are disputed and exceedingly difficult to verify, given in the lack of clear documentation of child actors' work in that era. By the age of 12, Berle was appearing in vaudeville, honing his comedic skills.

Although Berle was successful as a stage performer, he also did a great deal of work on radio, in movies, and in television. He was a regular on a number of radio programs, eventually becoming the host of *Stop Me If You Heard This One*, a show where comedians would finish the openings of jokes that were sent in by listeners. Later, on *The Milton Berle Show*, Berle began working with Arnold Stang, who would eventually become his regular sidekick.

In 1941, Berle married his first wife, Joyce Matthews. The two divorced in 1947 and remarried in 1949, only to divorce again two years later.

In 1948, NBC moved its then radio show, *Texaco Star Theater*, to television, using Berle as one of the regular hosts. It was here that Berle earned his nicknames "Uncle Miltie" and "Mr. Television," with the latter stemming from the high level of success the show received. Berle's mother was regularly in the audience, where she was often referenced by Berle due to her distinctive laugh. In addition to Berle's dominance of the early days of television, his show was noteworthy because Berle broke the color line, bringing African American acts like the Four Step Brothers, Lena Horne, and Bill Robinson onto his show, where they often appeared on television for the first time.

Although Berle achieved a high level of success in his show, by the mid-1950s his career as a television host had begun to wane. After his show was canceled, he appeared on a wide variety of shows, including *The Jack Benny Show*, *Get Smart*, and *Laugh-In*, among numerous others. In 1953, Berle married his second wife Ruth, to whom he would stay married for more than 30 years.

While many of Berle's post-1950s performances were successful, not all of them were. Berle's domineering approach to performance resulted in him being banned from *Saturday Night Live* after he hosted the show in its early days.

Known as "Mr. Television," Milton Berle had a long and storied career. He was well known for his quick wit and his outlandish costumes. (Library of Congress)

Still, Berle continued to perform and be honored for both his charity work and his performance career. He was one of the first seven people to be inducted into the Television Hall of Fame. Berle was also one of the founding members of the Friars Club of Beverly Hills, a group known for its celebrity roasts.

Berle was outspoken in his criticisms of many other comics. When others would act in a way that Berle perceived as upstaging him, Berle would deliver one-liners to attack them. He also criticized other comics—Lenny Bruce and George Carlin, in particular,—or their use of obscenity.

In 1991, two years after divorcing his wife Ruth, Berle married Lorna Adams, to whom he would remained married until his death.

Berle carried his vaudeville background with him throughout his career. Even in his later work, he would often demonstrate oversized reactions and feature broad comedy. This sometimes did not translate well to younger audiences, and this gap was only widened by his criticism of younger comics like Bruce and Carlin. Nevertheless, Berle had genuine staying power and succeeded in both comedy and many dramatic works. He was also influential in the careers and success of a number of younger comedians and performers, from Ruth Buzzi to the Osmonds to Will Smith. Although he did not fit every television landscape, Berle's substantial body of work has left an indelible impact on America's cultural landscape.

Further Reading

Berle, Milton. *BS I Love You: Sixty Funny Years with the Famous and Infamous*. New York: McGraw-Hill, 1987.

Berle, William. *My Father, Uncle Miltie*. Fort Lee: Barricade Books, 1999.

Dim, Joan Marans. "Milton Berle Turned on the National TV Craze." *Investors Business Daily*, December 13, 2013, A03.

Zeke Jarvis

BROOKS, ALBERT (1947–)

Albert Lawrence Einstein was born in Beverly Hills, California, to Thelma Leeds and Harry Einstein. He attended Beverly Hills High School with Richard Dreyfuss and Rob Reiner. Following high school, Brooks attended Carnegie Mellon University for one year before dropping out to pursue his comedy career. It was at this point that he changed his surname to "Brooks" to avoid confusion with the physicist Albert Einstein.

Brooks made regular appearances on variety and talk shows in the late 1960s and early 1970s, including *The Tonight Show.* After releasing two comedy albums, including the Grammy-nominated *A Star Is Bought* in 1975, Brooks began pursuing filmmaking. His first film was an early mockumentary called *The Famous Comedians School.* He would go on to direct six short films for *Saturday Night Live* in 1975–1976. In 1976, he appeared in Martin Scorsese's *Taxi Driver,* where he was allowed to improvise most of his lines. Brooks's ability to improvise lines would become one of the true hallmarks of his work.

Brooks directed his first full-length film, *Real Life*, in 1979. Throughout the 1980s and 1990s, he continued his directing and acting work, while also being one of the handful of comics to offer his voice to *The Simpsons* multiple times. Some of his work during this era includes *Modern Romance* (1981), *Lost in America* (1985), and *Defending Your Life* (1991). He received an Academy Award nomination for his role in *Broadcast News* (1987).

In 1997, Brooks married Kimberly Shlain. He continued his acting and voice work through much of the 2000s, highlighted by a role in *Finding Nemo* (2003), *The Simpsons Movie* (2007), and *Drive* (2011); the last role earned him several awards.

Brooks is known for his on-stage persona of a narcissistic, nervous comic. Because he was allowed to improvise many of his lines in Scorsese's *Taxi Driver,* screenwriter Paul Schrader has said that Brooks's character was the only one he could not understand. Brooks's best-received work is *Lost in America.* In other films, Brooks is known for being understated with many of his performances, playing the befuddled straight man to more off-the-wall characters. He also consistently strikes a balance between being intelligent and being easy to understand. As is the case with Woody Allen, his work incorporates both high-brow references and thoughts about sex, sports, and other, more base ideas and practices. IGN ranked Brooks as the best guest star in *The Simpsons'* history, specifically for his portrayal of super-villain Hank Scorpio.

Brooks has been nominated for many awards over the years, has been the recipient of the National Society of Film Critics Award for Best Screenplay (*Lost in America,* 1985; *Mother*, 1996) and the American Comedy Award (*Broadcast News,* 1987), and received 17 awards and an additional 10 nominations for his portrayal of Bernie Rose in 2011's *Drive*. Brooks's awards, the cameos that stars are willing to make in his films, and the way that other humorists discuss him all attest to the level of critical success that he has achieved and maintained.

Further Reading

Brooks, Albert. *2030: The Real Story of What Happens to America*. New York: St. Martin's Press, 2010.

Green, Daniel. " 'We're Getting a False Reality Here': Albert Brooks and the Comic Idea." *Film Criticism* 17, no. 1 (Fall 1992): 26–37.

Raab, Scott. "Albert Brooks Knows the Whole, Hellish Truth." *Esquire* 132, no. 3 (September 1999): 122.

Rhodes, Joe. "Albert Brooks Gives Himself the Business." *New York Times*, June 1, 2008, 26.

Brian Davis

BROOKS, JAMES L. (1940–)

James Lawrence Brooks was born in Brooklyn, New York, and grew up in New Jersey. Brooks was raised mainly by his mother. His father left his mother when she told him that she was pregnant, cutting off communication with his family when Brooks was 12. This abandonment led Brooks's mother to struggle financially and caused Brooks to feel like an outcast. Although Brooks did not excel in high school, he did work on the school newspaper, often getting the chance to interview celebrities. After graduating from high school, Brooks briefly attended New York University, studying public relations.

After he dropped out of college, Brooks obtained a job as an usher at CBS, which he got through his sister's connections. From there, Brooks receive opportunities to write copy for the news desk. In 1965, he moved to Los Angeles to write for documentaries. Brooks eventually moved into rewriting scripts for comedic films and writing for television shows such as *The Andy Griffith Show* and *My Three Sons*. In 1969, Brooks created his first show, *Room 222*, which ran on CBS until 1974. It was only the second television show in U.S. history to feature an African American in a lead role. After *Room 222*, Brooks and writing partner Allan Burns co-created *The Mary Tyler Moore Show*, cementing Brooks's status as a writer of significance in American television. Although the show was not initially received well, a move in time slot helped turn the show into a major success; it won the Emmy for Outstanding Comedy Series three years in a row.

In 1978, Brooks married for the first time. He and his wife had two children, but ultimately divorced in 1999.

Brooks went on to write a TV movie, do other television work, and create a *Mary Tyler Moore Show* spinoff, *Rhoda*, featuring Valerie Harper as Rhoda Morgenstern. He also departed from MTM productions (the company that had produced *Mary Tyler Moore* and *Rhoda*) to create *Taxi*, a sitcom set in a taxi company that included noteworthy figures like Danny DeVito, Christopher Lloyd, and Andy Kaufman in its cast. The show was a significant critical success. It also has been lauded as one of the earliest television comedies to use more realistic characters and conflicts, as opposed to the more broad comedy favored in earlier eras.

Although Brooks had done some film work, his first major success was *Terms of Endearment*. Released in 1983, the film won three Academy Awards. Brooks, however, had a sense of hesitance about his success, feeling that it would shift the

Top Ten Workplace Sitcoms

30 Rock (2006–2013)
Set on a TV show, this popular show played with the conventions of television.

Cheers (1982–1993)
Set in a bar, this very successful show launched the careers of a number of actors.

The Dick Van Dyke Show (1961–1966)
A show about a TV show, this helped to introduce the playful idea of writers writing about writers on TV.

Frasier (1993–2004)
A spin-off of *Cheers*, this show followed psychiatrist Frasier Crane to his radio call-in program.

The Mary Tyler Moore Show (1970–1977)
This breakthrough show portrayed a woman supporting herself for the first time on network television.

M.A.S.H. (1972–1983)
Set during the Vietnam War, this show looked at doctors getting by in the face of war-time pressures.

Newhart (1982–1990)
Set in a small inn owned by a couple, this show looked at the oddball small-town residents.

News Radio (1995–1999)
This show featured a strong ensemble cast working at a talk radio station.

The Office (2005–2013)
The American adaptation of the BBC show, this became a wildly successful sitcom.

Parks and Recreation (2009–2015)
Amy Poehler and Aziz Ansari starred in this playful look at local politics.

expectations of both audiences and people working in the entertainment industry (a similar concern would later be expressed by Adam Sandler's chef character in Brooks's movie *Spanglish*). Brooks has continued to work in film, seeing positive critical receptions of his movies *Broadcast News* and *As Good as It Gets*, among others. In the midst of his work in film, Brooks returned to television by producing *The Simpsons*, which he first helped to produce as a series of animated shorts on *The Tracey Ullman Show*. While Brooks did not write many of the episodes, writers from the show's early staff consistently credit Brooks with having a major impact on the show's humor and tone. The show went on to be a major critical and popular success, being dubbed the best show of the 20th century by *Time* magazine. Brooks also co-produced and wrote the film version of *The Simpsons*, while directing the voice cast, which the actors described as an intense experience.

Brooks has remarried and has one child with his current wife. He continues to live and work in Los Angeles.

Brooks has had a major impact on America's comedic and cultural landscape. From his boundary-breaking work in focusing on characters of color and prominent female comedians on television to his incorporating the lives of working-class figures into his material, Brooks has consistently given a voice and a view to traditionally marginalized groups. In addition, he has worked with a large number of prominent figures, including Mary Tyler Moore, Matt Groening, and Danny DeVito. While some of these figures had already established themselves prior to working with Brooks, a number of contemporary humorists regard Brooks as something of a mentor. In addition to including marginalized groups in his productions, Brooks is known for his deft knack for dialogue as well as his astute balance of bizarre situations and realistic, carefully crafted characters. In films such as *Spanglish* and *As Good as It Gets*, Brooks features offbeat and outcast characters who nevertheless convey an emotional depth and complexity that allows his work to balance a rhythm of emotional weight and light-hearted comedy. Although Brooks has already established his significance as a prominent figure in American comedy, he continues to produce major new texts while also carving out time for smaller, more personal projects.

See also: DeVito, Danny; Groening, Matt

Further Reading

Boskin, Joseph. *Rebellious Laughter: People's Humor in American Culture*. Syracuse: Syracuse University Press, 1997.

Lafayette, Jon. "Television Comedy's Humble Genius." *Broadcasting & Cable* 144, no. 4 (January 27, 2014): 4A.

Speidel, Constance. "Whose Terms of Endearment?" *Literature Film Quarterly* 12, no. 4 (1984): 271–273.

Zeke Jarvis

BROOKS, MEL (1926–)

Melvin James Kaminsky was born June 28, 1926, in Brooklyn, New York to Jewish parents. Kaminsky lost his father when he was only two years old. To add to his troubles, he was sickly as a child, often being picked on by his classmates. In high school, Kaminsky learned to drum under the legendary Buddy Rich. By age 14, he was beginning to earn money from his musical performances. After graduating from high school, Kaminsky became a corporal in the United States Army and served during World War II.

His career as Mel Brooks started soon after World War II. After a short career as a drummer and pianist in various nightclubs, in 1949, Brooks (who took his name to avoid confusion with a trumpet player who often performed in the same areas as Brooks) was given his first writing job as a joke writer for *The Admiral Broadway Revue* by Sid Caesar, who would eventually hire Brooks to write for his comedy series, *Your Show of Shows*. In 1953, Brooks married his first wife, with whom he had three children. The two would divorce in 1961. In 1964, Brooks married fellow performer Anne Bancroft, with whom he had one child.

Brooks began his ascent as a writer/director when he wrote and directed *The Producers* in 1968—a movie that would eventually be turned into a Broadway musical in 2001 and take home 12 Tony awards. Following the film's success, Brooks became an active moviemaker, usually serving as both writer and director for his films, and often acting in and producing them as well. After *The Producers*, Brooks would go on to write and direct 10 additional films between 1970 (*The Twelve Chairs*) and 1995 (*Dracula: Dead and Loving It*). Although Brooks has remained active in the field with various side projects—namely, voiceovers, occasional writing credits, and television specials—he has largely left filmmaking behind. Even so, his career has spanned multiple arenas and has led Brooks to be one of only 11 entertainers to be awarded an Emmy, a Grammy, an Oscar, and a Tony award for his work in the field of comedy.

In 2005, Brooks's wife, Anne Bancroft, died. Brooks had continually spoken of her with great admiration, and the two were generally regarded as one of the great couples of Hollywood.

Often using parodies in his films, Brooks extends the scope of his humor to include Adolph Hitler and Nazi Germany, no doubt on account of his Jewish heritage and his experiences during World War II. Farce and parodies are central to his work, which occasionally makes an effort to parody otherwise grave scenarios—the Spanish Inquisition and the French Revolution in *History of the World Part I* being two examples. Films like *Spaceballs*, *Young Frankenstein*, and *Dracula: Dead and Loving It* are more focused in the subjects they are parodying—*Star Wars*, *Frankenstein*, and *Dracula*, respectively. Brooks's comedic styling has often been built around the same actors and actresses across many of his films, similar to a repertory theater company for stage performances. In later years, Brooks acted and produced numerous works with his second wife, Anne Bancroft, prior to her death in 2005. During the height of his directing career, he relied heavily on the services of Gene Wilder, Dom DeLuise, Madeline Kahn, Harvey Korman, Cloris Leachman, Ron Carey, Dick Van Patten, and Andréas Voutsinas.

After his second film *Twelve Chairs*, many in Hollywood suggested that his work was too Jewish in nature. Brooks responded by moving into parody, which would become his niche, with *Blazing Saddles* in 1974. His excessive style began to generate some negative press, but when he went outside his realm of parody and farce (*Life Stinks*, 1991), his work was all but ignored. He followed up that brief departure by directing *Robin Hood: Men in Tights* (1993) and *Dracula: Dead and Loving It* (1995).

Many of Brooks's films acknowledge their own existence as films. *Spaceballs*, for example, spends a significant portion talking about how the movie itself will be marketed and merchandised. Brooks echoes this idea with multiple announcements for sequels to his films that never actually come to be. *History of the World Part I* closes with a "preview" montage of *History of the World Part II*. In this case, Brooks once again turns to his Jewish heritage ("Jews in Space") and his routine mocking of Adolf Hitler ("Hitler on Ice") to execute the humor.

Despite objections to his work being too Jewish, complaints about his excessive style, and individual films receiving mixed reviews, Brooks is looked on with almost universal acclaim for his overall body of work. Deemed his three greatest works, *Blazing Saddles*, *The Producers*, and *Young Frankenstein* were all named to AFI's top 100 comedy films of all time, coming in at sixth, 11th, and 13th, respectively. In 2011, the American Film Institute presented Brooks with its highest honor, the AFI Life Achievement Award. In 2010, Brooks was awarded a star on the Hollywood Walk of Fame, quite literally cementing him into the canon of the giants of modern comedy.

See also: Caesar, Sid

Further Reading

Brooks, Mel. *Heil Myself*. OnlineSheetMusic.com, 2013.

Hug, Bill. "*Blazing Saddles* as Postmodern Ethnic Carnival." *Studies in Popular Culture* 36, no. 1 (Fall 2013): 63–81.

McDonald, Paul. " 'They're Trying to Kill Me': Jewish American Humor and the War against Pop Culture." *Studies in Popular Culture* 28, no. 3 (April 2006): 19–33.

Parish, James Robert. *It's Good to Be the King: The Seriously Funny Life of Mel Brooks*. New York: Wiley, 2008.

Brian Davis

BURNETT, CAROL (1933–)

Carol Burnett is an American comedienne, actress, and writer. She was born in San Antonio, Texas, in 1933 to alcoholic parents who worked in the entertainment industry. Her mother was a publicity writer for movie studios and her father was a manager of a movie theater. Burnett spent much of her childhood with her grandmother because of her parents' alcoholism and divorce. She and her grandmother moved to a boarding house in Hollywood, where Burnett worked as an usherette for a movie theater on Hollywood Boulevard.

After Burnett graduated from Hollywood Hills High School, she studied theater and English at the University of California at Los Angeles. She soon discovered that she loved making audiences laugh. At a party thrown by a professor, Burnett told a man who was also at the party that she wanted to go to New York and try her hand at musical comedy. The man offered her an interest-free loan on two conditions: that she would never reveal his name and that if she became a success, she would help others also achieve success. Burnett failed to obtain any acting jobs during her first year in New York, but landed a small role on a television show in 1955, which led to a role in a short-lived sitcom in 1956. She also married for the first time. Burnett eventually made a name for herself by performing in cabarets and nightclubs, and these performances led to appearances on *The Tonight Show* and *The Ed Sullivan Show* in 1957. In 1959, Burnett was nominated for a Tony Award for her role on Broadway in *Once upon a Mattress*.

In 1962, Burnett won an Emmy Award for her role on television in *The Garry Moore Show*. In this show, she played a number of characters, including the charwoman who would become a permanent part of her repertoire and would appear later on her own variety show, *The Carol Burnett Show*. Also in 1962, Burnett divorced her first husband; she married Joe Hamilton (with whom she would have three children) in 1963.

Burnett won another Emmy Award for *Julie and Carol at Carnegie Hall*, a production in which she co-starred with her friend Julie Andrews. She also recorded two musical albums for Decca Records. She went on to make numerous appearances on a variety of television shows, including *The Twilight Zone*; *Gomer Pyle, U.S.M.C.*; and *The Lucy Show*. Her friendships with Jim Nabors and Lucille Ball became long-lasting relationships that led to many guest-starring appearances for all three performers on their respective shows over the years. Lucille Ball sent Burnett flowers every year on her birthday.

In September 1967, *The Carol Burnett Show* debuted on CBS as a result of a contract stipulation that Burnett be allowed to produce whatever show she wanted. *The Carol Burnett Show* was a one-hour variety show that featured comedy skits and music, with Harvey Korman, Lyle Waggoner, and Vicki Lawrence starring in an ensemble cast. Tim Conway became a cast regular in the eighth season. Dick Van Dyke joined the show in its 11th (and final) season as a replacement for Korman, who left the show after its 10th season. Taped at CBS Television City's Studio 33, *The Carol Burnett Show* became an instant hit. Its comedy sketches often parodied popular movies such as *Gone with the Wind*, soap operas such as *As the World Turns*, and television commercials of the day. *The Carl Burnett Show* consistently ranked with the top 30 shows in terms of ratings until 1972, when it began to slip. By the 11th season, ratings were sagging and Burnett decided to let the show end. For years after it ended, *The Carol Burnett Show* continued to enjoy success in syndicated reruns as the re-edited, half-hour *Carol Burnett & Friends*. During its run, *The Carol Burnett Show* garnered 25 Emmy Awards. Since its demise, it has placed high on lists of the best television shows of all time. No other television variety show since *The Carol Burnett Show* has been as successful.

After *The Carol Burnett Show*, Burnett occasionally returned to the theater stage and appeared on numerous game shows and television specials, including *Dolly and Carol in Nashville* on Valentine's Day in 1979 with Dolly Parton. That program was a music and comedy hour taped on the stage of the Grand Ole Opry. In the 1980s, Burnett occasionally appeared in her role as Eunice on the spin-off series *Mama's Family*, which starred Vicki Lawrence as Mama. In 1982, she played the role of Agatha Hannigan, the manager of the orphanage, in John Huston's *Annie*.

In 1984, Burnett divorced her husband, Joe Hamilton. In 1986, she published a best-selling memoir, *One More Time*, which chronicled her coming-of-age years in Depression-era Hollywood. In the early 1990s, Burnett and CBS attempted to revive *The Carol Burnett Show* with Meagen Fay and Richard Kind in the cast, but the series did not find its audience because of the changing nature of television comedy and was canceled after only nine episodes. Burnett appeared with the cast of the original *The Carol Burnett Show* in three reunion specials in 1993, 2001, and 2004.

In 2001, Burnett married for the third time. In 2002, her daughter Carrie died at the age of 38 of lung and brain cancer. Burnett's relationship with her daughter became the basis of a 2013 memoir, *Carrie and Me: A Mother-Daughter Love Story*, which followed Burnett's 2010 memoir, *This Time Together: Laughter and Reflection*, a recollection of her years on *The Carol Burnett Show* and her friendships with numerous comedy legends.

In addition to her Emmy Awards, Burnett has been the recipient of several Golden Globe Awards, a Peabody Award, the Kennedy Center Honors, a Presidential Medal of Freedom, and the Mark Twain Prize for American Humor. Her star on the Hollywood Walk of Fame is located in front of the theater where she worked as an usherette when she was a teenager.

On her own show, Burnett was known for her wild characters and ability to stay composed during comedic improvisation. Characters such as Mr. Tudball, Mrs. Wiggins, Eunice, Mama, and the charwoman became household names during the original run of *The Carol Burnett Show*, largely owing to her physical, high-energy performances. She also demonstrated a courage that not all performers possess in her use of improvisation. Most shows opened with Burnett saying, "Let's bump up the lights," and hosting an unrehearsed question-and-answer session with the studio audience. On numerous occasions during these sessions, an audience member would ask Burnett to do her trademark Tarzan yell; Burnett would willingly oblige. Burnett often ad-libbed funny answers to audience questions. Episodes were taped on Fridays, after a week of rehearsals. Each episode was filmed in only two takes. Actors flubbing their lines and breaking character became a trademark of the show; such events were popular with television audiences because they gave the illusion that the show was airing live. Burnett closed most shows with the song, "I'm So Glad We Had This Time Together," followed by Burnett tugging her ear, which was a signal to her grandmother. Burnett continued the tradition of tugging her ear at the close of each show even after her grandmother's death. Because of her significant commercial success and her versatility as a performer, Burnett has become a symbol of a successful female humorist in the American popular culture industry.

See also: Conway, Tim

Further Reading

Burnett, Carol. *This Time Together: Laughter and Reflection.* New York: Three Rivers Press, 2011.

Marc, David. "Carol Burnett: The Last of the Big-Time Comedy-Variety Stars." *Quarterly Review of Film & Video* 14, nos. 1/2 (July 1992): 149–156.

Martin, Peter. "Backstage with Carol Burnett." *Saturday Evening Post* 235, no. 10 (March 10, 1962): 36–40.

Taraborrelli, J Randy. *Laughing till It Hurts: The Complete Life and Career of Carol Burnett.* New York: William Morrow, 1988.

Stephen Powers

BUTTONS, RED (1919–2006)

Red Buttons was born Aaron Chwatt in New York. Both of his parents were Jewish immigrants and he grew up in a working-class neighborhood. He got his start performing while working as an entertaining bellhop at Ryan's Tavern in the Bronx. The striking look of his red hair and buttons on his uniform led him to gain the moniker "Red Buttons," under which he would later regularly perform. In the mid-1930s, he worked on the Borscht Belt, eventually becoming noticed and working his way up to Broadway. In 1943, Buttons was drafted into the army, where he worked to entertain the troops. After the war, he continued to perform on Broadway.

In 1947, Buttons married briefly, and he married again in 1949. His final marriage began in 1964 and lasted until his wife's death in 2001.

Over the course of Buttons's career, he starred in two television shows, several Broadway shows, and a number of movies, including a turn away from comedy in the dramatic film *Sayonara*, for which he won an Oscar for Best Supporting Actor. Buttons died in 2006; he was survived by his son and daughter.

Buttons worked in a variety of media and with a variety of performers, from Mickey Rooney to Jane Fonda to Marlon Brando. Despite his versatility, he is best remembered for his comedic television work. While his show was relatively short-lived, running for only three seasons, it was very well received in the early going. In addition to the performances mentioned previously, Buttons performed at venues in Las Vegas and wrote and recorded an album of children's poems. He often was willing to engage in self-deprecating humor, playing the buffoon to a straight man, as he did in the early part of his career, or simply appearing as a humorous character unto himself. His versatility and sense of humor about himself are likely two of the central components that allowed Buttons to successfully transition from the Catskills into television and film—a transition that not all comedians made.

Further Reading

Bernstein, Adam. "Comedian Red Buttons, 87: Star of Skits, Stage and Screen." *Washington Post*, July 14, 2006.

Blumberg, Esterita Cissie, and Red Buttons. *Remember the Catskills: Tales by a Recovering Hotelkeeper*. New York: Purple Mountains Press, 1996.

Mendez, Evelyn. *Red Buttons 126 Success Facts: Everything You Need to Know about Red Buttons*. New York: Emero, 2014.

Zeke Jarvis

CAESAR, SID (1922–2014)

Isaac Sidney Caesar was born in Yonkers, New York. The child of Jewish immigrants, he had two older brothers. Caesar's parents owned a small restaurant, where he worked while growing up. At the establishment, he began to hear a number of different voices, accents, and ways of speaking—an experience that would help Caesar develop his variety of characters and voices. Caesar began to perform for customers, much to their delight. At the age of 14, he went to the Catskills, playing the saxophone and performing in comedic sketches. After graduating from high school, Caesar moved to Manhattan, where he worked a number of odd jobs to support himself and studied music at Juilliard. In 1939, he joined the U.S. Coast Guard. While serving in the Coast Guard, Caesar regularly performed as part of the military revues.

In 1942, Caesar met his wife. The two married in 1943, and they would go on to have three children together. As part of his military service, Caesar was relocated to Florida. There, he continued to perform and became part of a national touring show, which helped launch his career. Caesar began to appear on television and in films, steadily rising to prominence. In 1950, he became part of *Your Show of Shows*, a highly successful sketch comedy show with noteworthy writers, including Mel Brooks. After the show ended in 1954, Caesar had a series of shows that he anchored, including *Caesar's Hour*, where he had creative control. Unfortunately, the heavy load of television performances began to wear Caesar down. He turned to drugs and alcohol and eventually dropped out of the public eye for some time. He still performed live from time to time, but in 1977 he passed out during a performance and decided to give up his addictions. After successfully leaving behind his substance abuse problems, Caesar began to have more positive public experiences, including his hosting spot on *Saturday Night Live* in 1983. At the end of the episode, he was made an honorary cast member.

Caesar was known for being able to stay in character no matter how ridiculous the scene he was part of, in contrast to many of the other performers of his day. He was also known for being able to sustain much longer sketches than usual, regularly running as long as 10 to 15 minutes rather than the more typical five-minute range. Caesar's range, endurance, and ability to sustain his career over the long run have made him a source of admiration for generations of humorists. In addition, he was noteworthy for being one of the earliest performers to have significant creative control over his show. Although he was not one of the writers, he had final say on all of the sketches performed on his shows. Another hallmark of Caesar's work was allowing a wide variety of voices, characters, and contexts on his show. For all of his innovations and successes, Caesar is well respected as a performer.

See also: Brooks, Mel

Further Reading

Auslin, Michael. "Sid Caesar and His World." *Commentary* 137, no. 4 (April 2014): 60–63.

Caesar, Sid, and Eddie Friedfeld. *Caesar's Hours: My Life in Comedy with Love and Laughter*. New York: Public Affairs, 2005.

Corliss, Richard. "Great Caesar's Ghost: On the Passing of Sid Caesar." *Time.com* (February 18, 2014): 1.

Zeke Jarvis

CAMPBELL, BRUCE (1958–)

Bruce Campbell was born in Royal Oak, Michigan, the youngest child in his family. His father was a part-time actor. Campbell began making movies with future director Sam Raimi while the two were still in high school. They made an early version of the first *Evil Dead* movie, then titled *Within the Woods*, that attracted investors and allowed the two to collaborate on what would turn into a series of films. Campbell would go on to regularly have small cameos in Raimi's movies, both smaller films like *Dead Man* and big-budget films like the *Spider-Man* series, as well in Raimi's television work.

Bruce Campbell as his signature character "Ash" from the *Evil Dead* series. Campbell achieved cult fame for his offbeat and physical performances. (New Line Cinema/Photofest)

As Raimi came more into the public eye with his commercial success, Campbell also gained a greater level of prominence, and he began writing, publishing two autobiographical works celebrating and satirizing his status as a beloved cult figure. In 1983, he married his first wife, with whom he had a son and a daughter. In 1989, the two divorced. Campbell later married a costume designer whom he met on the set of his film *Mindwarp*. The two live together in Jacksonville, Oregon.

Campbell has been featured in many minor movies outside of his work with Raimi, starring in the *Maniac Cop* series and appearing in the Coen Brothers' *The Hudsucker Proxy*. In *Bubba Ho-tep*, Campbell played Elvis Presley. In the plot of this movie, Elvis switches places with one of his impersonators, who then dies, leading everyone to believe that the true Elvis is dead. As the film begins, Elvis is in a retirement home, where he befriends an African American man (played by Ossie Davis), who believes himself to be John F. Kennedy. The two fight off a mummy that is sucking the souls out of the residents of the retirement home. This sort of absurd plot, along with the simultaneously pompous and ridiculous character of an aged Elvis Presley, is typical of Campbell's work, as is the tone of the film, which straddles the horror and comedic genres. While Campbell has appeared in more realist works, he generally is featured in films that have a science fiction or fantastic component.

In addition to Campbell's film work, he has appeared in both prominent roles and small roles in prominent series. He starred in *Brisco County Jr.*, regularly appeared in *Ellen* for one season, had a starring role for an episode of *The X-Files* while it was very popular, and, most recently, served as a cast member on the show *Burn Notice*. While Campbell is not necessarily a household name, his regular appearances and speaking appearances, often on college campuses, has kept him popular among his cult following.

Further Reading

Campbell, Bruce. *If Chins Could Kill: Confessions of a B Movie Actor*. Los Angeles: LA Weekly Books, 2002.

Pomerantz, Dorothy. "Why an *Evil Dead* Remake? Because Horror Is Hollywood's Only Sure Thing." *Forbes.com* (April 5, 2013): 21.

Ross, Dalton. "Bruce Campbell Lives!" *Entertainment Weekly* 773 (July 9, 2004): 48–54.

Zeke Jarvis

CARELL, STEVE (1962–)

Steve Carell was born in Concord, Massachusetts, and grew up in Acton, not far from Concord. During his high school years, Carell was part of a reenactment group and also played hockey. After graduating from high school, he attended Dennison University, where he earned a degree in history. At Dennison, he was also part of an improvisational comedy group.

In the early 1990s, Carell moved to Chicago, where he worked with the Second City comedy troupe. There, he met his future friend and frequent co-star Stephen Colbert as well as his future wife Nancy Walls, whom he married in 1995. Carell and Colbert began their national television careers on *The Dana Carvey Show*. Although the show was relatively short-lived, it gave a number of stars, such as Robert Smigel, some early exposure.

After the show's cancellation, Carell had a number of roles on sitcoms and in movies before landing a regular role as a correspondent on *The Daily Show* in 1999. Carell's friend Stephen Colbert and wife were also among the show's correspondents during that time. During their run on the show, Carell and his wife had two children, a son and a daughter. Carell remained with the show, sometimes hosting or cohosting in Jon Stewart's absence, until 2005, at which point he left to star on the American adaptation of the successful BBC show, *The Office*. It was also around this time that Carell starred in the Judd Apatow film *The 40-Year-Old Virgin*. Prior to that, Carell had had roles in major films like *Bruce Almighty*, but had not carried a film on his own. The success of the film and the television show brought Carell many film and television opportunities, including independent and critically acclaimed films such as *Little Miss Sunshine* and more mainstream fare like *Get Smart*.

In 2010, Carell announced that he would leave *The Office* to focus more exclusively on his film career. Carell has continued to work regularly, appearing in both live-action and animated films. Currently, Carell and his family live in Los Angeles, California.

Carell is known for his deadpan delivery, often playing awkward situations for laughs. While his characters are often very self-assured—as is true of his character Michael Scott on *The Office* and the title character in *Evan Almighty*—but he also has played more good-natured but insecure or inept characters in such hits as *The 40-Year-Old Virgin* and the Will Ferrell film *Anchorman: The Legend of Ron*

Burgundy. Although Carell will always be known for his comedic work, he has shown more dramatic, though still funny, range in films like *Dan in Real Life*. Carell is also regularly associated with Will Ferrell and other, similar performers who frequently play man-children and otherwise immature or idiotic characters. Carell is very well respected among both comic and dramatic actors, who note his professionalism and keen wit.

See also: Apatow, Judd; Stewart, Jon

Further Reading

Dockterman, Eliana. "Steve Carell Says You're Messing up the 'That's What She Said' Joke." *Time.com* (December 19, 2013): 1.

Happel, Allison. "Pageant Trouble: An Exploration of Gender Transgression in *Little Miss Sunshine*." *Gender Forum* (2013): 46.

Kirby, Mark. "*Evan Almighty*." *GQ: Gentlemen's Quarterly* 77, no. 9 (September 2007): 352–355.

Zeke Jarvis

CARREY, JIM (1962–)

Jim Carrey was born in Ontario, Canada. His father was a musician, though Carrey has stated that his father also worked in other jobs to support his family. When his father lost his job, the family became homeless and lived in a van. Because of his family's struggles, Carrey had to drop out of school at age 15 and begin working as a janitor. After his family moved, Carrey went to high school for a time again, but had to drop out once more to help support his family and care for his mother, who was suffering from chronic illness. Eventually, Carrey's family situation began to stabilize, so that he was able to focus on comedy, overcoming some of his early struggles in performance and gaining a strong reputation in the Ontario comedy club scene.

Carrey got a significant break when he was given the opportunity to open for Rodney Dangerfield. After living in Las Vegas for a time and working with Dangerfield, Carrey decided to move to Los Angeles to further pursue his career. While he regularly performed in stand-up clubs, the early portion of Carrey's television and movie career was not particularly successful. Although he appeared in films, they were often not well received by either audiences or critics. Nevertheless, he did meet Damon Wayans, who then introduced him to his brother Keenan Ivory Wayans. This connection led to Carrey becoming part of the cast of *In Living Color*.

Carrey subsequently starred in the movie *Ace Ventura: Pet Detective*, which he also cowrote. The film was a major box-office success, catapulting Carrey to international fame and leading to major roles in *The Mask* and *Dumb and Dumber*. From there, Carrey did have some struggles, receiving criticism for possibly exploiting his popularity to support films like *Batman Forever*, in which he played the Riddler, and *Ace Ventura: When Nature Calls*. Carrey rebounded with his more serious performances in *The Truman Show*, for which he received an Academy Award nomination, and *Man on the Moon*, in which Carrey played the comedic performer Andy Kaufman. Carrey's performance received positive reviews from both critics and many of the performers who knew Kaufman, including Danny DeVito and Christopher Lloyd. Carrey starred in a number of films following *Man on the Moon*, though his next major success was *Bruce Almighty*, which also featured major stars Morgan Freeman and Jennifer Aniston.

Sometimes referred to as a "rubber-faced" performer, Jim Carrey has a large array of characters and impressions. In addition, he has received positive critical reactions for several dramatic performances. (AP Photo/Eric Draper)

During this time, Carrey had a number of high-profile relationships, including his marriage to Lauren Holly, his *Dumb and Dumber* co-star, and his long-term relationship with Jenny McCarthy. He became a U.S. citizen in 2004. Carrey continues to live and work in California.

Although Carrey has a diverse body of work, his early performances were clearly grounded in his impersonations and his rubber-faced persona. Carrey brought back his oversized personas, such as Fire Marshall Bill, and his effective impersonations, such as his work playing Jimmy Stewart, in both his seasons on *In Living Color* and his more sporadic appearances, like his hosting work on *Saturday Night Live*. This sort of oversized performance also carried through into most of the film work he did as he rose to national prominence. In *Ace Ventura* and *The Mask*, Carrey played over-the-top characters that were measured for wild performances and extreme behavior. As Carrey became more popular, he settled into some more complex roles, like his portrayal of Andy Kaufman in *Man on the Moon*. Even so, many of his performances accepting awards or promoting films incorporated odd and striking elements not unlike Kaufman's performances. At one MTV Movie Awards ceremony, Carrey's unkempt appearance and Jim Morrisonesque behavior struck much of the audience as strange and surprising. Carrey has also used his own celebrity as a source of humor on multiple occasions. From his satirical exploration of his salary and personal life on various talk show appearances to his statements about himself while playing Jimmy Stewart on *Saturday Night Live*, Carrey regularly deflates his own persona in his appearances. While Carrey's career has clearly had its ups and downs, he has become known as a resilient and versatile performer, succeeding in both dramatic and humorous exploits.

See also: Kaufman, Andy; Wayans Siblings

Further Reading

Corless, Kieron. "*Ace Ventura*: King of the Quarter." *Sight and Sound* 18, no. 5 (May 2008): 12.
Ebert, Roger. "Jim Carrey Laughs in the Face of Success." Rogerebert.com. July 24, 1994.
Kehr, Dave. "The Lives of Jim Carrey." *Film Comment* 36, no. 1 (January–February 2000): 12–15.
Stein, Joel. "Can Jim Carrey Turn It around?" *Time* 169, no. 9 (February 26, 2007): 56–61.

Zeke Jarvis

CARSON, JOHNNY (1925–2005)

Johnny Carson was born in Corning, Iowa. His family moved around Iowa before settling in Nebraska when Carson was eight. At age 14, Carson began to perform his magic act with a kit that he had ordered. In 1943, he enlisted in the Navy, serving at the end of World War II. During this time, Carson continued to work on his magic act and also boxed. After leaving the military, Carson attended the University of Nebraska, where he wrote a thesis on Jack Benny's work. In 1950, Carson began his career in broadcasting.

Johnny Carson was a beloved late-night talk show host. With a 30-year run in that role, he was one of the most enduring stars on television. (AP Photo)

In 1949, Carson married his first wife. The two had three children together, though the pair would divorce in 1963.

In 1951, Carson moved to California to pursue his career further. While there, he developed a small but loyal following that included Red Skelton, who allowed Carson to fill in for him, giving Carson his first big break. Jack Benny also helped Carson rise to prominence. In 1962, Carson took over hosting duties for *The Tonight Show*. One year later, he married for the second time, this time divorcing in 1972.

Although Carson was initially nervous (he did, indeed, struggle in his first year of hosting), he steadily gained a following and had a long and successful career as host of *The Tonight Show*. In 1972, Carson married for the third time, this time divorcing in 1985.

Carson dominated the late-night slot in the 1980s. In 1987, he married for the final time.

In 1992, Carson retired from *The Tonight Show*. He rarely performed or appeared after his retirement, though he would sometimes write jokes for David Letterman. In 2005, Carson died after suffering multiple heart attacks.

Carson established the late-night talk show as a major cultural phenomenon. In fact, many comics saw Carson as a kingmaker, because many comedians first rose to prominence largely from their *Tonight Show* appearances. Partially because of his own help from Benny and Skelton, Carson took special pleasure in helping young comedians have breakthrough performances. David Letterman, Jay Leno, and Steve Martin all benefited from their *Tonight Show* appearances and guest hosting experiences. Carson was seen as a generally pleasant figure, sometimes making lewd jokes, but being relatively inoffensive. His "nice guy" persona helped to make him a beloved figure in American comedy. In fact, upon both his retirement and his death, positive stories and expressions of gratitude came from a wide variety of public figures and humorists.

See also: Benny, Jack; Leno, Jay; Letterman, David; Martin, Steve

Further Reading

Bushkin, Henry. *Johnny Carson*. New York: Houghton Mifflin, 2013.

McMahon, Ed. *Here's Johnny! My Memories of Johnny Carson, the Tonight Show and 46 Years of Friendship*. Nashville: Rutledge Hill Press, 2005.

Miller, John. "From the Great Plains to LA: The Intersecting Paths of Lawrence Welk and Johnny Carson." *Virginia Quarterly Review* 79, no. 2 (Spring 2003): 265–279.

Sweeney, Don. *Backstage at the Tonight Show: From Johnny Carson to Jay Leno*. New York: Taylor Trade Publishing, 2006.

Zeke Jarvis

CHEECH AND CHONG (CHEECH MARIN [1946–], TOMMY CHONG [1938–])

Thomas Chong was born in Edmonton, Alberta. His mother was of Scottish and French descent; his father was Chinese. While Chong was growing up, his family moved to Calgary, in an area with a conservative mindset that Chong quickly grew to dislike. Chong dropped out of high school, deciding to make a living as a musician. In 1960, he married his first wife. The two stayed married until 1970; they had two children, both of whom have appeared in a number of films. By the early 1960s, Chong moved to Vancouver, where he played in the group Bobby Taylor and the Vancouvers.

Richard Marin was born in Los Angeles. After graduating from high school, he received a degree from San Fernando Valley State College. However, as the Vietnam War expanded and the draft for the U.S. military began, Marin (who took on the name "Cheech" for his stage performances) moved to Vancouver, Canada. It was there that he met Tommy Chong. The pair began to perform stand-up

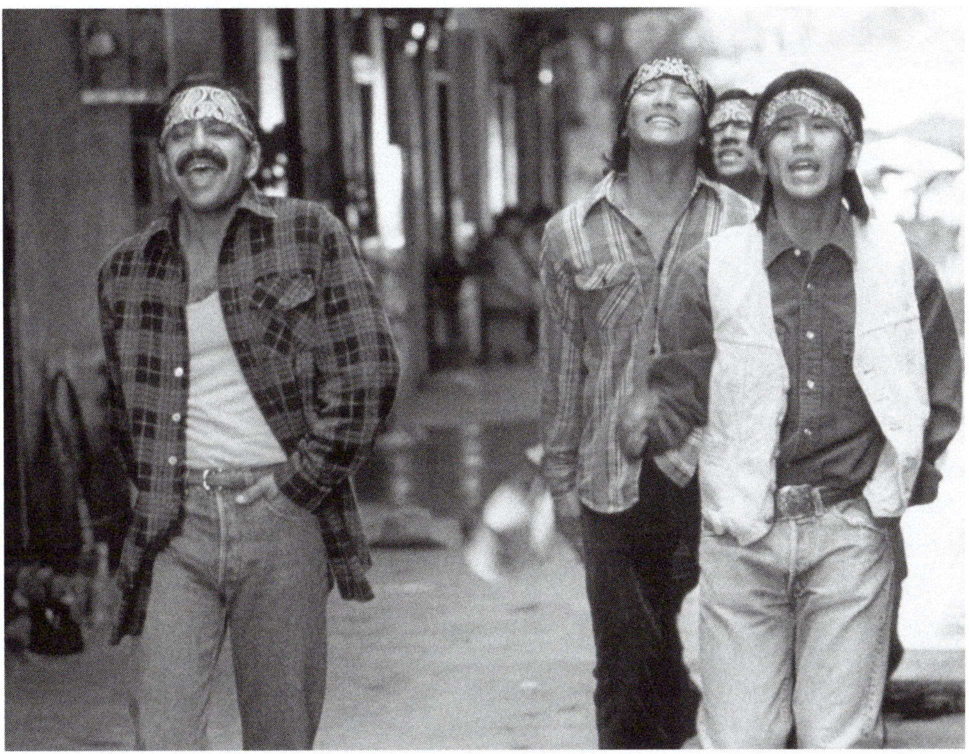

Cheech and Chong were the forerunners of "stoner comedy." Though they eventually went their separate ways, their time together made them significant figures in American culture. (Universal Pictures/PhotoFest)

comedy as a duo, focusing on the counterculture, particularly marijuana use. Throughout the 1970s, Cheech and Chong released numerous albums, having a strong niche following.

In 1975, Chong married for the second time, this time to his eventual creative partner, Shelby Fiddis. That same year, Marin married his first wife; the two divorced in 1984. They had one child.

Following the success of their albums, Cheech and Chong began making films, starting with *Up in Smoke* in 1978. Even with a small production budget, the film was very popular and commercially successful. The pair sometimes attempted to stray from their pot-smoking personas, but those efforts rarely produced success.

In 1986, Marin married for the second time, this time having two children. The couple divorced in 2009.

In 1987, Marin decided to leave the partnership, preferring to focus on a more mainstream acting career. Chong's place in the public eye diminished, though he continued to perform, eventually playing a stoner character on *That 70's Show* in the 1990s. Marin has had a number of roles, perhaps notably his appearances in Robert Rodriguez's films and on the television show *Nash Bridges*, where Chong appeared in an episode in 1997.

In 2003, the pair were slated to reunite for a film, but Chong was arrested for selling drug paraphernalia. This turned into a comic "release Chong" movement. Since Chong's release from prison, the two have performed together off and on, with rumors of a film to come. In 2009, Marin married again.

Although Cheech and Chong have had a long career, many fans focus most clearly and consistently on their albums, which contain some well-known routines. Perhaps most memorable is "Dave's Not Here," in which a pot-smoking character is so intoxicated that he does not realize that his roommate is knocking on his door, asking to be let in. Instead, the pot-smoking character thinks it is someone asking for his roommate, Dave. As was often the case, Chong played the buffoon character. Cheech and Chong are also known for bringing in odd or street characters—for example, giving noise artist Michael Winslow an extended scene in one of their films. In general, the duo were seen as giving voice to the countercultural movement of the 1960s and 1970s. Openly discussing drug culture and belittling the establishment, Cheech and Chong satisfied crowds looking for more boundary-pushing comedy than was offered by other, more straight-laced comedians of the time, and they have been an inspiration for a generation of drug-based humor.

See also: Barker, Arj

Further Reading

Cheech and Chong. *Cheech and Chong's Almost Legal Book for Stoners*. Philadelphia: Running Press, 2013.

Medina, John. "The Hippocampus Meets Cheech and Chong." *Psychiatric Times* 24, no. 3 (March 2007): 25–28.

Snierson, Dan. "Home Rolls with Cheech and Chong." *Entertainment Weekly* 1145 (March 11, 2011): 15.

Kristen Franz

COEN BROTHERS (JOEL COEN [1954–], ETHAN COEN [1957–])

Born in St. Louis Park, Minnesota, to Jewish parents Edward and Renee Coen, Joel and Ethan Coen's interest in filmmaking began when Joel purchased a camera at a young age. The pair focused initially on remaking movies viewed on television. Their first film attempt was *Henry Kissinger, Man on the Go*. Both graduated from Bard College at Simon Rock, with Joel receiving an additional undergraduate film degree from New York University, while Ethan received an additional degree in philosophy from Princeton University.

After working in a number of difficult jobs, the brothers made their first film, *Blood Simple*, in 1984. The film received a significant amount of praise and earned the director/writers awards from the Sundance Film Festival and Independent Spirit. Also in 1984, Joel Coen married actress Frances McDormand, one of the stars of *Blood Simple*. The brothers wrote *Crimewave* in 1985, then wrote and directed *Raising Arizona* in 1987. In 1990, Ethan Coen married film editor Tricia Cooke.

Cult favorites Joel and Ethan Coen have dabbled in both dramatic and comedic films. Major movies like *Fargo* and *O Brother, Where Art Thou?* straddle the line between serious subjects and humor. (AP Photo/Carlo Allegri)

The brothers' first major success was *Barton Fink*, which was released in 1991 and received Academy Award nominations, among other honors. It was on *Barton Fink* that the Coen's began working with cinematographer Roger Deakins, who became a routine collaborator for the next 15 years. *Fargo* was their next major success, taking several awards including two Oscars. In 1998, the brothers released *The Big Lebowski*, which has established a significant cult following since its release. Their first film of the 2000s, *O Brother, Where Art Thou?*, continued the brothers' success, both commercially as well as critically. After much of the 2000s saw the brothers depart from their normal style (and fall to win high praise from critics and audiences) with *The Man Who Wasn't There* (2001), *Intolerable Cruelty* (2003), and *The Ladykillers* (2004), they received universal acclaim and recognition for their adaptation of Cormac McCarthy's *No Country for Old Men*. The film netted the brothers eight Academy Award nominations and four wins, along with numerous other awards.

The brothers have continued their work in film writing/directing, directing more than six films since 2008 and having writing credits on four of them. Ethan Coen extended his scope into off-Broadway in 2008 by writing *Almost an Evening*, a series of three one-act plays. The TV series *Fargo* (2014) is based on the Coen's film and lists them as executive producers. They are often credited as editors under the alias "Roderick Jaynes." The brothers continue to write, direct, and produce films.

The Coen brothers have received widespread recognition for much of their work, including a total of 14 Academy Award nominations (four wins). Their films have been nominated for 28 BAFTA awards (five wins) and 14 Cannes Film Festival awards (seven wins). In 2011, the pair were awarded the Dan Davis Prize of $1 million.

The Coen brothers' work is defined by several distinct characteristics. They often employ the same actors in their films. For example, Joel Coen's wife, Frances McDormand, has appeared in six of their films. Other frequent collaborators are

Steve Buscemi, John Goodman, Jon Polito, John Turturo, and George Clooney, among others. The Coen brothers also employ similar crews on the majority of their films: Roger Deakins (cinematography), Carter Burwell (music), and Ethan's wife Tricia Cooke (editor). Their first film *Blood Simple* established many of the elements that became pillars of their style: paying homage to genre films, dark humor, wild plot twists over a normally basic storyline, and use of *mise-en-scène*—that is, using design (set, lighting, space) and movement of characters and objects to set the mood as well as establish a character's state of mind. *Mise-en-scène* ultimately can encompass any and all visual elements employed by the director.

See also: Apatow, Judd

Further Reading

Campbell, Neil. "From *Blood Simple* to *True Grit*: A Conversation about the Coen Brothers' Cinematic West." *Western American Literature* 48, no. 3 (Fall 2013): 312–340.

Corliss, Richard. "The Coen Brothers' *Inside Llewyn Davis:* Folk You." *Time.com* (December 5, 2013): 1.

Mottram, James. *The Coen Brothers: The Life of the Mind*. New York: Brassey's, 2000.

Rowell, Erica. *The Brothers Grim: The Films of Ethan and Joel Coen*. Lanham, MD: Scarecrow Press, 2007.

Brian Davis

COHEN, ANDY (1968–)

Andy Cohen was born in St. Louis, Missouri. After graduating from high school, he attended Boston University, earning a degree in journalism. From there, he interned at CBS, steadily rising through the ranks until he began producing *The Early Show*, *48 Hours*, and *CBS This Morning*. In 2000, Cohen left for an executive position at Trio, a pop-culture-themed network. In 2005, he became senior vice president of original programming at Bravo. In addition to his work as a producer, he hosted the show *Watch What Happens Live* and regularly blogs about pop culture. Cohen cohosts and appears on shows ranging from *Live with Kelly!* to *Late Night with David Letterman* to *Morning Joe*. In 2012, he released his first book, *Most Talkative: Stories from the Front Lines of Pop Culture*. Cohen continues to live and work in New York.

Cohen is best known for his celebration of camp. Like David Letterman, he regularly plays clips of B-level shows and movies from early in the careers of his guests. He also intermixes pop culture, status symbols, and slang to comedic effect. He regularly jokes about both the stars on the reality television shows that he produces and his own life. Although Cohen generally engages in lighter, less substantial interviews and humor, he is outspoken on gay rights, advocating for same-sex marriage and other issues. One of the most noteworthy aspects of Cohen's career is the fact that he used his behind-the-scenes success to become a star himself. Unlike many humorists who used performance to achieve fame, Cohen gained a measure of power and influence and then became an outspoken and prominent commentator, not only hosting his own show, but also maintaining a level of success in a variety of other media outlets.

Further Reading

Cohen, Andy. *Most Talkative: Stories from the Front Lines of Pop Culture*. New York: St. Martin's Griffin, 2013.

Keating, Caitlin. "Andy Cohen." *Fortune* 165, no. 8 (June 11, 2012): 22.

Littleton, Cynthia. "The Hosts: Conan O'Brien and Andy Cohen." *Variety* 324, no. 13 (June 18, 2014): 8–12.

Smith, Erin Copple. " 'Affluencers' by Bravo: Defining an Audience through Cross-Promotion." *Popular Communication* 10, no. 4 (October–December 2012): 286–301.

Zeke Jarvis

COLBERT, STEPHEN (1964–)

Stephen Colbert was born in Washington, D.C. He was raised in Charleston, South Carolina, as the youngest of 11 children. After losing his father and two of his brothers to a tragic plane crash, Colbert's mother relocated the family to a different neighborhood in Charleston. While attending Episcopal Porter-Gaud School, Colbert participated in school plays and wrote for the school newspaper. He was later accepted to Hampden-Sydney College in Virginia, but transferred to Northwestern University after only two years. At Northwestern University, he studied theatrical performance and fell in love with performing.

Stephen Colbert began as an improv comic and shot to fame on *The Daily Show* and, later, *The Colbert Report*. In 2015, he took over hosting duties in the late-night talk slot once occupied by David Letterman, marking his further entry into mainstream culture. (Martin Crook/Comedy Central)

While at Northwestern, Colbert became involved with the improvisation team No Fun Mud Piranhas. After an initial aversion to the group, Colbert joined Second City as an understudy for Steve Carell. Colbert, along with Amy Sedaris and Paul Dinello, left Second City to work on the sketch comedy show *Exit 57*. The show lasted for only 12 episodes. After it ended, Colbert worked on *The Dana Carvey Show*, served as a freelance writer for *Saturday Night*

Memorable Performances by Politicians

Although politicians have used humor in their speeches for decades, their appearances on popular television have been a more recent phenomenon. Richard Nixon attributed his upswing in popularity to his appearance on the playful show *Laugh-In*. In 1992, Bill Clinton appeared on *The Arsenio Hall Show*, playing the saxophone and taking lighthearted questions so that he could appear more approachable. When this strategy proved successful, politicians began to regularly use the exposure and endearment that comedic shows can offer.

Many appearances by politicians end up coming after unsuccessful runs for office. Examples include Bob Dole appearing on *Saturday Night Live* with Norm MacDonald (who portrayed Dole on the show) and Al Gore appearing on *Futurama* (his daughter was one of the staff writers). Although these appearances may not have had a significant impact on the outcome of any election, they have certainly changed the way that Americans think about their leaders and how leaders think about their public images.

Live, and became a script consultant for VH1 and MTV. Colbert began work on the Comedy Central program *Strangers with Candy* in 1998. The show lasted for 30 episodes, but received mixed reviews for its politically incorrect, raunchy humor.

While Colbert was working on *Strangers*, he was simultaneously working on Comedy Central's *The Daily Show*, serving as a writer and satirical news correspondent. In October 2005, Colbert began hosting a *Daily Show* spinoff series, *The Colbert Report*. The show parodies cable-personality talk shows like *Glenn Beck* and *The O'Reilly Factor*; Colbert portrays an opinionated, right-wing persona.

Colbert has published two books, *Wigfield: The Can Do Town That Just May Not* and *I Am America (And So Can You!)*. He has guest starred in numerous television shows, including *Curb Your Enthusiasm*, *Spin City*, and *Law & Order: Criminal Intent*.

Colbert resides in Montclair, New Jersey, with his wife, Evelyn McGee-Colbert, and his three children, Madeline, Peter, and John. He was tapped to replace David Letterman after the announcement of Letterman's retirement from television. Colbert was named one of *Time*'s 100 most influential people in 2006 and 2012.

Colbert is known for his daring performances. From his many confrontational interviews to his hosting of the 2006 White House Correspondents Dinner, where he received mixed reviews for his many jokes about then president George W. Bush and his associates, Colbert is known for not pulling punches but perhaps even more for not breaking character. While Colbert does occasionally laugh during his interviews or monologues, by and large he maintains his character's perspective and behavior during even contentious exchanges. Colbert also presents a satirical perspective on conservative and arrogant commentators like Rush Limbaugh and Bill O'Reilly. He often demonstrates the flaws in the thinking of these figures by slightly exaggerating their arguments to absurd ends. In fact, Colbert has overtly challenged the American political system by mounting a satirical bid for president and creating a political action committee, thereby illustrating the many problematic issues with fundraising for political candidates. Colbert's clear political and social engagement and well-observed satire have made him an important figure in both humor and politics.

See also: Carell, Steve; Sedaris, Amy; Stewart, Jon

Further Reading

Eggerton, John. "Super PAC Men Eating up Media Buys." *Broadcasting & Cable* 142, no. 6 (February 6, 2012): 14.

Lafayette, Jon. "Colbert vs. O'Reilly." *Television Week* 26, no. 4 (January 22, 2007): 2.

McGrath, Charles. "How Many Stephen Colberts Are There?" *nytimes.com,* January 4, 2012. http://www.nytimes.com/2012/01/08/magazine/stephen-colbert.html?pagewanted=all&_r=0.

Placone, Ronald A.; Tumolo, Michael. "Interrupting the Machine: Cynic Comedy in the 'Rally for Sanity and/or Fear'." *Journal of Contemporary Rhetoric* 1, no. 1 (2011): 10–21.

Kristen Franz

CONWAY, TIM (1933–)

Thomas Daniel Conway was born in Ohio in 1933. After graduating from high school, he attended Bowling Green State University, where he studied radio and speech. Conway graduated with a degree in speech and radio. From there, Conway served in the army. He then worked at a radio station in Cleveland, where, starting in 1960, he also began writing comedy material for a television station. He soon went to New York City and landed a regular spot for two seasons on *The Steve Allen Show*.

In 1961, Conway married for the first time. He and his wife, Mary Anne Dalton, had six children together.

As Conway rose to prominence, he changed his name to Tim Conway to avoid confusion with fellow actor Tom Conway. Conway gained fame with the role of Ensign Charles Parker on the sitcom *McHale's Navy*, where he began a lifelong friendship with co-star Ernest Borgnine. In 1964, Conway starred in two *McHale's Navy* theatrical spin-off films, *McHale's Navy* and *McHale's Navy Joins the Air Force*.

After *McHale's Navy* was canceled, Conway starred in *Rango*, a sitcom in which he played an inept Texas Ranger. *Rango* aired for less than a year. After it was canceled, Conway starred in the only episode of *Turn-On*, a sketch comedy show created by George Schlatter, who had also created *Rowan and Martin's Laugh-In*. The response to the show, which featured a countercultural treatment of sexuality, was largely negative.

Conway launched *The Tim Conway Show* on CBS in 1970. Running for only 12 episodes, it co-starred Joe Flynn from *McHale's Navy* and featured Conway as a bumbling pilot who ran a small charter airline. In the fall of 1970, Conway starred in another show, *The Tim Conway Variety Hour*, a variety show that featured sketch comedy, the music of the Nelson Riddle Orchestra, and Sally Struthers. *The Tim Conway Variety Hour* also proved unsuccessful, running for only 13 weeks.

In 1973, Conway starred in a Disney film, *The World's Greatest Athlete*. He found more success co-starring with Don Knotts in additional films for Disney. He played a bumbling gold robber first in *The Apple Dumpling Gang* and again in its sequel, *The Apple Dumpling Gang Rides Again*. Conway also starred with Knotts in *The Prize Fighter* and *Private Eyes*.

In 1975, Conway became a regular on *The Carol Burnett Show*, the role for which he is most well known. He made television icons out of the characters of Mr. Tudball and the Old Man Duane Toddleberry, earning five Emmy Awards for his work on the series. Conway often caused his co-stars to break character and laugh, usually without Conway speaking any lines of dialogue.

After *The Carol Burnett Show* ended in 1978, Conway starred once again in a show called *The Tim Conway Show*. This, too, was a one-hour variety show, although later in its run it was reduced to a half hour. It lasted for a year and featured Harvey Korman, his co-star from *The Carol Burnett Show*. *The Tim Conway Show* also featured guest appearances by Carol Burnett and Vicki Lawrence.

Also in 1978, Conway divorced his first wife. In 1984, he married for the second time.

In the late 1980s, beginning with *Dorf on Golf*, Conway popularized the character Dorf in a string of eight films focusing on different sports. Dorf, an apparently Swedish dwarf about as tall as a five-year-old, resurrected Mr. Tudball's accent from *The Carol Burnett Show*. Conway achieved Dorf's short height by standing stationary in a hole with shoes attached to his knees.

In 1990, Conway hosted *Tim Conway's Funny America*, a show much like *Candid Camera*. It, too, did not last more than a few weeks. Conway appeared in numerous other guest roles, including on *Married ... with Children*, in which he played Peg Bundy's father for four episodes; *Diagnosis: Murder*; *Hot in Cleveland*; and *30 Rock*. Conway reunited with Don Knotts on the direct-to-video series *Hermie and Friends*. He provided the voice for the character of Barnacle Boy on *SpongeBob SquarePants*. Conway continues to work and live with his family in California.

Conway is known for his wide range of colorful characters. From the incompetent Dorf to the decrepit old man, Conway regularly makes himself the object of humor. He also works well as part of an ensemble cast, as he did in *The Carol Burnett Show* and in some of his film work. He has a broad base of appeal, not being overly edgy or challenging with his work. Conway is known for his longevity as well, maintaining a career that many humorists aspire to, but very few attain. For these reasons, although Conway might not have the groundbreaking role of humorists like Richard Pryor or Andy Kaufman, he is clearly a major figure in American comedy.

See also: Burnett, Carol

Further Reading

Conway, Tim and Jane Scovall. *What's So Funny? My Hilarious Life*. New York: Howard Books, 2013.

Keveny, Bill. "Carol Burnett Recalls How Variety Spiced up TV." *USAToday.com*, April 6, 2010. http://usatoday30.usatoday.com/printedition/life/20100406/burnett06_st.art.htm.

Perret, George. *Tales from the Script: Behind-the-Camera Adventures of a TV Comedy Writer*. New York: Bear Manor Media, 2012.

Stephen Powers

COSBY, BILL (1937–)

William Cosby was born in Philadelphia, Pennsylvania. While his father was often away from the family working for the Navy, Cosby's family lived in Philadelphia for most of his life. Cosby excelled in sports in school, but he did not always devote the level of attention to his studies necessary to succeed. Indeed, Cosby describes himself as a class clown, more interested in humor than academic work. In middle school, Cosby also began to perform in school theater productions. After struggling academically in a magnet school, Cosby transferred to another high school; he did not fare much better there. After failing the 10th grade, Cosby dropped out and joined the Navy after serving a brief stint as an apprentice at a repair shop. While in the Navy, Cosby took correspondence courses to obtain his high school equivalency degree.

After leaving the Navy, Cosby enrolled in Temple University, where he had an athletic scholarship. He also began to work as a bartender, a role in which he developed his humor as he served the customers. As he saw people respond to his humor, Cosby decided to try stand-up comedy. Cosby worked first in Philadelphia, then in New York. Soon, he began touring, eventually getting performances on *The Ed Sullivan Show* and *The Tonight Show*, which helped him gain prominence.

In 1964, Cosby married Camille Hanks, with whom he would have five children. One year later, Cosby acted in the dramatic series *I Spy*, becoming the first African American to co-star in a dramatic television series. He won Emmy Awards for his

Breaking Through

Television comedies have had a longstanding role in representing groups that often do not otherwise have a strong presence in mainstream culture. From Billy Crystal's character on *Soap* (the first openly gay character on television) to *The Cosby Show* (the first show to have an African American family with two professional parents), sitcoms have the sense of play and the cultural prominence necessary to catch the public's eye without setting it too much on edge. Comedies like *I Love Lucy* and *The George Lopez Show* have given central roles to Hispanic characters before their presence on more dramatic shows.

Of course, not all portrayals have been flattering. Redd Foxx's *Sanford and Son* often relied on stereotypes, for example, and many viewers looking back on *Soap* find Billy Crystal's character to be overly flamboyant. Nevertheless, the tradition of comedy addressing underrepresented groups before dramatic television includes them demonstrates how important sitcoms can be.

work, though some viewers and stations did not respond well to an African American star. During this time, he continued to tour, doing stand-up comedy.

After *I Spy*, Cosby had two sitcoms, though neither was a major success. After doing some work on the children's show *The Electric Company*, he created the show *Fat Albert and the Cosby Kids*. The show ran for five years and was met with generally positive reactions. Cosby and Sidney Poitier also funded a number of comedies for African American actors in an attempt to balance out what they saw as violent and degrading films in the "Blaxploitation" genre.

In 1984, Cosby began writing for and starring in *The Cosby Show*, in which Cosby played a doctor and his wife, played by Phylicia Rashad, was a lawyer. This portrayal of African Americans as successful professionals was a shift in how they were often depicted in the mainstream media at the time. The show was very popular, breaking a number of records for ratings. It also spawned a spin-off, *A Different World*. The show ran until 1992, engaging in a minor rivalry with *The Simpsons* toward the end of its run.

Cosby had a variety of short television endeavors and some film work, including the unsuccessful film *Leonard Part 6*, during the last part of the show's run and after as it had finished. In 1997, tragedy struck Cosby's family when his son, Ennis, was murdered. In 1999, Cosby returned to children's programming, creating the show *Little Bill* for the Nick Junior network. The show featured many prominent actors doing voice work, including Phylicia Rashad and Gregory Hines.

Cosby also continued his education, receiving a doctorate in education, and is a well-respected jazz drummer. He continues to tour, performing stand-up comedy and delivering lectures on the state of education and race relations.

Cosby, like Bob Newhart and Jerry Seinfeld, has made a commitment to doing clean material. This perspective has sometimes led to disputes with other performers. Most notably, Eddie Murphy has discussed the conflicting conversations that he had with Cosby, who advised him to clean up his act, and Richard Pryor, who told Murphy not to let himself be bullied by Cosby. In general, Cosby strives for wholesome comedy, often telling humorous stories about parenthood, marriage, and other domestic topics. This has consistently carried through to his film and television work, where he generally strives to portray family situations without vulgarity or obscenity.

Cosby has been very outspoken not only regarding his stance on which sort of material he will do, but also on the topic of race in America. On the latter, he has attracted criticism from some African American leaders, who accuse him of not being in touch with contemporary African American life. Some argue that Cosby's views intensified after his son's death. In addition to this controversy, in 2014, rape accusations began to surface, seriously impacting Cosby's image and reputation.

Despite any controversies or debates about Cosby's work and his views, he has been able to maintain a consistent following for decades. Although he is well known for his stand-up work and well respected for his work on children's programming, most of the population remembers Cosby for his groundbreaking and popular sitcom in the late 1980s and early 1990s. Cosby's character on *The Cosby Show* was simultaneously professional and sometimes buffoonish, often being outsmarted or outmaneuvered by either his wife or his children. In this way, the Cosby family was very much like a number of other sitcom families, helping to bring African Americans into mainstream television in a way not previously done in a commercially successful way. For this breakthrough and for his masterful storytelling, Cosby has become a respected humorist.

See also: Murphy, Eddie; Newhart, Bob; Pryor, Richard

Further Reading

Cosby, Bill. *Fatherhood*. New York: Berkley, 1986.

Coleman, Robin R. Means. *African American Viewers and the Black Situation Comedy: Situating Racial Humor*. London: Routledge, 2000.

Gray, Herman. *Watching Race: Television and the Struggle for Blackness*. Minneapolis: University of Minnesota Press, 2000.

Zeke Jarvis

CRYSTAL, BILLY (1948–)

William Crystal was born in Manhattan, New York, and raised in the Bronx and on Long Island. His father owned a music store and worked as a music promoter. Crystal's father would bring comedy albums home from his store; Crystal, along with his two brothers, would regularly re-create the routines heard on the records. Unfortunately for the family, as the jazz movement wound down in popularity, Crystal's father lost his business.

After graduating from high school, Crystal attended Marshall University on a baseball scholarship. When the baseball program at Marshall was suspended, Crystal returned to New York, where he attended first community college and then New York University. While at NYU's Tisch School of the Arts, Crystal met Christopher Guest, with whom he would appear on *Saturday Night Live*. During this time, Crystal began regularly performing as a stand-up comic. In 1970, Crystal married, and he and his wife have two children.

In 1976, Crystal appeared on *All in the Family* as well as on one of the Dean Martin Celebrity Roasts. He also appeared on the show *Soap*, in which he played an openly homosexual character, one of the first to appear on mainstream television. In the late 1970s and early 1980s, Crystal began appearing in films, including Joan Rivers's film *Rabbit Test* and Rob Reiner's film *This Is Spinal Tap*. Crystal would work with Reiner on other notable films such as *The Princess Bride* and *When Harry Met Sally*.

Crystal was one of the stars of *Saturday Night Live*'s 1984–1985 season, which had an all-star cast and is often considered one of the best seasons in the show's history. In 1986, Crystal began hosting *Comic Relief* along with Whoopi Goldberg and Robin Williams. The trio regularly hosted the series for years. In 1991, Crystal hosted the Academy Awards ceremony; he returned to host the event several more times. For several of his hosting years, Crystal has won Emmys for his performance;

he is often thought of as one of the best hosts of the show. In 1992, Crystal wrote, directed, and starred in the film *Mr. Saturday Night*, which met with modest success. Crystal has continued to perform, including doing work on Broadway, and he had success on television and in film. He also does voiceover work, most notably as one of the characters for the *Monsters, Inc.* series from Pixar. Crystal has become a recognized and respected figure in American comedy, achieving enduring success.

Crystal is known for his wide variety of impressions, including both specific figures, such as Howard Cosell and Fernando Lamas, and Willie, an odd character appearing in sketches with Christopher Guest. In addition, Crystal is known for regularly referencing his passions, such as jazz and baseball. This material has been used in both his stand-up and writing work, creating a strong sense of persona that has endeared him to audiences for years. In many ways, Crystal is a family-friendly comic, not using harsh language or broaching vulgar topics. For this reason and for his generationally based references, Crystal has not been on the leading edge of comedy movements, but his lasting success, his range as an actor, and his consistent vision for comedy have installed him as a respected elder statesman in the comedy world. His appearances on *The Tonight Show* with his friend Robin Williams have come to be regarded as some of the best moments on late-night television. Overall, Crystal is a tremendously successful performer who has had a lasting impact on American comedy.

See also: Goldberg, Whoopi; Guest, Christopher; Williams, Robin

Further Reading

Crystal, Billy. *Still Foolin' 'Em: Where I've Been, Where I'm Going, and Where the Hell Are My Keys?* New York: St. Martin's, 2014.

Taylor, James C. "Down Memory Lane with Billy Crystal." *LA Times*, January 4, 2006. http://articles.latimes.com/2006/jan/14/entertainment/et-crystal14.

Zeke Jarvis

DAVID, LARRY (1947–)

Lawrence David was born to a Jewish family in Brooklyn, New York. He graduated from the University of Maryland with a degree in history in 1969, then obtained a degree in business administration from the Robert H. Smith School of Business in 1970. After graduation, he enlisted in the U.S. Army Reserve. During this time, David began to work on his stand-up career, but also worked several different jobs to pay bills. It was during this time that David lived in Manhattan Plaza, across the hall from Kenny Kramer—the eventual inspiration for Cosmo Kramer on *Seinfeld*.

In 1980, David got a position as a writer for ABC's *Fridays*. Andy Kaufman would appear on the show, disrupting the live broadcast by breaking character in the middle of a skit. Shortly after *Fridays* ended in 1982, David began to write for *Saturday Night Live*. He left the show in mid-season after being frustrated at how few of his sketches aired in the episodes. In 1988, David co-created a pilot episode for *The Seinfeld Chronicles* with Jerry Seinfeld. This effort would become the basis for the enormously successful sitcom *Seinfeld.* David penned 62 episodes of *Seinfeld.*

In 1993, David married Laurie Lennard. The two had two daughters, though they ultimately divorced in 2007.

David wrote and directed the film *Sour Grapes* in 1998 and later appeared in several movies and television series. After airing the one-hour special *Larry David: Curb Your Enthusiasm* in 1999, HBO expanded it to *Curb Your Enthusiasm*—a full series—in 2000, with David as the principal writer and star. The characters in each episode improvised their actions from an outline of only a handful of pages. The show also featured a wide variety of celebrities who were friends with David in real life, including Richard Lewis and Ted Danson. The celebrities play exaggerated versions of themselves, as is the case with David's character on the show. David, who lives in California, has also begun to write for *The Huffington Post.*

David has been widely recognized throughout the industry for his work on *Seinfeld* and *Curb Your Enthusiasm.* He won the Emmy Award for Outstanding Writing—Comedy Series for his *Seinfeld* episode "The Contest" in 1993. This episode was also recognized as the number 1 episode of all time by *TV Guide's* "TV's Top 100 Episodes of All Time." In *The Comedian's Comedian,* a poll of fellow comedians ranked David as number 23 among the greatest comedians of all time. He received the Laurel Award for TV Writing Achievement from the Writers Guild of America in 2010.

One of the clearest sources of admiration for David is his willingness to put his life on display, magnifying his insecurities, frailties, and moral weaknesses. His neurotic character finds increasingly convoluted strategies for avoiding conflict, but these approaches always backfire, leading to him enduring even greater discomfort. In addition to this fierce self-ridicule, David is well known for being a gifted improv performer, as are all of the regular cast members of *Curb Your Enthusiasm.* This skill set is admired by many comedic performers, and David's performances demonstrate his mastery of it. David is also particularly skilled at skewering the idea of celebrity, putting on display the odd aspects of commercial success. An example of this comes in the episode of *Curb Your Enthusiasm* in which David's character has a sandwich named after him at a deli; David is dissatisfied with the sandwich, which leads to him ultimately rejecting the honor in an indirect and absurd manner. This sort of awareness and imagination has helped make David a widely admired and commercially successful figure.

See also: Lewis, Richard; Seinfeld, Jerry

Further Reading

Gillota, David. "Negotiating Jewishness: *Curb Your Enthusiasm* and the Schlemiel Tradition." *Journal of Popular Film & Television* 38, no. 4 (Winter 2010): 152–161.

The Onion. "Interview: Larry David." April 22, 1998.

Rosenberg, Roberta. "Larry David's Dark Talmud; or Kafka in Prime Time." *Studies in American Jewish Literature* 32, no. 2 (2013): 167–185.

Wright, Benjamin. " 'Why Would You Do That Larry?': Identity Formation and Humor in *Curb Your Enthusiasm*." *Journal of Popular Culture* 44, no. 3 (June 2011): 660–677.

Brian Davis

DEGENERES, ELLEN (1958–)

Ellen DeGeneres was born in Metairie, Louisiana. She has one brother, Vance, who also worked in comedy, appearing on *The Daily Show*, before becoming a musician and producer. DeGeneres was raised as a Christian Scientist for the first 13 years of her life. At that point, her parents divorced, with Ellen staying with her mother and her brother moving with their father.

After high school, DeGeneres attended the University of New Orleans, where she majored in communication studies. After a single semester, she dropped out. She subsequently took a number of odd jobs, including being a waitress, a bartender, and a painter. In the early 1980s, DeGeneres began doing stand-up in small clubs and coffee houses. She steadily climbed in prominence, eventually starring in her own sitcom. While she had her sitcom, she came out as a lesbian, also having her character come out on the show. DeGeneres married Australian actress and model Portia de Rossi in 2008.

Ellen DeGeneres has had a major upward trajectory, starting as a stand-up comic and achieving significant success in both film and television. She was one of the first actresses to address issues of sexual orientation in her work. (ImageCollect/Dreamstime.com)

After the cancellation of her sitcom and a brief run on another sitcom, DeGeneres got her own daytime talk show, which has consistently been commercially successful. She has also been a spokesperson for a number of companies, most prominently JC Penny. While some groups protested DeGeneres's role given her sexual orientation, JC Penny has kept DeGeneres on as its spokesperson.

DeGeneres's style is often characterized by a neurotic, self-effacing delivery influenced by Bob Newhart and Woody Allen. DeGeneres has also stated that Steve Martin is an influence upon her work, and her observational style has led her to sometimes be labeled "the female Jerry Seinfeld," though this label faded away as she continued on in her career. Her stand-up earned her a good deal of commercial success and critical acclaim. She was the first comedienne to be invited to sit down for an on-screen talk with Johnny Carson on *The Tonight Show*. DeGeneres's character on her sitcom was very close in style and tone to her stage persona. As was true with Jerry Seinfeld or Ray Romano, DeGeneres's sitcom work overlapped with her personal life. While there is debate over how her sexual orientation affected the viewership and eventual cancellation of her sitcom, many feel that DeGeneres's career was stunted because of her coming out. DeGeneres has made reference to the struggles and pressures that she has felt in her professional and personal life as a result of her sexual orientation. This openness has helped pave the way for other comediennes such as Maria Bamford and Elvira Kurt, who have likewise discussed the reactions of audiences and their own families to their sexual preference.

DeGeneres has achieved some noteworthy success in her voiceover work. Her most striking success came with *Finding Nemo*, in which she played the very talkative and forgetful character Dory. While the motor-mouthed, pun-filled performance of Dory is cartoonish, it also is a slightly exaggerated version of DeGeneres's stage persona.

See also: Campbell, Bruce

Further Reading

DeGeneres, Ellen. *My Point . . . and I Do Have One*. New York: Bantam, 1996.

Elmer-Dewitt, Philip. "Ellen DeGeneres's Tweet Count: Android 5, Apple 4." *Fortune.com* (March 6, 2014): 1.

Nichols, James. "Ellen Page Discusses Coming out with Ellen DeGeneres." *The Huffington Post*, May 1, 2014. http://www.upworthy.com/ellen-page-discusses-her-coming-out-experience-with-ellen-degeneres-in-a-remarkable-segment.

Zeke Jarvis

DEVITO, DANNY (1944–)

Daniel DeVito, Jr., was born into a family of five in Neptune Township, New Jersey. At age 14, DeVito went to a boarding school, partly to keep him from getting into trouble as a young man. After graduating, he studied at the American Academy of Dramatic Arts. DeVito then performed in a variety of theaters and troops, including the Eugene O'Neill Theater Center and the Westbeth Playwrights Feminist Collective, where he met his future wife, Rhea Perlman, with whom he has three children.

DeVito's first major film appearance was as an inmate in the mental health facility in *One Flew over the Cuckoo's Nest*. A few years later, DeVito got a regular role on *Taxi*, a show co-created by James L. Brooks and also starring humorist Andy Kaufman and Christopher Lloyd, who had appeared alongside DeVito in *Cuckoo's Nest*. DeVito subsequently worked with Brooks on the movie *Terms of Endearment*. He also had notable roles in films such as *Romancing the Stone, Throw Momma from the Train*, and *The War of the Roses*. Although his work generally involves comedies, DeVito did have some successful dramatic turns in movies such as *The Rainmaker* and *L.A. Confidential*, as well as taking on the role of the Penguin in *Batman Returns*, which was met with mixed reviews.

In addition to his acting work, DeVito began producing and directing. *Throw Momma from the Train* was his directorial debut, and he went on to direct successful films such as *Matilda* and *The War of the Roses* as well as less commercially successful cult films as *Death to Smoochy*. DeVito's production credits include hit films such as *Pulp Fiction* and *Erin Brockovich*. Most recently, DeVito has been appearing in the television show *It's Always Sunny in Philadelphia*.

DeVito's work is often characterized by his gruff yet craven persona. He regularly plays crass characters who aspire to be wealthy and promiscuous, often at the expense of those around him. Many of DeVito's projects have taken on the issue of greed and wealth, particularly his work in the 1980s, known as the "Me Decade" for its rampant conspicuous consumption. DeVito also regularly plays working-class characters who fail to fit in with the more refined characters around them. DeVito's diminutive, rotund frame heightens the sense of awkwardness his characters have. At times, he will play against type, as in *The War of the Roses*, where he plays the voice of reason to the selfish and spiteful husband played by Michael Douglas. He has made appearances as himself on shows such as *Sesame Street*, where his kinder demeanor is on display. Nevertheless, DeVito is most known for his willingness to play immoral characters and participate in potentially humiliating situations, such as his appearing nude on *It's Always Sunny in Philadelphia* and as an unsuccessful male stripper on *Friends*. With his many prominent roles in a variety of media and his work as a producer and director, DeVito's impact on American humor has been both substantial and sustained.

See also: Brooks, James L.; Kaufman, Andy

Further Reading

Ellen, Barbara. "Danny DeVito: 'It All Worked out for Me. Life Is Good'." *The Guardian*, April 14, 2012. http://www.theguardian.com/film/2012/apr/15/danny-devito-interview-sunshine-boys.

Hueso, Noela. "Danny DeVito: The Master of Every Medium." *Hollywood Reporter* 417, no. 30 (August 26, 2011): 54.

Tannenbaum, Rob. "Danny DeVito." *Rolling Stone* 1191 (September 12, 2013): 28.

Zeke Jarvis

EDWARDS, BLAKE (1922–2010)

William Blake Crump was born in Tulsa, Oklahoma. His family had ties to show business, with his grandfather being a director of silent movies and his stepfather managing a film production company. It was his stepfather who moved Crump's family to Los Angeles. Edwards served in the U.S. Coast Guard for a time, but suffered a back injury that would cause him pain for years to come.

After graduating from high school, Crump, who would go on to be known as Blake Edwards, began working as an actor. In interviews, he indicated that he was difficult to work with as an actor, but also stated that he learned a great deal from the directors he encountered. Indeed, Edwards worked with notable directors such as Otto Preminger and John Ford. In the mid-1950s, Edwards worked in television, writing for both comedy shows, like Mickey Rooney's first sitcom, and more serious shows, such as *Richard Diamond, Private Detective*.

In 1953, Edwards married his first wife, actress Patricia Walker. The two divorced in 1967.

At the end of the 1950s, Edwards got his first experience directing big-budget feature-length films with *Operation Petticoat*. This film turned out to be a major success: it was the biggest success of the decade for Universal Studios and established Edwards as a director. In 1961, Edwards worked again with Mickey Rooney with the film *Breakfast at Tiffany's*, an adaptation of Truman Capote's book of the same name. The film, which starred Audrey Hepburn, was another success, gaining a significant and sustained positive response. In 1963, Edwards began the series of films for which he would be best known, *The Pink Panther*. His partnership with Peter Sellers, who played the bungling Inspector Clouseau, was commercially successful albeit sometimes tempestuous, though Edwards often spoke of the relationship with respect and reverence.

In 1969, Edwards married Julie Andrews, who appeared in a number of his films, including the acclaimed *Victor/Victoria*. The two had a total of five children. Edwards died in 2010.

Edwards's career has received mixed reviews. Many critics have put down his work for being popular or slick rather than complex and thematically deep. Other critics have pointed to his longevity as evidence of his success and achievement as an artist. In addition, many have recognized the influence of comedic luminaries on his visual style. This comes through particularly in his use of slapstick comedy in the *Pink Panther* series and other of his works. The use of broad comedy and complex setups for situations is a staple of much of Edwards's work, such as the elaborate skiing scene in *The Pink Panther*. In addition to his use of slapstick, Edwards often employs humorous situations relying upon sexual tension and ambiguity. From the jokes in the *Pink Panther* series to *Skin Deep* and *10*, much of his work has largely revolved around sexual desire and exploits. This focus helped both establish his commercial success and undermine his artistic integrity in the eyes of some critics. While his status as a pure artist is argued, Edwards's commercial success is clear, and his impact has been lasting.

Further Reading

Davis, J. Madison. "Richard Diamond, Peter Gunn and Jacques Clouseau: The Crime Writing of Blake Edwards." *World Literature Today* 85, no. 5 (September–October 2011): 9–11.

Fowkes, Katherine A. "From Gender to Genre: Blake Edwards' Roller Coaster of Comedy." *Studies in American Humor* 3, no. 22 (2010): 191–200.

Wasson, Sam. *A Splurch in the Kisser: The Films of Blake Edwards*. Middletown: Wesleyan University Press, 2009.

Zeke Jarvis

FALLON, JIMMY (1974–)

James Fallon was born in Brooklyn, New York. While Fallon was still a child, his parent moved to Saugerties to be closer to his father's job at IBM. Fallon attended Catholic school in his elementary school years and graduated from Saugerties High School in 1992. Growing up, Fallon and his sister would reenact skits from *Saturday Night Live*, giving him a start in practicing the craft of comedy. Fallon also began honing his impressions.

After graduating from high school, Fallon attended the College of St. Rose in Albany. He began as a computer science major, but eventually switched to communications before dropping out one semester before graduating. Fallon did eventually finish his work, receiving a degree from the college in 2009.

After leaving college, Fallon began performing at a variety of comedy clubs, including winning an impression contest at Bananas Comedy Club. As Fallon began to travel in support of his career, he took classes with the Groundlings in Los Angeles. After touring and performing stand-up (and taking a few minor roles in film and television) for a few years, Fallon was invited to audition for *Saturday Night Live*. He was accepted partly on the strength of his impressions of celebrities ranging from Hillary Swank to Adam Sandler to Bono from U2. In the 1998–1999 season, Fallon was a featured performer; he was promoted to a full-time cast member the following year. In 2000, Fallon and Tina Fey took over hosting duties for the Weekend Update segment on *SNL*. In 2004, Fallon left the show to pursue a career in film, which resulted in modest success.

Jimmy Fallon at Grauman's Chinese Theatre in Hollywood, California, February 2, 2009. Fallon has worked on two major television shows, *Saturday Night Live* and *The Tonight Show*. (S. Bukley/Dreamstime.com)

Fallon married in 2007, and he and his wife had a daughter, Juvonen, in 2013. In 2009, he returned to television, replacing Conan O'Brien in the *Late Night* time slot. One year later, Fallon hosted the Emmy Awards. After the tumultuous struggle between Jay Leno and Conan O'Brien, it was announced that Fallon would take over hosting duties for *The Tonight Show* in 2014. Fallon continues to host and perform in other venues.

Fallon is best known for his light, playful humor, often poking fun at himself. During his time on Weekend Update, Fallon would often play the likable but ill-informed counterpart to Tina Fey's sharper and more worldly critic. In his work in skits on *SNL*, Fallon was also known for his difficulties in keeping a straight face. In fact, he sometimes drew criticism for laughing during sketches while other cast members strove to maintain the reality of the scene. Even so, Fallon was a popular and versatile performer, not only doing impressions of a variety of celebrities, but also being able to act, sing, and play guitar, much like former cast member Adam Sandler. In some of his post-*SNL* performances, Fallon continued to incorporate music, even having respected musicians like Bruce Springsteen and Eddie Vedder appear on his 2012 album, *Blow Your Pants Off*. While Fallon's film work has not garnered the same level of success as that of some other *SNL* cast members, his hosting and performing career has enabled him to maintain a steady and admirable level of achievement.

See also: Fey, Tina

Further Reading

Carter, Bill. "Bullish on Boyish." *New York Times,* February 12, 2014. http://www.nytimes.com/2014/02/16/arts/television/nbc-hopes-jimmy-fallon-brings-younger-viewers-to-tonight.html.

Poniewozik, James. "The Smartest Thing Jimmy Fallon Did on His First *Tonight Show*." *Time.com* (February 20, 2014): 1.

Tsai, Diane. "Late Night Highlight: Michelle Obama Does 'Ew!' with Jimmy Fallon and Will Ferrell." *Time.com* (February 24, 2014): 1.

Zeke Jarvis

FEY, TINA (1970–)

Elizabeth Fey was born in a township of Philadelphia, Pennsylvania. From early on, Fey was both thoughtful and invested in comedy, doing an independent study of it as early as middle school. In high school, she continued her interest in comedy by writing a satirical column for the school newspaper, which she also edited. Fey attended the University of Virginia, where she majored in acting and playwriting.

After graduating from college, Fey began taking courses at Second City in Chicago, eventually getting regular work there. While at Second City, Fey met Jeff Richmond, her future husband. Also while working at Second City, Rey continually submitted scripts to *Saturday Night Live*, which eventually led to her getting a staff position as a writer. In 1998, Fey began working as an extra on the show as well. In 1999, when then head writer Adam McKay left, Lorne Michaels offered Fey the position, making her the first female head writer in the show's history. In 2000, Fey began performing regularly on the show, most notably as co-anchor of the Weekend Update segment, first sharing the desk with Jimmy Fallon, then with Amy Poehler.

Tina Fey arrives at the 64th Primetime Emmy Awards at the Nokia Theatre in Los Angeles, California, on October 14, 2012. Fey has achieved success as both a writer and a performer on shows like *Saturday Night Live* and *30 Rock*. She also has achieved success as an awards show host, appearing in tandem with Amy Poehler in that role. (Jordan Strauss/Invision/AP Photo)

In 2004, Fey began branching out into film, writing and co-starring in the movie *Mean Girls*. In 2005, she and her husband had their first child, a daughter. Their second daughter was born in 2011. Not long after the birth of her first daughter, Fey's sitcom *30 Rock*, which focused on a show very much like *Saturday Night Live*, premiered. While the show initially did not fare well in the ratings, it won an Emmy. Fey returned to *SNL* to portray vice-presidential candidate Sarah Palin during the 2008 election. She also continued to appear in movies and on television. When *30 Rock* ended in 2013, it was widely seen as a successful show. Fey continues to write and act, and she lives in New York with her family.

Fey is known for her quirky but intelligent humor, mixing broad sexual humor with incisive political commentary. She is also a gifted improvisational artist, having worked with Second City and on the improv show *Asssscat*! Fey has stated that her character on *30 Rock*, Liz Lemon, is inspired by Julia Louis-Dreyfus. This is in keeping with much of Fey's work as a neurotic female character navigating absurd and often contradictory gender expectations. That said, Fey is also seen as an influential female figure in contemporary comedy for her success as a writer and performer whose work stretches over various genres. In addition, Fey has won a large number of awards and honors. Of particular note, she is the youngest person to win the Mark Twain Prize. For her broad range of skills and consistent success, Fey is recognized as a major figure in contemporary comedy.

See also: Fallon, Jimmy; Poehler, Amy

Further Reading

Dowd, Maureen. "What Tina Wants." *Vanity Fair*, January 2009. Accessed August 26, 2013. http://www.vanityfair.com/magazine/2009/01/tina_fey200901.

Lauzen, Martha. "The Funny Business of Being Tina Fey: Constructing a 'Feminist' Comedy Icon." *Feminist Media Studies* 14, no. 1 (February 2014): 106–117.

Patterson, Eleanor. "Fracturing Tina Fey: A Critical Analysis of Postfeminist Comedy Stardom." *Communication Review* 15, no. 3 (2012): 232–251.

Zeke Jarvis

FOXX, JAMIE (1967–)

Eric Bishop was born in Terrell, Texas. Shortly after he was born, Bishop, who would adopt the stage name Jamie Foxx, was adopted and raised by his mother's adoptive parents. They were strict Baptists, and he grew up in the African American section of a heavily segregated town. Foxx was a Boy Scout and a member of the church choir growing up, and he played both football and basketball in high school. After graduating from high school, Foxx attended United States International University, where he studied composition and classical music.

At the end of his college career, Foxx began doing stand-up at comedy clubs. Foxx has said that he adopted his stage name in an effort to get on stage earlier, because he found that the female comedians typically got called up to the stage earlier. By 1991, Foxx had made it onto *In Living Color*, the show created by Keenan Ivory Wayans and featuring David Allen Grier and other prominent African American comics. Foxx played a wide range of characters on the show, with arguably his most memorable being "LaWanda the ugly girl." After *In Living Color*, Foxx was given his own sitcom, *The Jamie Foxx Show*, which ran for five years.

Foxx has also worked in film, appearing in both more humorous fare, like voice work in *Toys*, and more serious movies, like *Any Given Sunday*. But it was his portrayal of Ray Charles in the biopic *Ray* that garnered him the greatest attention and critical reception, even earning him an Academy Award.

In 2012, Foxx starred in the controversial Quentin Tarantino film, *Django Unchained*, in which he played an ex-slave taking revenge on a variety of oppressive white figures. The controversy surrounding the movie was exacerbated after Foxx told a joke while hosting *Saturday Night Live* in which he claimed to enjoy killing all the white people. Still, Foxx has not consistently been a lightning rod for controversy.

In addition to his film work, Foxx has put out a number of records. His musical work stems partly from his experience with the piano, which he has played since the age of five. Foxx has one daughter, and he currently lives in Hidden Valley, California.

Foxx has stated that his comedy idol is Richard Pryor. In some ways, this is not surprising given Foxx's exploration of race in much of his material, although Foxx does not always use the level of obscenity that Pryor regularly employed. Even so, Foxx has never shied away from openly stating his political or social views. During the controversy surrounding Michael Richard's use of racial slurs in his onstage work, Foxx was one of his most outspoken critics. Unlike some other humorists who leave comedy for a time only to refocus on their comedic career later, Foxx has tended to stick with dramatic acting and musical pursuits in the later portions of his career, but he still regularly incorporates humor into his public appearances and promotional work.

See also: Wayans Siblings

Further Reading

Amber, Jeannine. "Jamie Foxx." *Essence* 37, no. 4 (August 2006): 142–194.
Chiu, Melody. "One Last Thing Jamie Foxx." *People* 81, no. 17 (April 28, 2014): 102.
Torres, Sasha. *In Living Color: Race and Television in the United States.* Durham: Duke University Press, 1998.

Zeke Jarvis

FRANKEN, AL (1951–)

Alan Franken was born in New York City, but his family moved to a suburb of Minneapolis, Minnesota, in his childhood. After graduating from high school, Franken attended Harvard College, graduating cum laude with a degree in government. In his first year of college, Franken met the woman he would later marry. The two have two children.

After graduation, Franken and his writing partner, Tom Davis, initially struggled to find work in Los Angeles. They found their first success in show business as part of the original writing staff for *Saturday Night Live*. In this role, Franken earned a total of seven Emmy nominations. In addition to his work as a writer, Franken sometimes appeared as a performer on the show, with his most memorable character being Stuart Smalley. Franken later wrote the movie *Stuart Saves His Family* based on this character; in the film, the pathetic self-help guru has to confront his antagonistic family. Although Franken might be best known in his *Saturday Night Live* appearances as Smalley, his writing work often had a keen eye turned toward politics. Franken left the staff of *Saturday Night Live* when he was denied the head producer role after an incident in which he ridiculed the president of NBC. He came back a few years later, only to leave the show again when he did not receive the role of anchor for the Weekend Update portion of the show.

Originally a writer on *Saturday Night Live*, Al Franken achieved success as an author and a radio host. After a significant career in comedy, Franken ran for and won a seat as a U.S. Senator. (Al Franken for U.S. Senate)

Franken has written a number of humorous books concerning politics, including *Rush Limbaugh Is a Big Fat Idiot* in 1996 and *Lies and the Lying Liars Who Tell Them: A Fair and Balanced Look at the Right* in 2003. Although Franken did work in film and television after leaving *Saturday Night Live*, he is best known for his books and for his work on the radio network Air America, where, like Janeane Garofalo, he used his celebrity to attract attention to liberal views and causes.

Franken has also been very active in politics. After the death of Minnesota Senator Paul Wellstone, Franken decided to run as his successor. In 2008, he won an extremely contentious election. In fact, the call was so close that Franken was not officially sworn in (using the Bible of Paul Wellstone in a symbolic tribute) until the midpoint of 2009. In office, Franken has continued to work for liberal causes such as universal health care. During his senatorial tenure, Franken has had some noteworthy moments and accomplishments. These include both positive events, like the reasoned, civil debate about health care recorded between Franken and members of the Tea Party movement, as well as less positive moments, such as his eye rolling in response to a speech by fellow senator Mitch McConnell opposing the confirmation of Elena Kagan to the U.S. Supreme Court, though Franken did issue a public apology to McConnell later. Franken has also passed through significant legislation, including bills supporting disabled veterans and oppressed women. Currently, Franken splits his time between Minnesota and Washington, D.C., where he continues to serve as a U.S. senator.

Franken's work is most clearly characterized by his disappointment in both the conservative members of government and the ineffective work done by the media to create an informed and engaged electorate. In particular, Franken uses specific examples and facts to illustrate the hypocrisy of conservative politicians, then he adds his own acerbic or sarcastic commentary. In this way, his material is a clear precursor to *The Daily Show*, though his work tends to occupy more of a niche. Franken can often be aggressive with his humor, leading him to become a lightning rod for many conservative critics. Still, not all of his political humor has a specific ideology. In one noteworthy segment on Weekend Update, Franken looked at a series of fictional "dirty" campaign ads, critiquing the practice of going negative in election advertisements—a practice employed by both political parties. He satirized the absurd lengths that some journalists go to in an effort to get political scoops. He also has sometimes ridiculed Democratic candidates, perhaps most notably doing very unflattering impressions of Paul Tsongas during the 1992 Democratic presidential primary campaign. Even so, Franken clearly favors liberal goals and ideals, and this interest comes through in his comic work. While he has drawn back from performance since his election, he has made a noteworthy and lasting impact upon political humor in America.

See also: Miller, Dennis

Further Reading

Davey, Monica and Carl Hulse. "Franken's Win Bolsters Democratic Grip in Senate." *Nytimes.com,* June 30, 2009. http://www.nytimes.com/2009/07/01/us/politics/01minnesota.html.

Franken, Al. *Rush Limbaugh Is a Big, Fat Idiot*. New York: Delacorte Press, 1996.
Hirsh, Michael. "Al Franken Gets Serious." *Newsweek* 156, no. 2 (July 12, 2010): 38–40.

Zeke Jarvis

GOLDBERG, WHOOPI (1955–)

Caryn Elaine Johnson was born in New York City in 1955, though some sources list the year of her birth as 1949. Goldberg did not finish high school. In the late 1970s and early 1980s, she performed in various theater productions in East Germany. In 1973, Goldberg married for the first time; the marriage ended in divorce in 1979. She made her film debut in 1982 in the independent, avant-garde film, *Citizen: I'm Not Losing My Mind, I'm Giving It Away*, after which she developed a one-woman show of comedic monologues that ran on Broadway from 1984 to 1985.

As she became more prominent, Goldberg began to use her stage name. She got the idea for her first name from a whoopee cushion and adapted the last name Goldberg after her mother, a stern nurse and teacher, told her that her real surname did not sound Jewish enough. In its review of Goldberg's stage show, *The Spook Show*, the *New York Times* called her a "very funny character comedian with a distinctive point of view and rich comic potential." *The Spook Show* led to Goldberg's big break when director Steven Spielberg noticed her and cast her as Celie Harris in his film *The Color Purple*, adapted from Alice Walker's Pulitzer Prize-winning epistolary novel. *The Color Purple*, also starring Oprah Winfrey and Danny Glover, was released in December 1985 and achieved both box office success and widespread critical acclaim, with numerous critics making note of Goldberg's performance. Roger Ebert called it "one of the most amazing debut performances in movie history." Goldberg even received an Academy Award nomination for Best Actress for her work.

Whoopi Goldberg is one of the most versatile and successful performers in the history of American entertainment. From her stand-up work to her efforts to raise money for the homeless, Goldberg has had a huge impact on American culture. (ABC/Photofest)

Goldberg continued her film career by appearing in Penny Marshall's *Jumpin' Jack Flash* in

1986. In 1986, she married the second time, only to divorce again in 1988. After three more pictures, none of which achieved the success of *Jumpin' Jack Flash*, Goldberg starred in *Clara's Heart*, with Neil Patrick Harris, in 1988. She turned to television, making appearances on HBO's *Comic Relief* with Billy Crystal and Robin Williams and appearing in the short-lived CBS sitcom, *Bagdad Cafe*, with Jean Stapleton. During the run of *Bagdad Cafe*, Goldberg starred in the 1990 film *The Long Walk Home*, which dealt with the 1955 Montgomery bus boycott. Sissy Spacek also starred in the film.

Goldberg had another prominent role in 1990 in the film *Ghost*, with Patrick Swayze and Demi Moore. Goldberg won an Academy Award for Best Supporting Actress for her role of the psychic in that film, becoming only the second black woman in history to win an Oscar for acting (Hattie McDaniel had won the award for Best Actress in a Supporting Role in 1939 for her role as Mammy in *Gone with the Wind*).

Goldberg realized a lifelong dream of appearing on *Star Trek* when a recurring guest role on *Star Trek: The Next Generation* was created for her. In the second season and frequently throughout the series' run, Goldberg played the role of Guinan the bartender; she also reprised it (albeit uncredited) in two *Star Trek* movies, *Star Trek Generations* and *Star Trek Nemesis*.

Goldberg continued her film career in the 1990s by appearing in *Soapdish* as part of an ensemble cast that included Sally Field and Robert Downey, Jr. In 1992, she headlined the comedy film *Sister Act*, in which she played a lounge singer hiding from the Mob as a nun in a convent. The film received lukewarm reviews, but it was a box-office smash; it cemented Goldberg's place as a major Hollywood star and, for a time, the highest-paid actor in history. Goldberg reprised the role in the 1993 sequel, *Sister Act 2: Back in the Habit*. Other films in the 1990s included *The Lion King*, in which she voiced one of the hyenas in the hyena trio, and *Boys on the Side*.

Also in the 1990s, Goldberg hosted her own late-night talk show, *The Whoopi Goldberg Show*, which ran for only a year. In 1994, she hosted the Academy Awards for the first time. She returned to host the ceremony again in 1996, 1999, and 2002. In 1994, she also married for the third time, only to divorce in 1995. More film roles followed, including *Ghosts of the Mississippi* and *How Stella Got Her Groove Back*.

In 1998, Goldberg served as an executive producer of the retooled *Hollywood Squares* game show, hosted by Tom Bergeron. Goldberg occupied the center square until her departure from the show in 2002.

In 2001, Goldberg won the Mark Twain Prize for American Humor. In 2003, she was honored with a star on the Hollywood Walk of Fame. She also starred in her own sitcom, *Whoopi*, which aired for only one season. In 2006, she began hosting a morning radio show, *Wake Up with Whoopi*, and in 2007, she was offered a spot as moderator and cohost on *The View*, replacing Rosie O'Donnell. Goldberg remains on *The View* as moderator and cohost; she has largely retired from acting, except for occasional roles on Broadway and in London, and in guest bits on television and in film.

Goldberg's humor often examines the tensions and conflicts stemming from disempowered groups like women and minorities. For this reason, Goldberg is sometimes seen as edgy, though perhaps less so than some of her comic role models such as Richard Pryor. Still, she never shies away from expressing her political and social views. Appropriately, Goldberg is an activist known for supporting lesbian/gay/bisexual/transgender (LGBT) issues, appearing at a March on Washington in 1987 and becoming involved at a time when few celebrities were lending public support to the LGBT cause. She has appeared frequently at the biennial Stars over Mississippi benefit concert, which raises money for education in honor of Sam Haskell's mother, in Amory, Mississippi.

Much of Goldberg's comedic work takes the form of near-lectures rather than what are typically seen as jokes. In her time on *The View*, Golberg has stirred controversy for her outspoken opinions, including her remarks about Michael Vick and Roman Polanski, and for her frequent, sharp disagreements with fellow cohost Elisabeth Hasselbeck. That said, as shown by her appearances in *Star Trek* and the *Sister Act* films, Goldberg is also willing to engage in lighter forms of pop culture. Given her long career and list of accolades, Goldberg is clearly a prominent figure in humor as well as a voice for underserved groups.

See also: Pryor, Richard

Further Reading

Goldberg, Whoopi. *Whoopi Goldberg Book*. New York: William Morrow, 1997.

Goodman, Wendy. "Hollywood, New York: Whoopi Goldberg." *New York* 45, no. 15 (May 7, 2012): 76–78.

Parrish, James Robert. *Whoopi Goldberg: Her Journey from Poverty to Megastardom*. New York: Birch Lane Press, 1997.

Stephen Powers

GOLDTHWAIT, BOBCAT (1962–)

Robert Francis Goldthwait was born in Syracuse, New York. Although he grew up in a working-class family, Goldthwait, who would go on to adopt the stage name "Bobcat," formed a comedy troupe with his classmate Tom Kenny, who would eventually become the voice for the titular character of *SpongeBob SquarePants*. Goldthwait worked as part of the troupe for a time, but quickly emerged as an engaging stand-alone stand-up comic, having two breakthrough comedy specials during the 1980s. In 1986, Goldthwait married Ann Luly, who worked on a number of Goldthwait's projects, including his special *An Evening with Bobcat Goldthwait* and *Shakes the Clown*. The two would have one child and divorce in 1998.

During the 1980s, Goldthwait began acting in films, with his most striking role being that of Zed in the *Police Academy* series. He appeared on a number of television series and on late-night talk shows, often giving emphatic and sometimes dangerous performances, most notably when he set fire to the couch on

The Tonight Show with Jay Leno in 1994. Goldthwait also began a directorial career with the surrealistic, semi-autobiographical film *Shakes the Clown*. He continued writing and directing such well-received films as *Sleeping Dogs* and *World's Greatest Dad*. He also has begun directing *Jimmy Kimmel Live!*

After his first marriage ended, Goldthwait entered into a long-term engagement with actress Nikki Cox. He married Sarah de Sa Rego in 2009. Goldthwait continues to live and work in Los Angeles.

Goldthwait is best known for his dark comedy. In his stand-up act, he employed a grating voice and a high-energy delivery featuring odd turns and obscene language and references, though often with an underlying bit of political or social commentary. His early acting work employed a persona very close to his on-stage persona, portraying a maniac with little or no control over himself. This perception did change with other films, such as *Scrooged*, where he played a more uptight office worker who slowly unraveled. Nevertheless, he was most consistently associated with a wildman delivery, partially because of his stand-up and late-night talk show performances. In his later directorial work, Goldthwait began to tone down his humor. While *Shakes the Clown* had a madcap character and aggressive humor using clowns with superhuman powers who dealt with substance abuse and committed acts of violence against mimes, later films, such as *World's Greatest Dad*, dealt with very dark situations (i.e., a father processing his son's death) in a more realistic fashion. The darkness of *World's Greatest Dad* does hearken back to Goldthwait's transgressive and confrontational work as a stand-up comic. The film also was the first in which Goldthwait's friend and fellow comic Robin Williams took on a starring role, though the two had worked together previously and Williams had a cameo as a mime in *Shakes the Clown*. Goldthwait's work on *Jimmy Kimmel Live!* helped to establish the show, with its ratings climbing after he became part of the staff. Goldthwait's aggressive and surrealistic approach to humor have given him a distinctive and well-established position in contemporary American humor.

See also: Kimmel, Jimmy

Further Reading

Quinn, M., and W. Cole. "Emmet Killjoy." *Time* 139, no. 12 (March 23, 1992): 73.

Rabin, Nathan. "Bobcat Goldthwait Interview." *Onion AV Club*, August 20, 2009. http://www.avclub.com/article/bobcat-goldthwait-31890.

Zeke Jarvis

GRIER, DAVID ALAN (1956–)

David Alan Grier was born in Detroit. His father was a psychiatrist and author of the book *Black Rage*. After graduating from high school, Grier attended the University of Michigan and then the Yale School of Drama, where he received his MFA. After graduating, Grier got a role on Broadway, playing Jackie Robinson in *The First*. He worked in the theater on a number of plays, then got a small role on the sitcom *A Different World* and bit parts on a number of movies.

On the set of *I'm Gonna Git You Sucka*, Grier met Keenan Ivory Wayans, who would cast him on *In Living Color*. Grier played a wide variety of characters on the show, with his most notable regular character being one half of the flamboyant pair in the "Men on . . ." series of sketches. With the show's high ratings and critical success, Grier became a very visible figure on the comic landscape.

After the show's cancellation, Grier took on a variety of roles, hosting Comedy Central's stand-up showcase series *Premium Blend*, playing small roles in movies and sitcoms, and regularly filling in for Adam Corolla on the MTV show *Loveline*. He also has acted on Broadway a number of times, perhaps most notably in *Porgy and Bess* in 2012 and in David Mamet's play *Race*, for which he received his second Tony Award nomination.

Grier has been married and divorced twice. He has a daughter from his second marriage. He currently lives and works in New York.

Grier is known for his versatility, playing both uptight, more "white" characters and more militant African American characters, as well as a host of characters in between. In the same way, Grier is well known for his array of voices and impressions, including a running gag during his appearances on *Loveline* in which he would call out the names of various medications referenced by Dr. Drew, his cohost, as though they were the names of African American children being admonished by their parent. Not surprisingly, he has done voiceover work for animated shows and as a puppet on the show *Crank Yankers*. While Grier's range is, in many ways, an asset, it also means that he does not have a single, defining persona or character as other humorists do. In fact, like many other comic actors, he has appeared in dramatic movies, such as *BAADASSSSS!*, as well as a number of children's shows. Along the way, he has established himself as a regular fixture in a variety of media.

See also: Wayans Siblings

Further Reading

Bailey, Constance. "Fight the Power: African American Humor as a Discourse of Resistance." *Western Journal of Black Studies* 36, no. 4 (Winter 2012): 253–263.

Grier, David Alan. *Barack Like Me: The Chocolate-Covered Truth*. New York: Touchstone, 2009.

Torres, Sasha. *Living Color: Race and Television in the United States*. Durham, NC: Duke University Press, 1998.

Zeke Jarvis

GROENING, MATT (1954–)

Matt Groening was born in Portland, Oregon. He was the middle of five children and his father worked as a cartoonist, among other jobs. Groening spent all of his early life in Portland. Upon graduating from high school, he attended Evergreen State College in Olympia, Washington. While there, Groening both edited and drew cartoons for the school newspaper.

After graduating from college, Groening moved to Los Angeles to pursue writing. In his early years in the city, Groening held a number of undesirable jobs, including

The Animation Boom of the 1990s

In the 1990s, a number of animated television shows broke through and rose to national prominence. Cartoonist Matt Groening and producer James L. Brooks collaborated to create *The Simpsons*, which started as a series of small clips for *The Tracey Ullman Show*, but quickly became a show onto itself. Unlike previous animated humor shows such as *The Jetsons* and *The Flintstones*, *The Simpsons* had a contemporary setting and often included realistic conflicts in its early shows. It also has references and language that made it a show for adults as much as for children.

After the success of *The Simpsons*, networks began producing more animated shows—some successful (*Beavis and Butthead* and *South Park*, for instance), and some both unsuccessful and short-lived (*Family Dog* and *Fish Police*). The Fox Network, in particular, aired a number of animated shows, including *King of the Hill*, created by Mike Judge, who had risen to fame largely with *Beavis and Butthead*, and *Family Guy*, created by Seth MacFarlane.

Many of these shows pushed boundaries even further than *The Simpsons* did, using profanity and blatant references to sex. Other shows pushed boundaries in more conceptual ways, with the Cartoon Network's Adult Swim programming making bizarre reuse of old cartoon footage to create *Space Ghost Coast to Coast* as well as satirical or absurd shows like *The Powerpuff Girls* and *Aqua Teen Hunger Force*. While not every show had a long run or a lasting impact, the overall boom has helped to shape the U.S. television landscape, particularly its humor, and has influenced the references and terms used by generations of television viewers.

washing dishes at a nursing home and working at a sewage treatment plant. After floundering for a time, Groening began publishing his comic strip *Life in Hell* in alternative newspapers.

Shortly after *Life in Hell* began, his life changed in many ways. First, Groening met the woman whom he would soon marry; the couple eventually had two children. Also, James L. Brooks saw some of Groening's work and became interested in working with him. The first outlet for Groening's work was some short clips that appeared on *The Tracey Ullman Show*. Brooks and Groening discussed the possibility of animating the *Life in Hell* comic strip, but Groening did not want to give up rights to his strip. Instead, he proposed a new set of characters, which developed into the short clips that would evolve into *The Simpsons*. Though the animation in the early clips was relatively crude, the core dynamic of the family was well established, with the father, Homer, being a dim-witted character; Bart, the son, being a disobedient child; Lisa, the eldest daughter, being the most intelligent and well behaved of the children; Maggie being the baby of the family; and Marge being the well-intentioned but sometimes harried mother. Groening has pointed out that many of the Simpson family members take their names from his own family.

In 1989, *The Simpsons* debuted as a series with a Christmas special, followed by regular episodes a few months later. The series quickly became popular for its irreverent take on popular culture. After it established a fan base, the Fox Network moved the show against *The Cosby Show*, leading Cosby to criticize *The Simpsons* for his perception of its championing of the bad behavior of Bart. Even though *The Cosby Show* generally beat *The Simpsons* in the early days of their rivalry, the series has lasted a tremendously long time for a television show and was turned into a movie as well.

After years of success in writing for and producing *The Simpsons*, as well as continuing to write his *Life in Hell* comic strip, Groening and *Simpsons* writer David X. Cohen created the show *Futurama* in 1999. (That same year, Groening and his wife divorced.) Groening has openly discussed the struggles he had in dealing with the Fox Network to get the show on the air and secure support for keeping it on the air. Despite some of these struggles, *Futurama* developed a large and loyal fan base; indeed, after the show was canceled by Fox, Comedy Central began producing new episodes based on the strength of syndicated episodes and DVD sales.

Groening has engaged in a number of other pursuits, including working on titles from Bongo Comics (the publishing house named for one of his *Life in Hell* characters) and playing music in the Rock Bottom Remainders along with other notable writers, including Dave Barry. Although Groening has pulled back in some of his writing work—ending *Life in Hell* in 2012, for instance—he continues to be a force in producing and editing works. Groening lives and works in Los Angeles.

Groening blends his regard for previous generations of comedians (ranging from Harold Zoid to Monty Python) with incisive social commentary in his work, and he readily acknowledges the influence of these figures in interviews. Although he is clearly liberal or progressive in his politics, he is often critical of political structures. For example, he does not support the two-party system in general. When he does support one party over the other, he consistently leans Democratic. More broadly, his efforts look at the problems of humanity at large, pointing out examples of hypocrisy and short-sightedness that even he practices. In one Halloween-themed special episode of *The Simpsons* entitled "Citizen Kang," for instance, the show portrays Americans as preferring to vote for hideous space aliens that openly declare they intend to enslave humanity rather than for a candidate outside the two-party system. Although much of his work has a decided political slant, a significant component of Groening's humor is based on gender relations, the familial unit, and other, more personal issues. For example, *Life in Hell* largely revolves around relationships and selfishness or a lack of self-awareness, with another component being an expression of skepticism toward authority figures such as parents and teachers.

Beyond these facets, perhaps the most striking feature of Groening's humor is its self-awareness. Many episodes of *The Simpsons* include jokes about television or about the format being used to make a joke. For example, Sideshow Bob's complaints about television's lack of vision are echoed by the ending of the episode's use of phrases heard while Sideshow Bob is making the complaint. Other episodes have included discussions of what makes good television even as they employ or eschew the traits being discussed. While this approach to comedy has roots in the work of earlier performers, perhaps most notably Monty Python, it also has exerted a tremendous influence on subsequent television comedies. The association most frequently made is with Seth McFarlane's *Family Guy*, which is not surprising, given that many members of the writing staff for McFarlane's show established their careers by working on *The Simpsons*. While there are some clear departures between the two shows (e.g., *Family Guy* generally employs more vulgar and shocking humor), the idea of self-referential humor is clearly present in both. Indeed, McFarlane and Groening consider each other to be friends, though some writers tend to disparage the other show in some venues. Groening has stated that he appreciates McFarlane's irreverent take on the media, and McFarlane's other highly successful show, *American Dad*, satirizes conservative thinking in a way that is very similar to Groening's portrayal of Homer Simpson's unthinking political and social stances. While other animated shows, such as *King of the Hill* and *Beavis and Butthead*, were part of the animation boom that came out of the success of *The Simpsons*, *Family Guy* is likely to remain the one most closely associated with *The Simpsons*.

Groening has also spoken at length about his interest in boundary-breaking music, most clearly with Frank Zappa, whom Groening befriended before Zappa's death. In general, Groening supports independent films, music, and other transgressive or boundary-breaking art. In fact, many of Groening's idols, from comedians such as Bob Newhart and Mel Brooks, to marginal pop culture icons such as Adam West, to politicians such as Al Gore, have appeared on either *Futurama* or *The Simpsons*. Groening has spoken very positively about these experiences on the DVD commentaries linked to the episodes and in interviews. Although Groening will inevitably be primarily, if not exclusively, linked to *The Simpsons*, his impact can be felt over a variety of media and art forms: bands like Fallout Boy have even taken their names from characters or phrases from the show. Even focusing just on *The Simpsons*, Groening's impact is undeniable, given that the show is one of the longest continuously running animated or comedy shows in television history.

See also: Brooks, James L.; Judge, Mike; McFarlane, Seth

Further Reading

Conrad, Mark, William Irwin, and Aeon Skoble, eds. *The Simpsons and Philosophy: The D'oh! of Homer*. Chicago: Open Court, 2001.

Groening, Matt. *The Big Book of Hell*. New York: Pantheon Books, 1990.

Hull, Margaret Betz. "Postmodern Philosophy Meets Pop Cartoon: Michel Foucault and Matt Groening." *Journal of Popular Culture* 34, no. 2 (Fall 2000): 57–67.

Zeke Jarvis

GUEST, CHRISTOPHER (1948–)

Christopher Guest was born in New York City. His father was a British diplomat to the United Nations. Guest grew up in England, but returned to America to attend the High School of Music and Art in New York. After graduating from high school, Guest attended New York University, studying acting. He began performing in the theater in the early 1970s. By 1972, he added *The National Lampoon Radio Hour* to his experience. Here, he met many of the humorists with whom he would continue to collaborate over his career.

Guest continued to work on both stage and screen, but his breakthrough role came in 1984, when he was part of the mockumentary *This Is Spinal Tap*. Also in 1984, Guest became a member of what many believe to be the greatest cast ever of *Saturday Night Live*; that cast also featured Martin Short, Harry Shearer, and Billy Crystal. Around the same time, Guest married actress Jamie Lee Curtis; the two have adopted two children. Guest also had a major role in *The Princess Bride*, a cult classic film.

In the mid-1990s, Guest began writing, directing, and co-starring in a series of mockumentaries, beginning with *Waiting for Guffman*. The mockumentaries employ a fairly regular cast of actors and are largely improvised. They have met with both critical and commercial success. Guest has also had serious roles, and he wrote and produced the series *Family Tree* for HBO.

Guest is known for a very effective deadpan, maintaining his composure in live television and during the largely improvised mockumentaries. He has regularly incorporated some form of music into his work, including in *Waiting for Guffman, This Is Spinal Tap*, and *A Mighty Wind*. While Guest is a well-respected comedian, he is notorious for being willfully unfunny in his personal life. Well educated and thoughtful, he is known for being serious and dedicated off screen. Even so, his playful work with the mockumentary format has helped to establish him as an innovative, original, and effective humorist.

Further Reading

Geller, Lynn. "Christopher Guest." *BOMB* 29 (Fall 1989): 38–41.

Jones, Kent. "All in the Family: The Democratic Humor of Christopher Guest." *Film Comment* 42, no. 6 (November/December 2006): 46–50.

Muir, John Kenneth. *Best in Show: The Films of Christopher Guest and Company*. New York: Applause Theatre and Cinema Books, 2004.

Zeke Jarvis

HANDLER, CHELSEA (1975–)

Chelsea Handler was born in New Jersey to an interfaith family. Her father was Jewish and her mother was Mormon, though Handler was raised in Reform Judaism. Handler has stated that her family lived in an affluent neighborhood and that she felt less affluent by comparison, though she did not grow up poor by most standards. Still, Handler did have a tumultuous early life, losing a brother when she was 10 years old and having an abortion at age 16.

At age 19, Handler moved from New Jersey to Los Angeles to pursue a career in acting. Although she was not initially successful in her acting pursuits, she soon focused on stand-up, which helped her gain a level of prominence. Handler then began to receive more acting roles, most notably on *Girls Behaving Badly* on the Oxygen Network and on *The Bernie Mac Show*. In 2007, Handler began her show, *Chelsea Lately*, which gave many emerging comics a venue for their work and an opportunity to attain national prominence. Handler became a major figure in comedy as a result, which in turn led to more acting roles for her and a hosting spot on the MTV Music Awards in 2010. Handler continues to host *Chelsea Lately* and appeared in a number of shows, such as Whitney Cummings's (now canceled) sitcom *Whitney*.

Handler has been involved a number of high-profile relationships—for example, with Ted Harbert, a high-ranking official at E! Entertainment, and with the rapper 50 Cent. She is currently unmarried. Handler lives in California with her older brother, who is her personal chef and who occasionally appears on her show.

Handler is known for employing a mix of sharp-tongued humor and self-effacing jokes. Like earlier-generation female comics such as Joan Rivers, Handler does not shy away from discussing sex, bodily functions, or other vulgar topics that are typically seen as male-dominated areas. Handler also makes a large number of popular cultural references, discussing low-cultural topics and incorporating transgressive puns. This approach puts Handler in a very interesting position when it comes to feminism. Her openness about her abortion, her discussions of her interest in drinking and partying, and her frank explorations of sexual interest and desire have made Handler a complex and dynamic figure, with some critics seeing her as breaking boundaries for female comics and others seeing her as simplistic and reductive in her comedy. Interestingly, she also has clear roots in the work of earlier comics, and she honors those roots by discussing those influences, such as Rivers and Phyllis Diller (for her boisterous personality). Although Handler can be a controversial figure, her support for upcoming comics and the popularity of her show have established her role as a prominent American humorist.

See also: Diller, Phyllis; Rivers, Joan

Further Reading

Fox, Marisa. "Chelsea Handler Puts It All out There." *Redbook* 218, no. 3 (March 2012): 117–121.

Handler, Chelsea. *Are You There Vodka? It's Me, Chelsea*. New York: Gallery Books, 2008.

Lipsky-Karasz, Elisa. "Chelsea the Handler." *Harper's Bazaar* 3581 (April 2010): 210–213.

Zeke Jarvis

HENRY, BUCK (1930–)

Henry Zuckerman was born in New York City. Zuckerman, who would go on to become known as Buck Henry, is the son of silent film actress Ruth Taylor. After graduating from high school, he went to Dartmouth College. While there, he worked on the humor magazine, *Dartmouth Jack-o-Lantern*. After graduating, Henry appeared on a variety of television shows, sometimes as the fictitious figure G. Clifford Prout, the president of the Society for Indecency to Naked Animals. In addition, Henry was part of an improvisational group known as The Premise. He also appeared on *The New Steve Allen Show* and co-created the show *Get Smart*. Henry hosted *Saturday Night Live* 10 times, establishing regular characters in that view. Henry has appeared in a number of films and wrote a number of screenplays—most notably, the screenplay for *The Graduate*, for which he shared an Oscar nomination. He also has written for Broadway. Henry currently lives in New York.

Henry is well known for his dry humor, regularly employing a deadpan delivery. This mastery of deadpan and his use of it in his extended Prout prank could be considered a predecessor to Sacha Baron Cohen's work on *Da Ali G Show* and *Borat*. In addition, much of Henry's work relies on sexual innuendo and deviant impulses. One of his regular characters on *Saturday Night Live* was Uncle Roy, a pedophile who would snap pictures of Gilda Radner and Laraine Newman, who played young girls, or would make other inappropriate remarks and gestures. Henry's seemingly plain appearance helped to enhance the ironic distance of his disturbing and unseemly acts and statements. Despite the edginess of some of his material, Henry has found consistent work in a variety of media. While he does not have the visibility of some other humorists, he is well respected by other comedians and has had a part in a number of prominent and successful comedies.

Further Reading

Chumo, Peter N., II. "An Affair to Remember: Buck Henry on Writing *The Graduate*." *Creative Screenwriting* 12, no. 6 (November–December 2005): 69–72.

Georgakas, Dan. "From Words to Images: An Interview with Buck Henry." *Cineaste: America's Leading Magazine on the Art and Politics of the Cinema* 27, no. 1 (Winter 2001): 4–10.

Hill, Doug. *Saturday Night Live: A Backstage History*. New York: Untreed Reads, 2011.

Zeke Jarvis

HENSON, JIM (1936–1990)

Jim Henson was born in Greenville, Mississippi, to Betty (Brown) and Paul Henson. He and his family moved from Leland, Mississippi, to Hyattsville, Maryland in the late 1940s. While still a student at Northwestern High School, Henson began creating puppets for *The Junior Morning Show* on WTOP-TV. After graduating from high school, he enrolled in the University of Maryland, College Park; he ultimately received a BS in home economics.

As a freshman, Henson was asked to create the 5-minute puppet show *Sam and Friends* for WRC-TV. The puppets he created were the predecessors of the Muppets. While working on *Sam and Friends*, Henson began developing new methods of puppetry, including using rods to move the puppets' arms, which made the characters more expressive, making the characters from fabric-covered foam rubber instead of carved wood, and attempting to match mouth movements to dialogue to give the puppets the illusion of speaking.

After the success of *Sam and Friends*, Henson married his assistant from the project, Jane Nebel, in 1959. The couple had five children: Lisa, Cheryl, Brian, John, and Heather. The family moved to New York City in 1963, where they set up the headquarters for Muppets, Inc. After Jane quit working to raise the family,

Henson hired Jerry Juhl and Frank Oz to replace her. The breakout moment for the Muppets was acceptance of the piano-playing dog, Rowlf, on the *Jimmy Dean Show*. The character became a regular feature, much to Henson's delight.

In 1969, Henson was asked to work on *Sesame Street*, an up-and-coming children's TV show. Henson created some of the show's most famous characters—Grover, Cookie Monster, and Big Bird, among other puppets. The show gradually integrated the puppets into the live-action segments, which drew greater attention to Henson's work. Henson became worried that his puppets were being typecast as children's show features, so he began working with *Saturday Night Live*. After failing to work well with the comedy show, Henson moved on to create *The Muppet Show*, which garnered so much success that Henson created *The Muppet Movie*. The film did well critically and financially, giving Henson the courage to work on other projects like *Star Wars* and *Labyrinth*.

Henson separated from his wife in 1986. In 1989, he began negotiations to sell Muppets, Inc., to the Walt Disney Company in hopes that with Disney handling the finances, he would be able to become more creative. In 1990, Henson developed flu-like symptoms that led to streptococcal toxic shock syndrome and organ failure. He died from this condition in May 1990.

Henson spent his life seeking new challenges and projects. While many of these efforts, such as *Sesame Street* and the Muppets, were wildly successful, others were not. The efforts that seem to have yielded the best results are often the ones with a clear element of humor. Henson is largely known for the radical changes that he brought to children's programming, including the live interaction of people and puppets. His vaudevillian sensibility is evident in the characters Walter and Standorf, the wise-cracking fixtures of *The Muppet Show* who often criticized the show itself. Another example of the vaudevillian technique is apparent in the relationship between Ernie (the playful, good-willed imbecile) and Bert (the ever-frustrated straight man). These sorts of characters and the absurd puns were traditional in some formats but seemed new and different when put into the context of a children's show. Mostly, though, Henson is associated with promoting a sense of acceptance and tolerance, consciously seeking out a multicultural cast and highlighting themes of accepting difference in many of his shows and works. This sort of light-hearted approach and his willingness to incorporate silliness into his work make it easy to enjoy and have helped Henson achieve a lasting impact on American humor and pop culture.

Further Reading

Davis, Michael. *Street Gang: The Complete History of Sesame Street.* New York: Penguin Books, 2009.

Freeman, Don. "Muppets on His Hands." *Saturday Evening Post* 251, no. 8 (November 1979): 50–126.

Spinney, Carroll, and Jason Milligan. *The Wisdom of Big Bird (and the Dark Genius of Oscar the Grouch): Lessons from a Life in Feathers.* New York: Villard, 2007.

Kristen Franz

HODGSON, JOEL (1960–)

Joel Hodgson was born in Stevens Point, Wisconsin. While still in middle school, he began to perform magic and ventriloquist acts. After graduating from high school, Hodgson went to Bethel College in Minneapolis, Minnesota. While there, he began working comedy into his magic act. At Bethel, Hodgson also took a class on the theater of the absurd, which he cites as having a major impact on his comedy. In 1981 and 1982, Hodgson won two local comedy contests, one for the college and another for Twin Cities.

In November 1982, Hodgson moved to Los Angeles to pursue his comedy career. After being seen performing in clubs, he appeared on *Late Night with David Letterman*, *Saturday Night Live*, and a young comedians special on HBO, where Bill Maher and Paula Poundstone also appeared. Hodgson continued to write and perform, including cowriting an HBO special with Jerry Seinfeld. In 1988, he created *Mystery Science Theater 3000*, a show that featured Hodgson and puppets watching low-quality movies and making wisecracks. The show first aired on Comedy Central, then moved to the SciFi (now Syfy) Channel. Shortly before the show switched networks, Hodgson left the show due to creative struggles with one of the other writers.

Hodgson subsequently worked in short-term roles on a variety of shows, such as *Jimmy Kimmel Live!* and *Freaks and Geeks*. In 2012, he created a touring show, *Cinematic Titanic*, that used the same formula and some of the same contributors as the original *Mystery Science Theater 3000*. He also began touring with a one-man show. Hodgson lives in Los Angeles and continues to perform.

Hodgson is known for his offbeat humor and dry, deadpan delivery. He uses a variety of esoteric references, including humorous and offbeat references to low culture. Although he discusses low culture, Hodgson is able to incorporate experimental and intellectual approaches and references, showing his training and exposure from his academic work. Though Hodgson occupies somewhat of a cult or niche audience in his performances, he has had success in writing for mainstream shows and with mainstream comics.

Further Reading

Bonnstetter, Beth E. "The Legacy of *Mystery Science Theater 3000*: Text, Textual Production, Paracinema and Media Literacy." *Journal of Popular Film & Television* 40, no. 2 (2012): 94–104.

Long, Marion. "Behind the Screen at *Mystery Science Theater 3000*." *Omni* 14, no. 11 (August 1992): 34.

Rees, Shelley S. *Reading Mystery Science Theater 3000: Critical Approaches*. Lanham, MD: Scarecrow Press, 2013.

Zeke Jarvis

HUGHES, JOHN (1950–2009)

John Hughes was born in 1950 in Lansing, Michigan. He spent a quiet childhood in Grosse Pointe, Michigan, until 1963, when his family moved to a suburb of Chicago, where he had a hard time fitting in at Glenbrook North High School.

This school, and his experiences there, would become the inspiration for much of Hughes's later writing and film work.

Hughes attended the University of Arizona, but did not complete a degree. He began his comedy writing career by writing jokes for numerous well-known comedians, including Joan Rivers and Rodney Dangerfield, and landed a job as a copywriter for an advertising agency in Chicago. Hughes soon ended up in New York working for Philip Morris. In New York, Hughes made connections at the offices of *National Lampoon* magazine, a humor publication that specialized in parody and produced comedy films spun off of its print material. In 1970, Hughes married his wife, Nancy, with whom he had two children.

A story that Hughes wrote about a disastrous family vacation to Disneyland, "Vacation '58," gained Hughes a position on the staff of *National Lampoon* magazine. During his time there, he penned his first screenplay—for *National Lampoon's Class Reunion*, which was a flop in 1982. Hughes subsequently found success with his screenplay for *National Lampoon's Vacation*, based on "Vacation '58." Starring Chevy Chase, Beverly D'Angelo, Randy Quaid, and Anthony Michael Hall, *National Lampoon's Vacation* was a commercial success in 1983. *Mr. Mom*, another film penned by Hughes and starring Michael Keaton, was also a hit that year; it landed Hughes a three-picture deal with Universal Studios.

In 1984, Universal Studios released Hughes's directorial debut, *Sixteen Candles*, to wide commercial and critical acclaim. Starring Molly Ringwald, *Sixteen Candles* has been listed by numerous outlets as one of the best high school films of all time. Hughes wrote and directed a string of high school hits in the 1980s. Universal released *The Breakfast Club* in 1985, which once again showcased Molly Ringwald and Anthony Michael Hall. *Weird Science*, featuring Hall, was also released in 1985, and *Ferris Bueller's Day Off*, starring Matthew Broderick, followed in 1986. Hughes wrote the screenplays for each of these films, as well as for *National Lampoon's European Vacation* (1985), *Pretty in Pink* (1986), and *Some Kind of Wonderful* (1987).

By 1987, Hughes was looking to branch away from teen comedies, so he wrote and directed *Planes, Trains and Automobiles*, starring Steve Martin and John Candy. Hughes then directed a romantic comedy, *She's Having a Baby*, in 1988. This film received mixed reviews from critics, who often cited the film's fantasy elements as missteps. Hughes continued writing, churning out such favorites as *The Great Outdoors*, also starring John Candy, in 1988; *National Lampoon's Christmas Vacation* in 1989; and *Home Alone*, which was a mega-hit in 1990, largely due to its child star, Macaulay Culkin. In addition, Hughes directed *Uncle Buck* in 1989 and *Curly Sue* in 1991; the latter was his last directorial effort.

After *Curly Sue*, Hughes focused on producing and writing. In this role, he was responsible for *Beethoven* (1992), *Home Alone 2: Lost in New York* (1992), *Dennis the Menace* (1993), and *Baby's Day Out* (1994). Remakes of *Miracle on 34th Street* and *101 Dalmatians* also followed. In 2006, filming began on a documentary about Hughes, *Don't You Forget about Me*, which chronicles a group of four young filmmakers from Canada trying to find the reclusive Hughes, who had stepped away from the spotlight after 1991. The film includes interviews with many of the actors who appeared in Hughes's films, with the exceptions of Matthew Broderick, Anthony Michael Hall, and Molly Ringwald. The film aired on the Encore channel a few times after Hughes's death from a heart attack in 2009.

Hughes is known for his use of outsider characters, particularly his examination of high school students. For a generation, many considered Hughes to give voice to the struggles of fitting in as a teenager. Hughes also was known for his ability to balance ridiculous situations with genuine emotion, as in the *Vacation* movies. His sense of rhythm and comedic timing is one of the many facets of his work that people admire. He also made the Midwest a setting for movies when many other filmmakers tended to focus on larger cities on the coasts. As both a writer and a director, Hughes has established his influence and position as a major American humorist.

See also: Edwards, Blake

Further Reading

Bleach, Anthony C. "Postfeminist Cliques?: Class, Postfeminism, and the Molly Ringwald-John Hughes Films." *Cinema Journal* 49, no. 3 (Spring 2010): 24–44.

Christie, Thomas. *John Hughes and Eighties Cinema*. Maidstone, UK: Crescent Moon, 2009.

Clarke, Jaimie, ed. *Don't You Forget about Me: Contemporary Writers on the Films of John Hughes*. New York: Gallery Books, 2007.

Stephen Powers

HURWITZ, MITCHELL (1963–)

Mitchell Hurwitz was born in Anaheim, California. While still in middle school, Hurwitz founded a cookie company with his brother and father, which is still operating. After graduating from high school, Hurwitz attended Georgetown University, where he earned degrees in both English and theology. He graduated from Georgetown in 1985, then worked in television, writing on such notable shows as *The Golden Girls* and *The Ellen Show* along with well-received but less commercially successful shows, such as *The John Laroquette Show*. In 1999, Hurwitz married Mary Jo Keenan. The two have two daughters, May, who was born in 2000, and Phoebe, who was born in 2002.

Hurwitz's most significant professional success came with his show *Arrested Development*, which premiered on the Fox Network in 2003. The show received positive critical reviews, but it struggled to maintain high ratings. This led to significant criticism of the Fox Network, perhaps most notably from David Cross, for not giving the show adequate advertising or a consistent time slot. Despite its commercial struggles, *Arrested Development* won a number of awards, including an Emmy for Outstanding Writing in a Comedy Series in its first season, and it was nominated for 11 Emmy Awards in its second season. Nevertheless, Fox canceled the show after three seasons. On the strength of DVD sales, the show was revived by Netflix in 2013. In between the initial and second runs of *Arrested Development*, Hurwitz worked regularly, writing for American adaptations of British and Australian shows. He also did some acting work, appearing in the Comedy Central show *Workaholics*. Currently, Hurwitz lives and works in California.

In many of the shows on which he has worked, Hurwitz has been known for challenging established approaches to television comedy. While some of the techniques he would use in *Arrested Development* can be seen in his early work, it was *Arrested Development* that most critics appreciated the most, noting its heavy but playful use of referentiality (having actor Scott Baio replace actor Henry Winkler, for example—as had occurred decades earlier on *Happy Days*) and the layered, pun-filled approach to humor. Hurwitz is particularly noteworthy for being in the center of a public battle with a network, making jokes about the Fox Network's treatment of the show while still having episodes aired on the network. Although Hurwitz is likely to always be linked most strongly with *Arrested Development*, he has been involved with a number of successful projects that make him a significant figure in television and comedy.

See also: Cross, David

Further Reading

Heisler, Steve. "Interview with Mitch Hurwitz." *The Onion AV Club,* October 5, 2010. http://www.avclub.com/article/mitchell-hurwitz-talks-about-the-resurrection-of-i-98157.

Poniewozik, James. "It's Not TV. It's *Arrested Development*." *Time* 181, no. 19 (May 20, 2013): 36.

Snierson, Dan. "*Arrested Development*." *Entertainment Weekly* 1228/1229 (October 12, 2012): 46–49.

Zeke Jarvis

JONZE, SPIKE (1969–)

Adam Spiegel was born to Arthur H. Spiegel III and Sandra L. Granzow in Rockville, Maryland. Spiegel grew up in Bethesda, Maryland, and Gulph Mills, Pennsylvania, before attending the San Francisco Art Institute. Jonze acquired his nickname as a junior at Walt Whitman High School; a Bethesda community store owner tagged him with the sobriquet in reference to musician Spike Jones.

Jonze fronted the international BMX club, Club Homeboy; worked as a photographer for *Freestylin' Magazine*; and co-created the magazines *Homeboy* and *Dirt*. In 2006, his commercial work for companies including Adidas, IKEA, and The Gap earned him a nomination for "Outstanding Achievement in Commercials in 2005" from the Directors Guild of America. At the time, he was also a producer and co-creator of *Jackass* and *Jackass: The Movie*.

Spike Jonze has several alter-egos that he uses for his diverse interests. Richard Koufey, one of his favored personas, is the leader of the Torrance Community Dance Group, which performs in public areas. One of the group's performances outside a Westwood, California, movie theater, earned Koufey's troupe an invitation to perform at the 1999 MTV Video Music Awards.

That same year, Jonze married fellow director, Sofia Coppola; they later divorced in 2003. Also in 1999, Jonze began his feature film directing career with *Being John Malkovich*, written by Charlie Kaufman. The pair would reunite for the film *Adaptation*. In 2009, Jonze directed *Where the Wild Things Are*, which garnered fairly positive critical review. In 2010, he created the short film *Scenes from the Suburbs*, which was inspired by an Arcade Fire album, *The Suburbs*. In 2013, Jonze released his original film *Her*, which earned Jonze the 2014 Golden Globe award for Best Screenplay and the 2014 Oscar for Best Original Screenplay. Jonze also spent time as a music video director, creating videos most notably for Björk (with whom he has become close friends), the Beastie Boys, Jay-Z, Kanye West, Arcade Fire, and Lady Gaga.

Jonze is known for being fearless with the artistic chances that he takes. Both *Being John Malkovich* and *Adaptation* took unusual approaches to their stories: *Malkovich* had the title actor and Charlie Sheen play exaggerated or warped versions of themselves, while *Adaptation* reflected on the writing of the movie's script instead of actually adapting a book into a movie. Equally playful is Jonze's willingness to appear in the *Jackass* movies—some directors would view themselves as above this fare. Another characteristic often referenced by critics of Jonze is his highly energetic and experimental visual style, which may well be an influence gleaned from his experience directing films. Even with his playfulness, Jonze is very well respected for both his imagination and his craft. His humor is offbeat and surprising while still having a careful and consistent tone or atmosphere. While not all of Jonze's work is humorous in nature, much of it has a strangeness that makes him an interesting artist and humorist to watch.

See also: Kaufman, Charlie; Knoxville, Johnny

Further Reading

Annunziato, Sarah. "A Child's Eye View of *Where the Wild Things Are*: Lessons from Spike Jonze's Film Adaptation of Maurice Sendak's Picture Book." *Journal of Children & Media* 8, no. 3 (July 2014): 253–266.

Jonze, Spike. *Spike Jonze: I'm Here*. Zurich: Nieves, 2010.

Nessier, Vartan. "Desire and the 'Deconstructionist:' *Adaptation* as Writerly Praxis." *Journal of Adaptation in Film and Performance* 7, no. 1 (2014): 65–82.

Kristen Franz

JUDGE, MIKE (1962–)

Mike Judge was born in Ecuador, where his father (an archeologist) was doing non-profit work. When Judge was seven, his family moved to Arizona, where Judge grew up. After graduating from high school, he attended the University of California at San Diego, earning a degree in physics. After graduating, Judge worked programming jets and in other programming capacities. Judge disliked the corporate culture, and he found various outlets for his energies, such as taking graduate-level math courses and performing music. Eventually, he turned his sights on animation.

In 1991, Judge produced his first animated short, *Office Space*, which was followed by *Frog Baseball*. These shorts were the forerunners of *Office Space* (the feature-length film) and *Beavis and Butthead*, respectively. From 1993 to 1997, Judge worked on *Beavis and Butthead*, which also led to a feature-length film. Both the film and the show were very commercially successful. After the close of the series, Judge created *King of the Hill*, which ran for 13 years. Judge also directed the films *Office Space* and *Idiocracy*. Unlike his television work, Judge's films had stronger cult followings than commercial success. In 2012, Judge began work on a sitcom called *Silicon Valley* for HBO, which was partly inspired by his time in the corporate world. Judge has three children; he and his wife are divorced.

Judge is known for his observations about the "dumbing down" of American culture. In both *Beavis and Butthead* and *Idiocracy*, Judge portrays unintelligent and unmotivated characters as becoming more of the norm in America than the exception. These portrayals alternate between comical and unsettling as he looks at the long-term impacts of these trends. Judge also is known for bringing focus on Texas, an area of the country not as frequently used in television humor. Although some critics see Judge as being essentially conservative, he has stated that he critiques the structures of power and knowledge. Finally, Judge is part of the animation boom of the 1990s. Along with *The Simpsons* and *South Park*, Judge's work was part of the significant development of animated comedy shows that brought cartoons back into the mainstream of entertainment.

See also: Groening, Matt

Further Reading

Hagle, Will. "Mike Judge: Accuracy Aids *Silicon Valley*." *Broadcasting & Cable* 144, no. 24 (June 30, 2014): 19.

Judge, Mike. *Reading Sucks: The Collected Works of Beavis and Butt-head*. New York: MTV Books, 2005.

Leckart, Steven. "Mike Judge Skewers Silicon Valley with Satire of Our Dreams." *Wired.com*, April 2, 2014. http://www.wired.com/2014/04/mike-judge-silicon-valley/.

Zeke Jarvis

KALING, MINDY (1979–)

Vera Mindy Kaling was born in Cambridge, Massachusetts. Both her parents were Hindu: her father is an architect and her mother is a doctor. After graduating from a private high school, Kaling attended Dartmouth College, where she developed her creative process by being part of an improv group, writing for the college humor magazine, and drawing a comic strip. While attending Dartmouth, Kaling also served as an intern for Conan O'Brien's show, *Late Night with Conan O'Brien*.

In 2001, Kaling graduated with a degree in playwriting. In 2003, she appeared in the play *Matt and Ben* (which she also cowrote), in which she portrayed Ben Affleck. The play was a significant success, even being listed as one of *Time* magazine's "Top Ten Theatrical Events of the Year." Kaling subsequently began to get steady work writing and acting in television and film, including her appearances on *Curb Your Enthusiasm* and writing for an episode of *Saturday Night Live*. In the mid-2000s, she became a regular character on *The Office*, where she also had served as a writer. She continued to write and appear on the show until its end, also appearing in a variety of films, including her voiceover work in *Wreck-It Ralph*. In 2012, Kaling began work on the Fox television show *The Mindy Project*, where she writes and stars. This achievement makes her the first woman of Indian descent to star on a major network show. Kaling continues her work as both a writer and a performer, while also regularly blogging and working on webisodes.

Kaling is known for her self-effacing style, joking about her life, her fashion choices, and her romantic life. Although she does not make her ethnicity the core of her work, she does acknowledge it in a variety of humorous ways while also serving as a positive role model. Kaling lists other East Coast comics such as Denis Leary and Conan O'Brien as influences, and her willingness to laugh at herself and to incorporate quick and often gear-shifting jokes make that comparison clear. She is known as a quick wit who can improvise and work well live. Her broad array of talents and her influence on significant shows make her an important figure in American comedy.

Further Reading

Duca, Lauren. "Why You Should Be Upset of Mindy Kaling's *Elle* Cover, Even If She Isn't." *Huffington Post*, January 8, 2014. http://www.huffingtonpost.com/lauren-duca/mindy-kaling-elle_b_4561454.html.

Gonzalez, Sandra. "Mindy and Danny's Moment." *Entertainment Weekly* 1307/1308 (April 18, 2014): 94–95.

Kaling, Mindy. *Is Everyone Hanging out with Me? (and Other Concerns)*. New York: Three Rivers Press, 2012.

Zeke Jarvis

KAUFMAN, CHARLIE (1958–)

Charlie Kaufman grew up mainly in Massapequa, New York, though his family later moved to West Hartford, Connecticut, where he attended high school. After graduating from high school, Kaufman attended New York University's film school. Subsequently, he wrote articles for *National Lampoon* and eventually moved to California, where he began to work in television—initially on *Get a Life* and later on *The Dana Carvey Show*. In 1999, Kaufman's script *Being John Malkovich* was turned into a film directed by Spike Jonze. Kaufman was nominated for an Academy Award for his work. Kaufman also married, having two children with his wife. Kaufman continued to write screenplays, notably *The Eternal Sunshine of the Spotless Mind* and *Adaptation*. In 2008, Kaufman released the first film that he both wrote and directed, *Synecdoche, New York*. Kaufman continues to work as both a writer and a director.

Kaufman's work is known for being both very offbeat (sometimes confusing, according to critics) and very intellectual, drawing in influences from philosophy, literature, and other sources. While his work has found mixed results with mainstream audiences, his core group of supporters finds his work surprising, inventive, and cerebral. The undercurrent of careful thought helps to balance some of the stranger aspects of Kaufman's work, making viewers willing to give his work repeated viewings to catch the significance of the seemingly haphazard details. In fact, Kaufman has won high praise from significant critics, including Roger Ebert and other well-known commentators.

See also: Jonze, Spike

Further Reading

Hill, Derek. *Charlie Kaufman and Hollywood's Merry Band of Pranksters, Fabulists and Dreamers: An Excursion into the American New Wave*. Hertfordshire, UK: Oldcastle Books, 2008.

Marks, Peter. "Adaptation from Charles Darwin to Charlie Kaufman." *Sydney Studies in English* 34 (2008): 19–40.

Nessier, Vartan. "Desire and the 'Deconstructionist:' *Adaptation* as Writerly Praxis." *Journal of Adaptation in Film and Performance* 7, no. 1 (2014): 65–82.

Zeke Jarvis

KEATON, BUSTER (1895–1966)

Joseph Keaton was born in Piqua, Kansas, though the town was not his family's home. His father owned a traveling show that employed Harry Houdini, and Keaton was raised in the vaudevillian scene. Though the story may be part exaggeration, Keaton claimed that he got the nickname "Buster" at a young age when Houdini saw him fall down a flight of stairs and remarked, "That was a real buster." Whatever the true origin of his nickname, it suited his incorporation into the family comedy act, where he would tease or disobey his father on stage, resulting in Keaton being tossed around. Keaton was so skilled at taking falls that his father was sometimes accused of (and occasionally even questioned by the police for) child abuse. Keaton would have to show the authorities that he was unharmed and unbruised. Keaton also began to adopt his deadpan expression for his pratfalls as a child, allowing the audience to not be either afraid or unsurprised by the act. Keaton was billed as "The little boy who can't be damaged." Unfortunately, though the family's show had some success, it ran up against child-labor laws and his father's emerging alcoholism. By the time Keaton turned 21, he and his mother had left his father behind, moving to New York.

During World War I, Keaton served in the army. Though he survived the war, an ear infection permanently damaged his hearing. Upon returning from the war, Keaton befriended actor Fatty Arbuckle. Though Keaton was skeptical about film as a medium prior to his meeting Arbuckle, after some exploration he became interested in both its artistic and technical aspects. Keaton's first film appearance was in an Arbuckle film, *The Butcher Boy*. By 1921, Keaton had released *The Saphead,* the first feature film in which he was the sole star. Also in 1921, Keaton married his first wife, Natalie Talmadge. The two would have two children.

Actor/director Buster Keaton is pictured in costume in 1939. Keaton may be the most acclaimed physical comic in American film history. (Library of Congress)

After a number of successes, Keaton was given his own production company. He released a number of films in the early 1920s. Keaton quickly became known for employing complicated and seemingly dangerous stunts. In 1927, he released what many consider to be his greatest film, *The General*, which is well known for its extended and striking train scene. Although the film is now very well respected, some audiences at the time felt that it was too serious for a comedy and were unsettled by the fact that Keaton portrayed a Confederate soldier.

The following year, Keaton signed with MGM, but he struggled after losing creative control over many of his projects. There were a number of other struggles, over issues such as MGM's insistence on Keaton using stunt doubles and having to shoot films in three different languages. Keaton's struggles led him to begin drinking heavily and to ultimately depart from MGM, even though a number of his films were financially successful. Also during this period, Keaton's first marriage ended. He married again in 1933, but divorced slightly more than two years later.

After briefly leaving the film world, Keaton returned as a writer and performer. He married again in 1940, this time staying married until his death. Keaton had roles and cameos in a number of films and, in 1950, had his first television show, *The Buster Keaton Show*. Keaton continued to appear in a combination of films and television shows late into his life. In 1966, he died of lung cancer.

Keaton is most widely recognized for his seeming reckless abandon in performing physical comedy. A number of his films include complex and elaborate stunts, including a train derailing in *The General* and a house falling apart over Keaton in *Steamboat Bill, Jr.* The boldness and creativity of his stunts have influenced humorists and performers ranging from the writers of *Arrested Development* to martial arts star Jackie Chan. Keaton is also known for his masterful deadpan, not reacting to the madness surrounding his characters; this treatment of one's surroundings as natural is both deeply rooted in vaudeville tradition and still practiced in absurd humor performances. One of Keaton's trademark features was his porkpie hat, which was often demolished in the course of a stunt. The hat was so distinctive that it was sometimes used as a direct reference to Keaton, as in the film *Benny and Joon*, where Johnny Depp's character imitates some of the stunts and mannerisms of Keaton and fellow silent film star Charlie Chaplin.

One of Keaton's major impacts was the level of control that he exercised over his early work, serving as writer, performer, and producer. His keen awareness of and interest in the technical aspects of film set him apart from some other vaudeville performers; likewise, his willingness to move into films with sound set him apart from some other silent film stars. Keaton's daring, careful attention, and vibrant imagination helped to make him a significant and enduring figure in both film and humor.

Further Reading

Bengston, John. *Silent Echoes: Discovering Early Hollywood through the Films of Buster Keaton*. Santa Monica: Santa Monica Press, 1999.

Fay, Jennifer. "Buster Keaton's Climate Change." *Modernism/Modernity* 21, no. 1 (January 2014): 25–49.

Smith, Imogen Sara. *Buster Keaton: The Persistence of Comedy*. New York: CreateSpace Publishing, 2013.

Zeke Jarvis

KEY AND PEELE (KEEGAN-MICHAEL KEY, 1971–; JORDAN PEELE, 1979–)

Keegan-Michael Key was born in Southfield, Michigan, though he grew up in Detroit. He is an adopted child of mixed race. He attended the University of Detroit after graduating from high school, then studied theater at the Pennsylvania State University School of Theatre, where he received a master of fine arts degree. Key is married to Cynthia Blaise.

Jordan Peele was born in New York City. He originally intended to be a puppeteer, but decided to pursue comedy during college. He also performed at Second City in Chicago, where he and Key first met. Peele auditioned for *Saturday Night Live* and was originally accepted, but was not able to join the cast because of a writers' strike.

Key and Peele auditioned against each other for the show *Madtv*, but their chemistry together led to both being hired. In 2012, the pair began work on their Comedy Central show, *Key and Peele*, which has met with significant success and has had a variety of well-known stars appear in small roles.

Key and Peele are known for pushing boundaries both in their discussions of race and in their willingness to incorporate vulgar and edgy material. Even more than that, they are renowned for their open and frank discussions of political and social issues. This can take the form of discussing statements by celebrities or engaging in impressions of President Barack Obama. In fact, one of the memorable running sketches from the show involved Peele doing an impression of Obama speaking in a polite, mannered way and Key performing the role of the angry African American man speaking what Obama was "actually" thinking during his speeches. Of course, not all of their sketches have that political bent, but with their incisive observations and willingness to laugh at edgy topics, Key and Peele have established themselves as respected and popular cultural commentators.

Further Reading

McGlynn, Katia. "Key and Peele Laud the Power of Comedy at the Peabody Awards." *Huffington Post,* May 30, 2014. http://www.huffingtonpost.com/2014/05/30/key-and-peele-peabody-award-speech-video_n_5418216.html.

Rahman, Ray. "Dissecting Key and Peele." *Entertainment Weekly* 1231 (November 2, 2012): 58–59.

Swartout, Harry. "Key and Peele: 'It's All Downhill from Here.'" *Time.com* (April 26, 2014): 1.

Zeke Jarvis

KIMMEL, JIMMY (1967–)

Jimmy Kimmel was born in Brooklyn, New York. At age nine, Kimmel and his family moved to Las Vegas, where he spent the remainder of his childhood. In school, Kimmel excelled in both academics and art. During his high school days, he began to watch and idolize David Letterman. To pursue his interest in comedy and performance, he worked as a radio disc jockey at both the University of Nevada at Las Vegas and Arizona State University. At 21, Kimmel began to pursue his radio career professionally, working in Seattle, Tucson, and Phoenix before landing a regular slot on a Los Angeles radio show as "Jimmy the Sports Guy." In 1988, Kimmel married his first wife, with whom he had two children.

From his radio exposure, Kimmel got a host job on the Comedy Central game show *Win Ben Stein's Money*. In that role, he served as the comic foil to Ben Stein, a former speech writer for Richard Nixon, who would compete against the winning contestant each episode in the final round. Shortly after landing this job, Kimmel began work on *The Man Show* with cohost Adam Carolla. Along with Daniel Kellison, the pair formed Jackhole Productions, which produced both *The Man Show* and *Crank Yankers*, a show that had puppets reenact prank phone calls spoken by a mix of prominent comedians like Sarah Silverman and David Allen Grier and lesser-known but more regular staff members. Both shows drew significant audiences and significant criticism, largely for the crassness and use of what many saw as stereotypical or simplistic portrayals of various groups. The taxing aspects of Kimmel's career ultimately took its toll on his marriage in 2003, when he and his wife divorced. That same year, Kimmel got a hosting job on his own late-night talk show, *Jimmy Kimmel Live!*, finally gaining the same position as his idol, David Letterman.

After his divorce, Kimmel began a well-publicized relationship with fellow comic Sarah Silverman. The pair split and then reunited, only to split again, though they remain good friends. In 2012, Kimmel got engaged to Molly McNearny, a writer

Jimmy Kimmel arrives at *TV Guide* magazine's 2012 Hot List Party at the Mondrian Hotel in West Hollywood, California, on November 12, 2012. Kimmel first achieved success on *The Man Show*, but has since developed a lasting career as a late-night talk show host. (AP Photo/ Todd Williamson/Invision)

for his show; they married in 2013 and had a daughter in 2014. Kimmel lives and works in New York.

Kimmel's early career is mainly known for his sarcastic and simple humor, shown through a number of bits on *The Man Show*, which portrayed Kimmel and cohost Carolla as men of simple desires and interests—mainly women, drinking, and sports. As he has evolved into his host persona with his own show, Kimmel's humor has become more akin to that of Letterman's, utilizing more off-the-wall jokes, referencing shortcomings of particular bits, and using family and staff members as on-air personalities rather than professional performers and personalities.

Kimmel has also been particularly outspoken about the competition between David Letterman and Jay Leno for late-night ratings. Kimmel has consistently derided Leno, even going so far as to appear to ridicule Leno when he was a guest on *The Tonight Show*. Kimmel has consistently maintained that Letterman performs with an eye toward humor whereas Leno performs with an eye toward ratings, even going so far as to complain about the intelligence level of viewers who consistently tune into Leno rather than Letterman.

Kimmel has taken on a number of noteworthy hosting duties, including the Friars Club Roast of *Playboy* publisher Hugh Hefner and the Emmys. Kimmel also was interviewed by Oprah, putting to rest any speculation that the two disliked each other from Kimmel's statements that he and Carolla were "the anti-Oprah" during their run on *The Man Show*. With Kimmel's popular success, his consistent work, and his outspoken views on comedy, he has earned the respect of many contemporary comedians, and he continues to impact the American comedy scene.

See also: Silverman, Sarah

Further Reading

Chiarella, Tom. "Kimmel Is the Jimmy." *Esquire* 161, no. 4 (April 2014): 78–84.

Palmer-Mehta, Valerie. "Men Behaving Badly: Mediocre Masculinity and *The Man Show*." *Journal of Popular Culture* 42, no. 6 (December 2009): 1053–1072.

Rolling Stone. "Jimmy Kimmel." Weiner, Jonah. January 2013. http://www.rollingstone.com/movies/news/heres-jimmy-kimmel-20130301.

Zeke Jarvis

KNOXVILLE, JOHNNY (1971–)

Philip John Clapp was born in Knoxville, Tennessee. His mother taught Sunday school and his father was a tire salesman. After graduating from high school, Knoxville moved to California to pursue a career in acting, taking up the name Johnny Knoxville. Although he got bit parts, he did not achieve any major role. In 1995, Knoxville married his first wife, with whom he has one child. The two would divorce in 2008.

Frustrated with his lack of success in Hollywood, Knoxville decided to take an unusual approach, pitching unusual ideas to different publishers. One such

Classic Comedy Pranks or Stunts

Pranks are an essential part of American humor. The television show *Candid Camera* showed regular people being surprised in a variety of ways, making it an early example of reality television. Major stars have also carried out many successful pranks. Johnny Carson once had an elderly woman on his show who had a collection of potato chips that she said looked like different celebrities or historical figures. During the segment with her, Carson reached into his desk and pulled out a potato chip that he quickly ate. The woman was shocked for a few seconds, thinking that Carson had eaten one of her prized pieces. Carson also tricked Don Rickles, surprising him on a broadcast and making Rickles believe that he was angry.

More recently, there have been more conceptual pranks, such as Stephen Colbert encouraging viewers to wreak havoc with Wikipedia's pages and Dan Savage's fans making sure that vulgarities are the first results when people type conservative politician Rick Santorum's name into Google. Perhaps most famous of all is Andy Kaufman's long, fake feud with pro wrestler Jerry Lawler, which exploded on a famous segment of David Letterman's talk show. With figures like Johnny Knoxville and Spike Jonze, the prank remains part of America's humor tradition.

successful project was a review of self-defense equipment after it had been applied to himself. With a background in these sorts of odd projects, Knoxville and his close friend Jeff Tremaine filmed a pilot that they eventually sold to MTV under the name *Jackass*. The show became a major success, eventually leading to three films. The show revolved around Knoxville and the other cast members performing stunts or pranks.

After the success of *Jackass*, Knoxville began receiving parts in films, including *The Dukes of Hazzard* and *Men in Black II*. He had his first solo starring role in the film *The Ringer*, to modest success.

In 2010, Knoxville married for the second time. He and his second wife have two children together.

In 2013, Knoxville starred again in *Jackass Presents: Bad Grandpa*, in which he donned make-up and a costume to appear to be an elderly man, then played pranks on passersby. Knoxville continues to act, though his closest tie remains to his work from *Jackass*.

Knoxville is known for taking serious risks with his own personal safety, and he has sustained lasting damage from some of his pranks. Because of the unusual nature of his celebrity, Knoxville has received both high praise and significant criticism. After the success of *Jackass*, a number of viewers attempted to re-create stunts from the show or perform stunts that they believed could get them on the show. Owing to these events, Knoxville became a lightning rod for a variety of cultural critics. Nevertheless, many other humorists, from Conan O'Brien to Jon Stewart, have expressed admiration for the combination of imagination and courage exhibited by Knoxville and his crew.

See also: Jonze, Spike

Further Reading

Cliver, Sean, ed. *Jackass: 10 Years of Stupid*. New York: MTV Books, 2010.

Itzkoff, Dave. "Autumn of the Jackass: What's Next for Johnny Knoxville." *New York Times Magazine* (October 13, 2013): 18–21.

Lindgren, Simon, and Maxime Lelievre. "In the Laboratory of Masculinity: Renegotiating Gender Subjectivities in MTV's *Jackass*." *Critical Studies in Media Communication* 26, no. 5 (December 2009): 393–410.

Zeke Jarvis

LAWRENCE, VICKI (1949–)

Victoria Axelrad was born in Inglewood, California. Axelrad, who would eventually take the stage name Vicki Lawrence, was the valedictorian of Morningside High School. Early in her career, she became part of the group known as the Young Americans. After reading a review stating that she resembled Carol Burnett, Lawrence sent a copy of the review to Burnett along with an invitation to attend a performance. Burnett attended a show and was impressed enough to hire Lawrence to play her younger sister on *The Carol Burnett Show*. Other than Burnett herself, Lawrence was the only cast member to be on the show for the entirety of the show's 11 seasons.

After the Burnett show finished, Lawrence and her husband Al Schultz, moved to Hawaii for a brief time before moving back to Los Angeles. Prior to her marriage to Schultz, Burnett was married to songwriter Bobby Russell, who wrote the song "The Night the Lights Went out in Georgia." Lawrence's recording of the song reached number one on the Top 100 Chart and stayed there for two weeks.

In 1983, Lawrence reprised her role as Mama in a spin-off of her work on *The Carol Burnett Show*. That show, *Mama's Family*, ran until 1985 in its first run, and then again from 1986 to 1990 in its first-run syndication. Lawrence has played the character or characters closely related to Mama in tone and personality on a number of shows, including *Hannah Montana* and as part of a one-woman show. She has also had a good deal of work on game shows, hosting the game *Win, Lose or Draw*. Lawrence and her husband still live in California. They have two children, one son and one daughter.

Lawrence's characters are often outspoken and boisterous, drawing comedy from the reaction of the confusion and awkwardness of the other characters. Lawrence is also known for her comedic timing and delivery, working as part of a very successful ensemble cast on *The Carol Burnett Show*. Although her characters can be overbearing, her comedy has generally not been edgy or offensive. While there were some double entendres and innuendos on *The Carol Burnett Show* and *Mama's Family*, these shows were mainstream successes that appealed to large audiences.

See also: Burnett, Carol

Further Reading

Goldblatt, Henry. "*The Carol Burnett Show*." *Entertainment Weekly* 1176/1188 (October 14, 2011): 62–65.

Lawrence, Vicki, and Marc Eliot. *Vicki! The True Life Adventures of Miss Fireball*. New York: Simon & Schuster, 1995.

Schneider, Michael. "Now, Vicki after Breakfast." *Electronic Media* 16, no. 35 (August 25, 1997): 39.

Zeke Jarvis

LEAR, NORMAN (1922–)

Norman Lear was born on July 27, 1922, in New Haven, Connecticut. He was raised in a Jewish household. He briefly attended Emerson College in Boston, but dropped out to fly 52 bombing combat missions as a gunner and radio operator in the U.S. Army Air Forces during World War II.

After his discharge in 1945, Lear began writing comedy sketches for television, including for Rowan and Martin. He worked with his writing partner, Ed Simmons, on these television sketches until 1954, when he joined the writing team of the CBS sitcom *Honestly Celeste!* The show was soon canceled, so Lear moved on to *The Martha Raye Show* as a producer. Lear had married twice by this point, the second time to Frances Lear, with whom he had two children and to whom he stayed married for 30 years.

In 1959, Lear created his first television show, *The Deputy*, a half-hour Western starring Henry Fonda. *The Deputy* ran for 76 episodes until 1961. Lear then turned to film as producer and writer of *Divorce American Style*, a comedy satire directed by Bud Yorkin and starring Dick Van Dyke and Debbie Reynolds. The film earned praise from critics, with Roger Ebert calling it a "comedy with teeth in it." Lear directed 1971's *Cold Turkey*, also starring Van Dyke.

CBS then picked up Lear's sitcom about a working-class family after ABC rejected the first two pilot episodes. Based on the long-running British sitcom *'Til Death Do Us Part*, Lear's version, known as *All in the Family*, starred Carroll O'Connor as Archie Bunker, a bigoted but likable dock worker living in the Queens neighborhood of Astoria, and Jean Stapleton as his simple-minded but always kind-hearted and good-intentioned wife. Sally Struthers and Rob Reiner rounded out the cast as Bunker's daughter and son-in-law. *All in the Family* premiered in January 1971 as the first major American series to be filmed in front of a studio audience with multiple cameras. The show was shot on videotape as opposed to film, which give it the look of live television. It received disappointing ratings for its premiere, but its popularity increased during summer reruns of first-season episodes. In addition, the show won numerous Emmy Awards in its first year, including for Outstanding Comedy Series. Starting with the second season, *All in the Family* claimed the number one spot in the TV ratings for the next five years; it stayed in the top 10 for the rest of its run.

Lear's second sitcom, *Sanford and Son*, adapted from the British show *Steptoe and Son*, debuted in 1972. It starred Redd Foxx in the role of Fred G. Sanford, a junk dealer in the Watts neighborhood of Los Angeles. *Sanford and Son* was a hit, running for five years.

Later in 1972, Lear turned his attention to the first of numerous spin-off series from *All in the Family*. That show eventually spawned five spin-offs, and two spin-offs of those spin-offs, each developed by Lear and each noted for its treatment (often for the first time openly on television) of major political and social issues of the day, much like in *All in the Family*. The first spin-off, *Maude* in 1972, starred Bea Arthur in the titular role. In 1974, *Good Times*, a spin-off of *Maude*, premiered. *Good Times* featured an African American working-class family living in the housing projects of south-side Chicago. The next spin-off, *The Jeffersons*, premiered in 1975 and ran for 11 seasons. Sherman Hemsley played Archie Bunker's former next-door neighbor, George Jefferson, who found success with his chain of dry cleaning businesses and moved to a luxury apartment in a high-rise on New York's Upper East Side. Other spin-offs included *Checking In* (a short-lived spin-off of *The Jeffersons*); *Gloria*, which premiered in 1982 and ran for only one season; and *704 Hauser*, which aired for only five episodes in 1994.

In 1987, Lear married for the third time, this time having three children. He served as host for *Quiz Kids* on CBS in the early 1980s. He continued his career with acquisitions of communications companies and by financing Rob Reiner's directorial debut, *This Is Spinal Tap*. One of Lear's companies produced Reiner's next three films and, in 1991, *Fried Green Tomatoes*. In the 1990s, Lear returned to television with *The Powers That Be*, but the series proved unsuccessful. The recipient of numerous awards, most for *All in the Family* and its spin-offs, Lear has remained active with civil advocacy and numerous Democratic and progressive causes, especially causes related to the First Amendment.

One of Lear's most memorable shows, *All in the Family*, was significant for its progressive treatment of such subjects as racism, homosexuality, rape, abortion, women's rights, and the Vietnam War. It showcased the always conservative Archie Bunker arguing with his liberal son-in-law, Michael "Meathead" Stivic, about numerous issues of the day. Bunker usually ended an argument by blowing a raspberry. Lear has stated that part of the inspiration for Bunker was Lear's own father, whom Lear describes as a bigot. One of the most impressive aspects of both *All in the Family* and *Sanford and Son* is that both bigots and more progressive audiences alike would laugh at the jokes. The first audience would laugh in agreement with Bunker and Sanford, while the more progressive audiences would laugh at the ignorance of the bigot.

Lear has influenced a generation of humorists, perhaps most notably Seth MacFarlane, creator of *Family Guy*, who has cited Lear as one of his core influences. Indeed, the humorists whom Lear has influenced continue to influence new and aspiring humorists, making him a powerful figure in American humor.

See also: MacFarlane, Seth

Further Reading

Bartholome, Lynn. "Loud Mouthed and Liberated: The Women of Norman Lear." *Popular Culture Review* 5, no. 1 (February 1994): 139–147.

Landy, Thomas M. "What's Missing from This Picture? Norman Lear Explains." *Commonweal* 119, no. 17 (October 1992): 17–20.

McCrohan, Donna. *Archie, Edith, Mike & Gloria: The Tumultuous History of* All in the Family. New York: Workman, 1988.

Stephen Powers

LENO, JAY (1950–)

James Leno, later known as Jay Leno, was born in New Rochelle, New York. His mother was a Scottish immigrant and his father was the child of Italian immigrants. While he was still young, Leno's family moved to Andover, Massachusetts. Leno struggled in school, likely because of his dyslexia. Despite a guidance counselor's suggestion that Leno drop out of high school, he finished and went on to earn a bachelor's degree in speech therapy from Emerson College. It was there, in Boston, that Leno began his work as a stand-up comic. In addition to his regular work in this venue, Leno wrote for television, including the show *Good Times*, and appeared in a number of films. While none of his acting performances garnered success or critical acclaim, Leno did find regular work, landing appearances on noteworthy shows such as *Laverne and Shirley* and in the movie *Almost Heaven*. In 1980, Leno married Mavis Leno, and the two remain together.

Leno's rise to prominence came less through acting than through his stand-up performances and regular appearances on television talk shows. Leno has a reputation for performing frequently even while maintaining his schedule hosting. In the late 1980s, he began regularly substituting for Johnny Carson as host on *The Tonight Show*. While Leno was generally acknowledged as successful in filling in for Carson during absences, a minor controversy occurred during the transfer from Carson's regular hosting duties to Leno's assumption of the full-time role of host of *The Tonight Show*. Many viewers expected David Letterman, who had hosted the show following Carson's for a decade, to be given the helm of *The Tonight Show*. A number of comedians rallied to Letterman's side after he was denied the full-time hosting job and went to CBS in a time slot that was in direct competition with Leno's show. In addition, another comedian, Arsenio Hall, was given a show on the Fox Network that was in direct competition with *The Tonight Show*; Hall publicly declared that he would beat Leno in the ratings. All that said, Leno consistently received solid ratings and was supported by NBC. While not all comedians have supported him (Bill Hicks has a famous bit skewering Leno as a sellout for interviewing subpar performers on *The Tonight Show* and appearing in advertisements for Doritos), Leno has enjoyed sufficient commercial success to keep him in the public eye.

Even so, a second controversy emerged in relation to Leno's status as *Tonight Show* host. As fellow talk-show host Conan O'Brien's contract was expiring with NBC, significant discussions took place about O'Brien's future. As with Letterman and Carson, O'Brien, who served as the host of the show following *The Tonight Show*, was the presumptive successor to Leno's position. At one point, Leno declared on *The Tonight Show* that he would welcome O'Brien as a successor, stating that he was "no Johnny"—in reference to the fact that Johnny Carson was able to helm the show well into his elder years and that Leno would be in his sixties at the time that O'Brien's contract would be expiring. Nevertheless, after O'Brien took over *The Tonight Show*, NBC (the network broadcasting the show) pushed O'Brien's show back to make room for a shortened version of *The Tonight Show* being hosted by Leno. Many prominent comedians, led by Patton Oswalt, who was the first to publicly discuss the conflict, indicated their dissatisfaction with Leno's approach to the conflict. Rosie O'Donnell also weighed in, referring to Leno as "a bully" for how he handled the conflict. Still other comedians—most notably Jerry Seinfeld and Paul Reiser—expressed support for Leno, claiming that his decision was motivated by business concerns and the demands put upon Leno by NBC executives rather than out of jealousy for O'Brien.

The two conflicts—first with Letterman and then with O'Brien—have had a lasting impact on public perception of Leno's overall career arc. Despite the negative aspects, Leno continues to work both on screen and in clubs, putting out a large volume of material.

Much of Leno's work focuses on pop cultural satire. One of his most popular segments on *The Tonight Show*, "Jaywalking," would show Leno interviewing people on the street, asking them questions to which they should know the answer and watching the people fall well short of the correct response. In one notable example, Leno asked a person on the street, "What was the Gettysburg Address?" and was met with the response, "I don't know the actual address"—indicating that the person being questioned understood the title to refer to a postal address rather than the speech that Lincoln gave at Gettysburg.

See also: Carson, Johnny; Hicks, Bill; Letterman, David; O'Brien, Conan

Further Reading

Carter, Bill. *The Late Shift: Letterman, Leno and the Network Battle for the Night*. New York: Hyperion, 1995.

Grove, Lloyd. "The Twilight of Jay Leno." *Newsweek Global* 161, no. 27 (July 24, 2013): 1.

Poniewozik, James. "Jay Leno Says Goodbye to *The Tonight Show*, Probably for Real This Time." *Time.com* (February 10, 2014): 1.

Zeke Jarvis

LETTERMAN, DAVID (1947–)

David Letterman was born in Indianapolis, Indiana, near the Indianapolis Motor Speedway. Growing up, he was a fan of racing and collected model cars. While Letterman was growing up, his father had a heart attack; Letterman has talked about the impact of worrying about his father's health. During his high school years, Letterman worked as a stock boy in a grocery store. After graduating from high school, he attended Ball State University, where he did not perform well academically. In 1968, Letterman married his first wife; the couple divorced in 1978.

The Comedians Strike Back: The Comedy Store Trouble

In the 1980s, stand-up comedy was booming. While this created opportunities for many comics, it also eventually led to a surplus of comedians which generated a real sense of competition. While this friction existed in some level throughout the United States, it was perhaps most intense in California, where stand-up comedians formed a sort of union and picketed outside of The Comedy Store, asking for wages for their performances and more opportunities for stage time. Rising but prominent comics like David Letterman and Jay Leno carried signs and demanded changes, which greatly upset club owner Mitzi Shore. Eventually, the dispute ended after one comedian, Steve Lubetkin, committed suicide in despair over having been shut out of The Comedy Store.

Even though the conflict was resolved, it served as a major transitional moment for many stand-up comics. In their field, the competition for real and sustained careers in stand-up comedy became less attainable and more competitive. It also left some long-lasting anxieties and frustrations for both comedians and club owners.

At Ball State, Letterman graduated from the department of radio and television. While there, he worked for the college radio station. After graduating, Letterman worked as a weatherman, where he was known for his odd antics, such as claiming that the area would experience hail the size of canned hams or that the borders between states had been erased.

Letterman eventually moved to Los Angeles after being encouraged to do so by his friends and his wife. In Los Angeles, he began working as a writer, first writing for comedian Jimmie Walker, then for a number of television shows. He also appeared on variety shows and sitcoms. Although Letterman gained some attention from his variety show appearances, it was his appearances on *The Tonight Show* that gave him the greatest public prominence. Letterman also began hosting the show in Johnny Carson's absence, which led him to getting a morning comedy show on NBC. While the show did well with the critics, its irreverent comedic style was not popular with mainstream audiences. Rather than continue the morning show, NBC gave Letterman a late-night talk show in 1982, called *Late Night with David Letterman*. The first guest was Bill Murray, who helped establish the offbeat comedy that would become the show's trademark.

Letterman's late-night show was both a critical and popular success. In 1992, when Johnny Carson was retiring from his hosting duties on *The Tonight Show*, many expected Letterman to be announced as Carson's replacement, including Letterman himself. When the job was given to Jay Leno, Letterman became angry and announced that he would be leaving NBC. Letterman moved to *The Late Show* on CBS, which competed directly with Leno's version of *The Tonight Show*. While Letterman's show originally beat Leno's in the ratings, Leno's show eventually began to consistently beat Letterman's. Some attribute this shift to Letterman's decision to tone down some of the more bizarre humor that had been popular in a later time slot. In 2000, Letterman had to take a leave of absence from his show while he had heart surgery. While Letterman was recovering, the spot was filled with a mix of reruns and guest hosts. Letterman's show also featured the final television appearance for Johnny Carson, which took place in 2005. Some see this as an indication that Carson sided with Letterman in the dispute between him and Leno.

In 2009, Letterman married his long-time girlfriend. The two are still married and have a child, despite a scandal involving Letterman's sexual relations with a staff member of his show. Letterman continues to live in Connecticut and host his show, but plans to retire from this position in 2015 (Stephen Colbert will take his place).

Letterman is generally known for his offbeat humor and unconventional approach to hosting, often using staff members such as the cue card holder or director as performers rather than professional performers. He is also well known for bringing his mother onto the show, particularly during holidays, as a way to further undercut the appearance of professionalism and seriousness that many other talk shows attempt to accomplish. In addition, Letterman departs from expectations for talk shows by referring directly to awkward aspects of the show or satirically discussing struggles or uncomfortable topics in his personal life.

With his unconventional approach, Letterman has exerted a tremendous influence on a generation of comedians with late-night talk shows. From the creation of bizarre personas for his staff on Conan O'Brien's show to the use of family members by Jimmy Kimmel, Chelsea Handler, and Kathy Griffin, Letterman's influence can be seen throughout the late-night television landscape. Many comics have also been supportive of Letterman in his battles with NBC and Jay Leno. Kimmel has been particularly vociferous in his support and, though he never stated it outright, many perceive Carson as having favored Letterman over Leno. That said, Letterman has also engaged in some very public feuds and disagreements with celebrities. After allowing one of Bill Hicks's routines to be cut from his show, Letterman caught some backlash, though he eventually apologized and had Hicks's mother on the show, also airing the bit in its entirety. Letterman has sparred with Oprah Winfrey and Cher after a series of jokes and challenged Madonna during an appearance on his show when he felt that she had been overly provocative. Ultimately, Letterman has settled his differences with most of these figures, appearing with Madonna on an MTV Awards ceremony and having Oprah on his show as well as granting a rare interview with her. Given the many comics who emulate his work and the many years he has spent hosting, Letterman is clearly a major figure in television comedy.

See also: Carson, Johnny; Hicks, Bill; Leno, Jay

Further Reading

Browne, David. "David Letterman: Year One." *Rolling Stone* 1140 (September 29, 2011): 74–82.

Carter, Bill. *The Late Shift: Letterman, Leno and the Network Battle for the Night*. New York: Hyperion, 1995.

Poniewozik, James. "David Letterman Is Ending *Late Night*'s Great Run." *Time.com* (April 5, 2014): 1.

Zeke Jarvis

MAC, BERNIE (1957–2008)

Bernard McCullough was born in Chicago, growing up on the city's South Side as part of a large family and in a rough neighborhood. He attended Chicago Vocational Career Academy. Growing up, McCullough was influenced by a combination of watching the Three Stooges and listening to Redd Foxx and Richard Pryor. He began his own stand-up work in the Cotton Club in Chicago.

McCullough, who adopted the stage name Bernie Mac, rose to minor prominence after winning the Miller Lite Comedy Search. Thereafter, he opened for a variety of performers, including one of his comedy idols, Redd Foxx. Mac began a slow but steady climb to fame that culminated with him becoming one of the four Original Kings of Comedy and receiving his own sitcom. On his path to stardom, Mac had appeared in many cult films, including *Friday*, and had an HBO special, "Midnight Mac." He also starred in a number of commercially successful films, including the

Ocean's 11 series and *Transformers*. In 2008, Mac died from complications of sarcoidosis and pneumonia.

Mac was known for his observations about family life, particularly his undercutting of his own masculinity and desire to be stoic in his sitcom work. As with many family-based sitcoms, Mac often played the well-intentioned but bumbling father who was manipulated or outsmarted by his children or wife. His show was unconventional in its breaking of the fourth wall: Mac would address the viewers directly, always referring to them as "America." It also had captions or comments that appeared to be handwritten, adding to the humor and instability of the visual presentation. In addition, the show was unconventional in that it portrayed Mac taking care of children who were not his own. According to the show's narrative, Mac and his wife took the three children in after his sister entered rehabilitation. This backdrop helped to heighten the awkwardness and uncertainty with which Mac's character tried to navigate his new life.

In his stand-up work, Mac was quite similar to his television persona. He was well known for not only his funny material, but also, like Pryor, for his careful use of facial expressions to emphasize punchlines and establish the various personas that he might use on stage. As part of *The Original Kings of Comedy*, Mac helped to establish a revival of African American stand-up comics, bringing another level of diversity to the American cultural landscape.

Further Reading

Christian, Margena A. "Bernie Mac." *Jet* 114, no. 7 (August 25, 2008): 44–47.

Coleman, Robin R. Means. *African American Viewers and the Black Situation Comedy: Situating Racial Humor*. London: Routledge, 2000.

Fernandez, Jay A. "Papa Don't Take No Mess." *Savoy: Power, Substance, Style* 2, no. 4 (May 2002): 53–57.

Zeke Jarvis

MACFARLANE, SETH (1973–)

Seth MacFarlane was born in Kent, Connecticut. From a very young age, he had a keen interest in animation, sketching figures like Fred Flintstone and Woody Woodpecker. At age nine, MacFarlane was already publishing a comic strip in Kent's local newspaper. After graduating from high school, MacFarlane attended the Rhode Island School of Design. During his time at RISD, MacFarlane also directed films. His thesis, *The Life of Larry*, would become the foundation for his show *Family Guy* and would also get him a job working for Hanna-Barbera Studios.

Although MacFarlane had studied animation, he was actually hired as a writer. At Hanna-Barbera, he focused on shows such as *Dexter's Laboratory* and *Johnny Bravo*. After working on a number of small projects, MacFarlane landed a prime-time animation show on Fox in 1999. As with Mike Judge on *King of the Hill*, MacFarlane worked in a variety of capacities on *Family Guy*, voicing some of the characters, writing and running the show, and even doing some of the animation early on. Although the show drew a cult following, its time slot was switched and it struggled in its competition against some highly rated shows. In 2002, the show was canceled. On the strength of syndicated episodes on the Cartoon Network's *Adult Swim* programming and DVD sales, the show was revived by Fox starting in 2005. That same year, Fox signed MacFarlane to create another show, *American Dad!*; again, MacFarlane performed both voice and writing work on this series. MacFarlane also created a *Family Guy* spin-off called *The Cleveland Show*, but it was significantly less successful than either of his other two shows.

MacFarlane has also directed films, most notably the movie *Ted*, about a grown man and his living teddy bear, who behaves in vulgar and offensive ways. The movie achieved both commercial and critical success. MacFarlane has also performed in other ways, releasing an album of big-band songs, hosting a number of Comedy Central Roasts, and hosting the Oscars in 2013. MacFarlane continues to work both on and off the screen.

MacFarlane readily acknowledges the influence that other humorists and series have had on his comic sensibilities—most notably, the impact of *The Simpsons* and *All in the Family* on his work on *Family Guy*. With their combination of irreverent treatments of popular culture and prominent figures and edgy playing with stereotypes and other controversial topics, the impact of both shows clearly comes through in his work. Likewise, the send-up of conservative politics in *American Dad!* is very much in keeping with the work of figures like Matt Groening and one of MacFarlane's other stated influences, Bill Maher. Nevertheless, some of MacFarlane's satire has received significant criticism from viewers and cultural commentators who fail to differentiate between the views of MacFarlane and the views of idiotic or satirical figures like Peter Griffin from *Family Guy* and Stan Smith of *American Dad!*; this perception has led many critics to cite these shows as a sign of American culture's further decline. MacFarlane has also received criticism for his references to former vice-presidential candidate Sarah Palin's daughter, who suffers from Down syndrome. MacFarlane has often been the focus of criticism from conservative commentators, because, in addition to maintaining his shows' edgy styles, he is outspoken in his support of both the Democratic party and gay rights. MacFarlane has consistently stood by his shows, arguing that their satirical nature should undercut the seriousness with which his critics approach his work. Despite many of the criticisms that MacFarlane has received, he has achieved critical and commercial success in a number of venues, and the impact that his work has had on contemporary American culture is undeniable.

See also: Groening, Matt

Further Reading

Rabin, Nathan. "Seth MacFarlane Interview." *Onion AV Club,* January 26, 2005. http://www.avclub.com/article/seth-macfarlane-13910.

Ricke, LaChrystal D. "Funny or Harmful? Derogatory Speech on Fox's *Family Guy*." *Communication Studies* 63, no. 2 (April–June 2012): 119–135.

Sienkiewicz, Matt, and Nick Marx. "Click Culture: The Perils and Possibilities of *Family Guy* and Convergence-Era Television." *Communication & Critical/Cultural Studies* 11, no. 2 (June 2014): 103–119.

Zeke Jarvis

MAHER, BILL (1956–)

Bill Maher was born in New York City to Catholic and Jewish parents. Maher was unaware of his Jewish heritage during his early years as he was raised Catholic. The religious background of his life was further disrupted when his father left the Catholic Church because of its position on birth control. For the largest portion of Maher's life, his family lived in New Jersey. After graduating from high school, Maher attended Cornell University, where he earned a degree in English in 1978.

After graduating, Maher began his stand-up career. He steadily gained recognition, eventually becoming the host at Catch a Rising Star, a comedy club in New York. While performing there, Maher gained sufficient attention to land some TV time on Johnny Carson's *Tonight Show*. Carson was an idol for Maher, and he even wrote an article about Carson for *Rolling Stone* shortly after Carson's death.

Maher continued to appear on television and in small parts in B-movies until he was given his own show on Comedy Central, *Politically Incorrect with Bill Maher*. The show was a critical success and featured a wide variety of guests, including comedians, politicians, musicians, actors, authors, and other prominent figures. Eventually, the show transitioned from Comedy Central to ABC. *Politically Incorrect* continued for five years, until, after the attacks on September 11, 2001, the show was canceled. In an exchange with a guest, Maher contended that the terrorists, while being reprehensible, were also brave. Maher later apologized for his remarks (and cited his long-standing support for the U.S. military), but he did receive an award for defending free speech from the L.A. Press Club as well as a significant groundswell of support from his viewers. About one year after *Politically Incorrect* was canceled, Maher began his show *Real Time with Bill Maher* on HBO. Unlike *Politically Incorrect*, *Real Time* tended to have more socially significant guests. During his run on *Real Time*, Maher also made the documentary *Religulous*, which focused on extremists and other figures who undercut the validity of religious expression in America. In addition, Maher wrote the novel *True Story*, which was about the era of stand-up comedy in which Maher established himself.

Although Maher has been romantically linked to a wide variety of women, he has never married, and he has regularly been critical of marriage. Maher continues to work on television and as a political commentator on a variety of shows. Currently, he lives in Los Angeles.

Maher is a complex figure. While he consistently has been interested in social and political commentary, Maher (like fellow comedians Bill Hicks, Lenny Bruce, and Mort Sahl) defies a simplistic political classification. While Maher is aligned with conservative thought in some aspects, such as in his unfailing support for the military, he also promotes a liberal viewpoint in many ways, such as by supporting the legalization of marijuana and gay rights. Although Maher could be classified as a libertarian, he criticizes the Libertarian party when it clings too closely to certain causes, not showing careful or thoughtful approaches to issues. Another prominent example of this sort of political flexibility is his relationship with People for the Ethical Treatment of Animals (PETA).

That said, not all of Maher's comedy is focused on politics. Maher often grounds his jokes in pop cultural references, joking about hip-hop culture or the less appealing aspects of popular culture. Even so, Maher remains known primarily for his political commentary in both his television work and his stand-up.

In his position as host for a comedy club and on two shows, he has also served as the gatekeeper for many stand-ups looking to establish their careers. In this way, Maher is very much like his role model, Johnny Carson, who was able to launch the careers of many comedians. Maher has been outspoken in his observations of other comics, particularly Jay Leno, whom he referred to as a robot at one point. Maher's forthright positions on both comedy and politics make him an interesting public figure to watch.

See also: Tompkins, Paul F.

Further Reading

Dickinson, Tim. "Bill Maher Is, Duh, Winning." *Rolling Stone* 1129 (April 28, 2011): 80–83.

Maher, Bill. *The New Rules: A Funny Look at How Everybody But Me Has Their Head up Their Ass*. New York: Plume, 2012.

Parker, Kathleen. "Bill Maher Makes a Point." *Washington Post*, May 14, 2014. http://www.washingtonpost.com/opinions/kathleen-parker-bill-maher-speaks-his-mind-unfortunately/2014/05/13/1256ff28-dadc-11e3-b745-87d39690c5c0_story.html.

Zeke Jarvis

MARSHALL, GARRY (1934–)

Garry Marshall was born in the Bronx in New York. His father was an industrial filmmaker and his mother taught tap dancing. While still a child, Marshall appeared on *The George Burns and Gracie Allen Show*. After graduating from high school, he attended Northwestern University and served in the U.S. Army. He began his writing career as a joke writer for various stand-up comics, eventually landing a job on *The Tonight Show* with Jack Paar. He then began working on a number of iconic television shows, including *The Dick Van Dyke Show*, *Happy Days*, and *Laverne and Shirley*, among others. In the early 1980s, Marshall began his movie directing career, which has spanned decades and included a number of commercial successes. Marshall has also acted on a number of television shows. He is part of a large family of humorists, which includes his sister Penny Marshall and former brother-in-law Rob Reiner. Marshall is the father of three children. His son, Scott, is also a movie director.

Marshall is principally known for directing romantic comedies. The reception of his work has been mixed. While he has consistently achieved a high level of commercial success, some critics feel that his work is predictable or tame. Even so, his work contains a striking sense of dialogue that fits with many other humorists. In addition, he often displays an intricate sense of plotting and story that adds to the overall effect of the comic situations that he puts on display in the core of his work. While some critics see the plots dominating his sense of characterization, by having relatively flat characters who behave in ways that serve the plot and the sympathies of the audiences rather than themselves, many appreciate his focus on tradition.

One source of admiration for Marshall along these lines comes from audiences who appreciate more wholesome humor, though Marshall's work does also have some sexual themes. *Valentine's Day*, for instance, features suggestions of nudity, a homosexual relationship, and a strong sense of sexuality. One of his most successful films, *Pretty Woman*, features a woman (played by Julia Roberts) who is a prostitute and is portrayed in a positive light. Some viewers see this as demonstrating Marshall's ability to adapt to a variety of eras and social contexts. Whether seen as a practitioner of high art or not, Marshall has created iconic films and characters for decades, and his sense of timing and dialogue has been respected among multiple generations of viewers and humorists.

Further Reading

Goldman, Andrew. "The Shark Jumper." *New York Times Magazine* (April 29, 2012): 12.

Marshall, Garry. *My Happy Days in Hollywood: A Memoir*. New York: Crown Archetype, 2012.

Scala, Elizabeth; "Pretty Women: The Romance of the Fair Unknown, Feminism, and Contemporary Romantic Comedy." *Film and History* 29, nos. 1–2 (1999): 34–45.

Zeke Jarvis

MARX BROTHERS (CHICO, 1887–1961; HARPO, 1888–1964; GROUCHO, 1890–1977; GUMMO, 1892–1977; ZEPPO, 1901–1979)

The Marx Brothers (born Leonard, Adolph, Julius Henry, Milton, and Herbert Manfred, respectively) were all born in New York City, sons of Jewish immigrants. Their father was French and their mother was German. The children were encouraged to pursue artistic endeavors from an early age, even performing with their uncle, Al Shean. Harpo, in particular, excelled, becoming adept at various instruments, including the harp, from which he earned his name. Although the group began as musical performers, they began to explore comedy when Groucho delivered a series of jibes at an audience after an interruption. When the audience found his lines funny rather than aggressive, the group began to focus on using humor as the core of their act.

During World War I, the group began to downplay their German heritage, which led them to develop the comic personas that they would continue to use for most of their careers. Groucho was the wise-cracking ringleader of mischief, Harpo was a silent jokester who had wild hair and carried a bicycle horn, Chico used a heavy Italian accent and often provided comical misunderstandings, and Zeppo played the straight man, often having the romantic angle in their movies. By 1920, the Marx Brothers had become a tremendously popular theater act, performing both sketches and improvisational acts. The brothers credit both some of their material and their stage personas to their uncle Al Shean.

Around this time, films with sound ("talkies") were beginning to become popular, and the Marx Brothers found this format to be an effective vehicle for their humor. They signed a deal with Paramount Pictures that led to a number of highly

The Marx Brothers, left to right: Chico, Groucho, Harpo, and Zeppo. The group's bizarre humor helped them to successfully transition from vaudeville to Hollywood films. (AP Photo)

successful films, including *Horse Feathers* and *Duck Soup*. Around this time Groucho and Chico also began working on a popular radio show. After the brothers stopped working for Paramount, Zeppo and Gummo left performing to work as agents, founding an agency that would represent major figures like Jack Benny and Lana Turner. Groucho, Chico, and Harpo signed with MGM, continuing to work in film, albeit with more plot-driven movies than they had at Paramount. Perhaps their biggest success with MGM was *Night at the Opera*. After working at MGM, then ROK, and finally United Artists, the brothers began to further separate. Chico and Harpo worked sometimes alone and sometimes together. Groucho consistently worked on his own, first on the game show *You Bet Your Life*. The brothers' final television appearance together came on a precursor to *The Tonight Show* in 1957. Five years later, Groucho would appear on the show to introduce Johnny Carson as the new host. In 1970, the brothers (with the exception of Chico, who had died, and Zeppo, who had left performing) did voice work for the animated show *The Mad, Mad, Mad Comedians*. The brothers also made sporadic appearances and received a variety of honors over the final years of their lives.

The Marx Brothers were known for their highly imaginative conceits and performances. They even inspired surrealist artist Salvador Dali to write a short screenplay for the group, albeit one that was unproduced and so bizarre as to be essentially unfilmable. Nevertheless, the Marx Brothers were able to balance a zany brand of humor with mainstream success in a way that few comics have. They were also well steeped in the vaudevillian tradition, such that much of their humor incorporated puns, comic misunderstandings, and outlandish characters. While these forms of humor were not necessarily invented by the brothers, they certainly are some of the most well-known practitioners of it. While the Marx Brothers may now be less prominent than they once were, their impact remains clear across a variety of media, including the film *Brain Donors* and the animated series *Animaniacs*, in addition to more subtle, but still prominent, examples.

Further Reading

Flaig, Paul. "Lacan's Harpo." *Cinema Journal* 50, no. 4 (Summer 2011): 98–116.

Louvish, Simon. *Monkey Business: The Lives and Legends of the Marx Brothers*. New York: Thomas Dunne Books, 2000.

Marx, Harpo. *Harpo Speaks!* New York: Bernard Geis Associates, 1961.

Zeke Jarvis

MILLER, DENNIS (1953–)

Dennis Miller was born in Pittsburgh and grew up in the suburbs. His parents divorced while Miller was a child, with Miller subsequently being raised by his mother. He graduated from high school in 1971 and attended Point Park University in Pittsburgh, where he majored in journalism.

In 1979, Miller won a prize for writing the runner-up for Joke of the Year for *Playboy*. Shortly thereafter, he began work hosting a Saturday afternoon show for teenagers as well as writing humorous essays and performing stand-up. He also appeared on *Star Search*, where he lost to Sinbad. Although he may not have won the contest, Miller honed his craft and gained in prominence through this experience.

In 1985, Miller was given the opportunity to anchor the Weekend Update desk on *Saturday Night Live*. Miller's work on Weekend Update was characterized by a combination of sharp political commentary and silly observations about odd images from the week. He also had a very clearly developed persona, having clearly styled long hair, a high-pitched laugh, and small physical mannerisms. This led a number of people on the show to do impersonations of him.

After leaving *Saturday Night Live*, Miller got his own show, *The Dennis Miller Show*, where he had on a number of up-and-coming stars and employed a staff of writers who would go on to make significant contributions to humor, including Norm MacDonald and Bob Odenkirk. After two seasons, Miller moved his show to HBO, where he had considerable success, with the writing staff winning five Emmys. In 2002, his show was canceled, but by then he had begun his short-lived stint on *Monday Night Football*. Miller's commentary often employed esoteric references that went unappreciated by most of the viewing audience. After the failure on *Monday Night Football*, Miller began a phase of his career devoted more clearly to political commentary, having appearances first on CNBC and then on the Fox News Network. Miller also began hosting a radio show, to which he now devotes much of his time, although he has continued to regularly appear on shows like Bill Maher's *Politically Incorrect* and in movies such as *Thank You for Smoking* and *Bordello of Blood*.

Miller married Carolyn Espley in 1988. The two live in Santa Barbara with their two sons.

During the *Saturday Night Live* phase of his career, Miller's work was often characterized by a laidback style where he established a persona of cool distance from the subjects that he was observing. He would frequently belittle conservative politicians from his position on Weekend Update, though he was generally not leftist and did sometimes support conservative figures with his comedy. Still, there is considerable debate about a perceived shift in Miller's politics after the terrorist attacks of September 11, 2001. Many consider Miller to have shifted his politics significantly, having become an overt and consistent conservative. Miller himself maintains that he has not changed his essential political beliefs, but does admit that the attacks changed some of his feelings about his relationship to America. Other comedians have agreed that Miller has not changed as significantly as some critics claim. Miller's colleague from *Saturday Night Live*, Al Franken, also claims that Miller has always had a conservative streak and that the changing nature of media outlets simply put it on more visible display. Still, the perception clearly exists. Miller regularly discusses his politics in a defensive way, though his perceived change has not kept him off of many shows, including Howard Stern's radio programs and Bill Maher's shows.

In addition to his political beliefs, Miller is most known for making very obscure references. In parodies and impressions of him from *The Simpsons* and *Saturday Night Live* both during his run (performed by Dana Carvey and Tom Hanks, respectively) and after he had left *SNL* (performed by Jimmy Fallon), portrayals of Miller have included his use of surprising connections and esoteric references, his trademark high-pitched laugh, and his head-shaking and other mannerisms. While Miller can be a divisive figure due to his political stances and audience-specific references, he continues to maintain a significant audience with his radio show, television appearances, and other performances.

See also: Franken, Al

Further Reading

Dunne, Michael. "Dennis Miller: The Po-Mo Comic." *Humor: International Journal of Humor Research* 13, no. 1 (2000): 77–89.

Miller, Dennis. *The Rants*. New York: Main Street Books, 1997.

Waisanen, Don. "Satirical Visions with Public Consequence?: Dennis Miller's Ranting Rhetorical Persona." *American Communication Journal* 13, no. 1 (Spring 2011): 24–44.

Zeke Jarvis

MILLER, LARRY (1953–)

Larry Miller was born in Valley Stream, New York. After graduating from high school, he went to Amherst College, where he studied music and graduated with honors. Miller then moved to New York City in hopes of becoming a professional musician. While working clubs, he began doing stand-up comedy. Miller quickly became successful enough as a comic that he left his musical career behind. In 1978, he began working in film. He continued landing small parts in movies and television, breaking through into mainstream recognition with his role in the movie *Pretty Woman*, directed by Garry Marshall, who uses Miller in many of his films. Miller is close friends with a number of prominent stand-up comedians, most notably Jerry Seinfeld, on whose sitcom he appeared as a doorman who antagonized

Jerry for no discernible reason. Miller auditioned for the role of George Costanza on the show, but lost it to Jason Alexander. In addition to his regular television and movie work, Miller continues to perform stand-up as well as write a column for *The Daily Standard* and perform a weekly podcast for the ACE Network. He is married to Eileen Miller, who is also a writer and producer.

In Miller's acting work, he often plays a pompous or arrogant character, appearing multiple times as a college dean and as the overbearing father in *10 Things I Hate about You*. Miller has appeared in a number of Christopher Guest's mockumentaries, which rely heavily on improvisational work and exchanges with a strong sense of comedic timing. In his stand-up work, Miller is known for his sharp wit and patient, cool delivery.

See also: Seinfeld, Jerry

Further Reading

Borns, Betsy. *Comic Lives*. New York: Touchstone, 1987.

Miller, Larry. *Spoiled Rotten America: Outrages of Everyday Life*. New York: Harper Entertainment, 2006.

Shydner, Rich. *I Killed: True Stories of the Road from America's Top Comics*. New York: Three Rivers Press, 2007.

Zeke Jarvis

MOORE, MICHAEL (1954–)

Michael Moore was born in Flint, Michigan. His mother worked as a secretary and his father worked on an automobile assembly line. When he was 18 years old, Moore served on the school board in Davison, Michigan, where he had grown up in a Catholic household and attended a Catholic elementary school. After dropping out of the University of Michigan-Flint, Moore founded and wrote for *The Michigan Voice*. From there, he moved to *Mother Jones*, a liberal periodical based in California. He was fired after only a few months.

Moore started his first film, *Roger & Me*, with settlement money he received from *Mother Jones* in a wrongful dismissal lawsuit. This award-winning documentary takes an unflinching look at the unemployment problem in Moore's hometown of Flint after General Motors CEO Roger Smith closed auto factories there; it was released in 1989 to wide acclaim. Moore's short follow-up to *Roger & Me*, entitled *Pets or Meat: The Return to Flint*, aired on PBS in 1992.

In 1991, Moore married producer Kathleen Glynn. They filed for divorce in 2013.

In 1994 and 1995, Moore hosted a BBC newsmagazine series called *TV Nation*. The series aired on NBC and Fox in the United States. Moore's next film, *Canadian Bacon*, was released in 1995, but was not a critical or commercial success. *The Big One*, a documentary about a tour for his book, *Downsize This! Random Threats from an Unarmed American*, followed in 1997. Both the film and the book criticize American corporations for mass layoffs in a time of record profits. Moore published *Stupid White Men*, a book of political humor and criticism of U.S. foreign policy, in 2001.

Moore's next film, *Bowling for Columbine*, was released in 2002 to wide commercial success that was unusual for a documentary. Earning praise from critics, *Bowling for Columbine* won an Academy Award for best feature documentary and was the highest-grossing mainstream documentary of all time until Moore's *Fahrenheit 9/11* was released in 2004. *Fahrenheit 9/11*, with Moore pictured on the promotional poster holding hands with President George W. Bush on the White House lawn, fiercely attacked the Bush administration and its decision to go to war in Iraq in 2003. The film also questioned much of the media coverage of the War on Terror; depicts Bush as largely unresponsive when he first learned, in a classroom in Florida, that the terrorist attacks of September 11, 2001, had just occurred; and chronicles the Bush family's ties with the family of Osama bin Laden. Infuriated conservative groups pressured theaters not to show the film; the resulting publicity pushed *Fahrenheit 9/11* to break box office records for a documentary. It also won the Palme d'Or prize at the 2004 Cannes Film Festival. The film broke more sales records when it was issued on DVD, with sales in excess of 2 million copies on its first day of release alone.

In between *Bowling for Columbine* and *Fahrenheit 9/11*, Moore published *Dude, Where's My Country*, another book of political humor that attacks President Bush, the Iraq War, and corporate America. Moore released the film *Sicko*, which is a look at the flaws of the U.S. health care system, especially the profit-driven motives of the pharmaceutical and insurance industries, in 2007. *Capitalism: A Love Story*, a film exposé of the financial crisis of 2007, followed in 2009. Moore has also directed videos for the band Rage Against the Machine and been a frequent guest on talk shows like Bill Maher's *Real Time* and *The Rachel Maddow Show*.

Moore is best known for his harsh criticism of the wealthy in America. From his portrayal of Roger Smith as being a greedy and heartless boss to the discussions of the entire Bush family in *Fahrenheit 9/11*, he has consistently tried to highlight problems with corporate America and America's distribution of wealth. However, Moore also makes a point of incorporating unusual and humorous approaches in his work, such as staging a funeral rehearsal for a man unable to get sufficient medical treatment from his HMO and running a ficus tree for public office to demonstrate the general voter apathy in America. While Moore has received a number of very vocal criticisms for both his politics and his antics, he has broadened the understanding of what documentaries can be, adding a strong sense of humor and sarcasm to material that might have been more dully factual and alienating for mass audiences.

See also: Spurlock, Morgan

Further Reading

Kramer, Matthew H. "Michael Moore on Torture, Morality and Law." *Ratio Juris* 25, no. 4 (December 2012): 472–495.

Moore, Michael. *Downsize This! Random Threats from an Unarmed American*. New York: Harper Perennial, 1996.

Poindexter, Mark. "Art Objects: The Works of Michael Moore and Peter Watkins." *Journal of Popular Culture* 44, no. 6 (December 2011): 1268–1288.

Stephen Powers

MURPHY, EDDIE (1961–)

Edward Murphy was born April 3, 1961, in the Brooklyn neighborhood of Bushwick. His father was a transit police officer, but pursued comedy and amateur acting as a pastime. His father died when Murphy was young and his mother became ill, leaving Murphy and his brother in foster care. His mother later recovered and remarried, taking back custody of her children.

Murphy began a career in stand-up comedy in the 1980s, releasing his first comedy album in 1982 and filming his first performance in 1983. He combined his love of acting and comedy by working on the sketch show *Saturday Night Live* in the early 1980s. He became most well known for his character of Buckwheat from the Little Rascals. After his success on television, Murphy made his film debut in the film *48 Hrs.* His first starring role came with the comedy *Beverly Hills Cop* in 1984.

Murphy married Nicole Mitchell in 1993, and the pair had five children. In August 2005, Mitchell filed for divorce, which was finalized in 2006. He exchanged marriage vows with film producer Tracey Edmonds in January 2008, but that relationship eventually ended.

In the 1990s and early 2000s, Murphy appeared in a number of films in which he played multiple roles, as in *The Nutty Professor* and *Norbit*. He also had significant commercial success voicing the role of "Donkey" in the *Shrek* films. Murphy has experienced considerable success in his dramatic acting career as well. His work on the motion picture *Dreamgirls* won him a Golden Globe for best supporting actor, Screen Actors Guild and Broadcast Film Critics Association awards, and an Academy Award nomination.

Murphy's early career was largely defined by his discussions of race, sex, and other matters that were seen as taboo for the time. He also directly referenced other African American comedians, such as Bill Cosby (who advised Murphy to use less profanity in his act) and Richard Pryor (who advised Murphy not to leave the profanity behind). In his film career, Murphy has shown a great degree of versatility. Even when he played a single character, like Axel Foley in the *Beverly Hills Cop* movies, he often had the character impersonate other people or people of other backgrounds. Murphy's largest impact may actually be providing a new model for stand-up comics of his generation, particularly comics of color. Along with Steve Martin, Murphy achieved a level of success that many comedians may have not even dreamed of, filling arenas and selling large numbers of records, rivaling rock stars for prestige and commercial success.

See also: Cosby, Bill; Pryor, Richard

Further Reading

Hiatt, Brian. "Eddie Murphy." *Rolling Stone* 1143 (November 10, 2011): 34–41.

Rottenberg, Josh, Vanessa Juarez, and Adam B. Vary. "How Eddie Got His Groove Back." *Entertainment Weekly* 917 (January 26, 2007): 30–37.

Sanello, Frank. *Eddie Murphy: The Life and Times of a Comic on the Edge*. New York: Birch Lane Press, 1997.

Kristen Franz

MURRAY, BILL (1950–)

William Murray was born in Wilmette, Illinois, a suburb of Chicago. He grew up in a working-class family. His father died when Murray was just 17. To help pay for his tuition to a private high school, Murray worked as a golf caddy during his teenage years. He also was the singer in an amateur rock band and participated in his high school's theater productions.

Murray briefly attended Regis University, majoring in pre-med studies, but he dropped out and returned to Chicago, where he began work with Second City. In 1974, Murray followed his fellow Second City performer John Belushi to New York, where he began to write for *Saturday Night Live*. During this time, Murray had a brief romantic relationship with fellow cast member Gilda Radner. It was also rumored that Murray would sometimes write the first half of a sketch and then write, "Then Gilda does something funny," usually to much success.

In 1979, Murray enjoyed his first starring role in the film *Meatballs*, which was modestly successful. His subsequent films *Caddyshack* and *Stripes* met with much greater success and helped establish Murray as a rising star.

In 1981, Murray married for the first time. He and his wife had two children but divorced in 1996. In 1997, Murray married his second wife, with whom he had four children. The two divorced in 2008.

Murray tried his hand at more dramatic work with *The Razor's Edge*, but the effort was not received well. However, in 1984, he once again achieved significant success with his role in *Ghostbusters*. After his mixed luck with *Ghostbusters* and *The Razor's*

David Letterman at the taping of his first talk-comedy hour, *Late Night with David Letterman*, with guest Bill Murray. Murray has appeared in a number of significant pop culture touchstones, such as *Saturday Night Live*, *Caddyshack*, and *Ghostbusters*. (AP Photo/Nancy Kaye)

Edge, Murray left performing for a short time to study philosophy and history at the Sorbonne in Paris. In 1988, he returned to Hollywood, achieving success in *Scrooged* and *Ghostbusters II*. Murray continued to work regularly, achieving varying levels of success. In 1998, he achieved significant critical acclaim for his performance in *Rushmore*. The film marked the beginning of Murray's work with director Wes Anderson, with whom Murray would collaborate multiple times, typically to high critical praise. Murray continues to appear in a variety of films, both comic and dramatic, but he is still best known and most closely associated with his iconic roles in comedies like *Caddyshack* and *Ghostbusters*.

Not surprisingly, given the smart aleck roles that he occupied in *Stripes*, *Caddyshack*, and *Ghostbusters*, Murray is regarded as a gifted improv comic. His role in *Caddyshack*, for instance, was much smaller than what appeared in the final film, but Murray's extemporaneous bits helped to make him a central part of the film. Even in roles where Murray's character does not have a sharp tongue, his improv background comes through with the odd non sequiturs and absurd misunderstandings between his character and the others. Most of all, Murray is associated with certain lines from his films. *Saturday Night Live* featured the skit "The Quotable *Caddyshack*" which featured many of Murray's most beloved one-liners and further demonstrating the cult following that many of Murray's films have. Murray has also worked with his brothers in a number of films (the siblings had a brief show on Comedy Central featuring them arguing and playing golf), and he is a regular fixture on shows like *Late Night with David Letterman*, where his off-the-wall comedy and natural improvisation match well with Letterman's strange sense of humor. Perhaps the most interesting aspect of Murray's career is the fact that his work has been seen and enjoyed by multiple generations—first as a wild and goofy character in the 1980s and then as a more subdued but equally odd performer in the 2000s and beyond.

Further Reading

Labrecque, Jeff. "The Curious Case of Bill Murray." *Entertainment Weekly* 1109 (July 2, 2010): 48–54.

Murray, Bill, and George Peper. *Cinderella Story: My Life in Golf*. New York: Three Rivers Press, 2000.

Raab, Scott. "Bill Murray." *Esquire* 157, nos. 6/7 (June/July 2012): 41–48.

Zeke Jarvis

NEWHART, BOB (1929–)

George Robert Newhart was born in Oak Park, Illinois, where he lived during his youth with his parents and three sisters. He attended Catholic schools and, after graduating from high school, Loyola University in Chicago, from which he graduated with a degree in business management. Newhart was then drafted into the U.S. Army. He served stateside during the Korean War for two years.

After the war, Newhart held jobs in accounting and business, eventually working in advertising for a Chicago film producer. Newhart and his coworkers would entertain each other by participating in absurd phone calls, which they taped and then sent to various radio stations as audition tapes. While the calls were well received, Newhart's coworkers did not follow him into the realm of public performance. This led to Newhart's tactic of staging half of a phone conversation where he would give a bumbling, nervous response to a strange, unheard speaker on the other end.

Newhart's recordings and albums became quite successful. His 1960 comedy album *The Button-Down Mind of Bob Newhart* was so popular that it surpassed Elvis Presley, hitting number one on the charts. This album, along with its follow-up, *The Button-Down Mind Strikes Back*, held the number one and number two spots on the *Billboard* charts simultaneously. In 1961, Newhart was given a variety show on NBC, *The Bob Newhart Show*. Although the show lasted only a single season, it was very well received, earning both an Emmy and a Peabody Award. In the mid-1960s, Newhart was very active, appearing regularly on *The Ed Sullivan Show* and *The Dean Martin Show*. In 1963, Newhart married his wife, Ginny, with whom he has four children.

In 1972, Newhart got his first starring role on a sitcom, *The Bob Newhart Show*. Many performers who appeared on the show went on to have prominent careers, sometimes—as in the case of Tom Posten—with Newhart on other shows. The show was initially successful, but it began to struggle in the ratings; in 1978, the show ended.

In 1982, Newhart began work on a new show, *Newhart*, which was set in Vermont and incorporated a series of odd, humorous locals who played well against Newhart's befuddled, intentionally stumbling delivery. Like his previous show, *Newhart* was quite successful, staying on the air until 1990.

After *Newhart* ended, Newhart continued to work in television, having two more short-lived sitcoms and a number of appearances, sometimes playing himself, as he did on *The Simpsons*. His appearances were often comedic but sometimes dramatic, as his role on *ER* was. He also did some film work, most notably in *Elf* and *Legally Blonde 2*, as well as voice work in *The Rescuers Down Under*.

Newhart occupies a position of respect among many comics, being best friends with Don Rickles and often being mentioned as an influence by other comedians, including Woody Allen. He has won a number of awards for humor and television performances. He continues to work and is still married to his wife of more than 45 years.

In both his television and stand-up work, Newhart is known for his stammering and discomfort. When surrounded by odd or overbearing characters (sometimes offstage, as in his phone call bits), Newhart's patient insistence on some sort of rational discussion counterbalances the strangeness of the scene, adding a sense of reality and enhancing the humor of the performance. His low-key delivery also helps audiences to sympathize with Newhart. Newhart's ordinary, straight man persona has influenced a number of comics in both stand-up and performance. He has further discussed his approach to comedy and his life in his book *I Shouldn't Even Be Doing This*. Newhart's stated influences include Jack Benny (also well known for occupying the straight man role), Fred Allen, and Robert Benchley, whose bumbling, awkward delivery can be seen in Newhart's performances. Newhart also has a reputation for being a patient, kind performer, as demonstrated by how well liked he is by the majority of his former co-stars. His success in a variety of eras and media has firmly established his position as a significant figure in American humor.

See also: Allen, Woody; Rickles, Don

Further Reading

Martin, Pete. "Backstage with Bob Newhart." *Saturday Evening Post* 234, no. 41 (October 14, 1961): 118–121.

Newhart, Bob. *I Shouldn't Even Be Doing This!: And Other Things That Strike Me as Funny*. New York: Hyperion, 2007.

Sorenson, Jeff. *Bob Newhart*. New York: St. Martin's Press, 1988.

Zeke Jarvis

O'BRIEN, CONAN (1963–)

Conan O'Brien was born in a suburb of Boston, Massachusetts. His father was a doctor and his mother a lawyer, and O'Brien was the third of six children. O'Brien excelled in school, editing his high school newspaper, being honored as the valedictorian of his graduating class, and winning a short-story contest put on by the National Council of Teachers of English. After graduating from high school, O'Brien attended Harvard University, where he studied history and literature and wrote for *Harvard Lampoon*.

After his college graduation, O'Brien moved to Los Angeles to pursue a career in comedy. He wrote for HBO's program *Not Necessarily the News* and performed in the improvisational group known as the Groundlings. Not long after his move to Los Angeles, O'Brien earned a spot as a staff writer for *Saturday Night Live*. In 1991, the pilot episode for *Lockwell*, written by O'Brien, aired, though it was not picked up. Still, the episode has become a cult favorite, being hailed by humorists such as Bill Maher.

That same year, O'Brien left *Saturday Night Live*, getting a job on the writing staff of *The Simpsons*. O'Brien was highly respected by the rest of the writing staff, and some of the episodes that he wrote—"Marge vs. the Monorail," in particular—are fan favorites.

In 1993, O'Brien left the staff of *The Simpsons* to replace David Letterman as the host of the late-night talk show following Johnny Carson's *The Tonight Show*. The early years of his program did not fare well in the ratings. Critics often said that O'Brien's humor was too intellectual or too absurd. Slowly, though, O'Brien gained a steady following, balancing his manic persona with cohost Andy Richter's more sardonic wit and more naturally incorporating the offbeat humor of writer Robert Smigel. O'Brien himself indicated that he felt things had turned around when Letterman appeared as a guest on the show in 1994. O'Brien became a strong force on the late-night landscaping, even negotiating a contract in 2004 that guaranteed him the *Tonight Show* hosting duties, which at the time were held by Jay Leno.

In 2002, O'Brien married. He and his wife have two children.

In 2009, O'Brien replaced Leno as the host of *The Tonight Show*, and Leno was given an earlier talk show. Leno's program struggled in the ratings, and he expressed desire to have a later slot. To accommodate Leno's preferences, NBC pushed back the starting time of *The Tonight Show* by a half hour. After this and other struggles, O'Brien left the show, stating that he saw the time slot move as damaging an important television franchise. Because he was still under contract with NBC, O'Brien could not perform on television for one year. In turn, he began the Legally Prohibited from Being Funny on Television Tour, which was chronicled in the documentary *Conan O'Brien Can't Stop*.

In 2010, O'Brien began work on his new talk show, *Conan*, which runs on TBS. In addition to his work as a talk-show host, O'Brien has made guest appearances on a variety of shows, including *The Simpsons*, and hosted the Primetime Emmys. He currently lives with his family in California.

O'Brien is known for his unconventional humor, including the surrealistic turn *The Simpsons* took during his tenure and odd characters appearing on his first show, including Pimpbot and the Masturbating Bear. He has a dynamic, energetic personality with a keen sense of physical performance and a variety of voices and personas in his performance. Despite the well-publicized struggles between O'Brien, Leno, and NBC, O'Brien has spoken in a level-headed fashion about the turn of events, including very positively about his time as host of *The Tonight Show*. This even-handedness helped to further establish O'Brien's characterization as a likable, intelligent celebrity who focuses on the pursuit of comedy more than fame itself or competitive accomplishments. Although O'Brien will always primarily be associated with his talk-show work, his time on *The Simpsons* and *Saturday Night Live*, as well as his work on *Harvard Lampoon*, has made a significant impact on some of the largest franchises in American comedy.

See also: Leno, Jay; Smigel, Robert

Further Reading

Carter, Bill. *The War for Late Night: When Leno Went Early and Television Went Crazy*. New York: Plume, 2011.

Dinelli, Mark. "Conan Unbound." *Rolling Stone* 1117 (November 11, 2010): 48–83.

Hirschberg, Lynn. "Heeeere's . . . Conan!!!!" *New York Times Magazine* (May 24, 2009): 30–35, 42, 45–46.

Zeke Jarvis

ODENKIRK, BOB (1962–)

Bob Odenkirk was born in Berwyn, Illinois, but grew up in the nearby city of Naperville. Odenkirk had some feelings of antagonism toward both his father, who was an alcoholic, and his hometown, feeling that it lacked opportunities. Odenkirk's parents divorced not long before his father died.

After high school, Odenkirk left Naperville to attend Columbia College in Chicago. He then worked as a DJ at Southern Illinois University, though he eventually moved back to Chicago, where he began pursuing his comedy career through his work at Second City. There, Odenkirk met Robert Smigel and Chris Farley. After working at Second City for a time, Odenkirk got a job writing for *Saturday Night Live*. He wrote a number of successful sketches, including creating Chris Farley's wildly popular character Matt Foley, a motivational speaker whose life had unraveled and who lived, as his catchphrase indicated, "in a van down by the river." Though Odenkirk has indicated that he learned valuable lessons in writing by working under established writers like Al Franken and with friends Conan O'Brien and Robert Smigel, and though Odenkirk did get some minor parts acting on *Saturday Night Live*, his desire to perform led him to leave the writing staff.

Odenkirk subsequently had a variety of acting and writing jobs, working on *The Ben Stiller Show*, *The Larry Sanders Show*, and back at Second City. It was in 1995 that Odenkirk achieved his most notable fame, when he and David Cross created *Mr. Show*. In addition to boosting his own career, the show helped Odenkirk create a venue for several emerging comedians, such as Sarah Silverman, Paul F. Tompkins, and Brian Posehn, among others. During the run of the show, Odenkirk also married, and he and his wife have two children.

Since *Mr. Show* ended, Odenkirk has continued to work in a variety of television shows and films. He has made notable appearances on *Arrested Development* and filled regular roles on *Tom Goes to Mayor* and *Tim and Eric Awesome Show, Great Job*, along with taking on more dramatic work like his role on *Breaking Bad* and *Better Call Saul*, though even these parts often served as comic relief in the shows.

Odenkirk is known for playing characters that are equally confident and incompetent. Like the character he created for Chris Farley, Matt Foley, many of Odenkirk's characters tend to be loud and obnoxious. In terms of his writing, Odenkirk often tends toward the absurd. While David Cross went on to incorporate politics and socially relevant issues into his comedy, Odenkirk has stayed more firmly rooted in pure comedy, as in his work on some of the shows on the Cartoon Network's *Adult Swim* block. He also played an oversized character on a more dramatic series, *Breaking Bad*. His character, Saul Goodman, was a bit of a stereotype—a sleazy accountant who helps a drug dealer to launder his money. Not surprisingly, Odenkirk has listed Monty Python, Steve Martin, and Woody Allen as influences. While his performances are what have given Odenkirk the most attention in the popular sphere, his impact as a writer has been both clear and sustained in the comedy world. From his work on *Saturday Night Live* to his co-creation of the groundbreaking *Mr. Show*, Odenkirk has been and continues to be a major player in the comedy scene.

See also: Cross, David; Posehn, Brian; Stiller, Ben; Tim and Eric

Further Reading

Odenkirk, Bob. *A Load of Hooey (Odenkirk Memorial Library)*. San Francisco: McSweeney's, 2014.

Ryfle, Steve. "Run, Ronnie, Run: The Ronnie Dobbs Story." *Creative Screenwriting* 9, no. 2 (March–April 2002): 18–19.

Saval, Malina. "Absolutely Alternative Duo Challenges Norm." *Variety* 324, no. 9 (June 11, 2014): 33–35.

Zeke Jarvis

POEHLER, AMY (1971–)

Amy Poehler was born in Newton, Massachusetts, and grew up in nearby Burlington. After graduating from high school, Poehler attended Boston College, where she was part of the established improv comedy troupe, My Mother's Fleabag.

In 1993, Poehler graduated from Boston College with a degree in media and communications. She then moved to Chicago, where she studied improv at Second City. During this time, Poehler met Tina Fey. She also became part of the comedy troupe, Upright Citizens Brigade, and began to work with other future *Saturday Night Live* writers and performers, including Horatio Sanz and Adam McKay. The group performed around Chicago before moving to New York, where they produced a sketch comedy show on Comedy Central and opened a theater and training center.

After Comedy Central canceled the Upright Citizens Brigade sketch comedy show, Poehler joined the cast of *Saturday Night Live* in 2001. Her first show was the first *SNL* episode to air after the terrorist attacks of September 11, 2001. In 2004, Poehler took on co-anchor duties for *SNL*'s Weekend Update segment.

Poehler married Will Arnett in 2003, and she appeared on *Arrested Development* multiple times, playing the wife of Arnett's character, GOB Bluth. In 2008, Poehler had a child, stepping away from *SNL* for a brief time.

Poehler subsequently took on a starring role in the television series *Parks and Recreation*. The show was well received and helped a number of comics gain a level of prominence. Poehler was nominated for multiple Emmy awards for her work on the show.

In 2010, Poehler had her second child; she also hosted *SNL* that year. In 2012, Poehler and her husband divorced. Poehler continues to work in both film and television, having established herself as a major force in contemporary comedy.

Poehler is known for her high-energy comedy, often playing manic or over-the-top characters, like her hyperactive Girl Scout character in the animated series *The Mighty B!* She is a versatile impersonator, doing impressions of both respected figures like Hillary Clinton and Katie Couric and more low-brow figures like Britney Spears. Poehler also has strong and lasting ties to many other comics, often appearing on Conan O'Brien's show with other members of the Upright Citizens Brigade and having worked in film with Tina Fey after their successful performances on Weekend Update. Poehler is well respected within comic circles, having established herself both in smaller improv circles and on the larger scale of mainstream television and film.

See also: Ansari, Aziz; Fey, Tina

Further Reading

Guzman, Isaac. "How They Crushed It: Tina Fey and Amy Poehler's Opening Act." *Time.com* (January 14, 2014): 1.

Luippold, Ross. "Amy Poehler Did a Fake Interview for Seth Meyers on 'Late Night.'" *Huffington Post*, February 25, 2014. http://www.huffingtonpost.com/2014/02/24/amy-poehler-seth-meyers-late-night_n_4853782.html.

Rothman, Lily. "They Came Together: Amy Poehler, Paul Rudd and David Wain Champion a New Era of Spoofs." *Time.com* (June 28, 2014): 1.

Zeke Jarvis

ROCCA, MO (1969–)

Maurice Rocca was born in Washington, D.C. After being educated Georgetown Preparatory School in Bethesda, Maryland, he attended Harvard University, graduating in 1991 with a degree in literature. While at Harvard, Rocca served as the president of Harvard's Hasty Pudding Theatricals. Not long after his graduation, Rocca went on the tour of *Grease* in Southeast Asia.

Rocca began his work in television by writing for the children's series *Wishbone*. He continued to participate in children's television, writing for *The Wbubulous World of Dr. Seuss* and *Pepper Ann*, before landing a correspondent role on *The Daily Show*. In 2004, Rocca took a more serious turn as the correspondent for Larry King at the presidential party conventions.

Since leaving *The Daily Show*, Rocca has struck a balance between serious journalism and humorous pieces, appearing on Broadway, on *The Early Show*, and as a guest on NPR's *Wait, Wait . . . Don't Tell Me*. Rocca is openly gay, though he does not spend a good deal of his airtime discussing his personal life.

Like many of *The Daily Show*'s correspondents, Rocca is known for his deadpan delivery. His odd associations (Rocca has compared himself to President Barack Obama as a skinny man with a funny name) and absurd claims or perspectives serve to both undercut the reliability of his persona and satirize the general validity of many media outlets. Interestingly, Rocca's education positions him in a unique way: he has a level of intellectual credibility that many find to enhance the humor of his irreverent and absurd observations. Although Rocca has not achieved the breakout fame of some of the other correspondents, such as Steve Carell and Stephen Colbert, he has found consistent and prominent outlets for his humor and social commentary.

Further Reading

Benwick, Bonnie S. "Mo Likes to Stir Things up." *Washington Post,* January 15, 2013. http://www.highbeam.com/doc/1G1-317086543.html.

Rocca, Mo. *All the Presidents' Pets: The Story of One Reporter Who Refused to Roll Over*. New York: Crown, 2004.

Zeke Jarvis

SANDLER, ADAM (1966–)

Adam Sandler was born in Brooklyn, New York. His family moved to Manchester, New Hampshire, when Sandler was five. While in high school, Sandler began to develop his comedic talents; he first put them to the test at age 17 when he went on stage at an open mic event in a Boston comedy club. He continued to pursue comedy during his time at New York University's Tisch School of the Arts.

During the second half of the 1980s, Sandler began to appear on a variety of television shows, including *The Cosby Show* and MTV's *Remote Control*. In 1988, he graduated from NYU. After being seen by Dennis Miller, Sandler was given a position as a staff writer on *Saturday Night Live*, where he also began to perform. Sandler made a name for himself not only by playing characters in skits but also by performing songs like "The Chanukah Song" and "The Thanksgiving Song."

In 1995, Sandler had his first starring role in the film *Billy Madison*. While the film did not receive a positive critical reception, it did gain a significant positive response from fans. This led to other films such as *Happy Gilmore* and *The Wedding Singer*. Slightly before and during this period, Sandler also released comedy CDs, including *Stan and Judy's Kid*, that were a mix of stand-up comedy bits, songs, and short skits with Sandler playing a variety of characters.

Although Sandler would continue to perform stand-up and play roles in more purely comedic films, he also began to appear in more critically acclaimed films such as *Punch Drunk Love* and *Spanglish*, which was directed by James L. Brooks. Sandler struck a balance between humor and serious work in Judd Apatow's film *Funny People*, which was released in 2009.

During the filming of his 1999 film *Big Daddy*, Sandler met Jacqueline Samantha Titone, whom he would marry. The two have two daughters. Sandler currently lives and works in Los Angeles.

Sandler is known for playing idiotic characters stuck in absurd situations and worlds. This is an extension of his stand-up work, where he would ridicule himself in various ways, including making fun of his car and joking about his Jewish heritage. As Sandler's career took off, however, his display of dramatic range began to change critical reaction to his overall body of work. While some critics, such as Roger Ebert, saw his more dramatic turns simply as a sign that his earlier works were a waste of his talent, others saw his vacillating between more strictly comedic turns and more complex roles as a sign of Sandler's breadth. Whether critics see his overall body of work as complex or not, few have denied the impact that Sandler has had on the pop cultural landscape, with a variety of lines from both his characters and his stable of supporting characters (often played by Rob Schneider, Steve Buscemi, and other regulars) being quoted regularly. Sandler generally occupies a position of respect among other comedians, having starred as a prominent comedian in *Funny People* and filled in as a guest host for David Letterman during Letterman's absence for medical issues. While Sandler does not seem to seek out critical success or respect, his steady and sustained success have helped him to achieve it.

See also: Apatow, Judd; Smigel, Robert

Further Reading

Brodie, Ian. "Vladimir Propp, Meet Happy Gilmore: Adam Sandler and Vernacular Cinema." *Culture & Tradition* 27 (2005): 7–23.

Crawford, Bill. *Adam Sandler*. New York: St. Martin's McGriffins.
Pomerantz, Dorothy. "Why Adam Sandler's Ten Razzie Awards Won't Hurt His Paycheck." *Forbes.com* (April 2, 2012): 26.

Zeke Jarvis

SCHNEIDER, DAN (1966–)

Dan Schneider was born in Memphis, Tennessee. He was successful in high school, even attending Harvard University. However, he dropped out of college after one semester, returning to Memphis and working in repairing computers. After growing tired of that venture, Schneider moved to Los Angeles to pursue his career in performance. He met with success, first co-starring in films such as *Better off Dead* and *The Big Picture* during the mid-1980s. In 1986, Schneider played a regular character on the sitcom *Head of the Class*. The show ran until 1991.

Not long after that, Schneider began his work as a producer and writer. Beginning in 1994, he engaged in a long and productive career writing for shows on the children's network Nickelodeon. Beginning with the show *All That*, which some consider to be the young adult version of *Saturday Night Live*, Schneider wrote for a series of successful shows, including cultural touchstones like *iCarly*, *Victorious*, and *Drake and Josh*. These shows also led to spin-off movies such as *Good Burger* and helped to launch the careers of a number of stars, including Kenan Thompson, who became a cast member of *Saturday Night Live*, and Ariana Grande, who has a successful singing career. Schneider lives and works in California.

Schneider has been called "the Norman Lear of children's shows" because he has such a sustained and successful career writing for and producing shows. His shows often have a wild feel, using quick switches and ridiculous characters to provide humor. As his career progressed, he sometimes became more daring. The show *Sam and Cat* had characters with little interest in either behaving well or obeying any kind of consistent logic. Still, the show was quite successful, earning a Kids' Choice Award in its first year. Although Schneider might not be a household name, an entire generation of children has grown up watching his work, which makes him an important figure in American humor.

Further Reading

Frankel, Daniel. " 'Head of the Class' Actor Now Creating at Nick." *Variety.com*, October 4, 2007. http://variety.com/2007/scene/news/dan-schneider-1117973402/.
Littleton, Cynthia. "Nick Nets *iCarly* Guy." *Daily Variety* 306, no. 47 (March 10, 2010): 1–11.

Zeke Jarvis

SCHUMER, AMY (1981–)

Amy Schumer was born in Manhattan, New York, and grew up on Long Island. She comes from a mixed-faith household, with her mother being Protestant and her father being Jewish, and she was raised more in line with Jewish traditions. While in high school, Schumer was not known for her academic performance: she was voted "Teacher's Worst Nightmare." Still, she attended Towson University, graduating in 2003 with a degree in theater.

After graduation, Schumer moved to New York City, where she worked as a bartender and waitress while attending the William Esper Studio. There, she pursued both acting and comedy, appearing in the off-Broadway play *Keeping Abreast* and performing in comedy clubs. Schumer steadily gained recognition, recording a special for Comedy Central and making it to the finals of the reality competition *Last Comic Standing*. She continued to make small but steady appearances, ranging from guest spots on Fox News shows to writing for *Cosmopolitan* to appearing in an episode of *Curb Your Enthusiasm*.

In 2011, Schumer released her first stand-up comedy album, *Cutting*. The album and her 2012 Comedy Central special, *Mostly Sex Stuff*, generally received favorable reviews. They subsequently led to Schumer's Comedy Central sketch comedy show, *Inside Amy Schumer*, which premiered in April 2013. Schumer continues to live and work in New York, balancing stand-up performing with acting roles.

Schumer is well known for her frank and sometimes controversial discussions of sex and female sexuality. In interviews, she has frequently stated that her stage and television persona is an exaggerated version of herself. She consistently has discussed her desires and sexual experiences in a bold and striking way, similar to other comics such as Louis CK, Richard Pryor, and Kathy Griffin, all of whom included their anxieties and desires in their performances to both laugh at them and to open a space to discuss what many people feel uncomfortable discussing. That said, the ironic distance that Schumer creates between herself and her persona sets her apart from some of these comics—Louis CK particularly—in that she clearly separates her personality in interviews and her on-screen persona. Still, her boldness and inventive work makes her a strong comic figure.

Further Reading

Dockterman, Eliana. "Comedy Central Renews *Inside Amy Schumer*." *Time.com* (June 11, 2014): 1.

" 'Inside Amy Schumer:' It's Not Just Sex Stuff." NPR, June 25, 2013. http://www.npr.org/2013/06/25/188698578/inside-amy-schumer-its-not-just-sex-stuff.

Snierson, Dan. "Amy Schumer." *Entertainment Weekly* 1305 (April 4, 2014): 58.

Zeke Jarvis

SEDARIS, AMY (1961–)

Amy Sedaris was born in Waldicott, New York, though she grew up in Raleigh, North Carolina. In her youth, Sedaris could be a difficult student and worker, sometimes making fake announcements while working as a clerk at a Winn-Dixie supermarket, and once stealing and hiding her boss's car keys after being fired for being late. She also failed first grade.

Although Sedaris had started a bakery business with her mother in North Carolina, she left for Chicago after graduating from high school. In Chicago,

Sedaris began working at Second City and Annoyance Theatre. It was at Second City where she met her future cowriters Stephen Colbert and Paul DiNello. The trio left Chicago for New York, where they began to build their national prominence on television, first working on *Exit 57* and then breaking through with the Comedy Central series *Strangers with Candy*. That show featured Sedaris as an aging former prostitute who returns to high school; Colbert and DiNello played inept teachers who were also closeted gay lovers. As the trio gained more national attention, Sedaris began to get small parts in a variety of sitcoms, such as *Just Shoot Me*, and films, such as *Maid in Manhattan* and *Elf*. She also began what has become a long string of appearances on *The Late Show with David Letterman*, where Letterman gave her free reign to put her strange antics on display in the same way that he had with Andy Kaufman in an earlier era. Sedaris also began crafting, sometimes appearing on Martha Stewart's programs, balancing genuine know-how with wisecracks. In fact, Sedaris actually makes and sells crafts like home-made cheeseballs. She continues to live and work in a variety of fields in New York.

Sedaris is known for her outrageous characters and her willingness to appear physically unattractive. In *Strangers with Candy*, she appeared in a fat suit, wore copious amounts of make-up, and used exaggerated facial expressions to appear old and unattractive. In his own work, her brother David Sedaris has discussed how Amy would often wear the fat suit in public and even in front of her father in an effort to make him believe that she was putting on weight. Indeed, it can be difficult to determine where Amy Sedaris's work leaves off and her life begins, with performances like the one on *The Colbert Report*, where she and Colbert appeared to have an awkward conversation about a past relationship that some viewers mistook for a real moment of awkwardness. Ironically, Sedaris did have a real-life relationship with her other *Strangers with Candy* co-star, DiNello. Sedaris has also displayed a willingness to appear immature, playing an overly serious and sarcastic version of Snow White and using tape to give herself a "pig nose" on one of Martha Stewart's shows.

That said, Sedaris can play likable and more subdued characters, as she has in *Elf*. She also has mixed the childlike or wholesome references with vulgar or unappealing aspects of life, as in her satirical craft books. Although some see Sedaris as principally immature or relying on base humor, the positive support and respect that she has consistently received from David Letterman and other prominent humorists and cultural figures have helped to make Sedaris a well-known name within comedy circles.

See also: Colbert, Stephen; Sedaris, David

Further Reading

Goldberg, Whoopi. "Amy Sedaris." *Interview* 36, no. 6 (July 2006): 90–94.

Martin, Tyler. "Standing Ovation: Amy Sedaris on *Strangers with Candy*." *Back Stage* (19305966) 55, no. 18 (May 1, 2014): 56.

Sedaris, Amy. *I Like You: Hospitality under the Influence*. New York: Grand Central Publishing, 2008.

Zeke Jarvis

SHORT, MARTIN (1950–)

Martin Short was born in Hamilton, Ontario, the youngest of five children. By the time that Short was 19, he had lost an older brother, David, in a car accident, his mother to cancer, and his father to complications of a stroke. Nevertheless, Short was able to successfully complete his studies, graduating from McMaster University with a degree in social work in 1972.

Rather than pursuing social work, Short took up acting after being cast in a production of *Godspell*. The cast for the play was quite remarkable, including Gilda Radner, Dave Thomas, and Eugene Levy, and having Paul Shaffer as musical director. It was also on *Godspell* that Short met his wife, actress Nancy Dolman. The two married in 1980.

Short continued to act, landing a spot on *SCTV*, the seminal Canadian comedy show. With this and other television work, he gained in prominence. He was eventually brought onto *Saturday Night Live* in the 10th season as part of a large group of established comedians who were added to revive the show after the departure of some key cast members.

In addition to his work in television, Short has worked extensively in film, starring in some well-received movies, such as *!Three Amigos!*, and a variety of smaller projects. He has also appeared in a variety of plays and toured extensively.

After leaving *Saturday Night Live* and doing film work, Short had the show *Primetime Glick*, which featured him playing the inept interviewer Jiminy Glick. Glick interviewed a variety of prominent comedians, committing clear gaffes and blunders and forcing the interview subjects to decide between playing along or laughing in spite of themselves. This sort of refusal to break the premise is similar to the work of Jonathan Winters, Sacha Baron Cohen, and Andy Kaufman. Short has continued to appear on television shows, including *Arrested Development*, and as the voice of the Cat on *The Cat in the Hat Knows a Lot about That*.

Short and his wife had three children. In 2010, his wife died of ovarian cancer; Short has been active in his support of cancer research. He has dual citizenship and lives in California in addition to maintaining a home in Ontario.

Short's work is often characterized by boisterous personas and excellent execution of physical humor. Although his work sometimes is a bit more subdued, such as his portrayal of a neurotic, unscrupulous executive in the *60 Minutes* spoofs on *Saturday Night Live* or the good-natured buffoon in *Pure Luck*, he generally gives dynamic performances with a striking sense of physicality. He also plays strong characters with striking personas, such as the overweight, pompous windbag Jiminy Glick and the spastic man-child Ed Grimley, both of which had over-the-top costumes and appearances. Although Short has not shied away from sexual innuendo in his work, he rarely uses curse words. In fact, on *Inside the Actor's Studio*, when asked what his favorite curse word was, Short replied, "Poo." This is indicative of the sense of innocence that Short can capture with his characters, even while they are being boisterous or unsophisticated. For this reason, and for his striking delivery, Short's performances often convey a sense of vaudeville. Still, his work seems more classic than anachronistic, affording him significant staying power over the course of his career.

Further Reading

Goldberg, Robert. "Martin Short's Very Long Odds." *TV Guide* 42, no. 42 (October 15, 1994).

Shales, Tom. "My Favorite Martin . . . Short, That Is." *Electronic Media* 20, no. 29 (July 16, 2001): 4.

Short, Martin. *I Must Say: My Life as a Humble Comedy Legend*. New York: Harper, 2014.

Zeke Jarvis

SKLAR BROTHERS (1972–)

Randy and Jason Sklar are twin brothers who were born and raised in St. Louis, Missouri. After graduating from high school, both attended the University of Michigan. Following their college graduation, the two moved to New York to pursue their comedy careers. The brothers worked in comedy clubs, developing their act. In 1997, they had writing and acting work on MTV's sketch comedy show, *Apt 2F*. Although the show lasted only one season, it gave the brothers the recognition to get more work both together and separately. The two have appeared on a variety of TV shows, including *Curb Your Enthusiasm* and *Grey's Anatomy*, as well as in films, including *Wild Hogs* and *My Baby's Daddy*. The two are best known, though, for their appearances as themselves on shows like late-night talk show *Chelsea Lately* and *The United Stats of America*, a show on the History Channel that examines odd statistics as a way to both learn about American history and showcase the brothers' humor. The brothers also have worked for ESPN on the satirical show *Cheap Seats*.

Randy Sklar is married and has two children with his wife, Amy. Both brothers work on a variety of television shows, including VH1's *Best Week Ever*, which features short riffs on minor pop cultural matters.

Like the members of the Algonquin Round Table, the Sklar brothers are known for sharp puns, incisive jabs, and acerbic send-ups of various cultural figures. Generally speaking, they tend to focus on figures and events that draw short-lived attention, which fits the weekly or daily format of the shows on which they frequently appear. The brothers are also known for puns and odd combinations of references that suit the fast-delivery contexts in which they appear. They are credited with a keen ability to employ self-deprecating humor. While as yet the Sklar brothers have not had a single, major show or film to themselves, their ubiquitous presence as part of the cultural landscape make them significant figures in American comedy.

Further Reading

Chadwick, Alex. "Interview: Jason and Randy Sklar Discuss March Madness." *Day to Day* (NPR), March 16, 2005.

Thorn, Jesse. "Sklar Brothers Interview." *Onion AV Club*, February 28, 2012, http://www.avclub.com/article/sklar-brothers-69856.

Zeke Jarvis

SMIGEL, ROBERT (1960–)

Robert Smigel was born in New York City. His father, Dr. Irwin Smigel, is the founder and president of the American Society for Dental Aesthetics. Smigel attended Cornell University in the pre-dental program, but ultimately graduated from New York University in 1983 with a degree in communications. He first began working with comedy at the Players Workshop in Chicago.

Smigel's comedic break into Hollywood came when he became a writer for the sketch comedy show *Saturday Night Live*. He began writing for the show after the network began to threaten cancellation. To remedy this situation, the producers fired most of the cast and writers and brought in new comedic talent. Following the 1987–1988 season of *SNL*, Smigel joined a writers' strike and wrote an improvisational comedy program called *Happy Happy Good Show*. He then co-wrote *Lookwell*, which never went to series, and became the first head writer at *Late Night with Conan O'Brien*. In 1996, Smigel wrote and performed on the *Dana Carvey Show*, debuting his first cartoon, *The Ambiguously Gay Duo*. Upon the cancellation of the show, Smigel continued to develop cartoons and began airing them on *SNL*. Smigel's most famous creation, Triumph the Insult Comic Dog, debuted on *Late Night with Conan O'Brien* in 1997. The dog continued to make appearances on the show for years to come.

Smigel has been involved with films as well. In 2000, he provided the voice of a character in *Little Nicky* and cowrote the film *You Don't Mess with the Zohan*. He later cowrote and executive produced the film *Hotel Transylvania*.

Smigel lives in New York with his wife. The couple has a child with autism and serves on the board of New York Collaborates for Autism.

Smigel is known for his very edgy humor, which ranges from challenging exchanges as Triumph (even creating feuds with celebrities like Eminem) to often vulgar or offensive material on *TV Funhouse* and cartoons on *SNL*. Even so, he has enjoyed a consistent and generally successful career, being associated with a number of successful fellow comedians. Although Smigel himself is not a household name, his work is very well known, and he has had a hand in many commercially successful projects.

See also: O'Brien, Conan; Sandler, Adam

Further Reading

Koch, Stephen. "Robert Smigel's Dog Days." *Rolling Stone* 935 (November 13, 2003): 45.

Shales, Tom, and James Andrew Miller. *Live from New York: An Uncensored History of Saturday Night Live, as Told by Its Stars, Writers and Guests*. New York: Back Bay Books, 2003.

Smigel, Robert. "It's a Ruff Gig, But Someone Has to Do It." *Daily Variety* 280, no. 50 (September 12, 2003).

Zeke Jarvis

SMITH, KEVIN (1970–)

Kevin Smith was born in Red Bank, New Jersey. He was raised in a Catholic household and attended Henry Hudson Regional High School in Highlands. Smith's first film, *Clerks*, was shot at the convenience store where he worked. Despite the meager budget, it went to the Sundance Film Festival in 1994, won a Filmmaker's Trophy, and was picked up for distribution by Miramax. *Clerks* later went to the Cannes International Film Festival, where it won the Prix de la Jeunesse and International Critics' Week Prize. Smith's second film, *Mallrats*, did not perform as well as *Clerks*. Smith's next film, *Chasing Amy*, has sometimes been heralded as his best film.

In 1999, Smith married his wife, Jennifer, who appeared in *Jay and Silent Bob Strike Back*. The couple has one daughter.

Smith has also directed *Dogma*, *Jay and Silent Bob Strike Back*, *The Green Hornet*, *Jersey Girl*, *Clerks II*, and *Zack and Miri Make a Porno*, none of which garnered Smith the recognition he received from *Chasing Amy*. Following his direction of two horror films, *Red State* and *Tusk*, as well as *Clerks III*, Smith began to voice his desire to retire from directing, but stated he would return to direct sequels of movies that were uniquely his.

Smith worked briefly as a writer for a Superman movie, but was replaced when the film was handed off to Tim Burton. He also rewrote the film *Overnight Delivery* for New Line.

Smith published his first book, *Silent Bob Speaks*, in 2005. His second, *My Boring-Ass Life: The Uncomfortably Candid Diary of Kevin Smith*, reached number 32 on *The New York Times* Best Sellers List. His third book, *Shootin' the Sh*t with Kevin Smith: The Best of the SModcast*, was released in September 2009.

Smith's steps into making comic books commenced with a short Jay and Silent Bob story and a series of *Clerks* comics. He followed this with *Chasing Dogma* and, in 1999, wrote "Guardian Devil," an eight-issue story arc of Marvel's *Daredevil*. He has continued his activity with Batman and a Green Hornet story that came from an unused script from the *Green Hornet* movie. Smith also owns and operates Jay and Silent Bob's Secret Stash in Red Bank, New Jersey, which is a comic book store. This store is the setting for the reality television show *Comic Book Men*.

Smith is known for his balance of high-brow references and low cultural jokes—one of the traits that fans of Smith like best about his work. In the Jay and Silent Bob movies, for example, he employs a wide variety and large number of marijuana jokes. Smith himself has indicated that he makes "dumb movies for smart people," and his continued success seems to demonstrate that his straddling of this "smart/dumb" line has created a consistent audience for his work.

Further Reading

Eells, Josh. "Kevin Smith's Happy Ending." *Rolling Stone* 1130 (May 12, 2011): 48–51.

Muir, John Kenneth. *A View Askew: The Films of Kevin Smith*. New York: Applause Theatre & Cinema Books, 2002.

Percec, Dana, and Alexandru Oravițan. " 'Everything We Do Is Political': An Interview with Kevin Smith." *European English Messenger* 23, no. 1 (Summer 2014): 52–56.

Kristen Franz

SMOTHERS BROTHERS (TOM, 1937–; DICK, 1939–)

Both of the Smothers brothers were born on Governors Island, New York. Their father, an officer in the U.S. Army during World War II, died while a prisoner of war in Japan. After their father's death, the family moved to Los Angeles, where the pair were raised by their mother. They graduated from high school in Redondo, California, and attended San Jose State University.

After being part of a folk quintet for a time, the Smothers Brothers struck out on their own. They performed regularly and put out a number of records, most notably *The Smothers Brothers at the Purple Onion*. Their first television appearance was on *The Jack Paar Show*.

The brothers initially had a sitcom that was both brief and unsuccessful. This effort was followed by the very successful and boundary breaking show, *The Smothers Brothers Comedy Hour*. The show had a noteworthy writing staff, including Steve Martin, Rob Reiner, Bob Einstein, Albert Brooks, and a number of others. It also featured many prominent musicians, including the Who, Cream, Simon and Garfunkel, and other groups and musicians popular with younger audiences at the time. There were a number of striking performances—most notably, the Who's appearance finished with pyrotechnics exploding, slightly injuring Keith Moon and Pete Townshend. Not all the performances (either comedic or musical) were so dramatic, but many were progressive and anti-authoritarian. The show was well received by audiences, but its controversial material led to its cancellation after many struggles between the brothers and the show's network, ABC. Despite the cancellation, the show's writing staff won an Emmy, which many of the writers and performers saw as vindication after the network's decision.

The Smothers Brothers continued to work on television and in movies, both independently and together. They had another comedy hour starting in 1989; the series was short-lived, but it did help a number of musicians receive national air time, including singer k. d. lang. In 2010, the duo announced their retirement from touring; that same year, they were inducted into the Television Academy Hall of Fame.

Tom is married to Marcy Smothers, who was his producer. The two have two children, and Tom has one child from a previous marriage. Tom and his wife own and operate a vineyard in California. Dick has also had two wives; he has six children. Dick lives in Florida.

The Smothers Brothers have balanced music and comedy in their performances throughout their careers. They have also maintained a consistent dynamic, with Dick playing the exasperated, normal straight man to Tom's free-wheeling and sometimes dim-witted brother. There is some grounding in the actual personalities of the brothers in this dynamic, with Tom often being looser and more committed to being active and vocal in liberal politics. Still, in the original carnation of their variety show, both allowed seemingly transgressive material on the air, including a hippie character who regularly dropped coded drug references to the delight of younger crowds and befuddlement of older audiences on her segment, "Share a Little Tea with Goldie." This use of subtext and playfulness with television forms was a regular component of the show. In one famous sketch, the Smothers Brothers interact with fictitious censors, having each successive censor laugh at a page of their script, then rip it out until the script reaches the final censor, who finds nothing funny in it and then hands it to the Brothers. Their clear and unapologetic antagonism toward authority figures and structures was a fairly natural outgrowth of their background in folk music clubs and the San Francisco area, where they often performed. Despite their edgy material, the Smothers Brothers have settled into a perceived role as elder statesman of comedy, maintaining the personas and dynamic between each other.

See also: Martin, Steve

Further Reading

Bianculli, David. *Dangerously Funny: The Uncensored Story of "The Smothers Brothers Comedy Hour."* New York: Touchstone, 2010.

Fox, George. "The Smothers Brothers, Tom and Dick." *Saturday Evening Post* 240, no. 19 (September 23, 1967): 32–35.

Silverman, David S. *"You Can't Air That:" Four Cases of Controversy and Censorship in American Television Programming*. Syracuse, NY: Syracuse University Press, 2007.

Zeke Jarvis

SPURLOCK, MORGAN (1970–)

Morgan Spurlock was born in Parkersburg, West Virginia, and grew up in nearby Beckley. After graduating from high school, he attended New York University's Tisch School of the Arts, where he earned a BFA in film. In addition to his interest in film, Spurlock wrote plays, including the award-winning play *The Phoenix*. He also produced an Internet show, *I Bet You Will*, which featured people performing odd tricks or stunts for money. The show was eventually picked up by MTV.

In 2004, Spurlock's film *Supersize Me* was released. The documentary, which was nominated for an Academy Award, chronicled an experiment Spurlock performed in which he ate nothing but McDonald's food for 30 straight days. Over the course of the film, Spurlock gained 25 pounds and began to experience severe negative health consequences. On the heels of the film's success, Spurlock created a series on the FX network called *30 Days*, in which Spurlock or another worker on the show would live with a group or in a setting for 30 days; examples included working as a coal miner and being in prison.

In 2006, Spurlock married his long-time girlfriend; that same year, they had a son. The two would ultimately divorce.

Since Spurlock's FX series was cancelled, he has continued to make documentaries, including *Where in the World Is Osama bin Laden* and *The Greatest Movie Ever Sold*. He works and lives in New York City.

Spurlock's work is generally known for its keen interest in social relevance. With *30 Days*, Spurlock sought to expose the realities faced by various groups, such as people working for a minimum wage. With *The Greatest Movie Ever Sold*, he addressed the impact that advertising and product placement have on American culture. While not all of his work is funny, Spurlock's presence in the films and television shows often serves to add a level of satirical commentary and to establish a sense of entertainment beyond the serious investigations. Like Michael Moore, Spurlock makes no claims of objectivity while making his films; instead, he explicitly states his agenda and viewpoint, thereby shifting some of the conventional

Filmmaker Morgan Spurlock after a McDonald's meal in his 2004 documentary *Super Size Me*. Spurlock is known for blurring the edges of documentary and political commentary. (Photofest)

expectations of documentaries. Feedback on Spurlock's work has been mixed. While *Supersize Me* generally received high critical praise, some of his subsequent work has been accused of being less substantial than his first documentary. Although he has, perhaps, not equaled his initial success, Spurlock remains a vibrant and active figure in American culture.

See also: Moore, Michael

Further Reading

Beer, Jeff. "Morgan Spurlock." *Canadian Business* 85, no. 10 (June 11, /2012): 63–64.

Odeh, Omar. "*Jackass II*: Downsizing Morgan Spurlock's *Supersize Me*." *Bright Lights Film Journal* (August 2004): 45.

Spurlock, Morgan. *Supersized: Strange Tales from America's Fast-Food Culture*. Milwaukee: Dark Horse Books, 2011.

Zeke Jarvis

STEWART, JON (1962–)

John Stuart Leibowitz was born in New York City. His family moved to Lawrenceville, New Jersey, when he was young and lived there for the entirety of his childhood. When he was still a child, his parents divorced and the boy lost contact with his father. This is one of the reasons why he left behind his last name for performance, taking on the stage name Jon Stewart.

After graduating from high school, Stewart attended the College of William and Mary in Virginia, where he received a degree in psychology. He then held a wide variety of jobs, from busboy to puppeteer to bartender.

Two years after his college graduation, Stewart moved back to New York City to pursue his career in comedy. He began at some well-known New York clubs, including the Bitter End and the Comedy Cellar. Stewart honed his act and got a variety of writing jobs, eventually hosting the MTV show *You Wrote It, You Watch It*,

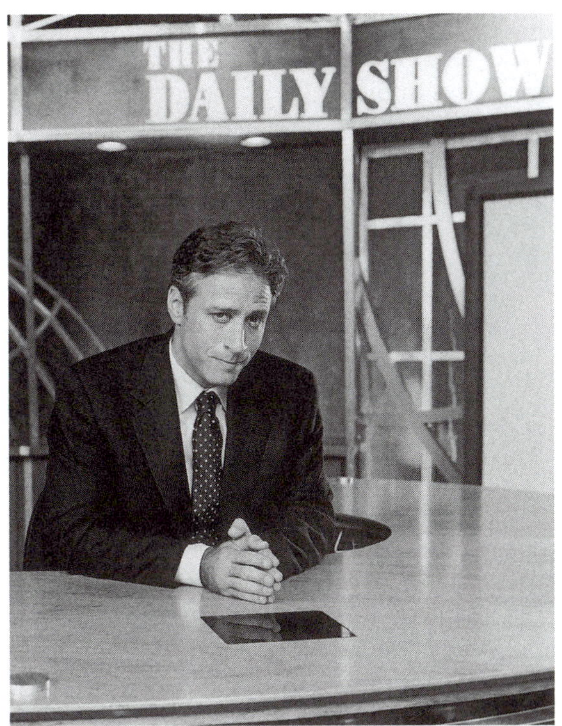

Jon Stewart appears on the set of *The Daily Show*, Comedy Central's award-winning satiric look at politics. Originally a stand-up comic, Stewart has evolved into one of the most highly respected figures in both comedy and political commentary. (Norman Jean Roy/Comedy Central)

which featured performers from the MTV sketch comedy show *The State*. In 1993, Stewart hosted *The Jon Stewart Show* on MTV. The show was very well received, but was canceled in 1995. David Letterman was among the fans of the show: he not only was the guest on Stewart's final show, but also had Stewart on his show after *The Jon Stewart Show* was canceled. In addition, Letterman signed Stewart to his production company, World Wide Pants. This led Stewart to frequently guest host for Tom Snyder in the talk show that followed Letterman's.

After working in this capacity and appearing in minor roles in films, Stewart was given the host position on *The Daily Show* after Craig Kilborn stepped down. It was on Stewart's watch that the show adopted a decidedly more political tone and became tremendously successful, winning two Peabody Awards and a number of Emmys. *The Daily Show* also helped to launch the careers of several prominent performers, including Stephen Colbert and Steve Carell, among others.

In addition to his work hosting *The Daily Show*, Stewart has written or cowritten multiple books. *Naked Pictures of Famous People* was a combination of satirical takes on American history and ironic musings on popular culture. *America (the Book): A Citizen's Guide to Democracy Inaction* was a mock history textbook in the idiom of *The Onion* and *The Daily Show*. Stewart has also hosted the Emmys and the Oscars. Nevertheless, Stewart's focus remains *The Daily Show*, though he has begun to branch out, writing and directing the feature film *Rosewater*.

In 2000, Stewart married; he and his wife have two children. Stewart and his family live in New York.

Even before his work on *The Daily Show*, Stewart was known for his irreverence and self-deprecating humor, even making many jokes about the fact that his MTV show had been canceled in numerous public appearances. On *The Daily Show*, Stewart has maintained his keen sense of satire and absurdity, but directed it more toward the political realm than he was able to do on MTV, given its pop culture slant. In addition to openly criticizing politicians, Stewart has been outspoken in his criticism of the news media. In fact, many attribute the cancellation of the political debate show *Crossfire* to Stewart's appearance, in which he accused the cohosts of being hacks who worked to further partisan bickering rather than engaging in thoughtful political discussion. In addition, Stewart's show regularly airs clips of political figures making absurd or directly contradictory statements as a way to undercut their ability to use the temporary nature of a constant newsfeed to encourage voters to forget about pledges or claims that they made earlier. For this reason, Stewart has been referred to by some as "the most trusted man in America," a title formerly held by legitimate news anchor Walter Cronkite. While Stewart often downplays the legitimacy of his show's ability to genuinely inform people, many insist that, like *The Onion* and *The Colbert Report*, *The Daily Show* is a source held in great esteem by critics and viewers, and Stewart remains the principal figure associated with the show.

See also: Carell, Steve; Colbert, Stephen; Rocca, Mo

Further Reading

Berkowitz, Dan, and Robert E. Gutsche, Jr. "Drawing Lines in the Journalistic Sand: Jon Stewart, Edward R. Murrow, and Memory of News Gone by." *Journalism & Mass Communication Quarterly* 89, no. 4 (Winter 2012): 643–656.

Cutbrith, Joe Hale. *Satire as Journalism:* The Daily Show *and American Politics at the Turn of the Twenty-First Century*. Dissertation, Columbia University, 2011, http://academiccommons.columbia.edu/catalog/ac:132290.

Garrett, H. James, and Mardi Schmeichel. "Using *The Daily Show* to Promote Media Literacy." *Social Education* 76, no. 4 (September 2012): 211–215.

Zeke Jarvis

STILLER, BEN (1965–)

Ben Stiller was born in New York City to comedians and actors Jerry Stiller and Anne Meara. Stiller was inspired by *Second City Television* and sought to be a part of sketch comedy. He attended the Cathedral School of St. John the Divine and graduated from the Calhoun School in New York in 1983. He enrolled as a film student at the University of California, Los Angeles, but left school after only nine months and moved back to New York City.

Stiller's first time on camera came at the age of 15 on a television soap opera, *Guiding Light*. Shortly after his short-lived role ended, Stiller produced a parody of the Martin Scorsese film *The Color of Money*, which caught the attention of producers of *Saturday Night Live*. In 1989, Stiller wrote and appeared on *Saturday Night Live*, but left after four episodes. He then began developing the film *Back to Brooklyn* for MTV. Executives were so impressed with Stiller's work that they decided to create *The Ben Stiller Show*. The show lasted 13 episodes, but Fox Network picked up the idea and created its own *Ben Stiller Show*. Twelve episodes were aired on Fox. Although the show did not perform well in terms of ratings, it won an Emmy Award for "Outstanding Writing in a Variety Show" after it ended.

Stiller then turned his attention to writing, recruiting cast members for, and directing the film *Reality Bites*. Danny DeVito produced the film, which debuted as the highest-grossing film at the box office on its opening weekend, but garnered mixed reviews. After this, Stiller developed the character Derek Zoolander for his hosting of the VH1 Fashion Awards. He continued working on the character, eventually growing it from a short film to a movie.

Actor, comedian, writer, director, and producer Ben Stiller is the son of veteran comedians and actors Jerry Stiller and Anne Meara. Stiller has achieved lasting success in a variety of media. (AP Photo/Evan Agostini)

Stiller married Christine Taylor in May 2000. The couple lives in New York with their two children, Ella Olivia and Quinlin Dempsey.

Along with his Emmy award, Stiller has been nominated for 12 Teen Choice awards, winning only once. He has also been nominated for 13 MTV movie awards, winning three. In 2007, Stiller received the Hasty Pudding Man of the Year award, which is given to performers who "give lasting and impressive contributions to the world of entertainment." In 2009, Stiller received MTV Movie Awards' highest honor, the MTV Generation Award. He was also awarded the 2011 Charlie Chaplin Britannia Award for Excellence in Comedy by BAFTA Los Angeles.

Stiller is known for his off-kilter humor that is rooted in subtle cultural critique. Although Stiller does not typically take a clear political angle, he often pokes fun at certain generational or pop culture figures and expectations. The film *Reality Bites* took on yuppies and hipsters in its parodying of their largely morally bankrupt interests and practices. Likewise, in his acting work, Stiller is regarded as being particularly skilled at portraying an everyman character, as in his work in the *Night at the Museum* films. Stiller's balance of absurd humor and mainstream likability have made him a versatile performer with genuine staying power.

See also: Garofalo, Janeane; Odenkirk, Bob; Stiller, Jerry

Further Reading

"A Tip from Ben Stiller: On Set, a 'Chicken' Is Not What It Seems." NPR, June 13, 2014, http://www.npr.org/2014/06/13/321697784/a-tip-from-ben-stiller-on-set-a-chicken-is-not-what-it-seems.

Gant, Charles. "*The Secret Life of Walter Mitty*." *Sight and Sound* 24, no. 1 (January 2014): 14–15.
Strauss, Neil, and Ringo Starr. "Why Isn't Ben Stiller Laughing?" *Rolling Stone* 1101 (April 1, 2010): 58–88.

Kristen Franz

STILLER, JERRY (1927–)

Gerald Isaac Stiller was born in Brooklyn, one of four children in a Jewish family. Gerald, who would go on to be known as Jerry Stiller, attended Syracuse University, earning a degree in speech and drama. He made his stage debut in *The Silver Whistle* with Burgess Meredith. Shortly after graduation, Stiller appeared in a Phoenix Theatre production of Shakespeare's *Coriolanus,* along with Gene Saks and Jack Klugman.

Stiller married actress Anne Meara in 1954. The two worked as a comedy team, appearing on *The Ed Sullivan Show* as Stiller and Meara. Their partnership was very successful for a time, but, as the variety show began to decline on the television landscape, their access to prominent venues diminished. The two continued to work both together and independently.

Stiller's return to national prominence came on *Seinfeld*, where he played George Costanza's father opposite Estelle Harris. After the series' end, Stiller worked on *The King of Queens*, playing Carrie Heffernan's father, who lives with the two main characters. Stiller continues to work in television, in movies, and on commercials.

Stiller and Meara have two children, Ben and Amy, both of whom have careers in entertainment. Stiller has worked with his son on a total of 11 movies.

Stiller's humor is often characterized by a boisterousness and buffoonish quality. On *Seinfeld*, his character regularly embarrassed his son with both his unconventional behavior and his absurd theories and opinions. His work on *The King of Queens* was similar to his work on *Seinfeld*, though without the similarly buffoonish counterpart that he had in Estelle Harris on *Seinfeld*. Stiller is also well known for his rhythmic, dynamic performances, which incorporate both emphatic deliveries and physical comedy.

See also: Stiller, Ben

Further Reading

Fussman, Cal. "Jerry Stiller." *Esquire* 131, no. 6 (June 99): 112.
Ross, Lillian. "Ritual Humiliation Dept." *New Yorker* 75, no. 31 (October 18–25, 1999): 82.
Stiller, Jerry. *Married to Laughter: A Love Story Starring Anne Meara*. Norwalk, CT: Easton Press, 2000.

Zeke Jarvis

TIM AND ERIC (TIM HEIDECKER, 1976–; ERIC WAREHEIM, 1976–)

Tim Heidecker was born in Allentown, Pennsylvania. He attended Temple University. Heidecker is married with one child.

Eric Wareheim was born in Norristown, Pennsylvania. He also went to Temple University.

Both Heidecker and Wareheim played in indie rock bands prior to and during their comedic careers. When the two began working together, they made a comedic film about fathers. Eventually, the pair got a show on Cartoon Network's *Adult Swim* line-up, *Tom Goes to Mayor*. The show drew a strong cult following, and the pair went on to have a second *Adult Swim* show, *Tim and Eric Awesome Show, Great Job!* In 2012, the duo released *Tim and Eric's Billion Dollar Movie*. They continue to create films and television shows.

Tim and Eric are known for using very low production values in their work. Often engaging in parodies of local news figures, child stars, and other pop culture phenomena, the pair walk a very thin line between poor production and genuine parody. Still, they have received support from a number of prominent comedians and performs, perhaps most notably Weird Al Yankovic, John C. Reilly, and Zach Galifianakis. These sorts of associations, along with their success both on screen and on tours have cemented Tim and Eric's position as important figures in American humor.

See also: Yankovic, Weird Al

Further Reading

Abrams, Simon. "Q & A: Tim and Eric's Really Big Movie." *Esquire*, March 2012, http://www.esquire.com/the-side/qa/sundance-2012/tim-and-eric-movie-interview-6642876.

Brown, Scott. "Awesome Guys, Great Job." *New York* 45, no. 7 (March 5, 2012): 55–58.

Snierson, Don. "*Tim and Eric, Awesome Show Great Job!*" Entertainment Weekly 995/996 (June 6, 2008): 55.

Zeke Jarvis

TOMLIN, LILY (1939–)

Lily Tomlin was born in 1939 in Detroit, Michigan, to Southern Baptist parents who had been forced by the Great Depression to relocate from Kentucky. After her graduation from Cass Technical High School, Tomlin attended Wayne State University, where she planted the seeds for her interest in performing. She soon began performing stand-up in Detroit and in New York City. In 1965, she landed an appearance on *The Merv Griffin Show*. In 1969, she began hosting the short-lived *Music Scene* on ABC, which featured top rock and pop acts of the time, including the Beatles.

Tomlin then joined *Rowan and Martin's Laugh-In*, where she created one of her best-known characters, Ernestine, a telephone switchboard operator with a 1940s hair style who showed little interest in helping her callers. Tomlin created and played numerous other characters on the sketch comedy show, including male drag characters and the popular character of Edith Ann, a five-year-old girl who frequently blew raspberries at the end of her monologues.

In 1971, Tomlin released a comedy album, *This Is a Recording*, which featured sketches of her character Ernestine. That same year, Tomlin began her relationship with long-time partner Jane Wagner, whom Tomlin married in 2013. Tomlin followed up *This Is a Recording* with another comedy album in 1972: *And That's the*

Truth, a collection of Edith Ann monologues. *Modern Scream* (1975) features many characters, including Ernestine and Edith Ann. Tomlin's Broadway show of 1977, *Appearing Nitely*—the first one-woman show on Broadway—was released as a comedy album as well, entitled *Lily Tomlin on Stage*. All of Tomlin's comedy albums in the 1970s were successful and earned Tomlin multiple Grammy nominations and awards.

Tomlin appeared in a CBS sketch comedy variety show special, entitled *Lily*, in 1973. This show, which co-starred Alan Alda and Richard Pryor, earned Tomlin her first Emmy Award. It was also the first of three television specials, with the next two following in 1974 and 1975.

Tomlin made her big-screen debut in 1975 in Robert Altman's *Nashville*, an ensemble-cast musical drama with numerous characters and multiple story lines about the country music scene that also starred Ned Beatty, Keith Carradine, and Shelly Duvall. Tomlin earned an Academy Award nomination for Best Supporting Actress for her role of Linnea Reese, a gospel singer raising two deaf sons.

Tomlin also starred in a 1977 film, *The Late Show*, with Art Carney, and 1978's *Moment by Moment* with John Travolta. *Moment by Moment* was written and directed by Tomlin's life partner, Jane Wagner.

Tomlin went on to star as Violet Newstead in one of the top-grossing films of 1980, *9 to 5*. This film, which co-starred Jane Fonda, was Dolly Parton's big-screen debut. The film chronicles the humorous exploits of three working women who take revenge on their misogynist boss, played by Dabney Coleman. The film holds the number 74 spot on the American Film Institute's 100 Funniest Movies list. She followed up her big-screen success in *9 to 5* with 1981's *The Incredible Shrinking Woman* and 1984's *All of Me*, which co-starred Steve Martin. Tomlin also won an Emmy for *Lily: Sold Out*, which was taped in Las Vegas and aired on CBS in 1981.

In 1985, Tomlin returned to Broadway with a one-woman show, *The Search for Signs of Intelligent Life in the Universe*, written by her partner Wagner. The show earned Tomlin a Tony Award.

In 1989, Tomlin joined Bette Midler on the big screen in *Big Business*, playing the dual role of twin sisters separated at birth. She worked with director Robert Altman again in his 1993 film *Short Cuts*, which also featured an ensemble cast that included Jack Lemmon, Robert Downey, Jr., and Andie MacDowell.

From 1994 to 1997, Tomlin voiced the character of Mrs. Fizzle on PBS's *The Magic School Bus*. She also played a guest role on *Murphy Brown*. In 2000, she revived *The Search for Signs of Intelligent Life in the Universe* on Broadway, then toured the show around the United States. On television, she appeared several times on *The West Wing*, *Will & Grace*, and *Desperate Housewives*. In 2005, she had a guest role on *The Simpsons*. In 2006, she appeared in Robert Altman's last film, *A Prairie Home Companion*, as half of a singing duo with Meryl Streep. In 2009, she premiered her one-woman Las Vegas show, *Not Playing with a Full Deck*, at the MGM Grand.

Tomlin has remained active on television. She appearing in HBO's *Eastbound and Down* in 2012 and co-starred with Reba McEntire in the short-lived *Malibu Country* from 2012 to 2013. She is also active in social causes supporting feminist and gay issues. She received the Mark Twain Prize for American Humor in 2003.

Like Carol Burnett and Tim Conway, Tomlin is known for her creation of memorable characters whose wacky behaviors and mannerisms are the grounding for their comedy. It is not surprising, then, that although Tomlin is mainly known for her humorous work, she is one of a handful of comics who are also respected for the range and depth of their careers. Tomlin did experience some minor controversy when scenes of she and David O. Russell (director of *I Heart Huckabees*) shouting at each other in front of other cast members became public. Tomlin and Russell appeared to have reconciled after the film was released. More generally, Tomlin is seen as a great comic mind and a gifted performer who has maintained a long and critically acclaimed career.

Further Reading

Reed, Jennifer. *The Queer Cultural Work of Lily Tomlin and Jane Wagner.* Basingstoke, UK: Palgrave Macmillan, 2013.

Sorenson, Jeff. *Lily Tomlin: Woman of a Thousand Faces.* New York: St. Martin's Press, 1989.

Tomlin, Lily. "Lily Tomlin's Short List." *Time* 175, no. 4 (February 1, 2010): 54.

Stephen Powers

TYLER, AISHA (1970–)

Aisha Tyler was born in San Francisco. When she was 10, Tyler's parents divorced; she was subsequently raised by her father. After graduating from a school for the arts in San Francisco, Tyler attended Dartmouth College, where she earned a degree in environmental policy. While at Dartmouth, Tyler co-founded an a capella group. After college graduation, Tyler worked at an advertising agency, but quickly left that behind to pursue her career in performance. In 1992, Tyler married her husband.

In 2001, Tyler took over hosting duties for *Talk Soup* on the E! Network. Not long thereafter, Tyler wrote, directed, and starred in the independent film *The Whipper*. She began to work regularly on a variety of television shows, including *Friends* and *Nip/Tuck*. Tyler also branched out into print publication and podcasts. In 2011, she began working as a cohost on the daytime talk show *The Talk*. Tyler continues to work in a variety of venues, including live performances.

Tyler is known for being open with her views on a variety of topics. She is an outspoken advocate for lesbian/gay/bisexual/transgender rights. In addition, Tyler is interested in a variety of pop culture pursuits, including gaming, poker, and fashion. Although she is not as crass as some other comics of her generation, she is willing to discuss her personal life and personal views in a way that makes her a dynamic and engaging figure.

Further Reading

Christian, Margena A. "Sheryl Underwood and Aisha Tyler." *Ebony* 68, no. 6 (April 2013): 38.

Johnson, Pamela K. "Conversations with a Postmodern Sister: Actress-Comedian Aisha Tyler Is Distinctive among Celebrity Authors: She Wrote Her Own Book Proposal and Her Own Book!" *Black Issues Book Review* 6, no. 4 (July/August 2004): 12–14.

Tyler, Aisha. *Self-Inflicted Wounds: Heartwarming Tales of Epic Humiliation*. New York: It Books, 2013.

Zeke Jarvis

WAYANS SIBLINGS (KEENAN IVORY, 1958–; DAMON, 1960–; KIM, 1961–; SHAWN, 1971–; MARLON, 1972–)

The Wayans children were born in New York to devout Jehovah's Witness parents. The second oldest child, Keenan, dropped out of high school in his senior year to pursue comedy. Although Keenan did not have striking success with his own stand-up comedy career, he did garner both praise and prominence for his writing on Eddie Murphy's special, *Raw*. This led to two films, *The Hollywood Shuffle* and *I'm Gonna Git You Sucka*. The first film was a satirical look at the roles available to African Americans in Hollywood; the second was a more parody-driven film sending up many of the conventions of the 1970's "Blaxploitation" films. While some critics preferred *The Hollywood Shuffle*, *I'm Gonna Git You Sucka* was clearly the greater commercial success. The latter film also included some of Keenan's siblings, including Damon and Kim.

On the strength of these films, Keenan and Damon created *In Living Color* for the Fox Network in 1990. It was one of the first sketch comedy shows to have a predominantly African American cast, including Jamie Foxx, David Allen Grier, Tommy Davidson, and Keenan and Damon's siblings Kim, Shawn, and Marlon. Other performers who rose to prominence on the show included Jim Carrey and singer and dancer Jennifer Lopez. The show ran for five seasons, closing in 1994 after struggles with the network over censorship and other matters.

After the show ended, the siblings began to pursue different avenues, with Damon and Marlon appearing in both comic films and more dramatic or action-oriented matter, such as *The Last Boy Scout* for Damon and *Requiem for a Dream* for Marlon. Damon also starred in the sitcom *My Wife and Kids* for five seasons. Keenan stayed out of the spotlight for a time, eventually returning to form with the *Scary Movie* franchise, which satirized horror films and, as with his earlier work, starred a number of his siblings.

Keenan Ivory Wayans has been married and is the father of five children, though he and his wife have filed for divorce. Damon has also been married and divorced; he has four children. Shawn has three children. Marlon is married, with two children, and Kim is married as well. All of the siblings, along with some of their children, continue to work in show business.

The Wayans family is known for having brought an African American voice into both film and sketch comedy. While many of the siblings also have considerable dramatic talent and have enjoyed success in stand-up comedy, they are closely associated with comedy heavily grounded in referentiality, often addressing issues of

African American culture on *In Living Color* and more mainstream pop culture in the *Scary Movie* franchise. The latter also employs the sense of self-referential humor that is often associated with *The Simpsons*, the work of the Zucker Brothers, and Monty Python. In *I'm Gonna Git You Sucka*, the humor often penetrates the fourth wall, calling attention to the cliché or familiar aspects of the film's structure. In both the *Scary Movie* franchise and *In Living Color*, the Wayans family has not shied away from commenting directly on pop culture figures, including Michael Jackson and Connie Chung, among many others. Although figures such as Redd Foxx and Bill Cosby also helped break down a number of barriers for comics of color, the Wayans family sought to reestablish and redefine African American comedy for a new generation. In this way, the siblings are significant as both comedic and cultural figures, and their impact will continue to be felt for years to come.

See also: Carrey, Jim; Foxx, Jamie; Grier, David Alan

Further Reading

Hesse, Monica. "Wayans Brothers: Spoof, They Did It Again." *Washington Post*, May 22, 2009, http://urbanmecca.net/news/2009/05/28/wayans-brothers-spoof-they-did-it-again/.

Sanneh, Kelefa. "The Wayans Brothers Become the Wayans Sisters." *New York Times* 153, 52893, June 27, 2004, Arts & Leisure p. 10.

Torres, Sasha. *In Living Color: Race and Television in the United States*. Durham: Duke University Press, 1998.

Zeke Jarvis

WILLIAMS, ROBIN (1951–2014)

Robin Williams was born in Chicago, Illinois, though he grew up in Michigan, near Detroit. Williams described himself as a shy child, but did begin to perform at an early age, doing impressions of his maternal grandmother for his mother's amusement. In 1973, Williams was accepted into Juilliard, a very exclusive and prestigious theater school. Only Williams and Christopher Reeve were accepted into the John Houseman advanced program; the two would remain friends for years. Williams excelled in his studies, mastering dialects particularly quickly. In 1976, Williams left Juilliard.

After working on *The Richard Pryor Show*, Williams appeared on *Happy Days* as Mork, the character he would play in a successful spin-off show, *Mork and Mindy*. Mork was an alien living on Earth with a woman who tried to help him manage his life. Mork typically was a good-natured but ridiculous character, which suited Williams's wild, energetic performances. Fittingly, Jonathan Winters, one of Williams's comedy idols, appeared on the show as Mork and Mindy's son, despite the fact that he was clearly older than Williams.

In 1978, Williams married for the first time. The marriage would result in one child and end in divorce after Williams's extramarital affairs.

Williams capitalized on the widespread popularity that his role as Mork brought by having stand-up comedy specials on HBO, which introduced audiences to his wide range of characters and voices beyond the character of Mork. He also appeared

Comedian Robin Williams, wearing his University of Moscow T-shirt, poses as "Joey Stalin" in Los Angeles on June 3, 1977. Williams was known for his manic performances and wide array of impressions and characters. (AP Photo)

in a large number of movies, including such offbeat fare as Terry Gilliam's *The Tales of Baron von Munchhausen*. In 1987, Williams appeared in *Good Morning, Vietnam*, which garnered him praise not only for his comedic performance but also for the depth of character he brought to the role. Although he was nominated for an Academy Award for this depiction, it was not until 1998 that he would win an Oscar for Best Supporting Actor for his role in *Good Will Hunting*.

In 1989, Williams married his second wife, with whom he had two children. The couple divorced in 2010.

In the time between *Good Morning, Vietnam* and *Good Will Hunting*, Williams appeared in a wide variety of films and performed stand-up on a regular basis. He also did some notable voiceover work, such as in the film *Aladdin*, where he played the wild genie.

In addition to his comedic work, Williams was known for his work with charity. Most notably, he hosted the Comic Relief series with his friends Billy Crystal and Whoopi Goldberg to raise money for the homeless. In addition, he helped to raise money for St. Jude Children's Research Hospital and performed on the USO tours a number of times.

In 2014, Williams committed suicide. His family and publicists indicated that this was likely the result of issues with depression and Parkinson's disease, though the exact reasons were never fully determined

In both his stand-up work and many of his film roles, Williams was known for his manic delivery and free-associative approach to comedy. Like Jonathan Winters, he often took a variety of surprising turns in his extemporaneous comic efforts. Although Williams changed in some ways as he aged and worked through his substance abuse issues (in fact, he spoke at length in interviews and on stage about watching John Belushi's problems with cocaine), he generally retained the wildly imaginative and energetic persona of his early days. In addition, Williams

Ten Great Comedic Remakes

The Birdcage, 1996 (original: *La Cage au Folles*, 1978)
Robin Williams and Nathan Lane play a hilarious gay couple in this American remake of the French film.

Dinner for Schmucks, 2010 (original: *The Dinner Game*, 1998)
Steve Carrel and Zach Galifianakis play good-natured imbeciles in this offbeat remake.

Dirty Rotten Scoundrels, 1988 (original: *Bedtime Story*, 1964)
Con men played by Michael Caine and Steve Martin are outfoxed in this update.

Down and Out in Beverly Hills, 1986 (original: *Boudu Sauve des Eaux* 1932)
Class comedy gets revisited in this American update.

Down to Earth, 2001 (original: *Heaven Can Wait*, 1978, which was itself a remake of *Here Comes Mr. Jordan*, 1941)
Warren Beatty had intended the main character to be an African American in the original, and his wish was granted in this remake.

Father of the Bride, 1991 (original: *Father of the Bride*, 1950)
Steve Martin and Martin Short combine for hilarious effect in this remake.

Hairspray, 2007 (original: *Hairspray*, 1988)
John Waters's classic goes from film to Broadway musical to musical film with a bigger budget and bigger stars.

The Producers, 2005 (original: *The Producers*, 1968)
The Mel Brooks comedy film gets an update as a musical after a successful run as a Broadway musical.

Ruby & Quentin, 2003 (original: *Les Fugitifs*, 1986)
Madcap comedy abounds in this remake.

Victor/Victoria, 1982 (original: *Viktor and Viktoria*, 1933)
Even 50 years after the original, the update seemed bold and funny; it was subsequently turned into a successful Broadway musical.

regularly employed a wide array of voices and characters in his performances. These two facets of his persona often led him to be the more rapid-fire, outspoken member within comedy pairs. Most notably, Williams appeared with Crystal multiple times on the *Tonight Show* in very striking performances.

In the same way that Williams was influenced by Winters, a number of comics point to Williams's breadth of characters and imaginative turns as a source of inspiration. Dana Carvey, for instance, has a similarly animated and off-the-wall delivery. Williams worked to balance his image as a live wire with more subdued and dramatic turns in much of his later film work, garnering him a position of respect among both humorists and dramatic actors that few performers have achieved. It also enabled him to take on roles that required both in a single movie, as he did in *The Bird Cage* and *Mrs. Doubtfire*. Although Williams earned a high level of respect from many fans and critics for his dramatic work, he will always be closely associated with the lively, humorous performances of his early career.

See also: Crystal, Billy; Goldthwait, Bobcat; Winters, Jonathan

Further Reading

David, Jay. *The Life and Humor of Robin Williams: A Biography*. New York: Harper Perennial, 1999.

Dougan, Andy. *Robin Williams*. New York: Thunder's Mouth Press, 1998.

Time.com. "Robin Williams: 1951–2014." August 14, 2014, 1.

Zeke Jarvis

ZUCKER BROTHERS (JIM ABRAHAMS, 1944–; DAVID ZUCKER, 1947–; JERRY ZUCKER, 1950–)

The ZAZ (Zucker, Abrahams, Zucker) team met while attending the University of Wisconsin at Madison. While there, they formed a theater group called "Kentucky Fried Theater." In addition to their work on the theater, some members of the group incorporated humor into their life on campus, taking part in student government to gain resources and publicity for their pranks. Abrahams, in particular, was part of the group that built a replica of the Statue of Liberty's upper portion. This replica was then placed on the ice on a lake in Madison, with a story being circulated that the Statue of Liberty had been flown across the country and dropped into the lake.

As they gained local attention and support, the ZAZ trio began to explore filmmaking. Their first film, a collection of sketches, was called *Kentucky Fried Movie*. While the trio wrote the script for the movie, it was directed by John Landis. The group's first proper film, *Airplane!*, established the group as significant figures in American humor. They continued to explore purely silly films and spoofs with works like *The Naked Gun* and *Top Secret!* The group members also struck out on their own, sometimes straying from pure comedy. Most notably, Jerry Zucker found significant commercial success with the dramatic film *Ghost*.

Like the Coen Brothers, the ZAZ trio tends to work with the same actors in multiple films, such as Leslie Nielsen, who starred in both *Airplane* movies as well as all of the *Naked Gun* movies. They also sometimes cast their family members as minor characters in their movies. The trio continues to work, sometimes together and sometimes independently, and gives lectures on comedy and film on college campuses.

The ZAZ trio is most consistently noted for slapstick comedy, parodying for pure humor rather than for political commentary or social satire. Still, their deft wordplay, clever referential humor, and effective use of anchors and callbacks have helped to establish the group as master craftsmen of comedy. In terms of their spoofs, their consistent and often family-based casting decisions, and their heavy use of pop culture references, the group can be seen as clear influences on the Wayans siblings and, to a lesser extent, on shows like *Family Guy* and

The Simpsons, which have often employed strange overlaps and echoes in their observations about popular culture.

Although the element is not as present in films like *Ghost,* the trio is generally known for not shying away from crass, sexual-based humor. This type of humor has been present from their early career work, such as the skit "Catholic School Girls in Trouble," to the jokes about a stewardess preforming oral sex on an inflatable autopilot in *Airplane!* To the wide variety of sexual jokes in the *Naked Gun* series, the trio have regularly added edgy jokes. Moreover, they have used stunt casting for comic effect, including O. J. Simpson as a clumsy, easily injured police officer and Kareem Abdul-Jabbar as a co-pilot. This sort of imaginative casting is very much in keeping with their overall approach to referential humor; it has been emulated by later film series such as the *Scary Movie* franchise, which used figures such as Dr. Phil and Carmen Electra for comic effect. Although the group's work does not always receive the critical acclaim accorded to some other humorists, the ZAZ films are quoted and referenced often enough to establish the trio's place in American humor.

Further Reading

Abrams, Simon. "Back Before 'Scary Movie,' When Parody Films, and the Zucker Brothers and Abrahams Were Great." *Capital New York*, September 20, 2001, http://www.capitalnewyork.com/article/culture/2011/09/3305301/back-scary-movie-when-parody-films-and-zucker-brothers-and-abrahams-.

Busch, Anita M., and Dan Cox. "Zucker Bros. Take U Turn." *Variety* 361, no. 5 (December 4, 1995): 19.

Dale, Alan. *Comedy Is a Man in Trouble: Slapstick in American Movies*. Minneapolis: University of Minnesota Press, 2002.

Zeke Jarvis

Section IV: Stand-up and Performance

From the days of radio to the advent of the podcast, American humorists have consistently employed a strong sense of persona that is very much in line with the American traits of individuality and strength. Even comic duos balanced the roles of the loudmouth and the lovable oaf to wonderful comic effect from the days of vaudeville and well beyond. While many viewers feel that performed comedy, by its nature, often does not have the subtlety or complexity of literary work, it does capitalize on the immediacy and sharp turns that only performance can offer, making it an important art form onto itself, and American humorists have a strong tradition of challenging the boundaries of comic performances.

The gap between the character on stage and the performer's everyday life allowed many oppressed groups to come into national cultural consciousness even when those groups found it more difficult to break into other forms of entertainment. Female performers like Joan Rivers and Phyllis Diller took on brash, outspoken roles that paved the way for later female performers to touch on topics that would have been considered taboo among previous generations. But these two female comedic icons were not the first noteworthy female performers, nor were they inspirations for only outspoken and brash performers. Both Rivers and Diller were able to balance boldness with self-deprecating humor.

Just as Rivers and Diller helped to tear down barriers for female humorists, so figures like Dick Gregory, Bill Cosby, and Richard Pryor helped to dismantle the barriers for African American performers and humorists. In his stand-up material and his film and television work, Pryor both used and undercut stereotypes about African Americans and African American culture. Cosby, by contrast, worked to give a sense of bringing African Americans fully into mainstream culture, an approach that has sometimes created genuine tension between Cosby and other prominent figures in African American culture. This tension has even been referenced in the work of other performers, like Eddie Murphy in one of his bits on *RAW*. Nevertheless, both Cosby and Pryor ultimately helped to open roles for other African American performers.

Finally, Jewish culture has had a wide array of representatives in the world of humor, both as writers for performers and as performers themselves. Many of these performers examine their culture in a way that demonstrates a level of internal conflict. Richard Lewis, Jon Stewart, and, of course, Lenny Bruce examine the way that Jewish culture is discussed in American pop culture.

Beyond marginalized groups, many breakthroughs in the humor field have been made in terms of technique and persona. Bizarre, distinctive comics like Steven

Wright and Mitch Hedberg returned to the sorts of one-liners and offbeat inversions that are less prevalent in contemporary stand-up, which tends to be more rooted in storytelling than in joke telling. Comics like Mort Sahl used improvised remarks based directly on stories from the newspaper, making no attempt to apologize for or mask his political views. Comic performers like Andy Kaufman and Neil Hamburger challenged the boundaries of the comic persona by giving intentionally unfunny performances that forced audiences to rethink their role within the performance, laughing at themselves as they recognized their relative powerlessness in the typical audience-performer relationship. Whether it is Kaufman reading *The Great Gatsby* on stage, even while the audiences screamed at him to get off, or Hamburger dropping glasses on stage and having performance CDs that include planted hecklers in the crowd, many comic performers have crafted personas that change our understanding of what a successful performance is.

Just as Hamburger and Kaufman challenged the boundaries of performance, so many humorists are at the front end of new forms of media associated with online forms of expression. Marc Maron has successfully transitioned from a funny but not necessarily groundbreaking stand-up comedian to a major figure in contemporary humor through his podcast interviews of other prominent American humorists. Likewise, many writers and performers such as Josh Groban have established a fan base through online humor forums before moving on to more established media such as cinema and television.

During the peak of vaudeville, comedic performers often worked in troupes or as part of larger groups of performers. Many of these troupes or duos—such as Abbot and Costello, the Three Stooges, and the Marx Brothers—went on to find work in movies or on television. During the 1980s, there was a stand-up comedy boom. As comedic performers like Steve Martin, Bill Cosby, and Eddie Murphy began to fill stadiums, the public interest in stand-up comedy provided the demand needed to create and keep in business many comedy clubs on both the east and west coasts. While this expansion allowed many performers to find both venues and money for their work, it also made it difficult for stand-up comics to set themselves apart. In turn, many comics developed gimmicks. For example, Smirnoff, based much of his comedy in the stereotypical differences between America's financial stability and Russia's oppression and relative poverty, and Emo Phillips and Judy Tenuta took on exaggerated personas. Nevertheless, during the 1980s, there was a sharp divide between the established comedians and their lesser-known counterparts, which made it very difficult for newer comics to break into professional humorist circles.

In the 1990s and beyond, large personas took a backseat to odd observational humor and strong political views, with major figures like Lewis Black and Jerry Seinfeld having well-defined but relatively realistic personas. Stand-up comics also sometimes competed with spoken-word artists, such as former punk rock icons Henry Rollins and Jello Biafra, for audiences, particularly as stand-up comedy evolved into anecdotes and observations rather than a series of jokes. Nevertheless, with outlets like comedy clubs, online opportunities like Funnyordie.com, and a large number of television networks giving space for stand-up performers, stand-up comedians and more humorous performers like Weird Al Yankovic and Sandra Bernhard have been able to regularly find audiences and avenues to practice their craft.

As the barriers between live performances, online media, and recorded works erode (Louis CK, for instance, has begun to avoid record companies and television networks, recording and releasing performances on his own), new voices and new approaches to comedy have come into focus more widely and more quickly, making the new millennium an exciting time to watch the evolution of American humor. Comedic performances have been come in the forms of podcasts, video games, and other forms that continue to emerge.

ANSARI, AZIZ (1989–)

Aziz Ansari was born to Indian parents in Columbia, South Carolina. While growing up, he attended South Carolina Governor's School for Science and Mathematics and the Marlboro Academy. After graduating from high school, Ansari attended New York University, where he graduated with a degree in marketing.

After his college graduation, Ansari pursued a career in performance, both in television and in stand-up. His early television and performing work included both Upright Citizens Brigade and MTV's *Human Giant*. Due to his work on these shows and his stand-up work, Ansari was included on *Rolling Stone*'s 2005 "Hot List" for up-and-coming stand-up comics. He went on to play a regular role on *Parks and Recreation* and in films, such as *Funny People*, where he played the part of Randy, which he sometimes adopts in his performances. Ansari has also done some activism, including organizing and performing at a benefit for bullied children in Los Angeles. In addition, he has broken through into voice acting, appearing as a wise-cracking slug in 2013's *Epic*. Still, the core of Ansari's work remains his stand-up comedy, and he continues to tour regularly.

In terms of style, Ansari is known for his distinctive, high-pitched voice and quick delivery. His rapid-fire speech allows him to work in a number of funny lines as he tells a story. In addition to his high-energy delivery, Ansari is known for balancing hip references and self-deprecating observations. In his film and television work, he generally plays characters who work too hard to be cool, undercutting any chance of genuine popularity. Although Ansari does have some material dealing with political events, he generally comments more on personal issues, such as his dating life after he became a prominent cultural figure and popular culture issues. Like other pop culture-focused comedians such as Chelsea Handler and Joel Stein, Ansari appears comfortable with his persona and material. He has generally received positive critical and popular reception, as indicated

Aziz Ansari is one of the first successful American stand-up comics of Indian descent. He has also been featured prominently in several films and television shows. (Carrienelson1/Dreamstime.com)

by both his *Rolling Stone* acknowledgment and his consistent appearances in both film and television. These appearances are noteworthy in that Ansari represents one of the first humorists of Indian descent (along with Aasif Mandvi) to break through into the cultural mainstream.

See also: Poehler, Amy

Further Reading

Ansari, Aziz. "Aziz Ansari Interviews Aziz Ansari about Being Aziz Ansari." *Bulletmedia.com,* January 3, 2013. Accessed August 27, 2013. http://bullettmedia.com/article/aziz-ansari/.

Grossman, Samantha. *Time.com*. "Aziz Ansari Explains Why He's a Feminist and Why We Don't Need to Be Afraid of That Word." http://time.com/3478159/aziz-ansari-feminism-jay-z-beyonce/.

Horn, Leslie. "Aziz Ansari Releasing New Comedy Special Online." *PC Magazine* (March 2012): 1.

Zeke Jarvis

ATTELL, DAVE (1965–)

Dave Attell was born in Queens, New York. Although Attell had academic success (he earned a degree in Film and Television from New York University), he has stated that he always felt a degree of uncertainty after graduating. It was partly in response to this uncertainty that Attell began pursuing stand-up comedy. While he worked to develop his stand-up persona and career, Attell also labored at a variety of low-level jobs, which provided him with material.

Attell's early stand-up work met with mixed reviews. Attell claims that he bombed in some crucial early gigs, but he did earn a reputation for being a "comedian's comedian," cultivating a fan base that included such humorists as Jon Stewart, who would later help him land a spot on *The Daily Show*. In 1988, Attell started to become more widely known through his television work on VH1's comedy show; his colleagues on the show included such future luminaries as Lewis Black, Margaret Cho, and Wanda Sykes. From there, Attell continued to gain prominence, receiving slots on *The Late Show with David Letterman*, which in turn led to a season's worth of work on *Saturday Night Live* from 1993 to 1994. Attell continued to do regular television work, including spots on *The Daily Show*, where he rose to some level of fame like fellow comedians Lewis Black, Stephen Colbert, and Steve Carell. Attell also did some film work, though he did not achieve either consistent or singularly striking success with any particular role.

In 2001, Attell was given his own show on Comedy Central, *Insomniac with Dave Attell*. The show was a mix of Attell's stand-up and his visits to a wide array of oddities and late-night businesses in the towns where he performed while on tour. The show played on Attell's long-standing claim and persona that he is an insomniac. While exploring the nightlife of a given city, Attell would crack jokes at passersby and take pictures on a disposable camera.

Attell continues to tour and perform. He had his own hour-long HBO special, *Captain Miserable*, in 2007. In addition to his film and television work, Attell has been a regular performer on the USO tour. He lives in New York when not on tour.

Attell is known for being a vulgar but imaginative comedian, cracking jokes about sex in sometimes unsettling but often surprising ways. Part of what other comedians indicate that they appreciate most about Attell's approach is his methodical, disciplined structure, incorporating surprising shifts in focus and callbacks even as he covers somewhat familiar territory. Attell also manages to make subtle social commentary with his off-the-wall analogies, particularly in his work on *The Daily Show* and *Tough Crowd with Colin Quinn*, where he would simultaneously comment on social or political issues while working in double entendres and outright profane statements. Another source of Attell's respected status among comedians is his practice of touring and appearing with other comics. On one tour, Attell appeared with Lewis Black and Mitch Hedberg, alternating headlining duties with Black. Although Attell has not achieved the same sort of prominence as some of his colleagues, such as Lewis Black and Stephen Colbert, he has been in the popular eye consistently enough to earn a reputation as a significant American humorist.

Further Reading

"Dave Attell Interview." Team Coco. 30 April, 2014, http://teamcoco.com/category/tags/dave-chappelle.

Spitznagel, Eric. "Dave Attell on the Touring Grind." *Billboard*. 5/24/2014, Vol. 126 Issue 17, p37.

Wolk, Josh. "Night Rider." *Entertainment Weekly*. 4/19/2002, Issue 649, p19.

Zeke Jarvis

AUSTEN, TREVOR (1974–)

Stephen Rogers was born in Madison, Wisconsin, and grew up in a Sun Prairie, a suburb of Madison. Following his graduation from high school, Rogers attended the University of Wisconsin-Oshkosh. After taking some time off to travel, Rogers returned to school, earning a degree in English and French, then going on to receive his master's and PhD in creative writing from the University of Wisconsin-Milwaukee in 2005. During his graduate work, he began performing under the name Trevor Austen. Austen performed in clubs throughout the Midwest as well as in some national shows. Eventually, Rogers left comedy behind for a career teaching at the college level. Currently, Rogers lives and works near Atlanta, Georgia.

Trevor Austen was best known for his self-effacing comedy that was largely rooted in his disability, which was being hard of hearing. In the same way that some ethnic minority comics mine their struggles and strengths for humor, Austen broke barriers by bringing a sense of comedy to his struggles, helping to pave the way for future comics with disabilities. While his career was relatively short and he did not break through into the national consciousness, Austen remains a noteworthy figure in American comedy.

See also: Martin, Steve

Further Reading

Limon, John. *Stand-up Comedy in Theory, or Abjection in America.* Durham: Duke University Press, 2000.

Reid, D. Kim, Edy Hammond Stoughton and Robin M. Smith. "The Humorous Construction of Disability: 'Stand–up' Comedians in the United States." *Disability & Society* 21, no. 6 (October 2006): 629–643.

Shain, Alan. "Comment from the Field." *Journal of Literary & Cultural Disability* Studies 7, no. 3 (2013): 337–346.

Zeke Jarvis

BARKER, ARJ (1974–)

Arjan Barker was born in San Anselmo, California. He is of mixed European and Indian heritage. After graduating from high school, Barker began working on his stand-up career. He steadily built up a reputation, eventually breaking through first with appearances on Comedy Central's *Premium Blend* and *Late Night with Conan O'Brien*. In 2004, Barker, along with two cowriters and performers, began performances of *The Marijuana-Logues*, a satirical take on *The Vagina Monologues*, discussing frankly the performers' enthusiasm for marijuana. Barker has also dabbled in web content, writing for his series *Arj and Poppy*.

Barker is known for his open and satirical commentary on his generation's political views, particularly on recreational drug use. One of his lines, "I used to get high on life, but then I built up a tolerance," helps to show his satirical view on drug use along with his dark but humorous view on life in general. Barker also represents his generation's view on comedy in that he openly discusses his personal life in a comical and absurd way. His smart observations about relationships and social issues have made Barker a successful figure in American comedy.

Further Reading

Ashman, Angela. "Lost in Medication." *Village Voice* 51, no. 3 (January 17, 2007): 36.

Benson, Doug, Tony Camin, and Arj Barker. *The Marijuana-Logues: Everything about Pot That We Could Remember.* New York: Crown Archetype, 2005.

Stimac, Elias. "The Marijuana-Logues." *Back Stage* 45, no. 27 (July 2, 2004): 40.

Zeke Jarvis

BARR, ROSEANNE (1952–)

Roseanne Barr was born in Salt Lake City, Utah. Barr is the oldest of four children in a working-class family. Although Barr's family was Jewish, her parents became involved in the Church of Latter-day Saints to fit in with their Salt Lake City community. At age three, Barr was afflicted with Bell's palsy. She recounts her parents bringing in a rabbi to pray for her to no effect, but notes that her affliction passed after a Mormon preacher prayed for her. While she would later discover that Bell's palsy was typically temporary, at the time the turn of events had an impact on Barr. She began to speak as part of the Church of Latter-day Saints services, giving her some early experience with public performance.

When Barr was 16, she was in a serious car accident, resulting in a brain injury. After the accident, her behavior changed to the point that she was briefly institutionalized. At age 17, Barr had a child whom she gave up for adoption; she also dropped out of high school. At 18, Barr left her parents' house, moving to Colorado. There, Barr met and married her first husband, with whom she had three children.

Roseanne Barr achieved popularity thanks to her brash, outspoken style. Although she was once a cutting-edge comic, she has evolved into an established, well-respected figure. (Turkbug/Dreamstime.com)

It was during this marriage that Barr began pursuing comedy in earnest, slowly building a career until she appeared on *The Tonight Show* in 1985. This exposure led to more success, culminating in an HBO special. In her act, she began referring to herself as a "domestic goddess," undercutting the stereotypical role of wife and mother expected of women. During this time, Barr also began to build connections in the comedy world, including with another larger-than-life comic, Sam Kinison.

Based on the success of her stand-up work, Barr was asked to create a sitcom, *Roseanne*, on ABC. The show differed from many other sitcoms in that it showed a working-class family and examined struggles rooted in class issues. The show ran for nine seasons, earning Barr a host of awards. It also gave early work to future humorists such as Judd Apatow, whose first writing credit was on *Roseanne*.

During the run of the show, Barr divorced her first husband and married Tom Arnold, who also worked on the show. The couple divorced after four years. Their troubled marriage was the subject of much publicity and, after their divorce, the two would have very public conflicts. Ultimately, they reconciled, partly through Barr's Comedy Central Roast. Not long after her divorce from Arnold, Barr married for a third time, this time having one child. This marriage ended in divorce in 2002.

After Barr's first sitcom ended, she began appearing on a number of television shows, eventually getting her own talk show. In 2005, Barr returned to stand-up comedy, this time performing in both America and in Europe. In 2009, after working on a variety of projects, Barr began hosting a politically themed radio talk show. Building upon this effort, she announced in 2011 that she would be running for U.S. president on the Green Party ticket; she also claimed to be running for prime minister of Israel. Barr lost her fight to be nominated as the Green Party's candidate, but she continued to participate in politics and activism, making appearances as part of the Occupy movement.

Barr continues to work in both comedy and politics. She and her long-time partner Johnny Argent live in Hawaii, where they own a macadamia nut farm.

Barr is known for her boisterous, boundary-breaking persona. As a representative of working-class women, she touched on topics that many other female comics of her generation had avoided. She also has consistently been willing to ridicule her own struggles and personal issues, openly and courageously referring to her mental health and substance abuse issues.

Although Barr's comedy has generally been well received, this has not always been the case. In 1990, Barr was invited to sing "The Star-Spangled Banner" before a baseball game. She sang it intentionally off-key and finished by grabbing her crotch, as baseball players sometimes do. Her performance was booed and generally panned by the public. Barr has twice joked about the event, once on a *Saturday Night Live* appearance not long after the performance and once on her Comedy Central Roast.

In general, Barr has not been shy about engaging in controversy or feuds. In particular, she feuded with Judy Tenuta, whose outlandish persona was often compared with Barr's as the two were beginning in stand-up comedy. Nevertheless, Barr's bold work has been cited as an inspiration to a number of younger female comics, including Chelsea Handler and Kathy Griffin, and she has firmly established herself as part of the American comedy landscape.

See also: Arnold, Tom

Further Reading

Barr, Roseanne. *Roseannarchy: Dispatches from the Nut Farm*. New York: Gallery Books, 2011.

Dresner, Zita Z. "Roseanne Barr: Goddess or She-Devil." *Journal of American Culture* (01911813) 16, no. 2 (Summer 1993): 37.

Lovric, Michelle. *Women's Wicked Wit: From Jane Austen to Roseanne Barr*. Chicago: Chicago Review Press, 2001.

Zeke Jarvis

BELZER, RICHARD (1944–)

Richard Belzer was born in Bridgeport, Connecticut, into a Jewish family. Belzer characterizes his childhood as difficult because he felt like a misfit. He claims to have been kicked out of multiple schools. After high school, Belzer attended Dean Junior College in Massachusetts and worked as a reporter. Belzer's mother died of breast cancer when he was 18, and his father committed suicide when Belzer was 22. Around the time of his father's death, Belzer married his first wife, Gail Susan Ross. After divorcing her, Belzer moved to New York City.

In New York, Belzer began his work in stand-up comedy in earnest. He worked at many well-known clubs, including Pips, Catch a Rising Star, and the Improv. As he gained prominence and experience, Belzer took a major role in Channel One, a comedy troupe known for its cutting and incisive satirizing of television. This led the movie *The Groove Tube*, a collection of shorts that featured Belzer along with future comics Ken Shapiro and Chevy Chase. As Belzer's career took off, he began working in television and film, including having a role in *Fame* and warming up the crowd for *Saturday Night Live*.

In 1976, Belzer married his second wife, Dalia Danoch. By 1978, the two had divorced. Belzer continued to do stand-up work, and he appeared in multiple music videos and had a slot on the *National Lampoon Radio Hour* as well as cohosting his own radio show. In 1983, Belzer began work on the program *The Thicke of the Night*, hosted by Alan Thicke and starring other comics such as Gilbert Gottfried and Chloe Webb. Although the program was not successful, it did achieve a level of exposure for Belzer that he had not previously enjoyed. Subsequently, Belzer received his own show, on which he was once rendered unconscious while his guest, Hulk Hogan, was demonstrating a chokehold on him. After the show, Belzer engaged in a highly publicized lawsuit against Hogan; it was eventually settled out of court. In 1985, Belzer married his current wife, Harlee McBride.

In the early 1990s, Belzer's work expanded into dramatic television, when he took on the regular role of Detective Munch. The character first appeared on *Homicide* and later cropped up on a variety of other shows, including *Law and Order: Special Victims Unit*. Between his multiple series, Belzer has portrayed Munch for more than 20 consecutive years. In addition to his television work, Belzer has written multiple books on both stand-up and conspiracies and cover-ups. He has appeared as an occasional political commentator as well.

Belzer is primarily known for his sarcastic, biting style and cool persona. Often wearing dark glasses and ripping into hecklers, Belzer's hip persona is the perfect counterpart to his sometimes aggressive and edgy style. Belzer also has experienced an interesting past and trajectory as a stand-up performer, opening for musicians on tours, including the late Warren Zevon. Belzer is well respected by other stand-up performers, having been honored at a Friars Club Roast. His long and consistent career has earned him a spot as a significant cultural and comic figure.

Further Reading

Belzer, Richard. *How to Be a Stand-up Comic*. New York: Villard Books, 1988.

Kurtz, Judy. "Richard Belzer Says 'Republican Party Has a Medical Condition.'" *Hill* 19, no. 122 (October 17, 2012): 36.

Stein, Joel. "Richard Belzer." *Time* 154, no. 15 (October 11, 1999): 94.

Zeke Jarvis

BLACK, LEWIS (1948–)

Lewis Black was born in Silver Spring, Maryland, in 1948. He graduated summa cum laude from Springbrook High School and studied for a year at the University of Maryland before transferring to the University of North Carolina at Chapel Hill to study theater. Black went on to earn a master of fine arts degree from the Yale School of Drama.

In the 1980s, Black worked as a playwright in New York City at the West Bank Cafe Downstairs Theatre Bar, where he composed numerous one-act plays. He also collaborated with Rusty Magee on a musical, *The Czar of Rock and Roll*. Black began doing stand-up comedy when his plays needed opening acts. By the end of the 1980s, he was doing stand-up comedy full time and occasionally appearing in small roles on television and in films such as *Hannah and Her Sisters* and *Jacob's Ladder*. While working as a stand-up comic, Black honed the style for which he is known today.

In the 1990s, Black made additional guest appearances on television in programs such as *The Days and Nights of Molly Dodd*, *Law & Order*, *Homicide: Life on the Street*, and *Mad about You*. In 1998, he starred in his first stand-up special on Comedy Central, which was part of the series *Comedy Central Presents*.

In 2000, Black was arrested for his involvement with the Naked Teen Voyeur Bus, which featured topless young women in a bus with glass walls that drove around New York City. He was released the next day and went on *The Daily Show* to assert his Constitutional rights.

Black appeared on *Comedy Central Presents* again in 2000 and in 2002. Also in 2002, he appeared in another special on Comedy Central, *Taxed beyond Belief*. Black hosted *The World Stupidity Awards*, founded by filmmaker Albert Nerenburg in 2003, to honor the year's stupidest man and the year's stupidest woman. Award recipients included politicians and pop culture figures such as John Kerry and Paris Hilton. Black hosted the awards several times at Montreal's *Just for Laughs* comedy festival in subsequent years. In 2004, Black starred in the HBO special *Black on Broadway*. This performance was also issued on a CD of the same name that year.

Nothing's Sacred, Black's autobiography, was published in 2005. In the book, Black openly recounts his family experiences, past drug use, and political opinions. At this time, he was also providing the voice for the character of Manobrain in the animated series *Duck Dodgers*. Black followed his book with another HBO special, *Red, White, and Screwed*, which was released on DVD a few months later. In 2007, Black won a Grammy Award for his album *The Carnegie Hall Performance*.

In 2008, Black began his stint as host of *The Root of All Evil* for Comedy Central. The show—which took the format of a mock trial pitting comedians against each other, with Black moderating them and deciding at the end which one was more evil—ran for two seasons. Also in 2008, Black published his next book, *Me of Little Faith*, which he supported with a book tour. In the same year, he released a comedy album, *Anticipation*, which drew material from his *Let Them Eat Cake* comedy tour.

Black continued his voiceover work in shows such as *Scooby Doo!, Mystery Incorporated*, and a revival of *Teenage Mutant Ninja Turtles*. He also appeared in the film *Accepted* and in an episode of *The Big Bang Theory*. He continued his stand-up tours, including a USO tour of Iraq, Kuwait, and Spain, and published yet another book, *I'm Dreaming of a Black Christmas*, in 2010. Several additional comedy albums followed, including 2013's *Old Yeller (Live at the Borgata)*, which was also a pay-per-view stand-up special.

Black's comedic persona is that of a man approaching the brink of insanity while encountering the absurdities of politics, religion, and popular culture. He usually performs his comedy as an angry rant in which profanity and sarcasm are trademarks, and in which he advocates his socialist political views. In this respect, his mannerisms are like those of Denis Leary, but his views are more closely akin to those held by George Carlin and Bill Hicks. Despite his often biting comedy and regular use of profanity, Black has managed to build a fairly wide and consistently loyal audience. Although he does not affiliate himself specifically with politics as much as Jon Stewart or Hicks, Black does give a clear and consistent view of the world as a fundamentally flawed and both scary and ridiculous place.

See also: Stewart, Jon

Further Reading

Black, Lewis. *Nothing's Sacred*. New York: Gallery Books, 2006.
Ito, Robert. "Lewis Black Mouths off." *Cincinnati* 47, no. 1 (October 2013): 30–31.
Salter, Chuck. "The Agonies of Lewis Black." *Fast Company* 108 (September 2006): 64–66.

Stephen Powers

BRENNER, DAVID (1936–2014)

David Brenner was born and raised in a working-class area of Philadelphia. Even as a child, his sense of humor was keen and distinctive, leading him to be declared "class president" multiple years. After graduating high school, Brenner went from being unemployed to joining the U.S. Army. Upon being discharged, Brenner attended Temple University, where he majored in communications and graduated with honors.

After graduation, Brenner pursued a career in stand-up comedy. His success led him to appear on *The Tonight Show*, where he would become a regular guest. In fact, Brenner holds the record for most appearances, at more than 150. Brenner also appeared on a number of news shows (spanning the political spectrum from MSNBC to CNN to Fox) because of his focus on current events in his performances. In addition to his stand-up work, Brenner wrote extensively. His writing was produced on a number of television shows and he published a number of successful books.

Brenner was married twice and was the father of three children. Both marriages ended in divorce and acrimonious custody battles, all of which were won by Brenner. Brenner died in 2014.

Brenner's humor is often characterized by a close attention to current events. Following in the footsteps of Mort Sahl and Lenny Bruce, he regularly skewered political figures for their handling and bungling of a variety of issues. He eschewed simple puns or wordplay for more conceptually funny material. Still, Brenner maintained an air of silliness for much of his work, balancing out his headier material with non-sequiturs and self-deprecating humor. While not all humorists appreciate Brenner's work, his success was sustained and noteworthy, selling large numbers of books and recording high ratings for his stand-up specials. Brenner remains a respected practitioner of humor in both broadcast and print.

Further Reading

Brenner, David. *I Think There's a Terrorist in My Soup: How to Survive Personal and World Problems with Humor—Seriously*. Riverside: Andrews McMeel, 2003.

Morrison, John F. "Comedian David Brenner, 78, Was a Uniquely Philly Guy." *Philadelphia Daily News*, March 17, 2014. http://articles.philly.com/2014-03-18/news/48301351_1_david-letterman-west-philly-comedy.

Poniewozik, James. "David Brenner." *Time International* (South Pacific Edition) 183, no. 12 (March 31, 2014): 26.

Zeke Jarvis

BRUCE, LENNY (1925–1966)

Leonard Alfred Schneider was born in Mineola, New York. His parents, Myron and Dorothy Schneider, divorced when he was five years old, resulting in his living with relatives for the next 10 years. At the age of 16, Schneider, who would take the stage name of Bruce, joined the U.S. Navy and spent time on the U.S.S. *Brooklyn* during World War II. Following a comedy performance that saw Bruce dress in drag, and on account of his commanders being upset with that show, Bruce claimed to being experiencing homosexual leanings. He received a dishonorable discharge in 1945 on this basis. However, because he never admitted to breaking any naval regulations, he was able to get the discharge changed to "under honorable conditions . . . by reason of unsuitability for the naval service."

In 1947, Schneider changed his name to Bruce after first performing under the name "Lenny Marsalle." In 1951, Bruce met and later married stripper Honey Harlow. Bruce wanted to make enough money to allow his wife to stop working as a stripper. This motivation led Bruce to run a money-making scam under the guise of the "Brother Matthias Foundation," in which Bruce claimed to be a religious official collecting money for orphans; in reality, he took the donations from wealthy families and kept it for his own. Though he was never charged in the scheme, his arrest during this attempted scam marked the beginning of Bruce's contentious relationship with the law.

It was during his marriage to Harlow (and the subsequent time spent performing and working in strip clubs) that Bruce began to create his comedic identity. He began writing a series of screenplays: *Dance Hall Racket* (1953), *Dream Follies* (1954), and *The Rocket Man* (1954). During this time, Bruce also released four comedy albums that cemented his style and traditional themes of his work.

As his notoriety grew, he appeared on the *Steve Allen Show* several times. Bruce and Harlow's only daughter, Kitty, was born in 1955. Shortly thereafter, Bruce began an affair with jazz singer Annie Ross, which led to the breakup of his marriage. Bruce and Harlow divorced in 1957, though the divorce was not finalized until 1959.

Lenny Bruce was a major figure for an entire generation of stand-up comics. Both Jon Stewart and Richard Lewis have referred to Bruce and his work as being a touchstone for transgressive or political comedy. (Library of Congress)

As Bruce's career developed, so did his persecution by the law. He was arrested five times—three times in 1961, once in 1962, and once in 1964. The reasons for these arrests included drug possession, but his use of obscenity truly made him a target of officials. Bruce was eventually found guilty of obscenity in 1964 and sentenced to four months in a workhouse. He appealed, but before the appeal was finalized he died of a drug overdose in his home on August 3, 1966.

Bruce's career was marred by constant charges of obscenity, resulting in him being banned from almost every nightclub in the United States by the time of his death—most clubs feared being prosecuted for supporting his work. Bruce was also banned from several cities around the world. Though he did reach significant notoriety for his comedy, he appeared on network television only six times.

Jazz music, spontaneity, and free association were cornerstones of Bruce's act. His first four records—rereleased as *The Lenny Bruce Originals*—are where his noted themes of jazz, moral philosophy, politics, drugs, the Ku Klux Klan, and Judaism (among others) became evident. It was perhaps these sorts of challenges and the edgy material that he used that made him a target of police as much as his actual obscenity. After Bruce's death, many of the police officers who had been responsible for his arrests changed their feelings about his work, stating that his persecution was the product of a repressive era rather than the result of genuinely problematic material. Bruce always claimed that his quotes were taken out of context, and he frequently requested that he just be able to do his act in court to demonstrate the necessity of obscenity within his work. Bruce's commentary and the daring that he showed in his willingness to work largely extemporaneously made him and Mort Sahl inspirations for generations of comedians. Likewise, his interest in language and power clearly influenced some of the most highly regarded stand-up comic routines in history, perhaps most notably George Carlin's "Seven Words You Can't Say on Television" bit. After Bruce's death, he was portrayed by Dustin Hoffman in a film biopic of his life. He is mentioned in songs by R.E.M., Bob Dylan, Nico, and others, demonstrating his long lasting cultural impact. Bruce also appears on the cover of the Beatles' *Sgt. Pepper's Lonely Hearts Club Band* album from 1967. In 2004, Comedy Central placed Bruce at number three on its list of the 100 Greatest Stand-Ups of All-Time.

See also: Carlin, George; Hicks, Bill; Sahl, Mort

Further Reading

Collins, Ronald, and David Skover. *The Trials of Lenny Bruce: The Fall and Rise of an American Icon*. Chicago: Source Books, 2002.

Goldman, Albert Harry. *Ladies and Gentleman—Lenny Bruce!!* New York: Random House, 1974.

Marowitz, Charles. "Remembering Lenny Bruce." *New Theatre Quarterly* 30, no. 3 (August 2014): 214–217.

Brian Davis

BURNS, GEORGE (1896–1996)

Nathan Birnbaum was born into a large family in New York City; he was the ninth of 12 children. His parents, who had emigrated from Romania, were active in their local synagogue. While Birnbaum, who would come to be known as George Burns, was still a child, his father died as part of a flu epidemic. Burns went to work to support the family. Although he was working in various odd jobs, Burns left both those positions and school in the fourth grade to pursue show business after he and his siblings received positive feedback for their singing in the neighborhood. Burns adopted his stage name around this time, though various stories have surfaced about how he chose the name.

In his early performances, Burns tried out a variety of activities, including singing, dancing, and even roller skating. He also began partnering with female performers who would help him to develop comic banter. Burns married his first partner, though the marriage lasted for only half a year. Burns has stated that they married only so that her family would allow her to go away with him on tour. Not long after that, Burns partnered with another woman whom he would eventually marry, Gracie Allen. Allen had experience in performance as part of "The Four Colleens," an Irish dancing act. Burns and Allen developed a long and successful partnership, with Burns playing the straight man to Allen's seemingly dim-witted but likable character. The two began performing in vaudeville, then proceeded to receive work in radio, on television, and in films, with Burns typically writing their act. Burns and Allen married in 1926, with Jack Benny serving as Burns's best man. In 1934, the two adopted a daughter; in 1935, they adopted a son. The two would continue to perform for the next three decades, until Gracie Allen died of a heart attack in 1964.

After Allen's death, Burns continued to work regularly, perhaps most prominently in his role in *The Sunshine Boys*, which earned him an Oscar. Burns had taken the role in place of Jack Benny, who was not able to do so because of his failing health. Although Burns would appear in other well-received films, such as the *Oh God* series, none would receive the critical respect that *The Sunshine Boys* did. Burns continued to work, having cameos in a variety of pieces. Toward the end of his life, Burns slipped and fell in the bathtub, suffering a head injury from which he was unable to fully recover. In 1996, after turning 100, Burns passed away in his home.

Burns and Allen were very prominent performers for an extended period of time. In the format used by many other comic duos, such as the Smothers Brothers, Burns played the more serious half, trying to maintain a level of logic and professionalism even in the face of his partner's irrational and absurd behavior. While this dynamic did not originate with Burns and Allen, they were one of the leading practitioners of it. They also demonstrated the vaudevillian style of humor that is often characterized by wordplay and jokes of timing and rhythm. Their quick exchanges and witty banter fit a variety of performance venues, from clubs to radio to television. In addition to their role as representatives of an era of humor, Burns and Allen helped other comics, including Bob Hope and Bing Crosby, who began their "road pictures" partly thanks to Burns and Allen. The couple also featured voice artist Mel Blanc as a supporting cast member in a number of their performances.

Burns and Allen also are notable for the overlap between their comic personas and their real lives. Many audience members associated Burns and Allen very closely with the characters that they portrayed, because the public knew that the two were married. Their marriage was also noteworthy because it was an interfaith marriage—Burns was Jewish and Allen was Catholic—which was unusual for the time in which they were married. Part of what made Burns and Allen's marriage acceptable to the general public, of course, was the clear affection and engaging dynamic that the two had together. For this reason, and because of the gradual acceptance of interfaith relationships, the two of them will always be much more widely known for their comedic work than anything else. Indeed, for his long and storied career, Burns holds a unique place of esteem in the comedy world.

Further Reading

Burns, George. *100 Years, 100 Stories*. New York: Putnam, 1996.

Epstein, Lawrence. *George Burns: An American Life*. Jefferson, NC: McFarland, 2011.

Wolfe, Charles. " 'Cross-Talk': Language, Space, and the Burns and Allen Comedy Film Short." *Film History: An International Journal* 23, no. 3 (2011): 300–312.

Zeke Jarvis

CARLIN, GEORGE (1937–2008)

George Carlin was born in Manhattan. After his parents separated when he was two months old, he was raised by his mother. Carlin attended Corpus Christi School, then Cardinal Hayes High School until he was 15, at which point Carlin decided

George Carlin was a major figure in stand-up comedy. His "Seven Words You Can't Say on Television" bit was perhaps the most famous in stand-up history. (Dreamstime.com)

to leave the school. He next attended Bishop Dubois High School and then Salesian High School. Carlin joined the U.S. Air Force when he was old enough and began working as a disc jockey at radio station KJOE. He was labeled "unproductive," court-martialed three times, and discharged in July 1957.

Carlin met fellow comedian Jack Burns in 1959, and the two moved to California as a comedic duo in 1960. While they worked together on their radio show, *The Wright Brothers*, Carlin began appearing on variety shows. He became a frequent guest on *The Tonight Show*, first with Jack Paar, then with Johnny Carson. In the 1970s, in an attempt to stay relevant, Carlin began performing stand-up in small clubs, which reduced his income. He released the album *FM & AM*, which paid homage to his original style of stand-up while introducing his new style. As he gained relevance, he also perfected his most popular comedic routine, "The Seven Words You Can Never Say on Television." His performances once resulted in an arrest at Milwaukee's Summerfest, which led to him referring to the routine as "the Milwaukee Seven" for a time. In October 1975, Carlin hosted the premiere episode of *Saturday Night Live*, but was the only host not to appear in sketches.

In 1976, Carlin began a five-year hiatus from performing. Later, Carlin made public that the reason for hiatus was health issues. Upon returning to show business, Carlin began working in film. He acted in such films as *Outrageous Fortune*, *Bill & Ted's Excellent Adventure*, *Bill and Ted's Bogus Journey*, and *The Prince of Tides*. He also worked in television as Mr. Conductor on *Shining Time Station* and on his own show, *The George Carlin Show,* in 1993, though the show was neither a critical nor a commercial success. Carlin's book, *Brain Droppings*, sold almost 900,000 copies and spent 40 weeks on the *New York Times'* Best Seller List.

Carlin married Brenda Hosbrook in June 1961. The two had one daughter, Kelly, before Brenda died of liver cancer in 1997. Carlin remarried Sally Wade in June 1998; he died shortly before their 10th anniversary. Carlin was honored at the 1997 Aspen Comedy Festival with a retrospective, *George Carlin: 40 Years of Comedy*. In 2001, Carlin was given a Lifetime Achievement Award at the American Comedy Awards.

Carlin was largely regarded as picking up on the work of Lenny Bruce and Mort Sahl as a clear and cutting social commentator. From his "Seven Words" bit to his discussions of "filth" (the amount of unsanitary material allowed in certain food items like hot dogs), Carlin regularly served as the voice of a disenchanted population skeptical of mainstream views. Carlin was also particularly skilled at incorporating both conversational, street-style voices and more educated and refined delivery. In addition, his career is noteworthy because Carlin took an unusual approach, being refined and professional in his early work and then more transgressive and confrontational (growing his hair out and refusing to wear suits for his performances) in his later career. Also, for his daring, his social commentary, and his careful attention to language, Carlin is known as one of the most important and influential stand-up comics in the history of American humor.

See also: Bruce, Lenny

Further Reading

Altschuler, Glenn C. "Snarlin' Carlin: The Odyssey of a Libertarian." *Studies in American Humor* 3, no. 20 (2009): 42–57.

Carlin, George. *Brain Droppings*. New York: Hyperion, 1997.

Sullivan, James. *7 Dirty Words: The Life and Times of George Carlin*. New York: De Capo Press, 2010.

Kristen Franz

CHAPPELLE, DAVE (1973–)

David Chappelle was born in Washington, D.C., but grew up mainly in Silver Spring, Maryland. Both of Chappelle's parents were professors. When they separated, Chappelle began to split time between Washington and Ohio. Chappelle attended Washington, D.C.'s Duke Ellington School of the arts, where he studied theater.

After graduating, Chappelle moved to New York to pursue his comedic career. His first major attempt was at the Apollo Theater's amateur night. Although Chappelle was booed off the stage, he took it as a positive experience overall and continued to work on his act, eventually getting regular bookings in clubs. Chappelle also appeared in a variety of films and shows, including *Robin Hood: Men in Tights*, directed by Mel Brooks, and *Home Improvement*, with his friend Jim Breuer. The pair were scheduled to have a sitcom together, *Buddies*, but Breuer was pulled off the project; the sitcom was largely unsuccessful. After the failure of the show and his father's death, which happened shortly thereafter, Chappelle contemplated leaving show business.

In 1998, the marijuana-themed film *Half Baked* was released, with Chappelle starring in and having cowritten the film. Although it did not achieve financial

Dave Chappelle has had a truly unique career. At the height of its popularity, he walked away from his eponymous show on Comedy Central. Even so, he has remained an influential and respected figure in American comedy. (Comedy Central/Photofest)

success in its theatrical release, it did become a cult favorite. Also in 1998, Chappelle converted to Islam. In 2000, he had his first HBO stand-up special, *Dave Chappelle: Killin' Them Softly*. The special was generally viewed as a success, and it helped lead Chappelle to other opportunities.

In 2001, Chappelle married. He and his wife have had three children.

Chappelle continued working and pursuing his craft, eventually culminating in him co-creating a show on Comedy Central. *Chappelle's Show* began in 2003 and quickly became a critical and commercial success. Richard Pryor said that he saw Chappelle as his successor as a comic and cultural commentator, and the DVD sales of the show were tremendous. Chappelle appeared to be poised for even greater success, with a movie planned in which he would portray Rick James, based on the popularity of sketches from Chappelle's show. It was also announced that Chappelle had been offered a $55 million contract to continue with his show for two more seasons. Despite the financial incentives, Chappelle stepped away from the show, leaving on a trip to South Africa instead of finishing production.

In 2005, Chappelle came back into the public eye, giving stand-up performances. The following year, *Dave Chappelle's Block Party* was released. The film was a documentary that showed a combination of musical performances, impromptu interviews, and humorous commentary from Chappelle. Chappelle has continued to perform in stand-up and in other media. He currently lives in Yellow Springs, Ohio, with his wife and family.

Chappelle is known for his commentary on race relations, frankly examining many of the struggles of African Americans through satirical takes on stereotypes and proposed solutions to alleviate racial tension. His sketch comedy show in particular put on display many of American culture's anxieties about race. For the example, "The Racial Draft" sketch featured entire races laying claim to celebrities of mixed-race backgrounds. Another famous but controversial sketch portrayed a blind African American who, not knowing his own race, became a prominent figure in the white power movement. While these sketches were generally well received, Chappelle has commented that some of them seemed socially irresponsible, which is what led him to step away from the show at the height of its popularity. *Chappelle's Show* also featured more base comedy, skewering celebrities and making jokes about bodily functions and drugs and alcohol. Chappelle's stand-up is generally more grounded in realism than his sketch comedy show was, but it contains many of the same themes—in particular, tensions along class and racial lines and other cultural struggles. Although Chappelle has yet to regain the mainstream prominence that he once held, based on the success of his show and his stand-up, he remains an important figure in American comedy.

See also: Mooney, Paul

Further Reading

Bradley, Bill. "Dave Chappelle Explains He Never Quit 'Chappelle's Show,' He's Just Seven Years Late for Work." *Huffington Post*, June 11, 2014. http://www.huffingtonpost.com/2014/06/11/dave-chapelle-leaving-chappelle-show-letterman_n_5483964.html.

Locker, Melissa. "Dave Chappelle Describes the First Time He Met Kanye West and It's Amazing." *Time.com* (June 17, 2014): 39.

Powell, Kevin. "Heaven, Hell, Dave Chappelle." *Esquire* 145, no. 5 (May 2006): 92–147.

Zeke Jarvis

CHO, MARGARET (1968–)

Margaret Cho was born to Korean parents in San Francisco, California. When discussing her childhood, Cho generally reflects on the diversity of her community, including the racial, generational, and cultural diversity. Cho's parents ran a bookstore, and her father wrote joke books. Cho auditioned to get into the San Francisco School for the Arts when it was time for her to attend high school. Once there, she became part of the school's improvisational comedy group.

After graduating, Cho began performing, first developing her act by performing in the club adjacent to her parents' bookstore, then striking out into other clubs and television appearances. Early in her career, she gained some high-profile appearances for which she received high critical praise; for example, she opened for Jerry Seinfeld and won Best Female Comedian at the American Comedy Awards in 1994. That same year, Cho began to develop the sitcom *All American Girl*, which was largely based on her stand-up act. Unfortunately, Cho felt unhappy with the project, feeling pressure from both the East Asian community and the show's producers over her portrayal of East Asians. She also starved herself under pressure to look right for TV, which led to serious health issues. After the show was canceled, Cho turned to drugs and alcohol, once even being so inebriated during a performance that she was booed off the stage by the audience.

Cho eventually became and stayed sober, and she returned to prominence with her one-woman show and book about her struggles with substance abuse. Both were titled *I'm the One That I Want*. Cho has continued to work on stage and

Margaret Cho at the VH1 Rock Honors The Who event in 2008. Cho is one of the first Asian American comics to achieve mainstream success. (Aaron Settipane/Dreamstime.com)

on screen, often appearing in independent films and lesser-known shows, as with her regular role on *Drop Dead Diva*. In addition, Cho has appeared on mainstream shows like HBO's *Sex in the City* and *30 Rock*. In 2003, Cho married Al Ridenour and they filed for divorce in December 2014.

In addition to her comedy, Cho has pursued a wide variety of interests, including belly and burlesque dancing, fashion, and appearing in a wide variety of music videos. She has been an outspoken advocate of oppressed groups, most notably the gay and lesbian community. Cho, who continues to perform comedy and other artistic forms, currently lives near Atlanta, Georgia.

Cho is known for discussing both her personal life and her cultural background. She openly discusses her struggles with addiction and the painful effects of discrimination, though she tempers the harshness of these topics with lighthearted wordplay and absurd situations. Cho also speaks out for women and for the LGBT community in her act, making her political and social views an integral part of her work, akin to Janeane Garofalo and Al Franken. Part of her openness comes in her frank discussions of sexuality and sexual desire; for example, she often discusses her admiration for male adult film star Jeff Stryker. Cho does impressions of her mother as well. While some critics feel that she employs stereotypes in her act, others suggest that Cho is actually ridiculing or unpacking those stereotypes in her act, creating a space for open dialogue rather than perpetuating the stereotypes. In her transgressive and edgy material, Cho is working to undo the stereotype of the meek, proper Asian woman. She has become a prominent figure in a number of subcultures and continues to work in a wide variety of media and forms.

Further Reading

Cho, Margaret. *I'm the One That I Want*. New York: Ballantine Books, 2002.

Lee, Hyun Joo. "Imagining beyond the Here and Now in Margaret Cho's *I'm the One That I Want*." *Criticism: A Quarterly for Literature and the Arts* 55, no. 3 (Summer 2013): 423–446.

Reed, Jennifer. "Sexual Outlaws: Queer in a Funny Way." *Women's Studies: An Interdisciplinary Journal* 40, no. 6 (September 2011): 762–777.

Zeke Jarvis

CK, LOUIS (1967–)

Louis Szekely was born in Washington, D.C. His father was Mexican and his mother was of Irish descent. Szekely writes his surname as CK to simplify the pronunciation.

CK's family lived in Mexico City for much of his early childhood. When CK was seven, his family moved to Boston. There, CK discovered stand-up comedy, admiring such luminaries as Richard Pryor, George Carlin, and Steve Martin. When he was 10, his parents divorced. Along with his three siblings, CK was then raised by his mother in Newton, Massachusetts. After graduating from high school, he worked as an auto mechanic.

His early forays into stand-up were not successful, but over time CK began to establish himself and become comfortable on stage, even opening for Jerry Seinfeld. In 1989, he moved to New York to more fully pursue his comedy career. In addition to his work as a stand-up, he worked as a writer on a wide variety of shows, including The *Late Show with David Letterman*, *Late Night with Conan O'Brien*, and *The Dana Carvey Show*. CK has often performed his stand-up material on the shows for which he has written. CK married in 1995. He and his wife had children before divorcing in 2008.

In 2001, CK released *Pootie Tang*, which drew from his work on the sketches for *The Chris Rock Show*. While the theatrical release was not commercially successful, the film became a cult classic after its DVD release. In 2006, CK wrote and appeared in the series *Lucky Louie* on HBO. Though the series was canceled after one season, it gave CK experience that he would build on with his show on the FX network, *Louie*; that show, which debuted in 2009, has been a tremendous critical success. Also in 2009, CK recorded a live performance that he independently released. This effort marked the beginning of CK's leaving behind commercial labels and taking charge of the production and distribution of his work, making him the first major stand-up comic to do so. CK continues to regularly perform as a stand-up comic, both in the shows that he records and releases and on tour for the USO. He lives in New York while not on tour.

CK is best known for his surprising frankness on stage. Like one of his comic idols, Richard Pryor, he is very open about his personal life, including his frailties and his weaknesses. On an episode of *Louie*, for example, he defends masturbation and his stand-up, while discussing topics like his shallowness and his laziness. In addition to his honesty and directness, CK takes surprising but clear stances on social issues, most notably disdaining any acceptance of racism and challenging opposition to gay marriage. While CK does not specifically advocate for a singular political party, he clearly challenges conservative and exclusionary views of the world.

CK is also known for being interested in pushing the boundaries of comedy formats. In addition to his break from traditional methods of production and release of his comedy, his show *Louie* not only intersperses a sitcom structure with stand-up (much like *Seinfeld* did), but also takes on much more transgressive material and topics as well as weightier issues, such as selling out and the perceived feud between CK and Dane Cook over what many perceived as Cook plagiarizing CK. *Louie* has also featured a variety of notable stars in guest roles, including Joan Rivers, demonstrating the respect that CK has achieved within stand-up comedy circles. In addition, CK has championed some young comics, such as Tig Notaro, and has maintained long-time friendships and collaborations with comics like Conan O'Brien and Robert Smigel. CK has a strong and lasting output that has been acknowledged critically and continues to grow in terms of commercial success.

See also: Cook, Dane

Further Reading

"The 15 Funniest People Alive." *GQ Magazine,* January 2014. http://www.gq.com/blogs/the-feed/2014/04/the-15-funniest-comedians-in-america.html.

Rabin, Nathan. "Louis CK Interview." *Onion AV Club,* July 6, 2011. http://www.avclub.com/article/louis-ck-58516.

Rivers, Joan. "Louis CK." *Time International (Atlantic Edition)* 179, no. 17 (April 30, 2012): 30–31.

Zeke Jarvis

COOK, DANE (1972–)

Dane Cook was born in Cambridge, Massachusetts, part of a large Irish Catholic family. Although Cook describes himself as being shy at school, he began his work in stand-up comedy and acting during high school. After graduating, he studied graphic design and continued working at stand-up.

In 1994, Cook moved to New York City to pursue his career in comedy. After performing in New York for two years, he moved to Los Angeles. While there, he got a spot on Comedy Central's *Premium Blend*, helping him to gain a level of prominence. Two years later, Cook had a half-hour special on Comedy Central; not long after that, he put out his first CD. As Cook's stand-up career took off, he began pursuing acting as well, having small roles in movies like *Mystery Men* and leading roles in *Good Luck Chuck* and *Employee of the Month*. Cook has also hosted a number of shows, including two highly rated episodes of *Saturday Night Live* and the Teen Choice Awards, along with Jessica Simpson.

Although Cook has enjoyed tremendous commercial success, he is not without his troubles. In 2008, Cook's half-brother Darryl, who had been his manager up to that point, was convicted of embezzling from Cook. Darryl and his wife went to jail for their crimes. In addition, Cook's career has been encountered its share of controversy, with other comedians disparaging his material and accusing him of stealing material. While the most vociferous of Cook's accusers has clearly been Joe Rogan, the most well-known controversy surrounding Cook's alleged theft of material involved bits originally performed by Louis CK. While CK has been relatively noncommittal in his discussions of how intentional any plagiarism on Cook's part might have been, many have attributed this reluctance to assign blame to CK's professionalism and Cook's insecurity. Still, Cook and CK established a sense of peace when Cook appeared on CK's sitcom *Louie*, where each comic played himself and the pair openly discussed the controversy, albeit as exaggerated versions of themselves. Despite the controversies and other issues, Cook maintains a tremendous popular appeal, holding a number of records for sales and ratings for his work. Currently, he lives and works in Los Angeles.

Cook is known for both his high-energy performances and what he refers to as his puppy-dog demeanor, which draws on his attempts to cultivate an everyman persona. This persona carries over to much of Cook's screen work, where he often plays a likable slacker who ultimately succeeds despite struggles along the way. Ironically, this aspect, which seems to please audiences, has triggered some of his harshest criticism from his fellow comics, who sometimes refer to his work as predictable and unimaginative. Regardless of whether his material is distinctive or not, Cook's persona and performances continue to please audiences on stage and on screen.

See also: CK, Louis

Further Reading

D'Allessandro, Anthony. "Louis CK: Dane Cook a 'Good Guy,' Didn't Steal Jokes Knowingly." *Huffington Post*, June 19, 2012. http://www.huffingtonpost.com/2012/06/19/louis-ck-says-dane-cook-a-good-guy_n_1609526.html.

Vary, Adam B. "Dane Cook Shapes up." *Entertainment Weekly* 1048 (May 22, 2009): 50.

Zeke Jarvis

CROSS, DAVID (1964–)

David Cross was born in Atlanta, Georgia. His father was an immigrant from Leeds, England. While Cross was growing up, his family moved to New York and Connecticut before returning to Georgia, this time in the smaller town of Roswell. Cross's father left the family when Cross was 10. Cross, his two sisters, and his mother struggled financially, sometimes living with friends.

While still in high school, Cross began performing stand-up comedy. Upon graduation, he left for New York. After searching for work, Cross enrolled in Emerson College in Boston. While he dropped out after a single semester, Cross did make connections with others interested in comedy, becoming part of the group known as This Is Pathetic. While in Boston, Cross also became part of the alternative comedy scene with Janeane Garofalo and Louis CK, among others. Within this more experimental comedy scene, Cross formed the group Cross Comedy, which played tricks on the audience, such as using fake hecklers similar to those used by Andy Kaufman.

Cross made his first break into television on *The Ben Stiller Show*, where he met Bob Odenkirk. This friendship would be particularly productive, with the two creating *Mr. Show*, which helped to establish Cross and Odenkirk in the comedy world, and which also gave a number of comedians, such as Brian Posehn, launching pads for their careers. After *Mr. Show* ended, Cross worked on a number of films and television shows, including *News Radio*, *Aqua Teen Hunger Force*, and *The Drew Carey Show*. Cross also performed stand-up comedy, touring and releasing records. His next regular role on television came when he played Dr. Tobias Fünke on *Arrested Development*. While the show was a critical success and quickly gained a devoted cult following, it was canceled after only three seasons. Cross and others were vocal in their criticism of the Fox Network regarding its handling of the show, especially the fact that the network switched the show's time slot multiple times during its short run. Since the show's end, Cross has continued to tour and work in television and film. He also has created a show on IFC, *The Increasingly Poor Decisions of Todd Margaret*. In 2012, he married girlfriend Amber Tamblyn.

While Cross's early comedic work was more abstract and absurd, sending up television and cultural figures in a light-hearted way, his more recent work has been more explicitly political. Cross has taken on a number of other comics, most notably Larry the Cable Guy, whom Cross accuses of tapping into the homophobic and racist urges of audiences by employing thoughtless, unoriginal comedy. Cross has also made the same accusation about some of the comedians who were prominent in the Boston comedy scene while he was coming up. Cross has taken on the entertainment industry as well, most notably the producers of the *Alvin and the Chipmunks* series, in which Cross has had a part. Still, not all of Cross's comedy is based in attack. He promotes a positive, humanist worldview, though his material often contains an undercurrent of darkness. Like his fellow alternative comics such as Garofalo and Louis CK, Cross's work espouses a view that demonstrates an overall dissatisfaction with the world and civilization. This speaks to Cross's general approach to comedy, which is largely grounded in a sense of blistering honesty, confronting difficult truths and unlikable figures. Cross has made a number of strong connections throughout the comedy industry, and his wide base of work has helped to establish his importance to American comedy.

See also: Odenkirk, Bob; Posehn, Brian

Further Reading

Cross, David. *I Drink for a Reason*. New York: Grand Central Publishing, 2010.

Ringen, Jonathan. "David Cross." *Rolling Stone* 982 (September 8, 2005): 59.

Ryfle, Steve. "Run, Ronnie, Run: The Ronnie Dobbs Story." *Creative Screenwriting* 9, no. 2 (March–April 2002): 18–19.

Zeke Jarvis

DANGERFIELD, RODNEY (1921–2004)

Jacob Rodney Cohen was born on Long Island, New York. His father, Phil Roy, was a vaudevillian performer. Jacob, who would eventually adopt the stage name Rodney Dangerfield, has remarked that his father was often out performing—and frequently cheating on his mother—and that he felt unsupported by his mother.

Dangerfield began pursuing comedy at age 15, writing jokes at first and beginning to perform at age 20. His early attempts at comedy were not particularly successful. As he struggled, he began to pursue other performance outlets, including spending time as a singing waiter. In 1949, he married for the first time, having two children. To support his family, Dangerfield left performance and sold aluminum siding. In 1961, Dangerfield and his first wife divorced, and he began pursuing comedy again in earnest. Still, he struggled for a time, eventually coming to the conclusion that his struggles came partly from his lack of a clear persona. This struggle, ironically, led to his success, as he adopted the persona of a lovable loser. He also began using his stage name, which Dangerfield took from an unsuccessful cowboy character off of one of Jack Benny's shows. He began using the phrase, "I don't get no respect," to wind up some of his bits.

After an extremely successful appearance on *The Ed Sullivan Show*, many doors opened for Dangerfield, including regular performances in Las Vegas. As his career began to regain momentum, he remarried his first wife, though the two would end up divorcing again. Once Dangerfield's success was fully established through his regular performances and appearances on *Saturday Night Live* and other venues, he decided to devote significant money and energy to helping young comics. In addition to including comics like Sam Kinison in his films, such as *Back to School*, Dangerfield started a comedy club called Dangerfield's, which hosted a number of HBO specials featuring young comics such as Jerry Seinfeld, Bill Hicks, Roseanne Barr, and Jim Carrey. Even beyond these direct beneficiaries of his efforts, younger comics have regularly talked about Dangerfield's commitment to helping others gain popularity and recognition.

Over time, Dangerfield began to appear in films and advertisements. He was in huge cultural landmarks such as *Caddyshack* and lesser-known films such as *Meet Wally Sparks*. In 1993, Dangerfield married for the third time; he would remain married until his death in 2004. While his career slowed down in later years, he remained close friends with some of the comics whose careers he helped to launch, perhaps most notably Sam Kinison, who died in 1992, and Jim Carrey, who Dangerfield signed to open for him.

Dangerfield will likely always be associated with the bewildered, everyman persona that he crafted over the years both in his stand-up work and on screen. His signature line and self-effacing humor borrowed from Groucho Marx and W. C. Fields, but also strongly influenced an entire generation of comics, from Jim Carrey to Bill Hicks, though Dangerfield tended to bridle at being too closely associated with his persona in later years. Dangerfield is regarded with nearly universal respect by stand-up comedians and comedic performers. After his death, *Saturday Night Live* ran a sketch featuring Darrell Hammond playing Dangerfield at the gates of heaven; Dangerfield's name is also reported to be a popular choice for celebrity tattoos. Along with Richard Pryor, Dangerfield is one of the core comedians referred to as an inspiration and source of support by younger generations of comics. Dangerfield's extemporaneous wit is also well known, with his role in *Caddyshack* being greatly expanded (as was Bill Murray's) after his many ad libs. With his keen wit and consummate professionalism, Dangerfield clearly and fully established himself as a comedy giant in American culture.

See also: Kinison, Sam

Further Reading

Boliek, Brooks. "It's about Time We Give *Caddyshack* Its Due." *Hollywood Reporter* (International Edition) 397, no. 33 (January 2, 2007): 80.

Dangerfield, Rodney. *It Ain't Easy Bein' Me: A Life Time of No Respect But Plenty of Sex and Drugs*. New York: Harper, 2004.

Neill, Mike, J. D. Heyman, Michael Fleeman, and Frank Swertlow. "Rodney Dangerfield: 1921–2004." *People* 62, no. 16 (October 18, 2004): 69–70.

Zeke Jarvis

DILLER, PHYLLIS (1917–2012)

Phyllis Driver was born in Lima, Ohio. An only child, Driver, who went on to be known as Phyllis Diller, studied piano after graduating from high school. She first attended Columbia College at Chicago, then transferred to Bluffton College. After graduating, she spent time as a housewife (she was married to Sherwood Anderson Diller from 1939 to 1965), then as a copywriter at an advertising agency. In 1952, she began her performance career on radio. Shortly after her introductory work in radio, Diller began working in television and in stand-up, working at the Purple Onion in San Francisco.

In the 1960s, Diller began working in film and accompanied Bob Hope on tour for his USO work. In 1965, she divorced Anderson Diller (with whom she had had six children) and married Wade Donovan. In this era, she also appeared on a variety of shows, including *Martin and Rowan's Laugh-In* and *What's My Line?* On these shows, she continued to develop the self-deprecating and over-the-top persona that she had first forged during her stand-up work. At the end of the 1960s, Diller began her work on Broadway with *Hello, Dolly!* In 1985, Diller, having divorced Donovan nearly 10 years earlier, married Robert Hastings. She died at the age of 95 in her home in Los Angeles, California.

Diller was known for her boisterous laugh, her willingness to belittle herself, and her outrageous costumes. Like other comics of her era, she often performed with a large persona and relied on wordplay and comic turns. While some comics struggle as they age, Diller's self-effacing approach to comedy made her maturity an asset rather than a detriment, as she referred to her age and joked about her lack of physical appeal as she grew older. In fact, Diller actually thrived in a number of ways as she aged, doing voice work on animated children's material like *A Bug's Life* and *Hey Arnold!* as well as animated fare for older audiences such as *Family Guy* and *Robot Chicken*. Her trademark voice and laugh served her well in these performances, which introduced her to another generation of viewers. Indeed, Diller's boisterous persona suited cartoon work well. In her later years, Diller was often acknowledged as one of the early female comics, along with Joan Rivers, who helped to pave the way for female humorists of other generations.

Further Reading

Diller, Phyllis. *Like a Lampshade in a Whorehouse: My Life in Comedy*. New York: Tarcher, 2006.

Haley, Alex. "Phyllis Diller: The Unlikeliest Star." *Saturday Evening Post* 235, no. 13 (March 31, 1962): 26–29.

Mock, Roberta. "Stand-up Comedy and the Legacy of the Mature Vagina." *Women & Performance: A Journal of Feminist Theory* 22, no. 1 (March 2012): 9–28.

Zeke Jarvis

FOXWORTHY, JEFF (1958–)

Jeff Foxworthy was born in Atlanta, Georgia. His father was an executive for IBM. After graduating from high school, Foxworthy attended Georgia Tech, though he did not graduate. After leaving college, Foxworthy worked for IBM for approximately five years. While there, he became known for his humor. At the urging of his coworkers, Foxworthy entered and subsequently won the Great Southeastern Laugh-off in 1984. Shortly thereafter, Foxworthy met his wife while working at a club in Atlanta. The two married in 1985, and they have two children.

Foxworthy's career got a major boost first from an appearance on an HBO special at Rodney Dangerfield's club and then from winning the Cable Ace Award for best male stand-up special in 1990. In 1993, Foxworthy released the album *You Might Be a Redneck If* . . . which featured the catchphrase he would most consistently be associated with for most of his career. Foxworthy received his own sitcom, *The Jeff Foxworthy Show* in 1995, though it was short-lived. He also made a variety of TV appearances, though his next prominent role would be as host of the game show *Are You Smarter Than a Fifth Grader?*, which pitted adults against actual elementary school students in a trivia contest. During this time, Foxworthy also toured with Ron White, Bill Engvall, and Larry the Cable Guy as part of the Blue Collar Comedy Tour. Foxworthy put out a number of books and more albums and was the subject of a roast on Comedy Central. He continues to tour and work regularly. When he is not on tour, he lives in Atlanta with his family.

Foxworthy is best known for his simple, everyman persona, focusing on topics and views that appeal to the working class. As part of the Blue Collar Comedy Tour, he is self-effacing yet also celebratory of Southern culture. In the same way that other comics reference popular culture or particular pieces of ethnic cultures, Foxworthy explores and plays with stereotypes of the South and the working class. Interestingly, the Blue Collar Comedy Tour has been seen by many as the working-class, white version of the Original Kings of Comedy, which grouped African American comics (Cedric the Entertainer, D. L. Hughley, Steve Harvey, and Bernie Mac) together on a large tour. The material covered on these two tours was quite different, but the marketing of the tour, which focused on niche audiences, was similar in many respects and was a shift in how comedians thought about touring and interacting with their audiences. While some critics and comedians (David Cross, in particular) have been critical of the Blue Collar crew in general, finding their humor simplistic and reliant on negative, limiting classifications, the roast of Foxworthy demonstrated the respect that many had for him as both a humorist and a person. With his sustained success and the pervasiveness of his catchphrase in popular culture, where it appears in everything from books to advertisements to greeting cards, Foxworthy has had an indelible impact on American popular culture.

Further Reading

Ajaye, Franklyn. *Comic Insights: The Art of Stand-Up Comedy*. Los Angeles: Silman-James Press, 2001.

Flippo, Chet. "Jeff Foxworthy Segues from Rednecks to Relationships; Brooks Makes Nashville Debut." *Billboard* 110, no 21 (May 23, 1998): 36.

Serchuk, David. "Are You Smarter Than a Foxworthy?" *Forbes* 180, no. 1 (July 2, 2007): 92–93.

Zeke Jarvis

FOXX, REDD (1922–1991)

John Sanford was born in St. Louis, Missouri, though his family moved to Chicago's South Side while he was still a young child. After Sanford's father left the family, Sanford was raised by this mother and his grandmother. At age 17, he began to perform on an amateur radio program. Sanford also worked on the railroad, where he was tagged with his eventual stage name. The name came from a combination of Sanford's reddish hair and his respect for the baseball player Jimmie Foxx.

Becoming Redd Foxx, Sanford began performing in night clubs. He gained significant prominence when the singer Dinah Washington insisted that he would come to Los Angeles. When Foxx did, he received a recording contract. This success led to Foxx working on the Las Vegas strip, making him one of the first African American comics to perform in front of largely white audiences. In 1948, Foxx would marry for the first time, only to divorce three years later.

In the 1970s, following from his performance and recording success, Foxx was given a starring role in the sitcom *Sanford and Son,* which was adapted from the British series *Steptoe and Son*. Foxx used his prominent position on television to help out other comics and actors of color, perhaps most notably Pat Morita and LaWanda Page. In fact, Foxx was known for criticizing the network and producers for not giving more opportunities to writers and actors of color. Also during this time period, Foxx married for the second time, though he divorced in 1975. In late 1976, Foxx would marry again.

Foxx left *Sanford and Son* after six seasons, despite its success. He briefly hosted a variety show, then went back to stand-up performance. In 1981, Foxx divorced again. In 1989, the film *Harlem Nights* was released; in it, Foxx appeared with fellow comedy giants Eddie Murphy and Richard Pryor. Toward the end of his life, Foxx began acting on *The Royal Family*, with Della Reese, and he also married again. Both the show and his marriage were short-lived, as he died (of a heart attack while on the set, filming) the same year both began.

Foxx was known for his edgy material. He was a tremendous influence on many comedians of color, most notably Chris Rock and Jamie Foxx, who, like Redd Foxx, engage in frank and daring discussions of racial and cultural issues. In *Sanford and Son*, Foxx's comedy continued to examine cultural stereotypes, in many ways being the African American counterpart to *All in the Family*. Foxx's character regularly made ignorant statements, which were often corrected by his on-screen son. Not surprisingly, *Sanford and Son* was made by Norman Lear's production company. Foxx also explored sexual taboos in much the same way that Lenny Bruce had before him. For this reason, it is in some ways surprising that Foxx was one of the early African American comics to break through into mainstream success, given his mix of groundbreaking stature and challenging material. Still, Foxx's groundbreaking success helped pave the way for future comics such as Richard Pryor and Chris Rock and later television shows like *The Cosby Show*. For these reasons, in addition to his own memorable work, Foxx looms large as an American humorist.

Redd Foxx achieved mainstream success as one of the title characters in *Sanford & Son*. Foxx also worked to bring more performers of color into television. (AP Photo/NBC-TV)

See also: Foxx, Jamie; Lear, Norman; Murphy, Eddie

Further Reading

Dempsey, Travis. *The Life and Times of Redd Foxx*. Urbana, IL: Urbana Research Press, 1999.
Robinson, Louie. "Redd Foxx: Prince of Clowns." *Ebony* 22, no 6 (April 1967): 91–99.
Starr, Michael Seth. *Black and Blue: The Redd Foxx Story*. Montclair, NJ: Applause, 2011.

Zeke Jarvis

GALIFIANAKIS, ZACH (1969–)

Zachary Galifianakis was born in 1969 in Wilkesboro, North Carolina. He graduated from Wilkes Central High School, then majored in communications at North Carolina State University but did not complete a degree.

Galifianakis's first break came with a role as a recurring character in five episodes of the sitcom *Boston Common*, which lasted from 1996 to 1997. He next appeared in five episodes of *Apartment 2F*, a short-lived sketch comedy and stand-up series that aired on MTV. At this time, he also worked for two weeks as a writer for *Saturday Night Live*. Galifianakis made his big-screen debut with a small part in a 1999 comedy film, *Flushed*. In 2001, he had additional small parts in *Heartbreakers*, *Bubble Boy*, and *Out Cold*. That same year, he appeared on *Comedy Central Presents*, which showcased his comedic work on the piano. In 2002, Galifianakis hosted his own talk show on VH1, *Late World with Zach*, but the show was canceled after only nine weeks. From 2003 to 2005, he starred in *Tru Calling*, a television show on Fox in which he played a coroner. He also made a handful of appearances in *Reno 911!* and showed up several times on *Jimmy Kimmel Live!*

Along with Patton Oswalt, Brian Posehn, and Maria Bamford, Galifianakis participated in the Comedians of Comedy tour from 2004 to 2005. The comedians performed in indie rock clubs instead of in comedy clubs for a 2005 Showtime film and a short-lived Comedy Central television series of the same name. The film and show featured off-stage footage of the comedians in addition to the performances.

Dog Bites Man, a fake-news show on Comedy Central Show that debuted in 2006 and caught people in candid moments, featured Galifianakis in a regular appearance. He also appeared on *The Sarah Silverman Program* and in music videos for Fiona Apple and Kanye West. Galifianakis released his own hip-hop single, "Come on and Get It (Up in 'Dem Guts)," in 2006. In 2007, Galifianakis starred in the Sean Penn-directed survival film, *Into the Wild*, with Emile Hirsch, William Hurt, and Vince Vaughn. Also in 2007, Galifianakis released a comedy-performance DVD, *Live at the Purple Onion*.

Galifianakis went on to star in small roles in numerous other films (*What Happens in Vegas* and *Super High Me*, for example) and television shows, including ones in which he provided his voice for animated characters. It was the commercial and critical success of 2009's *The Hangover*, however, that made Galifianakis a bona fide star. In *The Hangover*, Galifianakis plays the role of Alan Garner, a future brother-in-law to a groom who disappears after a bachelor party. He reprised the role in the film's two sequels, *The Hangover Part II* (2010) and *The Hangover Part III* (2013).

In a live appearance on *Real Time with Bill Maher* in 2010, Galifianakis lit what looked like a joint. In the controversy that followed, Maher spoke in defense of Galifianakis and denied that the joint was real. In 2012, Galifianakis appeared with Will Ferrell in *The Campaign*. Also in 2012, Galifianakis married Quinn Lundberg. The two had a child in 2013.

In 2014, Galifianakis garnered a great deal of attention for interviewing President Barack Obama on his podcast *Between Two Ferns* in an attempt to aid Obama in promoting his changes in healthcare coverage. Galifianakis continues to live with his family and work as both a writer and a performer.

Galifianakis is best known for his playing imbeciles in both his stand-up and screen work. One thing that made his interview with President Obama so striking was his willingness to both make outlandish claims and appear hostile to the president. Likewise, in his work in *The Hangover* series, his character often pushes his friends to make bad decisions and generally behave in nonsensical ways, then completely sidesteps any responsibility. Galifianakis has also fully embraced the alternative comedy scene, working regularly with Tim and Eric and using unconventional approaches to comedy, such as his satiric podcast. The line between Galifianakis's persona and his personal life has sometimes become unclear, and his ability to laugh at his own antics and tribulations demonstrate his commitment to allowing himself to be the butt of jokes through his use of self-deprecating humor.

Further Reading

Bump, Philip. "Obama's Interview with Zach Galifianakis Is Terrific/Completely Awkward." *The Wire*. March 11, 2014. http://www.thewire.com/politics/2014/03/obamas-interview-zach-galifianakis-terrific-completely-awkward/359035/.

Stein, Joel. "Mock the Vote." *Time* 180, no. 6 (August 6, 2012): 52–55.

Yabroff, Jennie. "Go 'Schmuck' Yourself." *Newsweek* 156, no. 4 (July 26, 2010): 55.

Stephen Powers

GAROFALO, JANEANE (1964–)

Janeane Garofalo was born in New Jersey, though her family moved a number of times while she was growing up. Garofalo's family lived in California and Texas in addition to New Jersey. Her father was an Exxon executive, and her upbringing was conservative and Catholic. After graduating from high school, Garofalo attended Providence College, where she earned degrees in both history and American studies. While there, she began to consider a career in comedy and performing, particularly wanting to work on David Letterman's writing staff. With this goal in mind, Garofalo entered a Showtime network talent search, which led to her winning the title of "Funniest Person in Rhode Island." While she pursued her career in comedy, she worked a number of jobs, such as bike messenger and a temporary secretary.

During the late 1980s and early 1990s, Garofalo performed regularly at clubs, becoming part of the alternative comedy scene in Los Angeles during that period. While she was performing, she got a role on a short-lived television series, *The Ben Stiller Show*. This led to her role on *The Larry Sanders Show*. As *The Ben Stiller Show* was ending, Garofalo's career was expanding, including a number of appearances on a variety of shows and films. Toward the end of *The Ben Stiller Show*'s run, Garofalo also married her then-boyfriend, Robert Cohen, in Las Vegas. In interviews about the event, Garofalo and Cohen have both stated that the marriage was part of a joke. After the two broke up, neither thought seriously about it until Cohen wanted to marry his then-girlfriend and the two needed to divorce.

While Garofalo has landed notable roles in a number of films, such as *Reality Bites* (directed by Ben Stiller) and *The Truth about Cats and Dogs*, she also declined some key roles, such as the role of Gale Weathers in the first *Scream* film. Garofalo also cowrote a book *Feel This Book: An Essential Guide to Self-Empowerment, Spiritual Supremacy, and Sexual Satisfaction* with Ben Stiller. Part of the publicity for the book included Garofalo discussing her struggles with substance abuse in the past, although she has been sober for an extended period of time. Garofalo has continued to perform and tour. In 2004, she hosted a radio on Air America, the leftist radio station. She has also appeared on political talk shows on television and been a regular guest on Bill Maher's shows *Politically Incorrect* and *Real Time*. Garofalo splits her time between New York and Los Angeles.

Garofalo is known for her biting, acerbic style, often grounded in observations about political and social issues. She has eschewed a number of expectations, such as the strict boundaries for perceptions of female beauty and the formality of some stand-up styles. Still, Garofalo is often self-deprecating with her comedy, putting herself down for her appearance and her romantic history. She has used both her hand with notes written on it and a notebook with quotations and articles in her stand-up act. Garofalo is also known for consistently and overtly incorporating her political views into her stand-up material. She has toured with Margaret Cho, who similarly makes commentary about social issues and gender relations. On one occasion, Garofalo invited her own father, who has conservative views, on her radio program to conduct a debate. Garofalo has been a lightning rod for various conservative pundits, drawing fire for her comments about the Iraq War, her observations about the racism within the Tea Party, and several other topics. Still, Garofalo often strives to include factual information and a number of sources to demonstrate the legitimacy of her claims.

Beyond her political beliefs, Garofalo is noteworthy for the wide array of connections she has within the comedy world. From playing the female counterpart to Jerry Seinfeld's character on his sitcom to having worked with every member of *The Kids in the Hall* to appearing on the final episode of *Mad about You*, Garofalo has worked with or influenced many of her fellow comics, giving her a prominent place in contemporary American humor and culture.

See also: Stiller, Ben

Further Reading

DiNovella, Elizabeth. "Janeane Garofalo." *Progressive* 67, no. 5 (May 2003): 35.

O'Neal, Sean. "Janeane Garofalo Interview." *Onion AV Club*, June 25, 2010.

Wagner, Bruce, and Wayne Stambler. "Janeane Garofalo." *Premiere* 11, no. 4 (December 1997): 120. http://www.avclub.com/article/janeane-garofalo-42551.

Zeke Jarvis

GIRALDO, GREG (1965–2010)

Greg Giraldo was born in the Bronx and raised in a working-class area in Queens, New York. He excelled in school: after graduating from high school, he attended the prestigious Columbia University. He then went to Harvard Law School, graduating from that institution in 1990. During this period, Giraldo also played guitar in a band.

Following his graduation from law school, Giraldo worked in a law firm for nearly a year before leaving to pursue comedy. He played in clubs, building a reputation. In 1995, he began starring in the sitcom *Common Law*, though the show would be short-lived. He also appeared on a variety of shows and was a regular guest on both *Tough Crowd with Colin Quinn* and *Politically Incorrect*.

In 1999, Giraldo married for the first time, divorcing after two years. Shortly thereafter, Giraldo married for the second time, this time having three children. This marriage ended in divorce in 2009.

In addition to his talk-show performances and tours, Giraldo regularly appeared on the Comedy Central Roasts, including the roasts of Pamela Anderson, David Hasselhoff, and Joan Rivers, among many others. In 2010, after years of struggling with substance abuse problems, Giraldo died of a drug overdose. After his death, there were a number of tributes to him, including a short clip on *The Daily Show*, a dedication to him at the Comedy Central Roast of Donald Trump. and a special on Comedy Central honoring his work and his memory.

Like Louis CK, Giraldo was known for satirizing exclusionary views and hierarchical structures, cutting down the simplistic reaction of telling the homeless to simply "get a job" and belittling attacks on illegal immigrants. Although his work often had a strong streak of irreverence, his clear investment in issues of equality and social justice gave it a substantial weight. Also like CK, Giraldo was very open about the struggles in his personal life, discussing his substance abuse problems and the deterioration of his marriage. As shown in the tributes to him, Giraldo was clearly well thought of by many major humorists. Appearing on the Comedy Central tribute show were Conan O'Brien, Jon Stewart, and Denis Leary; at a tribute show aimed at collecting funds for Giraldo's children, performers included Jerry Seinfeld, Lewis Black, and Colin Quinn, among other significant figures. Though his career was short-lived, Giraldo clearly had a significant impact on the American comedy scene.

Further Reading

Gaffigan, Jim. "Stand-up Guy Greg Giraldo." *Entertainment Weekly* 1134/1135 (December 24, 2010): 69.

O'Connor, Anahad. "Greg Giraldo, 44, Insult Humor Comic." *New York Times* (September 30, 2010): 37.

Serota, Maggie. "Greg Giraldo Interview." *Onion AV Club*, September 17, 2009. http://www.avclub.com/article/greg-giraldo-32904.

Zeke Jarvis

GOTTFRIED, GILBERT (1955–)

Gilbert Gottfried was born in Brooklyn, New York. By age 15, Gottfried was already beginning his stand-up work, appearing first at open mic nights in New York City, but steadily building a reputation with other comedians. His first major national exposure came in 1980, when he became a cast member for *Saturday Night Live*. Gottfried stayed on the show for only one season, as he was not used regularly and did not use his trademark persona. Although his time on *SNL* was not considered to be a success, it did lead to Gottfried getting more work, including an appearance on *The Cosby Show*, work in commercials that did play on his persona, and several appearances on *Late Night with David Letterman*. Gottfried continued to do stand-up while also having roles in the *Beverly Hills Cop* movies, hosting USA's *Up All Night* program, and appearing regularly on *Hollywood Squares*. He also began to get regular voiceover work, beginning with his breakthrough role as the voice of Iago the parrot in the Disney film *Aladdin*.

Gottfried has been a regular guest on *The Howard Stern Show* and a regular performer on the Comedy Central Roasts. Gottfried's distinctive voice served as the voice of the insurance company AFLAC's duck mascot for some time, but he was asked to step down from this role when he made jokes about a natural disaster in Japan. Gottfried also made waves by joking about the September 11, 2001, terrorist attacks in a Comedy Central Roast. Still, Gottfried continues to work regularly. He married in 2007, and he and his wife have two children.

Gottfried is best known for his grating voice and squinting, awkward delivery. He is also known for his willingness to be transgressive, with his controversial comments sometimes landing him in trouble, as when he asked to step down as the voice of the AFLAC duck. Nevertheless, he does not limit the boundaries that he breaks to what is offensive. He started the more mainstream interest in "The Aristocrats" joke by telling a joke publicly that was typically reserved for inner circles of comedians. As was the case with Norm MacDonald's self-reflexive performance at Bob Saget's roast, Gottfried's roast performances often bring in old or overused structures to call attention to them, making him a "comedian's comedian." He has demonstrated a willingness to speak very openly about some of his career struggles, having discussed the problems with *Saturday Night Live* in a number of venues and without hesitation. Gottfried has achieved genuine longevity, appearing on everything from *Hollywood Squares* to *Arrested Development*, in which he had a small cameo. His balance of mainstream and cult success make Gottfried an interesting figure who has had a significant impact on contemporary American comedy.

See also: Stern, Howard

Further Reading

Gottfried, Gilbert. *Rubber Balls and Liquor*. New York: St. Martin's Press, 2011.

Itzkoff, Dave. "Vulgarity's Abrasive Master, But Not at Home." *New York Times* 162, no. 56072 (March 11, 2013): C1–C5.

Savitz, Eric. "Aflac Fires Gilbert Gottfried over Japan Earthquake Tweets." *Forbes.com* (March 14, 2011): 3.

Zeke Jarvis

GREGORY, DICK (1932–)

Richard Gregory was born in a working-class area of St. Louis, Missouri. Though clearly intelligent, Gregory did not excel in school. Nevertheless, he received the support of his high school teachers in winning a track scholarship to

Dick Gregory was one of the early African American comics to achieve mainstream success. He used his success to make pointed jabs at racism, the Central Intelligence Agency, and former President Richard Nixon. (AP Photo)

the University of Southern Illinois at Carbondale. While there, Gregory set records in both the half-mile and mile races. Partway through his college work, Gregory was drafted by the army. During his military service, Gregory cemented his interest in performance by winning multiple talent shows.

Upon returning to civilian life, Gregory eventually dropped out of the university to focus upon his new career. He moved to Chicago, where he became part of an early generation of African American stand-up comics, including Bill Cosby and Nipsey Russell. This meant that Gregory performed in clubs primarily frequented by African American crowds. During this time, he worked in the post office to help support himself.

In 1959, Gregory met Lillian Smith, whom he would marry. The two have had 10 children, and they remained married.

Gregory's first significant break came in 1961, when he was discovered by Hugh Hefner, who gave Gregory a prominent slot in the Chicago Playboy Club. After Gregory built his reputation, he appeared on *The Tonight Show Starring Jack Paar*. During this time, Gregory also became active in politics, traveling to Selma, Alabama, during the civil rights struggles and even running against Richard Daley for mayor of Chicago. Since then, Gregory has been involved with a number of causes, from feminism to healthy eating. All the while, Gregory has remained an active humorist, continuing to write and perform. He currently lives with his family in Massachusetts.

Gregory is respected by a wide variety of comedic and cultural figures, from Hugh Hefner to Bill Clinton. That said, many see Gregory as an extremist, citing his interest in conspiracy theories and his fascinating but often seemingly ineffectual political campaigns. Still, his longevity and incisive brand of comedy have established and maintained his reputation as a master comic who balances irreverence with genuine social commentary. Although Gregory never achieved the mainstream success of Bill Cosby, he has regularly performed and had success in stand-up comedy, writing, and social commentary.

Further Reading

Gregory, Dick, and Robert Lipsyte. *Nigger: An Autobiography*. New York: Pocket Books, 1990.

Moses, Sheila. "Dick Gregory." *Ebony* 65, no. 6 (April 2010): 54–55.

Wright, Mark H. "Sophistic Humor and Social Change: Overcoming Identification with the Aggressor." *JPCS: Journal for the Psychoanalysis of Culture & Society* 5, no. 1 (Spring 2000): 57–64.

Zeke Jarvis

GRIFFIN, EDDIE (1968–)

Eddie Griffin was born in Kansas City, Missouri. Raised by a single mother, he grew up in a working-class household. For three years running, Griffin was voted the class clown in his school. At age 16, he was married, though he and his wife divorced the following year. After graduating from high school, Griffin enrolled in Kansas City University, where he was to major in biological engineering, but he dropped out after one semester.

Originally taking the stage on a dare, Griffin found that his motor-mouthed delivery worked well on the comedy stage. He quickly landed the opening spot for a tour with Andrew Dice Clay. With appearances on Def Comedy Jam and a special of his own, Griffin soon gained a level of prominence. This led to small roles in films such as *Meteor Man* and *Coneheads*, which in turn led to his co-starring in the television show *Malcolm and Eddie*, along with former *Cosby Show* actor Malcolm-Jamal Warner. The show ran from 1996 to 2000 and earned Griffin an NAACP Image Award for Best Actor in a Comedy Series, though Griffin also had a heart attack during the taping of an episode. In 2002, Griffin married for the second time. Griffin has appeared in a variety of prominent shows and films, including *Chappelle's Show* and the Eddie Murphy film *Norbit*. While Griffin has not attained the fame of some comics, he has maintained a noteworthy career for some time.

Griffin is known for balancing a strong sense of performance, often playing confident but mildly inept characters that are a spin on his stage persona. His performances are frequently rooted in sense of strong masculinity. However, Griffin is not afraid to undercut that sense of masculinity by sometimes allowing himself to be the butt of a joke. More than anything, Griffin's performances have an energy and pace that other performers sometimes fail to attain. That level of enthusiasm and dedication have helped to make Griffin a favorite for many other humorists and audiences.

Further Reading

Johnson, Kevin C. "Comedian Eddie Griffin Gets His Act Cleaned up." *St. Louis Post-Dispatch*, June 14, 2012. http://www.stltoday.com/entertainment/music/comedian-eddie-griffin-gets-his-act-cleaned-up/article_15226662-b1cf-11e1-8dec-001a4bcf6878.html.

Koltnow, Barry. "Eddie Griffin Hopes *Undercover Brother* Opens the Right Doors." *Orange County Register*, June 3, 2002. http://www.highbeam.com/doc/1G1-86665104.html.

Waldron, Clarence. "Eddie Griffin: 'You Can Tell 'Em I Said It.' " *Jet* 119, no. 10 (March 14, 2011): 42.

Zeke Jarvis

GRIFFIN, KATHY (1960–)

Kathy Griffin was born in Oak Park, Illinois. Her parents were both first-generation Irish Americans. Griffin attended a parochial elementary school; she has claimed that her experiences there led her to be skeptical of organized religion. Griffin was the youngest of five children. When her older siblings left the house, she felt alone and frustrated, and she developed an eating disorder.

Kathy Griffin has carved out a unique position in American pop culture. While celebrating her "D-List" status, Griffin charms audiences with a mix of camp, sarcasm, and self-effacing humor. (Carrienelson1/Dreamstime.com)

After graduating from high school, Griffin moved to California, where she began taking classes with the Groundlings after seeing them perform. Eventually, Griffin was invited to join the troupe. She began to perform as part of Los Angeles's alternative comedy scene, working closely with Janeane Garofalo and Margaret Cho, and regularly sharing the stage as part of the "Hot Cup of Talk" performances. Griffin began getting small roles in a variety of movies and television shows, including *Pulp Fiction*, *Seinfeld*, and *X-Files*. In the mid-1990s, she achieved mainstream success, getting an HBO special and a role on the NBC show *Suddenly Susan*. Griffin continued to both tour and appear in films and television, eventually creating her reality show, *Kathy Griffin: My Life on the D-List*.

In 2001, Griffin married Matthew Moline. The two separated for a brief time and, after reconciling, divorced in 2006. While Griffin has not married again, she was in a serious relationship with Apple co-founder Steve Wozniak from 2007 to 2008.

Griffin continues to work in a variety of media, branching into publishing in 2009 with *Official Book Club Selection: A Memoir According to Kathy Griffin*. She also tours and hosts the show *Kathy* on Bravo.

Griffin is best known for her edgy comedy, which is often both vulgar and confrontational, cutting down other celebrities. In her second run on *Seinfeld*, this habit is satirized by Griffin's character making a career out of badmouthing Jerry Seinfeld. While not generally explicitly political, Griffin is a consistent proponent of gay and lesbian rights as well as an outspoken critic of organized religion. She is known for engaging in petty celebrity feuds, which is part of her persona. These feuds come against both minor or down-on-their-luck stars, such as Demi Lovato, and lighter targets, such as conservative figure Elizabeth Hasselbeck. While these feuds are rarely regarded as serious by Griffin and her fans, they demonstrate the influence of humorists like Andy Kaufman, who was able to engage in public events that put him in a bad light. Still, Griffin has a loyal and consistently supportive fan base.

Further Reading

Gaydos, Kristen. "Kathy Griffin Doesn't Hide from Controversy." *Citizens' Voice* (Wilkes-Barre, PA), April 10, 2014. http://citizensvoice.com/arts-living/kathy-griffin-doesn-t-hide-from-controversy-1.1664072.

Griffin, Kathy. *Official Book Club Selection: A Memoir According to Kathy Griffin*. New York: Ballantine Books, 2010.

Melton, Mary. "Kathy Griffin." *Los Angeles Magazine* 50, no. 6 (June 2005): 74–192.

Zeke Jarvis

HACKETT, BUDDY (1924–2003)

Leonard Hacker, who would go on to be known as Buddy Hackett, was born and raised in Brooklyn, New York. Hackett grew up near Sandy Koufax, who would achieve fame as a baseball player. While still in high school, Hackett began to perform in Catskills comedy clubs, though he claimed that his early performances did not receive a single laugh. At the beginning of World War II, Hackett enlisted in the army. After the war, he performed at the Pink Elephant, where Hackett first used his stage name. Hackett was very active at the time, performing in Los Angeles and Las Vegas, in addition to working on Broadway and in the Catskills.

In Las Vegas, Hackett began to refine his persona as a club comedian. Like Lenny Bruce, he was willing to "go blue," discussing vulgar topics and incorporating obscenity into his act. He also relied on stereotypes in his work, including his very stereotyped portrayal of an Asian in his early film work. Because of the prejudices of the time, his racial comedy was a hit. Hackett was able to rein in his persona and give more restrained performances, however, so that he could appear on network television—frequently *The Tonight Show* with Johnny Carson.

In 1955, Hackett married Sherry Cohen. The two had three children and remained together until his death.

In 1956, Hackett began work on his sitcom *Stanley*. Near this time, he gained media attention for his appearances on *Hollywood Squares* and his role in the movie *It's A Mad, Mad, Mad, Mad World*. In 1978, Hackett starred as Lou Costello in a movie about Abbot and Costello. He and co-star Harvey Korman did a version of the classic sketch "Who's on First" that was received well by both critics and fans when the movie was released. He also had some prominent voice work, most notably providing the voice of the seagull, Scuttle, in Disney's *The Little Mermaid*. He had done voiceover work in early years as well, including the role of "Pardon Me Pete," the groundhog in the Christmas special *Jack Frost*.

Late in his career, Hackett began experiencing panic attacks during his live performances. He curtailed his stand-up career, blaming gum surgery that he had undergone shortly before the onset of his panic attacks. Still, he made appearances on recorded television shows. In 2003, Hackett died in his Malibu home. Issues with a stroke and his struggles with diabetes were blamed for his death.

Although Hackett's performances seem relatively tame in terms of vulgarity by contemporary standards, they were quite transgressive at the time. While some of his work might still seem surprising to audiences, that is more likely to come from his use of racial and cultural stereotypes than from his use of obscenity or innuendo. Even during his time, Hackett's obscenity was softened by his goofy, likable persona. His delivery and crassness captured a sense of working-class humor that made him accessible even while he instilled a sense of professionalism and craftsmanship in his delivery. While he is seen as one of the pioneers of blue material, his voice and character are also associated with more innocent works, such as his performances in animated material, which maintained his goofy and charming persona.

Further Reading

D'Alessandro, Anthony. "Comics Yuk It up for Hackett." *Daily Variety* 281, no. 14 (October 23, 2003): 19.

Fritz, Ben, and Army Archerd. "Buddy Hackett: Irrepressible Comic-Thesp Was Sweet Yet Caustic." *Variety* 391, no. 8 (July 14, 2003): 52.

Hackett, Buddy. *The Naked Mind of Buddy Hackett*. New York: Nash, 1974.

Zeke Jarvis

HAMBURGER, NEIL (1967–)

Greg Turkington was born in Australia to American parents, but grew up in Arizona and California. Turkington worked on his performances in both comedy and music. In 1992, he started his own record store, which continued in business until 1999. During this time, Turkington began to release records as Neil Hamburger as well as under the name Anton LaVey. Hamburger toured as well, often opening for punk or alternative bands rather than other comics. Hamburger also appeared on television shows and in films, including *Tim and Eric Awesome Show, Great Job!* and the Tenacious D film, *The Pick of Destiny*, as well as appearing on late-night talk shows such as *Jimmy Kimmel Live!*

In 2008, Hamburger released a country-and-western album through Drag City records. The album included both original songs and covers, with backing from musicians like Prairie Prince of the Tubes, David Gleason, Atom Ellis of Dieselhed, and Rachel Haden from that dog. Hamburger has also done his own broadcasts, called *Poolside Chats with Neil Hamburger*, in which he interviews alternative and lesser-known performers such as King Buzz from the Melvins and Bonnie Prince Billy. While Hamburger is not likely to ever become a household name, he is one of the few performers to have picked up on the methods of Andy Kaufman. He has a small but loyal following among comedians and fans alike.

Hamburger plays the part of an inept comic on stage. He tells jokes that are typically and very intentionally unfunny, shuffles and drops the drinks he holds, and wears outdated clothes and has a bad comb-over. While this approach can have a cumulative effect of winning audiences over with his odd but steadily maintained persona, it also met with skepticism and outright hostility. In Ireland, for instance, Hamburger was booed off the stage more than once. Still, his bold experiments and inventive use of persona make him an interesting humorist to watch.

Further Reading

Gehr, Richard. "Happy Discomfort." *Village Voice* 58, no. 45 (November 6, 2013): 19.

Rabin, Nathan. "Neil Hamburger Interview." *Onion AV Club*. March 24, 1999. http://www.avclub.com/article/neil-hamburger-laments-the-great-entertainers-30313.

Sisario, Ben. "Neil Hamburger." *New York Times* 156, no. 53789 (December 1, 2006): E24.

Zeke Jarvis

HEDBERG, MITCH (1968–2005)

Mitch Hedberg was born in St. Paul, Minnesota, with a heart defect that required much treatment in his childhood years. After he graduated from Harding High School, Hedberg started his comedy career in Florida before moving to Seattle, Washington. At this time, he began touring in comedy clubs and comedy festivals around the country.

After he appeared on MTV's *Comikaze*, Hedberg got his big break when David Letterman invited him to appear on *The Late Show with David Letterman* in 1996. Hedberg would appear on this talk show several more times before his death.

Hedberg won the grand prize in the Seattle Comedy Competition in 1997. He guest starred in an episode of the Fox sitcom, *That '70s Show*, in 1998. Hedberg, who was noted for having a comedic style in which he wore sunglasses on stage and avoided eye contact with the audience by keeping his head down in an attempt to deal with stage fright, soon gained a cult following, with *Time* magazine calling him "the next Seinfeld."

In 1999, Hedberg married Canadian comedian Lynn Shawcroft. That same year, he appeared on *Comedy Central Presents* and released his first comedy CD, *Strategic Grill Locations*. The CD was recorded in Houston, Texas, at the Laff Stop, a comedy club known for launching the careers of many accomplished comedians. Also in 1999, Hedberg directed and starred in *Los Enchiladas!*, a comedy film based on his time working in a Mexican restaurant during his teenage years. The film premiered at the Sundance Film Festival, but has remained undistributed. Hedberg then played the small part of a road manager in Cameron Crowe's 2000 film, *Almost Famous*.

The year 2003 saw the release of his second comedy album, *Mitch All Together*, which Hedberg recorded at the Acme Comedy Club in Minneapolis, Minnesota. In the same year, he was arrested in Austin, Texas, for heroin possession. Hedberg frequently joked about his drug use in his act, even stating in a 2001 interview with *Penthouse* that he had always wanted to die of an overdose after becoming famous. In March 2005, Hedberg claimed in an interview with Howard Stern that he had his drug use under control, but he was found dead 12 days later in a hotel room in Livingston, New Jersey. The cause of death was an overdose of heroin and cocaine. Later in 2005, the film *Lords of Dogtown*, a tribute to skateboard culture and skateboarding as a sport, was dedicated to Hedberg and released posthumously. Hedberg filmed his brief appearance in the movie shortly before his death. In 2008, Comedy Central Records released Hedberg's third and final comedy album, *Do You Believe in Gosh?* The album, with an introduction written by his wife, was recorded at the Improv in Ontario, California, in January 2005, two months before Hedberg's death.

Hedberg is best known for his ambling stage persona and his odd non-sequiturs, often relying on strange puns and associations. He was known for wearing sunglasses and having hair that partly blocked his face. This and his sometimes mumbling delivery helped to demonstrate his lack of comfort with speaking in front of crowds. Hedberg also would regularly ridicule himself if his jokes did not meet with the audience's approval. Still, many other comics had great respect for Hedberg. Lewis Black and Dave Attell toured with Hedberg, helping him to get name recognition. Although Hedberg's humor was too offbeat for some audiences, his cult following and respect from his fellow comics have established him as a noteworthy figure in American comedy.

Further Reading

Fierman, Daniel. "Comedy's Kurt Cobain." *Entertainment Weekly* 829 (July 15, 2005): 42–47.

"Mitch Hedberg." *Rolling Stone* 973 (May 5, 2005): 36.

Stott, Andrew. *Comedy: The New Critical Idiom*. New York: Routledge, 2004.

Stephen Powers

HICKS, BILL (1961–1994)

Bill Hicks was born in a small town in Georgia. His family, including his parents and two siblings, moved frequently—to New Jersey, Alabama, Florida, and, finally, Texas. Raised as a Southern Baptist, Hicks gained the exposure to religion that he would later both incorporate and rebel against in his work. He also developed an interest in comedy early, sneaking into clubs at age 13 to perform stand-up.

After feeling that he had begun to stagnate as a comic, Hicks decided to try drugs, as two of his idols, Jimi Hendrix and Richard Pryor, had to enhance their work. While Hicks continued to ingest psychedelic mushrooms, directly discussing in his act his experiences with the drug, and smoke cigarettes, he eventually quit drinking alcohol, feeling that it did more to inhibit his creativity than to support it.

Although Hicks struggled in the mid-1980s, by the end of that decade he made two important connections. First, after being featured on a young comics special by Rodney Dangerfield, Hicks began performing regularly, first in New York and then nationally after signing with manager Jack Mondrus. His second connection was with one of the club owners, Colleen McGarr, whom he would later date and propose to.

In the early 1990s, Hicks toured not only in the United States, but also in the United Kingdom, where he was very well received. He began to gain a level of prominence, being named the "Hot Stand-Up Comic" by *Rolling Stone* in 1993. He also opened for the band Tool, who dedicated their album *Aenima* to Hicks, referring to him as "another dead hero."

Although Hicks gained widespread critical recognition, he had significant struggles as well. Many audiences were hostile to Hicks's unfiltered views, and he often received threats of violence, even once being assaulted by audience members after a show. In addition, Hicks was cut from *The Late Show with David Letterman* in 1993 after he made a joke that mentioned Jesus and the cross as a symbol of Christian faith. Hicks was vociferous in his complaints about the episode, both discussing it at length in an interview with Howard Stern and writing about it in a piece for *The New Yorker*. Letterman would later apologize to Hicks's mother and play the clip in its entirety. Hicks also had a significant feud with Denis Leary, whom Hicks accused of plagiarism, with a number of sources in comedy taking Hicks's side.

In 1993, Hicks was diagnosed with cancer. He died in 1994, having prepared his final words and developed a sense of peace according to his friends and family.

Hicks's style was both aggressive and deeply rooted in his honest communication of his social and political beliefs. Although he can hardly be characterized simply as liberal, Hicks was more antagonistic toward established institutions and modes of thinking than many other emerging structures, often referencing the idea of evolution and change as a positive force. He mixed factual and well-researched observations about religion and politics with wild accusations and profane imagery. In his manic delivery, edgy material, and unorthodox discussions of religion, Hicks was similar to Sam Kinison. Although Hicks's material and delivery kept him from mainstream popularity, his original and striking approach to comedy made him a favorite among many critics. He often espoused a strong belief in conspiracy theories, regularly discussing the Kennedy assassination and the U.S. government's role in the Branch Davidian compound conflagration, in which the government brought down cult leader David Koresh after reports of child abuse and sexual abuse. Hicks has, arguably, become more popular after his death than he was in life, with a documentary and Tool's promotion of his work. Even with this support for Hicks's work, his appeal is generally strongest among comedy aficionados rather than the larger population.

See also: Kinison, Sam; Leary, Denis

Further Reading

Stafford, Mark. "Like an Anaconda Blowing in the Wind." *Vertigo* (November 2009): 28.

True, Cynthia. *American Scream: The Bill Hicks Story*. New York: Harper Books, 2002.

Zeke Jarvis

HOPE, BOB (1903–2003)

Leslie Townes Hope was born in London, England. In 1908, the Hope family, which included two parents and seven sons, immigrated to the United States, settling in Ohio. Leslie, who would be known as Bob Hope when he became a public figure, began busking (performing in the streets) for money at the age of 12. He also worked a number of entry-level jobs, such as butcher's assistant, before deciding to pursue a career in performance by signing up for dance lessons. Hope was discovered by Fatty Arbuckle, who helped him get regular performance work that served as both his training ground and his entryway into public performances. Hope performed in vaudeville for years, working as part of a duo in the early going and sometimes performing in blackface, which was less offensive at the time than it is considered today. In the mid-1930s, Hope began performing on the emerging media of radio.

Hope was married briefly to his first wife in 1933. He married his second wife in 1934; their union lasted until his death in 2003. The pair adopted four children over the course of their marriage.

In 1938, Hope had his first significant hit in *The Big Broadcast of 1938*, which also starred W. C. Fields. Hope continued to work in film, keeping up an impressive pace, and toured in a number of USO shows, which would become one of the hallmarks of his career. Hope so frequently performed as part of the USO shows that, in 1997, he was declared an "honorary veteran."

Starting in 1940, Hope began the series of *Road* movies (beginning with *Road to Singapore*) with Bing Crosby and Dorothy Lamour. In 1950, he began working on television, where he would find an even greater level of success. On his first show on NBC, he became one of the first television performers to use cue cards so that he would not have to memorize jokes. Although this was new at the time, it has become standard practice for any live broadcast on television today. Hope continued to do many specials, with his Christmas specials being particularly popular.

Bob Hope on one of his many USO tours. Hope had a long and remarkable career as a live performer. (Department of Defense)

He continued to perform well into his 70s, maintaining a large and loyal audience. In his later years, he received numerous significant awards and honors, including a special at the Kennedy Center for his 80th birthday. The festivities included such luminaries as Ronald Reagan, Lucille Ball, and George Burns. He was also honored in England, being appointed an honorary Knight Commander in 1998. Hope died at age 100 in his home in Los Angeles.

Hope's style was characterized by his rapid delivery and effective use of one-liners. This style also suited Hope's voice well, which was unique and often endearing. For most of his career, he was known for his self-deprecation, joking about a variety of topics and particularly his age in his later years. He was also well known for joking about his golf game and telling jokes about various politicians, often connecting the two sources of humor. Largely because of his ability to make these kinds of general and easily understandable jokes, Hope was quite successful as a mass-media and mainstream figure. Although he was very successful for decades and very well regarded by many comedians and other public figures, younger audiences toward the end of his life often found his work to be predictable or tame in a way that ran counter to the comedy that they were used to, such as the biting, harsh satire of Lewis Black and the edgy, dynamic performances of George Carlin and Bill Hicks. This led Hope's simple, more innocent delivery sometimes being associated with an antiquated form of comedy. Indeed, several comedians would cite Hope as an out-of-touch comic. Interestingly, this line of criticism was actually in line with Hope's own joking about his age.

Given the body of work that Hope produced and the sustained success of his career, he has earned a position of respect among many humorists and the culture in general, as evidenced by the number of references to him and his many appearances with prominent cultural figures. Whether the general population appreciates the entirety of his work, a large percentage of the population recognizes Bob Hope's name as one of the foundational figures in American humor. Beyond his importance as a comic, Hope has become an important part of America's cultural references. His USO work has particularly made an impression, referenced by both *The Simpsons*, where Hope appeared with Lisa (who was Little Miss Springfield in the episode) at a USO show, and Stephen Colbert, who came out with a golf club (a reference to Hope's love of golf and many golf jokes) when he performed for the troops as part of his show, *The Colbert Report*. Perhaps even more than his jokes, Hope's prominence as a public figure will assure that he is remembered. Still, his interest in poking fun at politicians, his quick delivery. and his ability to make fun of himself make him an important figure in American humor.

Further Reading

Faith, William Robert. *Bob Hope: A Life in Comedy*. New York: Da Capo Press, 2003.

Hope, Bob. *My Life in Jokes*. New York: Hyperion, 2004.

Mills, Robert L. *The Laugh Makes: A Behind-the-Scenes Tribute to Bob Hope's Incredible Gag Writers*. Duncan: BearManor Media, 2009.

Zeke Jarvis

HUGHLEY, D. L. (1963–)

Darryl Lynn Hughley was born in Los Angeles, California. After getting kicked out of high school, he joined a gang in Los Angeles, eventually leaving the group when his cousin was shot. For a time, he worked as a telemarketer, then in management for the telemarketing company. It was during this time that he met his wife, whom he would marry in 1986. The two have three children.

At his wife's urging, Hughley began to work at stand-up comedy. He steadily worked in clubs, eventually being selected to host the BET show *Comic View*. A few years after finishing his hosting duties, Hughley got his own sitcom, *The Hughleys*, which he wrote, produced, and starred in from 1998 to 2002. During the run of this show, Hughley was also part of the Original Kings of Comedy tour, along with Bernie Mac, Cedric the Entertainer, and Steve Harvey. When the sitcom ended, Hughley appeared in a variety of films and television shows, eventually landing a regular spot on *Studio 60 on the Sunset Strip*. In 2008, he was also chosen to host *DL Hughley Breaks the News*, a show examining politics and pop culture on CNN. Although the show was successful, it ended in 2009 when Hughley decided to move back to Los Angeles and be closer to his family.

Hughley continues to work regularly as both an actor and a stand-up performer. More recently, he has branched out into other fields, including writing and hosting a radio program, among other things.

Hughley is known for his sharp wit, often focusing on political matters or political or pop cultural figures. He refers to his childhood regularly, demonstrating an ability to laugh at his own struggles and misfortunes. In addition, Hughley is well known for his quick wit, improvising comical observations about the audience in the Original Kings of Comedy and regularly appearing on talk shows. Even with Hughley's sometimes aggressive form of comedy, he typically maintains a low-key, inclusive sense of performance. Hughley also has achieved a mainstream success while maintaining a following with various specific groups. Indeed, the diversity of Hughley's work is one of the things that helps to make his career significant and is likely to keep him consistently in the public eye.

Further Reading

Goodson, David. "Nightlife: Keep Ya Head up Kanye." *New York Amsterdam News* 98, no. 47 (November 15, 2007): 9.

Haggins, Bambi. *Laughing Mad: The Black Persona in Post-Soul America*. New Brunswick, NJ: Rutgers University Press, 2007.

Williams, Miya. "5 Things: DL Hughley." *Jet* 122, no. 16 (November 4, 2013): 44.

Zeke Jarvis

KAUFMAN, ANDY (1949–1984)

Andy Kaufman was born in New York City. He was the son of Janice and Stanley Kaufman, a Jewish couple living in Long Island, New York. He first performed at the age of nine and would later attend Graham Junior College, from which he graduated in 1971. Following his graduation, Kaufman began performing stand-up comedy at small clubs.

Much of Kaufman's career success came from his portrayal of original characters that he would introduce during his acts. The beginnings of his success came from his character, Foreign Man—a man from "Caspiar" who would lip sync to the *Mighty Mouse* theme and give several inept impersonation attempts of various celebrities. The one notable exception was the character's impersonation of Elvis Presley, which became one of Kaufman's most-recognized pieces. Foreign Man was renamed Latka Graves for ABC's *Taxi*, which ran from 1978 to 1983, with Kaufman appearing regularly in 79 episodes.

Another character was Tony Clifton, a singer who often opened for Kaufman at comedy clubs. The history of this character is somewhat complex, as many people did not realize that Tony Clifton was a fictional character for some time. Sometimes he was played by Kaufman, at other times by his brother Michael, and sometimes by Kaufman's friend and frequent collaborator, Bob Zmuda. This type of unpredictability was a pillar of Kaufman's career.

Kaufman was granted a television special through his contract with ABC's *Taxi*. This led to *Andy's Funhouse*, which aired in 1979. It featured many of Kaufman's routine characters and gags. In 1983, *The Andy Kaufman Show* aired; it has often been confused with *Andy's Funhouse* given the similarity in content.

After growing bored with television, Kaufman became involved in professional wrestling, beginning as the self-proclaimed "Inter-Gender Wrestling Champion of the World." Through a series of connections, Kaufman was eventually challenged by Jerry "The King" Lawler, with whom he would stage an ongoing feud that was not revealed as a joke until 10 years after Kaufman's death.

To build confidence for his performances, Kaufman learned Transcendental Meditation in 1969. He practiced TM, along with yoga, practiced three hours a day.

Although Kaufman never married, he met Lynne Marguilies in 1983. They remained together until his death the following year. While suffering from a lengthy cough, Kaufman was diagnosed with a rare form of lung cancer. After exhausting treatment options and even seeking psychic surgery outside the United States, Kaufman died in West Hollywood, California, on May 16, 1984.

Kaufman was known for his wild stage antics and his large, elaborate hoaxes. These two practices were often combined together. He read parts of *The Great Gatsby* to his audience before asking them if they would prefer to listen to a record, which turned out to be just a recording of him reading from the point he left off. He invited his "grandmother" to the side of the stage to watch at Carnegie Hall. Only at the end was it revealed to be Robin Williams in disguise. At the same show, Kaufman took the entire audience (24 buses) out for milk and cookies. These elaborate hoaxes (along with Kaufman's reported interest in doing so) have led to widespread speculation that Kaufman's death was actually a hoax. Zmuda claims that Kaufman truly did die and would not be so cruel as to leave his family in the dark for such a long time.

Kaufman is widely recognized for his unique approach to comedy. According to Carl Reiner, Kaufman did not influence comedy because no one else in the world is doing what Kaufman did. Reiner extended his praise further by saying that Kaufman is responsible for comedians being able to be themselves and not following any predetermined stigmas: "You could do anything that struck you as entertaining." A group of wrestling fans known as "Andy's Army" have sought to persuade World Wrestling Entertainment (WWE) to induct Kaufman into the WWE Hall of Fame because of his fights with Lawler, which promoted the entertainment aspect of wrestling. Perhaps the most enduring trait of Kaufman's work can be summed up in Reiner's remark of Kaufman, "Nobody can see past the edges, where the character begins and he ends." Others have also commented on the fact that Kaufman was, unlike many performers, comfortable leaving a performance with the audience disliking the character they saw, because he was able to step away even though the blurring between character and performer was often unclear.

Further Reading

Keller, Florian. *Andy Kaufman: Wrestling with the American Dream*. Minneapolis: University of Minnesota Press, 2005.

Zehme, Bill. "Andy Kaufman." *Rolling Stone* 827 (December 9, 1999): 55.

Zmuda, Bob, and Lynne Margulies. *Andy Kaufman: The Truth, Finally*. Dallas: BenBella Books, 2014.

Brian Davis

KINISON, SAM (1953–1992)

Sam Kinison was born in Yakima, Washington. Kinison's father was a Pentecostal preacher, and the family moved around for his career. When Kinison was just three months old, his family moved to East Peoria, Illinois. When he was 11, his parents divorced; Kinison stayed with his mother, while one of his three older brothers lived with their father. Kinison's mother moved the family to Tulsa, Oklahoma, after remarrying.

Like his father, Kinison began preaching. At age 17, he began a preaching career that was neither successful nor rewarding. During this period, Kinison married and divorced for the first time. After finding preaching to be unfulfilling, Kinison moved to Houston, Texas, where he started his comedy career. During this time, Kinison met Bill Hicks, who would frequently refer to Kinison as a major influence. In 1980, Kinison moved to Los Angeles to further pursue his career. Shortly thereafter, he would marry for the second time, this time divorcing in 1989.

Kinison struggled both with achieving success in his comedy career and also with cocaine addiction. In 1984, he rose to prominence with an appearance on Rodney Dangerfield's Young Comedian Showcase. His star rose further after a noteworthy appearance on David Letterman's show. In 1986, Kinison appeared in the Rodney Dangerfield film *Back to School*. All the while, Kinison continued to tour and perform, though his drug addiction worsened. In 1992, Kinison married for the final time. Later that same year, he died in a car accident with a drunken driver.

Kinison was known for his blistering performances, which were filled with energy, noise, and sometimes shocking views. He did not shy away from controversy, making light of the assassination attempt on then-president Ronald Reagan. Still, Kinison frequently commented on issues of social justice, discussing income inequality and his own drug addiction. That said, he had many troubling views and performances, often expressing misogynistic views when discussing his ex-wives or other women. More than anything, though, Kinison helped to change what

Gone Too Soon: Comedians Who Died Young

Many comedians have had long lives and lasting careers, but too many have died young from disease, substance abuse. or other issues. Some figures, like Lenny Bruce and John Belushi, struggled with personal demons that led them to die of either overdoses or complications of chemical dependency. Others, like Bill Hicks and Andy Kaufman, died of cancer or other diseases. Still others, including Freddie Prinze and Sam Kinison, died from suicide or car accident. While one cannot know how things would have turned out had the comedians lived, it is impossible not to recognize the real tragedy of missing out on the potential of these comics.

Tragically, these deaths are not unique to stand-up comedians. Television comics like Phil Hartman and humorous writers like Robert Benchley and Hunter S. Thompson died younger than the typical age of death, leaving behind significant bodies of work as well as genuine sense of longing for what might have been.

many saw as the role of the stand-up comic. Part preacher and part rock star, Kinison was different in tone and persona than many other comics, and his legacy can be seen in other striking performers such as Lewis Black, Bill Hicks, and Denis Leary. He also had the respect of many other comedians, perhaps most notably Letterman and Dangerfield. For his strong sense of persona and the flash of career that he had, Kinison remains an important figure to consider in American stand-up comedy.

See also: Hicks, Bill

Further Reading

Handelman, D. "The Devil and Sam Kinison." *Rolling Stone* 546 (February 23, 1989): 24.
Hedley, Tom. "The Last Laugh." *Esquire* 118, no. 6 (December 1992): 140.
Kinison, Bill, and Steve Delsohn. *Brother Sam: The Short, Spectacular Life of Sam Kinison*. New York: William Morrow, 1994.

Zeke Jarvis

LAMPANELLI, LISA (1961–)

Lisa Lampugnale was born in Trumbull, Connecticut. Lampugnale, who would change the spelling of her name to Lampanelli, attended Boston College and Syracuse University after graduating from high school. She received a degree in journalism and then attended the graduate program at Harvard University. Subsequently, Lampanelli had minor jobs at both *Popular Mechanics* and *Rolling Stone* magazines.

In the early 1990s, Lampanelli began performing stand-up after doing some work as a DJ. She also studied improvisation. In 1991, Lampanelli married, though she and her husband soon divorced. After steadily building a reputation and bank of material while working comedy clubs in New York, Lampanelli rose to national prominence with her work on the Friars Club Roasts on Comedy Central in the early 2000s. In 2005, she released her first comedy DVD, *Take It Like a Man*. Since then, Lampanelli has appeared on a number of celebrity roasts, had cameos in several comedy films, and continued to perform stand-up in a variety of venues. She lives in New York and continues to tour regularly.

Like other insult comics, whose numbers include Don Rickles and Andrew Dice Clay, Lampanelli is known for using racial stereotypes and other offensive or transgressive forms of humor. Like her idol Rodney Dangerfield, Lampanelli also makes herself the butt of jokes, discussing her personal life regularly and in unflattering detail. Although some individuals find Lampanelli's performances offensive, many fans see her willingness to laugh at herself and her inclusion of a number of groups in her jokes as a sign that Lampanelli approaches her humor with an eye toward leveling the social playing field rather than looking to create or maintain a sense of hierarchy. Although she sometimes receives criticism for being more transgressive than even other brash female comics like Joan Rivers or Roseanne Barr, many critics feel that this is more a matter of generational difference than lack of control or meaning.

While Lampanelli tends to focus more on stand-up than on acting, she has developed and maintained a clear level of prominence and success.

Further Reading

Ajaye, Franklyn. *Comic Insights: The Art of Stand-up Comedy*. Los Angeles: Silman-James Press, 2001.

Martin, Douglas. "Lisa Lampanelli and Jimmy Cannizzaro." *New York Times* (October 17, 2010): 16.

Zeke Jarvis

LAWRENCE, MARTIN (1965–)

Martin Lawrence was born in Germany, where his father was serving on a military base. Lawrence was named after civil rights leader Martin Luther King, Jr. His middle name, Fitzgerald, is also taken from a prominent figure—assassinated president John Fitzgerald Kennedy. When he was eight, Lawrence's parents divorced. Lawrence went with mother to Maryland. To support her family, his mother worked a number of jobs and the family moved often, which led to Lawrence attending a number of high schools. Also during his teenage years, Lawrence boxed, becoming a Golden Gloves contender.

Following high school, Lawrence went to Denver, where he began his stand-up career. After working in clubs, Lawrence landed a spot on *Star Search*, where he made it to the finals. Although Lawrence did not win, the exposure from the show got Lawrence his first acting job, an appearance on *Good Times*. As Lawrence continued to gain notice for his film and television work, he was given the opportunity to host Russell Simmons's series *Def Comedy Jam*, which gave many African American stand-up comics the exposure that would propel them to fame, including Bernie Mac and David Chappelle, among others. While hosting *Def Comedy Jam*, Lawrence also began starring in his own sitcom, *Martin*. On the show, Martin played multiple characters, which he would continue to do in a number of movies. The show ran for more than five years and had considerable ratings success.

During this time, Lawrence hosted *Saturday Night Live*, where he made a number of controversial remarks about women. After his performance, he was banned from the show and his monologue was edited out during reruns and syndicated airings of the episode.

Lawrence has been engaged three times, marrying twice and divorcing both times. Lawrence has three children from his two marriages. Although Lawrence has enjoyed considerable success, he has also been known for his personal problems, which range from substance abuse issues to accusations of sexual and physical harassment from former co-stars to even falling into a coma after overheating. At times, Lawrence's personal problems have overshadowed his comedic work. Still, he continues to work. Lawrence currently lives in Beverly Hills.

Lawrence's work has a variety of characteristics, depending on whether he is working in film or on stage. While there are some consistent factors, including his high-energy, frenetic delivery, his film work is much less edgy and dark than his work as a stand-up comic. In movies such as the *Big Momma's House* series, Lawrence often plays more than one role, and at least one of his characters is bombastic and over-the-top. This is similar to the practice of some other humorists such as Eddie Murphy, Tyler Perry, and Peter Sellers, who play sharply defined characters. In his stand-up work, Lawrence often examines very edgy material, exuding a sense of confidence and a willingness to be vulgar. This was in keeping with much of the work that the comedians on *Def Comedy Jam* did. Lawrence has achieved considerable financial and popular success, and he has a number of connections and overlaps with other contemporary comedians.

Further Reading

Collier, Aldore D. "Martin Lawrence." *Jet* 109, no. 5 (February 6, 2006): 56–60.

Haggins, Bambi. *Laughing Mad: The Black Persona in Post-Soul America*. New Brunswick, NJ: Rutgers University Press, 2007.

Martel, Jay. "Martin Lawrence." *Rolling Stone* 680 (April 21, 1994): 68.

Zeke Jarvis

LEARY, DENIS (1957–)

Denis Leary was born in Worcester, Massachusetts. His parents were both Irish immigrants. After graduating from high school, Leary attended Emerson College in Boston. Other prominent comics attended Emerson at the same time as Leary, including Steven Wright and Mario Cantone. During his college years, Leary became a charter member of the Emerson College Comedy Workshop, where he would also work as a teacher for a time after his graduation. He also met his wife at Emerson College. The two have had two children and remain married.

In the 1980s, Leary was active in the Boston stand-up comedy scene, playing in clubs and appearing on his friend Lenny Clarke's local show, *The Late, Late Show*. Leary began to achieve national prominence partially due to short clips that aired on MTV where he would deliver brief, rapid-fire rants about various bands or societal trends. He began to receive roles in a number of films and released several albums. One of them, *No Cure for Cancer*, included the song "Asshole," which gave Leary exposure and some notoriety.

Shortly after the release of *No Cure for Cancer*, Leary and his former friend Bill Hicks had a falling-out, as many people criticized Leary for having stolen much of his material from Hicks. Hicks agreed, and the two began a rivalry that lasted until Hicks's death. Still, Leary's career continued on an upward trajectory, with Leary receiving roles in both comedic and dramatic films and television shows—most notably his role on *Rescue Me*, for which he received Emmy nominations. Leary also lent his notable voice and persona to many animated films, including *Ice Age* and *A Bug's Life*.

In addition to his performances, Leary is known for his charity work to help the families of fire fighters who died in the line of duty. Leary continues to perform in films and on television; he also writes. Currently, he lives in New York with his family.

Leary's style is characterized by its aggressive nature, employing both vulgarity and high-speed delivery. The content of his act is off-putting to some, focusing on sometimes taboo issues such as cancer, sex, and religion. Despite his time at Emerson College, Leary often portrays rough-and-tumble, working-class characters, and his stand-up persona clearly overlaps with these characters. Leary has connections to a number of comedians from the Boston area, including Colin Quinn, on whose show *Remote Control* Leary would sometimes appear before he broke through into the national spotlight. In addition, Leary is related through marriage to Conan O'Brien. Like some other edgy comedians, Leary often makes himself the butt of some jokes, ridiculing his smoking addiction, his issues with alcoholism, and other frailties or struggles. Although some controversy does remain around Leary's original rise to prominence, he remains an active participant of the American humor scene.

See also: Hicks, Bill

Further Reading

Haggins, Bambi. *Laughing Mad: The Black Persona in Post-Soul America*. New Brunswick, NJ: Rutgers University Press, 2007.

Hedegaard, Erik. "The Upside of Anger." *Rolling Stone* 1035 (September 20, 2007): 81–86.

Zeke Jarvis

LEWIS, RICHARD (1947–)

Richard Lewis was born in Brooklyn, New York, though he grew up in New Jersey. After graduating from high school, Lewis attended Ohio State University, where he graduated with a degree in communication and marketing. Shortly after graduating, he began his stand-up career. While he was starting out, Lewis worked at an advertising agency. He also wrote jokes for other stand-up comedians before performing on his own.

Lewis has consistently acknowledged the comedians whom he sees as helping shape his career, particularly David Brenner and Robert Klein. Lewis is also close friends with Richard Belzer, who, like Lewis, typically wears black while performing.

Lewis began to gain prominence with his appearances on *Late Night with David Letterman, The Tonight Show* with Johnny Carson, and his own HBO specials. In 1989, Lewis had a starring role in *Anything But Love*, opposite of Jamie Lee Curtis. Lewis has played some notable roles in films, such as a cameo in *Leaving Las Vegas* and a well-received turn in *Robin Hood: Men in Tights*, directed by Mel Brooks. Lewis has also written multiple books, although most of his efforts have directed toward his stand-up touring and specials. He regularly appears on *Curb*

Your Enthusiasm, Larry David's improvisational sitcom. Lewis and David are friends from childhood.

In 2005, Lewis married Joyce Lapinsky. The two of them remain together. Although Lewis has struggled with addiction for a large portion of his life, he has now been sober for more than a decade.

Lewis is most well known for his angst-ridden material, focusing on his struggles with dating, his phobia of germs, and his battles with substance abuse. His work is also characterized by his manic, stream-of-consciousness style and his clever use of references and offbeat analogies. In his work on *Curb Your Enthusiasm*, Richard plays a slightly exaggerated version of himself, filled with neuroses and petty anxieties and jealousies, which Larry David's character often exploits for his own amusement. On that show, Lewis has put himself up for ridicule by highlighting his claim that he originated the phrase, "the (blank) from hell," which he often used when describing the problems from his life.

Lewis is a prolific comic, often creating new material while on tour and regularly producing jokes for the stage and print. Like Dave Attell and Louis CK, he is often referred to as a "comedian's comedian," for his careful craftsmanship and intelligent material and approach. In addition, Lewis is known for emulating Lenny Bruce's approach to comedy, with his willingness to broach difficult material and his fast-paced, rhythmic delivery.

See also: David, Larry

Further Reading

Ajaye, Franklyn. *Comic Insights: The Art of Stand-up Comedy*. Los Angeles: Silman-James Press, 2001.

Burch, Cathalena E. "Nervous, Neurotic Comedy: Richard Lewis' Lack of 'an Act' Replaced by a Rambling Stream." *Arizona Daily Star*, March 18, 2010. http://tucson.com/entertainment/music/nervous-neurotic-comedy/article_87ab652e-8fea-5034-8ed6-90b7609bf89c.html.

Loeffler, William. "Richard Lewis Still Finds Plenty to Despise about Himself." *Pittsburgh Tribune Review*, July 17, 2008. http://www.greenatom.net/news/richard_lewis_still_finds_plenty_to_despise_about_himself/.

Zeke Jarvis

LITTLE, RICH (1938–)

Rich Little was born in Ontario, Canada, as the middle of three children. While still young, Little began working with Geoff Scott, a fellow amateur impression-based performer. They started doing impressions of Canadian politicians, including the Ottawa mayor at the time. By the age of 17, Little and Scott were performing in night clubs. In addition to doing his live work, Little had a job as a disc jockey, where he continued to grow his stable of voices.

In 1963, Little was invited to audition for a variety show starring Judy Garland. After this early television exposure, he continued to grow his popularity through work in film and appearances on talk shows. In fact, Little did impressions of a number of talk show hosts, including Johnny Carson and Jack Benny, much to the delight of both. He also imitated President Richard Nixon. In the early 1970s, Little was part of a cast of impersonators on the show *Kopycats* and was regarded as one of the best impressionists in the world.

Little has also used his copying talents to dub in the voice for David Niven in some of the *Pink Panther* movies. In addition to his comedic work, he has been active in raising funds for various children's funds, most notably for the Juvenile Diabetes Fund.

In 1971, Little married Jeanne Worden. The two had one daughter and divorced in 1989. Little married three more times after his first marriage, once with the marriage ending in divorce and once with his wife passing away. Little is still married to Catherine Brown, whom he married in 2012. The two live in Las Vegas, where Little performs.

Little is one of a handful of comics known overwhelmingly for their impersonations. While some subjects were not entirely appreciative of his efforts, the bulk of the celebrities impersonated by Little have reacted well to his work. Jack Benny even sent Little a gold money clip in gratitude for the accuracy and entertaining nature of his impression. Although Little is regarded highly by many audiences, some view his work as a bit dated. In particular, his hosting of the White House Correspondents Dinner in 2007 was met with a lukewarm response, with many claiming that his work was outdated and tame, especially compared with the previous year's work of Stephen Colbert, who delighted many of the attendees but also displeased then-president George W. Bush. By contrast, although some of the audience members were left unimpressed by Little's efforts, the president praised him. Nevertheless, the vast majority of humorists and audience members hold Little in high regard for the range of impressions that he can do and the consistency and longevity of his career. In fact, Little regularly appears as a voice on *Futurama*, announcing himself as "Rich Little impersonating Howard Cosell" as a nod to the writing staff's appreciation of Little's work.

Further Reading

Ajaye, Franklyn. *Comic Insights: The Art of Stand-up Comedy*. Los Angeles: Silman-James Press, 2001.

Baird, Kirk. "A Lasting Impression: Rich Little Brings His Friends to Toledo." *The* Blade (OH), October 28, 2010. http://www.toledoblade.com/Music-Theater-Dance/2010/10/28/A-lasting-impression-Rich-Little-brings-his-8216-friends-to-Toledo.html.

Carter, Judy. *Stand-up Comedy: The Book*. New York: Dell, 1989.

Zeke Jarvis

LOPEZ, GEORGE (1961–)

George Lopez was born in Mission Hills, California. He was raised by his maternal grandmother after he was abandoned first by his father and then by his mother. After high school, Lopez practiced his craft, working in stand-up for a number of years before getting small roles in film and television comedies. He also gained experience performing and incorporating humor into his work as a disc jockey in Los Angeles.

In 1993, Lopez married, having a daughter with his wife. In 2005, Lopez's wife donated a kidney to him after he suffered the consequences of a genetic disorder. In 2010, Lopez and his wife separated, with the two divorcing in 2011.

In 2000, Lopez, with the help of actress Sandra Bullock, created *George Lopez*, a sitcom that drew heavily from Lopez's personal life and stand-up work, incorporating a distanced mother for Lopez's character and looking at a working-class Hispanic family. The show ran for six seasons. Although it was not a major commercial during its original run, it did receive solid ratings in syndication on Nick at Nite. After the show finished, Lopez began hosting a late-night talk show, *Lopez Tonight*, on TBS as part of the network's effort to enter the late-night talk show fray. During the run of his sitcom and talk show, Lopez also appeared in a wide variety of films, both performing in live-action roles in films like *Valentine's Day* and *Real Women Have Curves* and also doing voiceover work in films such as *Beverly Hills Chihuahua* and *Rio*. Although his talk show was canceled in 2011, Lopez continues to tour and appear in films. Currently, he lives in Los Angeles.

George Lopez found success on both his sitcom and his late-night talk show. Lopez was one of the first Hispanic comics to achieve significant mainstream success. (Department of Defense)

Lopez has stated that one of his comedy idols is Richard Pryor. Not surprisingly, Lopez often looks to his own life—even the painful moments and struggles growing up—for comedy. Much of his early stand-up work revolved around Hispanic culture and cultural tensions and misunderstandings. Also like Pryor, Lopez is willing to make himself the butt of his jokes, though he can have a sharp tongue for other cultural figures.

While Lopez has not been a lightning rod for controversy, he has sometimes feuded with other figures, perhaps most notably Carlos Mencia. In an interview on *The Howard Stern Show*, Lopez accused Mencia of stealing 13 full minutes from Lopez's act. This claim was backed by Joe Rogan, who is known for calling out comedians whom he believes to plagiarize material. Lopez also was outspoken in his criticism of ABC after the cancellation of his sitcom, claiming that the network was not supportive of performers of color.

In general, Lopez has demonstrated a consistent commitment to the promotion of cultural equality, particularly in show business. In addition to regularly having writers and performers of color on staff for his shows, Lopez has twice hosted the Latin Grammy Awards and spoken out for increasing the diversity on television throughout his career. For both his comedy work and his breaking of barriers, Lopez is a significant figure in American popular culture.

See also: Prinze, Freddie

Further Reading

Rancilio, Alicia. "George Lopez's New Sitcom 'Saint George' Makes No Apologies." *Huffington Post*, March 29, 2014. http://bigstory.ap.org/article/comedian-george-lopez-makes-no-apologies.

Rodriguez, Marissa. "George's Way." *Hispanic* 21, no. 8 (August 2008): 52–55.

Suddath, Claire. "Nick at Nite's Unexpected Success Explained." *BusinessWeek.com* (January 10, 2014): 10.

Zeke Jarvis

MANDEL, HOWIE (1955–)

Howard Mandel was born in Willowdale, an area of Toronto, Canada. He was expelled from his high school after pulling a prank where he forged the signature of a member of the school board. After leaving school, Mandel worked as a carpet salesman, while he pursued performance. By 1978, he was regularly performing in Toronto, using physical comedy to great success. Mandel steadily built a reputation, moving to the United States in the early 1980s and landing a role on the television show *St. Elsewhere*. He also did a great deal of voice work for cartoons such as *Muppet Babies*, *Gremlins*, and his own show *Bobby's World*, where he played both the title character (a child) and Bobby's father. During this time, Mandel continued to perform stand-up comedy and appeared on a wide array of television shows.

In 1980, Mandel married Terry Soil, with whom he has had three children. The two remain married to this day.

In 2005, Mandel began his hosting duties on *Deal or No Deal*, a game show that was very popular. Outside of the program, he would frequently do parodies of his own show, appearing on shows ranging from *Studio 60 on the Sunset Strip* to *Sesame Street* to do humorous versions of *Deal or No Deal*. During his later stand-up work, Mandel has discussed the fact that he has obsessive-compulsive disorder as well as a fear of germs. This fear prompted him to tap fists with contestants on *Deal or No Deal* rather than shaking hands, which makes him uncomfortable. He has also discussed having attention-deficit/hyperactivity disorder. Mandel continues to host shows and perform comedy.

Mandel is known for his wild, dynamic approach to comedy. His manic and striking physical work often catches audiences off guard. In the early stages of his comic career, Mandel was known for pulling a latex glove over his head and inflating it with his nose. He is also willing to make himself the butt of jokes, regularly referring to his psychological issues in lighthearted and good-natured ways. In keeping with this sort of approach to humor, Mandel often plays the role of imbecilic or childlike characters, as he did in *Walk Like a Man* and *Bobby's World*. While these sorts of roles often give him a sense of innocence, he is able and willing to joke about topics of more adult nature, referring to sex and dating in his stand-up. Critical reception to Mandel has been mixed, with many audiences and critics appreciating the energy and unpredictability of his work and others finding his work undisciplined or less complex than that of other stand-ups. Still, his success in a variety of forums and over a sustained period of time have helped to make him an important figure in American humor.

Further Reading

Mandel, Howie. *Here's the Deal: Don't Touch Me*. New York: Bantam, 2009.
Pomerantz, Dorothy. "Howie Mandel's Next Act." *Forbes.com* (March 8, 2011): 19.
Wihlborg, Ulrica. "At Home with Howie Mandel." *People* 78, no. 6 (August 6, 2012): 107–109.

Zeke Jarvis

MARON, MARC (1963–)

Marc Maron was born in Jersey City, New Jersey. His family lived in various places in New Jersey until he turned six, at which point they moved to Alaska, where his father was stationed for his service in the U.S. Air Force. After two years, Maron's father left the Air Force. The family then moved to Albuquerque, New Mexico, where Maron spent the remainder of his childhood. After graduating from high school, Maron attended Boston University, where he earned a degree in English.

In his early stand-up days, Maron worked in Los Angeles, where he met and worked with Sam Kinison. Not surprisingly, Maron used drugs and alcohol during this period. Still, he performed regularly and later moved to New York, performing in comedy clubs and appearing on television shows, including *Dr. Katz, Professional Therapist*. Although Maron auditioned for *Saturday Night Live*, he was passed over for the job. He also organized a stand-up comedy series, "Eating It," with fellow alternative comedian Janeane Garofalo. In addition to his stand-up work, Maron had a one-man off-Broadway show in 2000.

Like Garofalo, Maron had a presence on the liberal radio network, Air America, from its early days. Maron cohosted the show *Morning Sedition* with Mark Riley. Although the show did develop a loyal fan base, the executives at Air America felt that the tone was a bit too acerbic for morning radio; at the end of 2005, the show was taken off the air. Shortly thereafter, Maron began hosting *The Marc Maron Show* on a Los Angeles radio station. This show, too, was canceled.

After becoming frustrated with radio, Maron began a successful podcast, *WTF with Marc Maron*. The podcast is put out twice a week and consists of interviews Maron conducts with fellow stand-up comics. In 2012, *WTF with Marc Maron* was honored by Comedy Central as the best podcast of the year.

Maron has been married twice, with both marriages ending in divorce. Currently, he lives in Los Angeles and continues to perform and broadcast *WTF*.

Like some other comics, most notably Maron's former associate Sam Kinison, Maron is very open about his troubles with alcohol and the problems that led to his divorces. His openness often makes himself the object of laughter, highlighting his difficulties resisting temptations and his anger issues. Maron also discusses his relation to Judaism, as he did with his one-man show, *Jerusalem Syndrome*, which he later adapted into a book. Like Dave Attell and other, lesser-known comics, Maron is a "comedian's comedian." The respect he claims among stand-up circles is demonstrated by the wide variety of shows that he has performed or appeared on—most notably, *Late Night with David Letterman*, *Dr. Katz*, and *Louie*, the semi-autobiographical show about Maron's close friend, Louis CK. His status is also indicated by the large number of comedians who are willing to appear on his podcast. The natural, open conversations about stand-up comedy Maron is able to hold with his guests shows both his knowledge of the business and the mutual respect he and his colleagues feel. With Maron's podcast and performances, he has cemented his position as a significant figure in contemporary stand-up comedy.

Further Reading

Liem, Simon. "The Loud Listener." *Columbia Journalism Review* 52, no. 4 (November/December 2013): 36–39.

Maron, Marc. *Attempting Normal*. New York: Spiegel and Grau, 2014.

Zeke Jarvis

MARTIN, DEMETRI (1973–)

Demetri Martin was born in New York City, though he grew up in New Jersey. After graduating from high school, Martin attended Yale University. He was accepted at Harvard Law School, but decided to attend the New York University School of Law on full scholarship.

Martin soon began exploring stand-up comedy, first receiving attention after appearing on Comedy Central's *Premium Blend*. He worked as a writer for Conan O'Brien as well as a correspondent on *The Daily Show*. Prior to his appearance during Jon Stewart's tenure on *The Daily Show*, Martin had been an intern during Craig Kilborn's run. In 2006, he released an album, *These Are Jokes*. The following year, Martin was given his first Comedy Central special and, not long after that, a sketch comedy show called *Important Things with Demetri Martin*. Martin has also appeared in more serious fare, such as *Taking Woodstock*. He continues to perform regularly and has begun to appear more frequently in films. Martin lives and works in New York.

Martin is well known for his absurdist, offbeat comedy. Not surprisingly, he lists his influences as including Steven Wright, Steve Martin, and Mitch Hedberg. While he does not use props per se, Demetri—like Steve Martin—often uses both musical instruments and visual aids in his comedy. For example, he might use charts to add a mock sense of seriousness and offset the absurdity of his claims and observations. Martin also uses a marker and large drawing pad on stage to comic effect. He relies on a keen sense of wordplay, often engaging in inventive and surprising twists on the construction of words. For this reason, Martin refers to his jokes as "nerd humor." While it is true that Martin has a more narrowly focused audience than some comics, he has won the respect of many of his fellow stand-up comics, and he continues to be an important figure in contemporary American humor.

Further Reading

Martin, Demetri. "Who Am I?" *The New Yorker*, February 2011. http://www.newyorker.com/magazine/2011/02/28/who-am-i.

Satow, Julie. "A New Generation's Serious Comic." *Crain's New York Business* 22, no. 5 (January 30, 2006): 18.

Zeke Jarvis

MARTIN, STEVE (1945–)

Steve Martin was born in Waco, Texas, but grew up in California. He drew inspiration from his father, who was an aspiring actor. After graduating from Garden Grove High School, Martin studied drama at Santa Ana Junior College. During college, he worked in various productions at a local theater and landed a job with a comedy troupe at Knott's Berry Farm, a theme park in southern California. He dropped out of the University of California, Los Angeles (where he had begun to study philosophy) to pursue comedy full time.

In 1967, Martin was hired as a writer for *The Smothers Brothers Comedy Hour*. His work with the show won him his first Emmy Award in 1969. He also contributed writing for other shows, and in 1969 he made his first television appearance on *The Steve Allen Show*. Martin appeared in comedy venues and opened for musical acts such as the Carpenters. Eventually, Martin landed spots on *The Tonight Show Starring Johnny Carson*, *The Gong Show*, and *Saturday Night Live*. His first two comedy albums, *Let's Get Small* and *A Wild and Crazy Guy*, released in 1977 and 1978, respectively, each went platinum and earned Martin Grammy Awards for Best Comedy Album. *A Wild and Crazy Guy* included Martin's novelty song, "King Tut," which reached number 17 on Billboard's Hot 100 chart and sold more than 1 million copies. The success of these albums enabled Martin to sell out large arenas for his performances.

After he made his first major film appearance in *Sgt. Pepper's Lonely Hearts Club Band* in 1978, Martin focused his attention on the big screen, which he has said was always his first desire. In 1979, he cowrote and starred in the Carl Reiner–directed film *The Jerk*, which was a commercial and critical success. Martin's next film in 1981, *Pennies from Heaven*, was a commercial failure, however. He received acclaim for his role in *All of Me* with Lily Tomlin in 1984. In 1986, he starred in *¡Three Amigos!*, with Chevy Chase and Martin Short, and a film version of *Little Shop of Horrors*. Also in 1986, Martin married his first wife; they divorced in 1994. The year 1987 saw *Planes, Trains and Automobiles*, a successful John Hughes–directed comedy co-starring John Candy, and the romantic comedy *Roxanne*, co-starring Daryl Hannah. In 1989, Martin delivered another acclaimed performance in the Ron Howard–directed *Parenthood*.

In addition to taking several other film roles in the 1990s, Martin turned to writing. His first full-length play, *Picasso at the Lapin Agile*, premiered at the Steppenwolf Theatre Company in 1993. In 2000 and 2003, Martin published two novellas.

In 2001 and 2003, Martin hosted the Academy Awards. In 2004, he landed at the number 6 spot on Comedy Central's list of the 100 greatest stand-up comics. In 2007, he published a memoir, *Time Standing up*. That same year, Martin married his second wife, with whom he has one child.

A proficient banjo player since his teens, Martin made his first appearance on the Grand Ole Opry in 2009. That same year, he released an album of bluegrass songs featuring his banjo playing. *The Crow: New Songs for the 5-String Banjo*, which included guest appearances by Earl Scruggs, Vince Gill, and Dolly Parton, won a Grammy Award in 2010 for Best Bluegrass Album. Although Martin no longer performs as a stand-up comic, he does continue to write, appear in films, and tour with his musical group, playing the banjo.

Martin is known for striking a balance between intellectual and silly humor. In his memoir, he discusses the influence of the nonsense writing from Lewis Carroll's logic textbook on his use of wordplay and off-the-wall transitions in his stand-up comedy. He also is well known for his use of surprising physical comedy, which comes partly from his background in performing as an amateur magician. One of Martin's trademark features was to wear an "arrow-through-the-head" headgear while performing, adding a note of goofiness while he acted in a serious manner. Martin also broke boundaries in the audience/performer dynamic, sometimes leading audiences out to the streets at the end of his performances in his early stand-up days. In the 1980s, he was one of the comics who led the stand-up comedy boom, filling arenas in a way that was previously reserved for rock bands. Although Martin has since left behind stand-up comedy, his effective use of deadpan delivery and absurd logic have made him a major figure in this field.

See also: Smothers Brothers

Further Reading

Buhler, Stephen M. "Antic Dispositions: Shakespeare and Steve Martin's *LA Story*." *Shakespeare Yearbook* 8 (1997): 212–229.

Martin, Steve. *Born Standing up: A Comic's Life*. New York: Scribner, 2008.

Spector, Josh. "Steve Martin on Screenwriting, Storytelling and *Shopgirl*." *Creative Screenwriting* 12, no. 5 (September–October 2005): 56–60.

Stephen Powers

MASON, JACKIE (1931–)

Yacov Moshe Maza, who would go on to become Jackie Mason, was born in Sheboygan, Wisconsin, and grew up on the Lower East Side of Manhattan. After high school, Mason received a degree from the City Colleges of New York. He went on to become a rabbi, as his three brothers were. After a brief period, he left his religious calling behind to become a performer. When asked about his decision later, Mason joked, "Someone in the family had to make a living."

Mason began performing at clubs in New York City and eventually received a spot on *The Tonight Show* with Steve Allen. While Mason achieved significant success, he also had his share of issues. During an appearance on *The Ed Sullivan Show*, he was accused of giving Sullivan the finger. He was banned from the show for a time before filing a libel suit with the New York Supreme Court to help clear his name. After the proceedings finished, Mason was invited back on *The Ed Sullivan Show*, where Sullivan apologized to him for banning him from the show. Mason also ran into trouble for using the title *Politically Incorrect* for a show while Bill Maher's show of the same name was airing. He has been called to question for his statements regarding race and prominent African American figures as well as issues concerning Israel and Palestine. Despite his controversies, Mason has maintained a prominent position among contemporary humorists, performing regularly and appearing in major television shows and movies, such as *The Simpsons*, *Caddyshack II*, and *The Fairly OddParents*. In 1991, Mason married Jyll Rosenfeld, his current manager.

Mason is known for his delivery and voice as well as his culturally grounded humor. He often draws on his Jewish background to mine referential jokes. He uses innuendo, puns, and other such sources of humor in both his stand-up work and his acting. His persona in films often is a slight extension of his on-stage persona. Although some audiences began to regard him as a throwback in the later stages of his career, many audiences felt that Mason's work was classic and timeless. Mason's longevity and success have garnered him a position of respect among many comedic performers.

Further Reading

Jangcu, Robert. "Jackie Mason's World according to Hollywood." *Judaism* 40, no. 2 (Spring 1991): 134.

Macomber, Shawn. "The Ultimate Jackie Mason." *American Spectator* 41, no. 3 (April 2008): 16–20.

Mason, Jackie, and Ira Berkow. *How to Talk Jewish*. New York: St. Martin's Griffin, 1991.

Zeke Jarvis

MOONEY, PAUL (1941–)

Paul Gladney was born in Shreveport, Louisiana. When he was seven years old, his family moved to Oakland, California. Mooney was mainly raised by his grandmother, who gave him the nickname "Mooney," which Gladney would adapt as his stage surname.

In his early work experience, Mooney was a ringmaster for a circus. It was in this role that he first began to write jokes and tell humorous stories. Although he did not achieve stardom as a performer early on, he wrote jokes for a number of comedians, most notably Richard Pryor and Redd Foxx, whose edgy, incendiary material suited

Mooney's interest in pushing boundaries and fostering frank, if funny, discussions of race relations in America. In addition to writing jokes for their stand-up routines, Mooney wrote for both Foxx's and Pryor's film and television performances, including Pryor's appearance on *Saturday Night Live* and semi-autobiographical film, *Jo Jo Dancer, Your Life Is Calling*, and Foxx's show *Sanford and Son*. He also helped to foster the careers of many young comedians, most notably Sandra Bernhard, with whom Mooney is still close friends. In addition, he mentored Robin Williams, albeit to a lesser extent.

Mooney's work found another generation of fans when he created the character Homie the Clown for Damon Wayans on *In Living Color*. Mooney continued to write and perform, but his next major, recurring appearance would be on David Chappelle's show on Comedy Central. In that show, he would appear on sketches like "Ask a Black Dude," in which audience members would ask him questions about race and he would ad lib incendiary or challenging responses. One of his responses even led Wayne Brady to appear on *Chappelle's Show* in mock anger. Mooney also hosted *25 Most @#%! Moments in Black History* on BET, which chronicled shameful incidents involving African American celebrities.

Mooney has been married once, and he has two children, both of whom are comedians. He works and lives in California.

Mooney is known for his examinations of race and racism in his work. In both his own stand-up work and the jokes that he writes for other performers, Mooney often discusses what it means to be African American as well as the pressures and limits felt by African Americans in America. While not all of his work is edgy or vulgar, a good deal of it is. In addition, Mooney can be relatively confrontational when it comes to discussing other celebrities, as was the case in his bit about Wayne Brady on *Chappelle's Show* and his comments on celebrities ranging from Oprah to Michael Jackson and Diana Ross. Mooney also changed his position on the use of "the n-word" after the incident involving Michael Richards's use of racial slurs while on stage. While Mooney has sometimes slipped back into the use of this term, he has repeatedly said that he would stop saying it, and he has generally stayed true to his word. Though Mooney was initially harsh toward Richards after the incident, Mooney later publicly forgave him. Mooney was also openly and consistently critical of George W. Bush during his presidency, once even being pulled from the stage for his statements. After the incident, Mooney maintained that he had a right to challenge the president on political matters.

Beyond the content of his material, Mooney is known for his deep voice and sometimes slow, careful delivery. This often offsets his controversial remarks, giving an air of seriousness to his absurd or extreme views. Mooney's presentation was generally well received in his "Negrodamus" performances on *Chappelle's Show*. This sort of delivery is also considerably at odds with some of the performers for whom he wrote, such as Foxx and Pryor.

Mooney's work in comedy has been sustained over multiple decades. Although he himself may not be the most visible or well-known contemporary comic, his work is both well known and groundbreaking.

See also: Chappelle, Dave; Pryor, Richard

Further Reading

Horton, Cleveland. "Magazine Relaunch Is Laughing Matter." *Advertising Age* 65, no. 7 (February 14, 1994): 27.
Mooney, Paul, and Dave Chappelle. *Black Is the New White*. New York: Gallery Books, 2010.
Waldron, Clarence. "Paul Mooney's Raw Reflections." *Jet* 117, no. 9 (March 8, 2010): 44–45.

Zeke Jarvis

MORGAN, TRACY (1968–)

Tracy Morgan was born in Brooklyn, New York, where he was raised in a housing project. His father, a Vietnam veteran, left his family when Tracy was six. Morgan's father would die young, suffering from AIDS. Morgan dropped out of high school, marrying at age 17. To support his wife and their first child, Morgan sold drugs, but found greater success performing comedy. He had two more children with his wife, though the two would divorce in 2009.

After the death of a close friend, Morgan more fully devoted his efforts to comedy. While having success as a stand-up comic, Morgan got his first high-profile role in 1994 on *Martin*, where he played a character who tried to sell various items. In 1996, he broke through to the mainstream when he became a regular on *Saturday Night Live*, where he played recurring characters such as Brian Fellow (an imbecilic nature-show host) and Astronaut Jones (a mentally imbalanced homeless man) and performed his impressions of Star Jones and Mr. T, among others. Morgan was used less frequently than some other cast members, but was very well received by audiences. In 2003, Morgan had his own show, *The Tracy Morgan Show,* though it was cancelled after a single season. Also in 2003, Morgan left *Saturday Night Live*. In 2006, Morgan reunited with *Saturday Night Live* performer and writer Tina Fey on *30 Rock*; that show ended in 2013.

In 2011, Morgan announced his engagement to Megan Wollover. The couple had a child in 2013.

In addition to his television work, Morgan has consistently performed as a stand-up comic and in a wide variety of films. In 2014, he was in a severe car accident, putting him out of work for some time. Morgan lives in New York with his family.

Like Richard Pryor and Andrew Dice Clay, Morgan is known for regularly incorporating vulgarity into his act. Also like Pryor, Morgan regularly discusses his personal life and his upbringing, recognizing the troubling aspects of both. While this often leads to startling but funny performances, it can sometimes lead to controversy, as when Morgan comments on gays and lesbians and the disabled. Morgan has issued multiple apologies for his more offensive comments. Overall, Morgan has consistently had both mainstream and critical success in his stage and screen performances, winning an Emmy for his work on *30 Rock* in 2009. Like some of his contemporaries such as Louis CK and Larry David, Morgan is willing to incorporate aspects of his own life into both his stand-up and his television work, with *30 Rock* satirizing his persona from *SNL* and including real-life details such as his suffering from diabetes. For his fearlessness as a performer and his sharp wit, Morgan is a significant force on the American comedy scene.

Further Reading

Cagle, Jess. "Tracy Morgan and Hollywood's Nasty Comedy Habit." *Entertainment Weekly* 1160 (June 24, 2011): 17.

Morgan, Tracy, and Anthony Bozza. *I Am the New Black*. New York: Spiegel and Grau, 2009.

Zeke Jarvis

OSWALT, PATTON (1969–)

Patton Oswalt was born in Portsmouth, Virginia. His father was a U.S. Marine, which led to Oswalt's family moving while he was a child, going from Virginia to Ohio to California and back to Virginia. After graduating from high school, Oswalt attended the College of William and Mary in Williamsburg, Virginia, where he received a degree in English.

In the early 1990s, Oswalt began performing stand-up comedy, eventually getting appearances on *Late Night with Conan O'Brien* and getting a job writing for *MADtv*. By 1996, Oswalt had his on HBO special, which led to him getting a regular role on the sitcom *King of Queens*. Once he began to have regular success, he engaged in a wide range of acting and writing roles, including writing for comic books, having the starring voice role in Pixar's animated film *Ratatouille*, doing voice work for video games, and appearing on a number of Comedy Central Roasts.

In 2005, Oswalt married his wife, with whom he has one child. That same year, the film *The Comedians of Comedy* was released, starring Oswalt along with Brian Posehn, Maria Bamford, and Zach Galifianakis. Oswalt continues to work in a variety of genres and formats, providing voice work for children's shows like *SpongeBob SquarePants* and *WordGirl* and working to punch up the dialogue on screenplays. He has also regularly worked with more offbeat fare such as *Aqua Teen Hunger Force* and *Tom Goes to the Mayor*. Currently, Oswalt lives in California with his family, though he continues to work and release comedy albums.

Oswalt is known for his keen eye in sending up popular culture. Like Brian Posehn and David Cross, he makes larger cultural observations by examining seemingly small or low-cultural objects such as comic books or blogging. Oswalt is also open about his atheism and general distrust of organized religion and other hierarchical structures. He is a well-known supporter of more independent performers. As part of the Comedians of Comedy tour, Oswalt performed in small clubs, eschewing the larger venues for comedy. He also released one of his CDs on Sub Pop Records, which is generally considered a punk rock music label. This approach is in line with his interest in more subcultural programs, like the shows from the Cartoon Network's *Adult Swim* programming and his work on *Reno 911*. That said, Oswalt has achieved mainstream prominence and commercial success with his film and television work. This balance is similar to that demonstrated by other comics like David Cross and Janeane Garofalo. While Oswalt has not attained quite the prominence of major comics like Robin Williams and Eddie Murphy, he has managed a sustained and diverse career that makes him a significant American humorist.

Further Reading

Cutruzzula, Kara. "Patton Oswalt, Heartbreaker." *Newsweek* 158, 23 (December 5, 2011): 65.

Oswalt, Patton. *Zombie Spaceship Wasteland: A Book by Patton Oswalt*. New York: Scribner, 2011.

Wilkinson, Amy. "Patton Oswalt Casts Away." *Entertainment Weekly* 1306 (April 11, 2014): 55.

Zeke Jarvis

POSEHN, BRIAN (1966–)

Brian Posehn was born in Sacramento, California. After graduating from high school, he attended Sacramento State University.

Posehn's earliest television work was in small parts, though he gained recognition with regular appearances on *Mr. Show*, where he worked with Bob Odenkirk and David Cross, among others. Posehn balanced his work by appearing in mainstream television shows like *Seinfeld* and *Friends* as well as more offbeat, experimental shows such as *Aqua Teen Hunger Force* and *Tom Goes to Mayor* from Comedy Central's *Adult Swim* programming and *The Sarah Silverman Program*. He also appeared in a wide array of movies, including *Fantastic Four: Rise of the Silver Surfer*, the horror film *The Devil's Rejects*, and *Dumb and Dumber: When Harry Met Lloyd*, and he has worked writing in comic books, most notably a run on *Deadpool*.

Posehn had performed stand-up for years before he released his first album, *Live in: Nerd Rage*. His album also included songs from musicians such as Anthrax's Scott Ian and White Zombies' John Tempesta. This was a natural overlap for Posehn, who often talks about metal music and metal culture in his work. It led to him participating in the Bonnaroo Music and Arts Fest along with Louis CK and Janeane Garofalo, among others.

Posehn, who lives in California, has appeared in a variety of other media, including doing voice work in video games. He has also written both a book and comic books.

Posehn is known for his awkward persona and deadpan, stoner-like delivery. This fits with his material, which often focuses on pieces of low culture and insignificant concerns such as the distinction between *Star Trek* and *Star Wars* or the fan base of Britney Spears. Posehn carries this persona over to much of his acting work, where he generally plays oafish, awkward, dull-witted characters. While Posehn's comedy does not have the same overtly political aspect as that of Garofalo or Louis CK, he is often associated with the alternative comedy movement due to his association with offbeat and groundbreaking shows like *Mr. Show* and the programs on *Adult Swim*. While Posehn has not fully broken through into mainstream prominence (he jokingly refers to himself as "that guy from *Just Shoot Me*"), he has created a body of work that connects to a wide variety of prominent and progressive comedy.

Further Reading

"Brian Posehn Interview." Team Coco, August 2, 2011. http://teamcoco.com/video/starstruck-brian-posehn.

Friend, Tad. "Hostile Acts." *New Yorker* 82, no. 48 (February 5, 2007): 76–77.

Zeke Jarvis

PRINZE, FREDDIE (1954–1977)

Freddie Prinze (born Frederick Pruetzel) was born in New York to a Puerto Rican mother and a German father. While he generally identified as Puerto Rican, Prinze would sometimes refer to himself as "Hungarican" for comic effect. This sort of awareness of and commentary on race and culture would appear in much of Prinze's work.

Prinze was raised in Washington Heights, a diverse neighborhood in New York. While he was a child, his mother enrolled him into ballet classes to help him deal with a weight problem. Through this experience, he gained the skills that allowed him to enroll in an arts school, which allowed him to continue ballet while also studying drama. It was also here that he began his work in stand-up.

In 1975, Prinze married Katherine Cochran, with whom he had a son, Freddie Prinze, Jr. Just two years later, Cochran filed for divorce from Prinze, citing his escalating drug use. Prinze committed suicide shortly thereafter.

Prinze achieved significant fame in 1973, when he appeared on *Jack Paar Tonight* and *The Tonight Show* with Johnny Carson. He was the first young comic invited to sit down with Carson. He also starred in the hit show *Chico and the Man*, along with Jack Albertson, from 1974 to 1977. In addition, Prinze appeared on many of the *Dean Martin Celebrity Roasts*. Many critics have speculated that his quick rise to fame might have intensified some of the struggles that led to his eventual suicide.

Much of Prinze's humor, both in his stage performances and his work on *Chico and the Man* revolved around exploring racial stereotypes. This focus, along with his racial background, made him an important figure in breaking down a number of barriers. Of course, not all audiences were enthusiastic about his approach. Many conservative white viewers were uncomfortable with the territory that Prinze examined, and members of the Hispanic community also took issue with some of the portrayals of their culture on *Chico*. Still, Prinze regularly insisted that his depictions were not done in spite. Rather, he claimed to be examining the fact that everyone is a victim, meaning that everyone's struggles deserve examination and exploration.

Prinze has been memorialized with a number of articles and comments and even in the movie *Fame*, where one character claims to have grown up around Prinze and been inspired by him. This character's arc in the movie includes falling into depression and drug use. A TV movie, *Can You Hear the Laughter?*, directly focused on

Prinze's life. Prinze's legacy has also been honored with a posthumous star on the Hollywood Walk of Fame.

See also: Lopez, George

Further Reading

Appelo, Tim. "The Lost Prinze of Comedy." *Entertainment Weekly* 259 (January 27, 1995): 64.
Deggans, Eric. "Freddie Prinze." *Hispanic* 18, no. 9 (September 2005): 22–24.
Preutzel, Maria. *The Freddie Prinze Story*. New York: Master's Press, 1978.

Zeke Jarvis

PRYOR, RICHARD (1940–2005)

Richard Pryor was born Richard Franklin Lennox Thomas Pryer in 1940 in Peoria, Illinois. His mother was a prostitute. Pryor grew up in a brothel run by his grandmother, who raised him after his mother abandoned him. Pryor suffered frequent beatings at the hands of his grandmother and was sexually abused as a child while living in the brothel.

After his expulsion from school, Pryor joined the army, but spent most of his two years while enlisted in an army prison in Germany for beating another soldier. After his discharge, Pryor moved to New York City and began his comedy career in nightclubs, with an act inspired by Bill Cosby. Before long, he began appearing in spots on television. Pryor performed on *The Ed Sullivan Show* and *The Tonight Show Starring Johnny Carson*, which led to success in Las Vegas when Pryor shortly began performing there.

In 1960, Pryor married for the first time. The couple had one child but divorced in 1961. In 1968, Dove/Reprise Records released Pryor's first comedy album, *Richard Pryor*, which was recorded in West Hollywood at the Troubadour. Also in 1968, Pryor married for the second time, again having one child and divorcing in 1969. In 1971, Laff Records released Pryor's second comedy album, *Craps (After Hours)*. This album, which was recorded at Redd Foxx's club in Hollywood, captures the beginning of the racially charged and profanity-laced humor for which Pryor would become famous, as well as controversial, in the 1970s.

While still relatively unknown, Pryor appeared in Mel Stuart's 1973 documentary film, *Wattstax*, which captures Pryor's appearance at the 1972 Wattstax music festival in the Los Angeles Memorial Coliseum. This led to a deal with Stax Records, which released his third comedy album, *That Nigger's Crazy*, in 1974. *That Nigger's Crazy*, which was recorded at Don Cornelius's Soul Train nightclub, proved to be Pryor's breakthrough success, with gold certification from the Recording Industry Association of America, a Grammy Award for Best Comedy Album, and four weeks at the number 1 spot on Billboard's R&B/Soul Albums chart. Pryor topped its success with the release of his fourth album, *. . . Is It Something I Said?* in 1975. This album went platinum and earned Pryor another Grammy Award for Best Comedy Album. It is also notable for offering the first recorded appearance of

Pryor's popular Mudbone character, which had begun appearing in Pryor's stand-up performances as a wino offering off-the-wall and satirical observations on black life. Pryor's next album, *Bicentennial Nigger*, recorded at the Roxy Theatre in West Hollywood and released in 1976, continued his success and added yet another gold certification and Grammy Award to Pryor's list of achievements.

Also in the 1970s, Pryor contributed writing for television shows such as *Sanford and Son* and a Lily Tomlin special; he won an Emmy Award for the latter. He became the first African American to serve as a guest host on *Saturday Night Live*. Pryor had his own show on NBC, *The Richard Pryor Show*, which was a comedy variety show; it ran opposite ABC's *Happy Days* and *Laverne & Shirley*, however, and was cancelled after only four episodes.

In 1977, Pryor married for the third time, divorcing in 1978. He married a fourth time in 1979 and a fifth time in 1986.

Pryor had appeared in small parts in various films throughout the late 1960s and early 1970s, but the late 1970s brought him his most notable film roles, including *Car Wash* and *Silver Streak* in 1976. *Silver Streak* was Pryor's first vehicle with co-star Gene Wilder; the pair would collaborate in three additional movies. Pryor also played the Wiz in 1978's *The Wiz*, an urbanized, African American musical retelling of *The Wizard of Oz*.

Richard Pryor: Live in Concert, which was released in 1979, was Pryor's big-screen concert performance. Capturing Pryor in his prime in front of a Long Beach, California, crowd, it has been considered by many critics to be the best and most influential filmed stand-up comedy performance of all time. Also in 1979, Pryor made a cameo in *The Muppet Movie*.

While working on the film *Bustin' Loose* in 1980, Pryor accidentally set himself on fire while freebasing cocaine and drinking heavily. He was forced to spend several weeks recovering in the hospital with severe burns covering half his body. This incident became the basis of a joke in 1982's concert film and comedy album, *Richard Pryor: Live on the Sunset Strip*. It also featured prominently in 1986's *Jo Jo Dancer, Your Life Is Calling*, a semi-autobiographical film written and directed by Pryor.

In 1984, Pryor starred in the children's television show *Pryor's Place*, which featured Pryor interacting with puppet characters. This show ran for 13 episodes. Pryor also appeared in several more films throughout the 1980s, including another concert film, *Richard Pryor: Here and Now* in 1983; *Superman III*; *Brewster's Millions*; *See No Evil, Hear No Evil* with Gene Wilder; and *Harlem Nights* with Eddie Murphy.

Pryor received a diagnosis of multiple sclerosis in 1986. In 1990, he had a heart attack—his second—that required a triple bypass operation. He began using a scooter in the early 1990s; indeed, his last film appearance, in 1997's *Lost Highway*, shows him with his scooter. Pryor received the Mark Twain Prize for American Humor in 1998, and in 2004 he landed at the number 1 spot on Comedy Central's list of the 100 Greatest Stand-ups of All Time. In 2001, Pryor married for the last time. He died of another heart attack on December 10, 2005.

Pryor was known for his daring as a stand-up comic, both in his use of obscenity and in his direct discussion of racial tensions, as well as his willingness to discuss his own troubles, including being raised by a prostitute and lighting himself on fire while using drugs. This total openness shocked audiences and influenced comedians like Greg Giraldo and Louis CK. Pryor's irreverent and bold social commentary has also invited comparisons with Lenny Bruce, who likewise used iconoclastic views and obscenity to upset the establishment while winning over audiences. Although Pryor had many film and TV appearances, he is still best known as a stand-up comic, and his influence over subsequent comics is hard to overstate.

See also: Carlin, George; CK, Louis; Cosby, Bill; Murphy, Eddie

Further Reading

Durham, I. "Richard Pryor: Melancholy and the Religion of Tragicomedy." *Journal of Religion & Health* 50, no. 1 (March 2011): 132–144.

Haskins, James. *Richard Pryor, a Man and His Madness: A Biography*. New York: Beaufort Books, 1984.

Henry, David, and Joe Henry. *Furious Cool: Richard Pryor and the World That Made Him*. New York: Algonquin Books, 2013.

Stephen Powers

RICKLES, DON (1926–)

Don Rickles was born in Queens, New York, to Jewish parents who were both children of immigrants. His parents spoke Yiddish as Rickles was growing up, and he was raised in a working-class area with many immigrant families. After high school, Rickles enlisted in the Navy, where he served in World War II before being honorably discharged. Rickles married his wife, Barbara, in 1965. The two have remained together ever since, and they have two children, a daughter and a son. Their son died in 2011 at the age of 41. Rickles has regularly noted that he and comedian Bob Newhart are best friends, referencing the fact that their families often vacation together. This might be surprising, given the significant difference in style of humor between the two comics, but their longevity in stand-up comedy and onscreen have allowed them to have many overlaps in their careers.

Rickles's stand-up career began partly because there was so little work available while he was studying at the American Academy of Dramatic Arts. Although he started with prepared material, he began relying heavily on insult comedy when he found that his responses to hecklers were received even more favorably than his prewritten work. This approach led to a major breakthrough for Rickles when Frank Sinatra attended one of his sets in a Miami Beach nightclub, Murray's Franklin. Sinatra was so amused by Rickles's stage assault on his work as an actor that he recommended other celebrities attend Rickles's performances so that they could be ridiculed as well. This led to Rickles's association with the Rat Pack. As Rickles became more popular, he was offered more work, such as roles in the movie *Run Silent, Run Deep* and the TV shows *Get Smart* and *Run for Your Life*. In addition to these sitcoms, Rickles would regularly appear on talk shows such as Johnny Carson's *Tonight Show*. He was a regular fixture on the Dean Martin

Celebrity Roasts, where his insult approach to comedy fit well with the overall approach to humor. While Rickles often used humor rooted in ethnic stereotypes, he made a point to touch on many different ethnicities to diffuse his sense of aggression toward any specific group.

While Rickles was generally on the giving end of the insults, one of his more noteworthy incidents, now referred to as "The Cigarette Box Incident," came out of a bit on *The Tonight Show*. While working with Bob Newhart, Rickles accidentally broke a cigarette box, a long-standing prop on Carson's desk. In good-natured retaliation, Carson and a camera crew went to the set of Rickles's show *Sharkey*, where Carson called Rickles "Big Dummy" and used Rickles's approach to insult comedy to insult Rickles himself. The footage of this incident has often been replayed in retrospectives of *The Tonight Show*.

As the popularity of some members of the Rat Pack waned in the late 1980s, Rickles found new respect and adulation for his work on projects such as the Martin Scorsese film *Casino*, which drew upon his experience in Las Vegas, and the movie series *Toy Story*, in which he played Mr. Potatohead. Rickles continues to appear on talk shows, including *Late Night with David Letterman*, *Jimmy Kimmel Live!*, and *The Late, Late Show with Craig Ferguson*. He also was the subject of *Mr. Warmth: The Don Rickles Project*, a documentary directed by John Landis.

See also: Carson, Johnny; Newhart, Bob

Further Reading

Busis, Hillary. "Don Rickles: The King of Comedy." *Entertainment Weekly* 1313/1314 (May 30, 2014): 28.

Luscombe, Belinda. "Don Rickles, Auteur Bait." *Time* 146, no. 6 (August 7, 1995): 77.

Rickles, Don, and David Ritz. *Rickles' Book: A Memoir*. New York: Simon & Schuster, 2008.

Zeke Jarvis

RIVERS, JOAN (1933–2014)

Born Joan Molinsky, Joan Rivers was raised in New York. She was born in Brooklyn to Russian, Jewish immigrant parents. Her family eventually moved to Larchmont, in Westchester County. After graduating from high school, Rivers went to Connecticut College before transferring to Barnard College, where she earned a degree in English and anthropology. Before breaking into show business, Rivers held a number of jobs, including working in fashion and advertising and being a tour guide in Rockefeller Center. In 1955, Rivers married James Sanger, though the marriage lasted only six weeks.

Rivers's early work included her role in the play *Driftwood*, where she played a lesbian character who desired a character played by Barbara Streisand. Both Streisand and Rivers were unknown at the time. Rivers played in a number of night clubs in New York before landing a spot on *The Tonight Show*, hosted by Jack Paar at the time. This led to more television work, including a spot on *Candid Camera*, where she would both write and take part in the pranks pulled on the show. During the

1960s and 1970s, Rivers was very active, appearing on talk shows such as Johnny Carson's *The Tonight Show*, *The Ed Sullivan Show*, *Hollywood Squares*, *The Carol Burnett Show*, and even the children's program *The Electric Company*. During this era, she also wrote and directed her first movie, *Rabbit Test*, which starred Billy Crystal, a close friend.

Joan Rivers was well known for her daring, edgy comedy. Before her untimely death in 2014, Rivers had experienced a resurgence of popularity. (Featureflash/Dreamstime.com)

In the 1980s, Rivers continued to perform, having a regular show in Las Vegas. She put out a hit comedy album, *What Becomes a Semi-Legend Most?* and wrote a best-selling humor book, *The Life and Hard Times of Heidi Abramowitz*. In 1986, Rivers was given a talk show on the Fox Network that aired against Johnny Carson's. The show, which was widely considered a failure, cost Rivers her friendship with Carson. The pair had been very close, with Rivers even referring to herself as Carson's daughter in recognition of his mentoring. After her show's cancellation, Rivers's husband, Edgar Rosenberg, committed suicide; Rivers blamed his death on the executives' harsh treatment of herself and her husband, who had been the show's producer. In 1989, Rivers began a daytime talk show, which ran for five years to great success, earning her an Emmy.

In 1994, Rivers hosted the pre-awards show for the E! Network's coverage of the Golden Globes. The following year, Rivers and her daughter Melissa hosted both the pre-awards shows for the Golden Globes and the Academy Awards. Mother and her daughter used their acerbic wit and keen sense of wordplay to take on prominent cultural figures in this venue. This helped Joan Rivers to land a regular show on the *E!* network, *Fashion Police*, where she regularly handed down judgments on celebrities and their fashion choices. Rivers remained close to her daughter, and the two even participated in a joint reality television show: *Joan and Melissa: Joan Knows Best?* Joan Rivers died on September 4, 2014, in New York City as a result of cardiac arrest following a medical procedure.

Rivers was known for her sharp tongue and unapologetic, brassy persona. Like her contemporary Phyllis Diller, Rivers was often outrageous and boisterous in her presentation. Unlike Diller, Rivers was willing to be more vulgar and daring in her delivery, regularly using double entendres. Although Rivers could be mildly aggressive with her comedy, she often softened the blows by undercutting herself, referring to her numerous plastic surgeries or her age. In her later years, Rivers was a respected elder stateswoman in comedy, having been roasted on Comedy Central and honored in numerous ways. She also appeared on Louis CK's show, *Louie*, where she gave him advice about doing stand-up and balancing his artistic integrity with commercial concerns. CK has stated that this was both an honor and an education for him. Ironically, the episode on which Rivers appeared revolved around Donald Trump, who chose Rivers as the winner for *Celebrity Apprentice* in the second season. Rivers often spoke highly of Trump and had stated that she was a Republican. Of course, Rivers's politics did not play a central role in her comedy. Instead, she regularly took on societal expectations and politeness codes and seemingly frivolous points like the fashion choices of celebrities. Nevertheless, Rivers's brashness, wit, and longevity have earned her a position of respect among many contemporary humorists.

See also: Carson, Johnny; Diller, Phyllis

Further Reading

Courtney, Jennifer. "Talk about the Style: Joan Rivers, QVC Discourse and Stardom." *Studies in Popular Culture* 28, no. 3 (April 2006): 111–128.

Rivers, Joan. *I Hate Everyone . . . Starting with Me*. New York: Berkley Books, 2012.

Ross, Christopher. "Joan Rivers." *Wall Street Journal Magazine* (February 16, 2014): 156.

Zeke Jarvis

ROCK, CHRIS (1965–)

Chris Rock was born Christopher Julius Rock III to Rosalie, a social worker for the mentally handicapped, and Julius Rock, a truck driver and newspaper delivery man. Chris was born in Andrew, South Carolina, but his family moved to Crown Heights, Brooklyn, New York, shortly thereafter. As a child, Rock went to predominantly white schools, where he was often bullied. As he grew old and began attending James Madison High School, the bullying only increased in severity. Eventually, Rock's parents pulled him out of school altogether, leaving him to work various low-paying jobs and receive a GED.

In 1984, Rock began to do stand-up comedy in New York City's Catch a Rising Star comedy clubs. As he became more well known, he earned roles in the film *I'm Gonna Git You Sucka* and the TV series *Miami Vice*. Actor Eddie Murphy once attended one of Rock's stand-up performances and helped him to get a role in *Beverly Hills Cop II*, Rock's first role in a major motion picture. Rock joined the cast of *Saturday Night Live* in 1990. He worked alongside comedians Chris Farley, Adam Sandler, Rob Schneider, and David Spade, becoming known as one of the "Bad Boys of SNL." The year 1991 saw the release of Rock's first comedy album, *Born Suspect*, which enhanced his national exposure obtained through *SNL*. Rock had success on

SNL, but eventually decided to leave to focus on his solo career. In 1993, he began filming comedy specials. In 1994, Rock filmed the HBO special *Big Ass Jokes*; in 1996, he filmed the special *Bring the Pain*, which earned him two Emmy Awards. He also earned an Emmy nomination for his role as a commentator on Comedy Central's *Politically Incorrect*, which aired during the 1996 presidential elections.

First gaining attention as a cast member on *Saturday Night Live*, Chris Rock has become one of the most well-respected stand-up comics in American history. His outspoken style has helped make him an important figure in both comedy and discussions of race relations. (Photofest)

In 1996, Rock married Malaak Compton-Rock, a founder and executive director of StyleWorks, a nonprofit salon. The couple has two daughters, Lola Simone, born in 2002, and Zahra Savannah, born 2004. Despite numerous rumors, the couple have adamantly defended their marriage and never considered divorce.

In 1997, Rock began a talk show, *The Chris Rock Show*, on HBO. The program ran from 1997 to 2000 and featured guests raging from attorney Johnnie Cochran to former NAACP president Kweisi Mfume. In addition to his stand-up work, Rock was involved with films like *Dogma, Beverly Hills Ninja, Nurse Betty, The Longest Yard, Death at a Funeral, Grown-ups,* and *2 Days in New York*. He has done voice work for the popular *Madagascar* franchise. Rock also produced a semi-autobiographical television show, *Everybody Hates Chris*, in 2005, for which he provided the voiceover. The show was nominated for a Golden Globe, a People's Choice Award, and two Emmy Awards. Rock consistently works in film and on stage, and he currently lives with his family in Alpine, New Jersey.

Despite his rave reviews as a director and an actor, Rock has never had much success at hosting Hollywood affairs. He was once cut off during a London Live Earth event for swearing and was thoroughly criticized for his hosting of the 77th Academy Awards ceremony. In fact, Rock has received criticism for his outspoken views on race, gender relations, and political issues. Even so, Rock has gained and maintained a significant following, including general audiences and many other comics. He is known for his energetic delivery, often pacing the length of the stage as he rants. His on-stage work also employs hard emphasis on the punchlines, sometimes getting laughs for his delivery as much as for his content. In his film work, Rock often takes a softer touch than in his stand-up efforts. His cultural prominence (he often humorously discusses the changes in his life that followed his interview by Oprah) and his scathing send-ups of the racism and ignorance found in mainstream culture make him a significant and successful figure in American comedy.

See also: CK, Louis; Sykes, Wanda

Further Reading

Carr, Joi. "The Paraphernalia of Suffering: Chris Rock's *Good Hair* Still Playing in the Dark." *Black Camera: An International Film Journal* 5, no. 1 (Fall 2013): 56–71.
Rock, Chris. *Rock This!* New York: Hyperion, 1997.
Zehme, Bill. "Chris Rock Isn't Laughing." *Rolling Stone* 1049 (April 3, 2008): 44–50.

Kristen Franz

ROGERS, WILL (1879–1935)

William Rogers was born in Indian Territory in what is now the state of Oklahoma, and his parents were both part Cherokee Indian. When Rogers was 11, his mother died. Although Rogers was one of eight children, only four (Rogers included) survived into adulthood. Rogers and his father, who remarried less than two years after his wife's death, sometimes disagreed. Rogers's father wanted him to focus on business matters, which conflicted with Rogers's more easygoing personality. Although Rogers had some success as a student, he dropped out of school in the 10th grade, instead focusing on rope and cowboy tricks.

After dropping out, Rogers traveled the world, working in both Argentina and South Africa. He worked in different fields before joining "Texas Jack's Wild West Circus," which began his career in performance. After learning under Texas Jack, Rogers went to Australia to pursue his career. He returned to the United States in 1904 and began performing on the vaudeville circuit. During one performance, a wild steer got into the crowd. After Rogers was able to successfully subdue it, he received the publicity that would help launch his career. It was shortly after this event that William Hammerstein signed him to work, and Rogers performed regularly.

In 1908, Rogers married Betty Blake. The two had four children, one of whom died in infancy. During this time, Rogers continued to perform, and he and his family managed a ranch.

Rogers's act was a combination of rope tricks and jokes about the news of the day. He often would remark that he had no jokes, only the headlines. He was eventually given a regular slot on the Ziegfeld Follies. During one of his performances, President Woodrow Wilson was in the audience. Rogers roasted Wilson to the delight of the audience (Wilson included), thereby establishing his improvisational skills.

As Rogers's fame grew, Hollywood became interested in him. In 1918, he starred in *Laughing Bill Hyde*. Rogers was wildly successful in films, appearing in 48 silent films and 21 features films. In addition to his film and cowboy work, Rogers toured on the lecture circuit. He wrote regularly for *The New York Times* and *The Saturday Evening Post* and published a number of books that came out of his jokes from his stage work.

Although much of his humor had a seemingly simplistic nature, Rogers never shied away from political commentary. In 1928, he embarked on a stunt presidential campaign, publishing quotes and updates in *Life*, to satirize the general act of campaigning.

In addition to his interest in politics and humor, Rogers was an avid supporter of aviation. In 1935, aviator and fellow Oklahoman Wiley Post, whom Rogers had regularly visited to follow his aviation exploits, were attempting a flight from Alaska to Russia. Sadly, the plane crashed, and both men were killed.

Rogers's style is most clearly characterized by his desire to challenge major political figures and structures in support of the common man. Although Rogers supported the Democrats, he challenged both political parties and even advocated for Republican President Calvin Coolidge. Drawing directly from newspaper headlines and regularly commenting on political debates, Rogers used his everyman persona to make astute but jokey observations about the nature of American political discourse. Unlike in his early film career, toward the end of his career Rogers's persona was so well established that he often played slightly exaggerated versions of himself in a variety of films.

Rogers was very well respected by a broad section of American culture. H. L. Mencken referred to him as "the most dangerous man in America," because his observations were so widely read and so often cutting. One particularly striking aspect of Rogers's work was the fact that he was able to make incisive observations about political figures while maintaining a strong sense of likability. This approach to observational humor was later put into practice by humorists such as Tom Smothers and, to a lesser extent, Anita Loos. Rogers was known for claiming that he "had never met a man [he] didn't like," meaning that every person is basically interesting and sympathetic—it is simply a matter of knowing enough of the individual's backstory to appreciate what is most worth knowing about someone. For both his sustained and multifaceted success as a performer and humorist and for his innovative and popular approach to humor, Rogers remains one of the most prominent figures in the history of American humor.

Further Reading

Ware, Amy M. "Unexpected Cowboy, Unexpected Indian: The Case of Will Rogers." *Ethnohistory* 56, no. 1 (Winter 2009): 1–34.

White, Richard Jr. *Will Rogers: A Political Life*. Lubbock: Texas Tech University Press, 2011.

Yagoda, Ben. *Will Rogers: A Biography*. Norman: University of Oklahoma Press, 2000.

Zeke Jarvis

ROMANO, RAY (1957–)

Ray Romano was born in Queens, New York, where he grew up with two brothers. He was in the same high school graduating class as Fran Drescher, whose show *The Nanny* would later be one of Romano's early TV appearances. Romano has also competed in a number of World Series of Poker events.

Romano married his wife, Anna, in 1987. They have four children together, one daughter and three sons. Romano and his wife announced that she had dealt with breast cancer, stating that they had hoped help others by publicly discussing her illness.

Romano competed in the Johnnie Walker Comedy Search in 1989, which helped to get him experience and some early attention. He also appeared on both *Star Search* and *Dr. Katz, Professional Therapist*, a cartoon on which he did voice work. He was originally cast as a character on *News Radio*, but was replaced by Joe Rogan before the show's regular run began.

One of Romano's big breakthroughs came from performing on *The Late Show with David Letterman*. That experience eventually led to his sitcom *Everybody Loves Raymond*, on which he played a sports writer and father. *Everybody Loves Raymond* enjoyed significant commercial success, lasting nine seasons. The show often featured humor that revolved around gender conflicts, looking at typical or stereotypical conflicts between spouses and parents and children. It also helped to establish other actors, including Patricia Heaton and Brad Garrett, and it featured the well-known talents Peter Boyle and Doris Roberts.

After *Everybody Loves Raymond* went off the air, Romano continued to do stand-up work. In addition, he co-starred in *Men of a Certain Age* along with Scott Bakula and Andre Braugher. He also appeared on *The Office*, *Parenthood*, and *The Middle*, which starred his television wife, Patricia Heaton. While Romano's persona on *Everybody Loves Raymond* was generally likable and laid-back, if perhaps lazy or self-centered, his work since then has expanded his character range. From the neurotic character created for *The Office* to the gruff, arrogant character on *Parenthood*, Romano has explored characters further removed from his on-stage, stand-up persona and which show a greater dramatic range in his acting.

Romano's early career was generally characterized by conventional notions of masculinity, with men liking sports and women. Nevertheless, he is very highly regarded by other comics, who respect the amount of material that Romano is able to generate even while working on his television career. In the second phase of his career, Romano has become known for the range of his dramatic performances, which is similar to the path taken by other comedic performers such as Will Ferrell and Jim Carrey. Still, Romano is likely to be associated primarily with his stand-up work and especially his breakthrough sitcom.

Further Reading

Dalton, Mary, ed. *The Sitcom Reader: America Viewed and Skewed*. New York: State University of New York Press, 2005.

Raab, Scott. "Sing a Song of Ray Romano." *Esquire* 139, no. 5 (May 2003): 120.
Stein, Joel. "Q&A: Ray Romano." *Time* 153, no. 23 (June 14, 1999): 227.

Zeke Jarvis

ROSS, JEFFREY (1965–)

Jeffrey Ross was born and raised in New Jersey. When Ross was 14, his mother died; his father died when he was 19. After high school, he attended Boston University, where he received a degree in communications. During his college years, Ross worked for the local National Public Radio station. With his interest in social issues and his exposure to performance and broadcast, Ross was able to approach his stand-up career with a solid background.

Ross performed in Boston a number of times. During this time, he built a number of connections with other humorists, including with Greg Giraldo, who once defended Ross in court after Ross was accused of inciting a riot. Although he had a number of appearances in films and onstage, Ross came to national prominence mostly through his performances on the Friars Club Roasts. He has become the Roastmaster General, has often receiving some of the biggest laughs at these events. In addition, Ross was the first guest on Marc Maron's podcast, *WTF with Marc Maron* in 2009, and has appeared a number of times on Comedy Central shows, including *Shorties Watching Shorties*. Ross has also been a regular perform on the USO tour. In mid-2012, he got his own show, *The Burn with Jeff Ross*. The show mixes Ross's stand-up and his acting-out shtick in the cities he visits on his tours. Ross has also engaged in some political activity, including his appearance at and support for the Occupy movement in Los Angeles in 2011.

Ross is known for his willingness to be playfully aggressive with his comedy. His wild analogies and daring references often surprise audiences. But if Ross takes

Painful Love: The Comedy Roast

While America loves its celebrities, it also enjoys seeing them taken down. The comedy roast represents a very rare ritual where the U.S. public can get both aspects at once, showing the quality of fellow celebrities who come to roast the party being roasted as well as their frailties and problems. During the height of the Rat Pack's popularity, comedians like Don Rickles and Phyllis Diller would tell jokes about Dean Martin, Frank Sinatra, and other well-known figures. Although the tradition became less prominent for a time, Comedy Central's airing of the Friar's Club Roasts has helped to bring this practice back into the public eye. Comedians like Lisa Lampanelli, Greg Giraldo, and Jeffrey Ross have begun to make their names through their successful appearances roasting Jerry Stiller, Pamela Anderson, and David Hasselhoff, among many others. Unlike the harsher send-ups of politicians or other public figures, the roast is often (though not always) structured to give several minutes of joking about a figure, followed by a short but earnest comment about what the roasted figure means to the performer.

on others with his comedy, he also consistently demonstrates a willingness to put himself in the position to be ridiculed. Whether it is appearing on stage in a bathing suit and leather jacket at the roast of David Hasselhoff or discussing one of his early sexual experiences on *The Burn*, Ross mines his own life for humor on a regular basis. With a variety of connections and his regular appearances on Friars Club Roasts, Ross has steadily established himself as a significant figure in American comedy.

See also: Giraldo, Greg

Further Reading

Dorsey, Kristina. "Jeffrey Ross Is the Toast of the Roast." *The Day (New London, CT)*, April 1, 2011. http://www.theday.com/article/20110401/ENT12/304019959.

Gaydos, Kristen. "Roastmaster Jeffrey Ross Puts Audience Members in the Hot Seat." *Citizens' Voice (Wilkes-Barre, PA)*, October 24, 2013. http://citizensvoice.com/arts-living/roastmaster-jeffrey-ross-puts-audience-members-in-hot-seat-1.1573186.

Ross, Jeffrey. *I Only Roast the Ones I Love: How to Bust Balls without Burning Bridges*. New York: Gallery Books, 2009.

Zeke Jarvis

SAGET, BOB (1956–)

Bob Saget was born in Philadelphia. While he was growing up, his family moved multiple times, first to Virginia, then to California, and finally back to Philadelphia. During high school, Saget was steered away from his original plan of becoming a doctor into pursuing a career in film after a teacher encouraged him to find an outlet for his creativity. After graduating from high school, Saget attended Temple University, studying film. In film school, Saget worked on dramatic films, but was also part of a sketch comedy group. He planned on attending graduate school at the University of Southern California, but dropped out fairly early on. He also suffered from a gangrenous appendix—an event that Saget credits with having a significant impact on his approach to life.

Saget gained significant exposure after touring nationally and then cohosting and writing for *The Morning Program* on CBS. Not long after his morning television work, he landed a role on *Full House*, which had strong ratings and a lengthy run, and the host job on *America's Funniest Home Videos*. In 1996, Saget directed the television movie *For Hope*, which was inspired by the story of his sister, who died from scleroderma. Even prior to his sister's diagnosis, Saget had done work to raise awareness and funding for scleroderma research.

In 1998, Saget had a cameo in *Half Baked*, where he played a recovering cocaine addict. This role, along with his edgy form of the core joke in *The Aristocrats*, helped bring Saget's more daring material to light. Prior to these performances, much of the public knew only the more clean-cut brand of comedy featured on *Full House* and *America's Funniest Home Videos*.

After touring and acting work, Saget once again received a hosting job, this time on the game show *1 vs. 100*.

Although much of the population knows Saget as a wholesome performer, owing to either his portrayals of a father or hosting of family-friendly shows, people more familiar with Saget's stand-up work recognize that he is willing to push boundaries, making vulgar jokes and even discussing what his young daughter's future sex life might be like. Saget is also known for being supportive of younger comedians. During the Comedy Central Roast dedicated to him, Norm MacDonald gave a surprisingly heartfelt closing statement about Saget's good nature and supportive approach to interacting with other comics. As is true with many comedians, Saget's commercial success in acting and hosting has allowed him to the freedom to explore the territory that interests him most in his stand-up work. During a tribute to Andy Kaufman, Saget discussed the fact that Kaufman also supported his more experimental performances by working on mainstream television programs like *Taxi*. Saget's work on more purely comedic movies such as *Dirty Work* and *Half Baked* demonstrate the level of respect that other humorists have for Saget. For this strategic approach to his career and the indelible stamp he put on the central joke in *The Aristocrats*, Saget has established himself as a prominent figure in the stand-up comedy community.

Further Reading

Ajaye, Franklyn. *Comic Insights: The Art of Stand-up Comedy*. Los Angeles: Silman-James Press, 2001.

Loeffler, William. "Bob Saget Is More Than Just Another Filthy Mouth." *Pittsburgh Tribune Review*, May 2, 2012. http://triblive.com/aande/1300752-74/saget-says-comedy-improv-pittsburgh-audience-bob-family-award-comedians#axzz3K3whhLg0.

Sager, Mike. "Bob Saget." *Esquire* 145, no. 1 (January 2006): 96–97.

Zeke Jarvis

SAHL, MORT (1927–)

Morton Sahl was born in Montreal, Quebec, but has spent most of his life in America. His family moved from Canada to Los Angeles while Sahl was still in school. Shortly after high school, Sahl enlisted in the U.S. Air Force and was stationed in Alaska. Upon being discharged, he attended the University of Southern California, where he graduated with degrees in city engineering and traffic management in 1950.

Shortly after his graduation, Sahl began performing stand-up comedy in San Francisco. His style and material were admired by a variety of audiences in the beginning. One prominent friend to Sahl was Hugh Hefner, publisher of *Playboy*. In fact, Sahl married playmate China Lee in 1967. The two had one son, who died at the age of 19, and they divorced in 1991. Sahl still lives in California, occasionally performing and teaching courses.

Sahl's political beliefs sometimes alienated audiences, particularly after the assassination of President John F. Kennedy. His reading from the Warren Report on stage led some audiences to reject his work. Ironically, Sahl's criticisms of Kennedy during his presidency also led Sahl's audience to diminish. Ed Sullivan would not let him do material disparaging the president on his show, which limited the amount of TV work Sahl could get while remaining true to his comic sensibilities. Still, a significant countercultural audience was enamored with this technique, leading Sahl to have a relatively small but very loyal audience. Woody Allen, in particular, has been a consistent supporter of what he referred to as an intellectual approach to stand-up comedy. Sahl would often appear on stage holding a newspaper from which he would read headlines and comment on the news and political figures of the day. Certainly, his heavy focus on current events has been influential on comics like Bill Hicks and Bill Maher, but his style has been imitated by many comics as well. Sahl's conversational style eschewed traditional jokes in favor of more conceptual humor. This comic examination of major social and political issues can be seen in comics like Chris Rock and Louis CK, among many others.

Although Sahl's career has been punctuated by both success and struggle, he is generally held in very high regard among stand-up comics, often being associated with Lenny Bruce as one of the major figures in modern stand-up comedy. In addition to the respect of his colleagues, his status as a major social figure has been supported by the Library of Congress's National Recording Registry: his work was the earliest recorded example of stand-up comedy to be so registered. In addition, Sahl has appeared on prominent magazines such as *Time* and has received numerous awards and honors.

See also: Bruce, Lenny; Maher, Bill

Further Reading

Lewis, Paul. *Cracking up: American Humor in a Time of Conflict*. Chicago: University of Chicago Press, 2006.

Wolcott, James. "Mort the Knife." *Vanity Fair* 564 (August 2007): 80–84.

Wright, Mark H. "Sophistic Humor and Social Change: Overcoming Identification with the Aggressor." *JPCS: Journal for the Psychoanalysis of Culture & Society* 5, no. 1 (Spring 2000): 57–64.

Zeke Jarvis

SEINFELD, JERRY (1954–)

Jerry Seinfeld was born in Brooklyn, New York, though he grew up in Massapequa. Both his parents were Jewish and, during his teenage years, Seinfeld spent some time volunteering in Israel. After graduating from high school, Seinfeld attended State University of New York-Oswego, though he later transferred to Queens College, from which he received a degree in communications and theater.

During his college years, Seinfeld developed such a strong interest in stand-up comedy that he began to pursue it exclusively as a career path immediately after graduating. Seinfeld rose through the ranks, beginning at open mic nights, then working in clubs, and eventually landing a spot on a Rodney Dangerfield HBO special for young comics. Seinfeld had one small acting role on the sitcom *Benson*, but his central work continued to be his stand-up comedy. In 1981, he began to receive attention for his performances on *The Tonight Show*.

As Seinfeld's stand-up comedy work became more prominent, he and friend Larry David developed the sitcom *Seinfeld*. Although the show experienced some struggles in its early seasons, by season four it had become tremendously successful both in its ratings and in its cultural impact, with small phrases from *Seinfeld* consistently popping up in the cultural vocabulary.

After the series ended, Seinfeld went back to performing stand-up more regularly, and he appeared in a variety of advertisements and cameos. In 1998, Seinfeld garnered a bit of controversy by dating Jessica Sklar, who was married when she and Seinfeld met. The two would eventually marry, and they have two sons and one daughter.

In 2007, Seinfeld provided the voice for the main character, a bee, in *Bee Movie*. It was his most prominent acting role since the end of his series. Although Seinfeld has had some short-lived shows and projects, the core of his focus remains his stand-up work, along with his charitable work, most notably with the Baby Buggy, an organization started by Seinfeld and his wife to provide clothing for underprivileged women and children. Seinfeld has discussed that, like Andy Kaufman, he is a long-time practitioner of Transcendental Meditation, and he credits much of his success to his dedication to it. Seinfeld currently lives with his family in New York.

Seinfeld credits much of his approach to humor to Jean Shepherd. With his focus on the everyday and childish concerns in *Seinfeld*, this impact can certainly be seen. Having performed comedy that developed into "a show about nothing" (another phrase taken from the show *Seinfeld* itself), Seinfeld has received some criticism that his work lacks real social merit. Other observers feel that his work's eye toward the everyday and the personal demonstrates a level of craftsmanship and keen insight that render any discussion of social issues irrelevant. While Seinfeld's stand-up material has never espoused any direct political agenda (in fact, in his cameo on *News Radio*, Seinfeld does a send-up of his own general disinterest in and ignorance of matters of national importance), some critics have argued that the lack of caring and the misdirected emphasis of the characters on the sitcom have a deeper significance. Indeed, both Seinfeld and his show have been mentioned as being linked to the school of literary theory known as deconstruction. While this is an arguable point, it is certainly the case that the characters' lack of real emotional connection was handled in a way that was subtle, yet genuinely distinctive. After many fans expressed disappointment with the series' end, comic Bill Maher opined that the reason for their anger was the final episodes' highlighting of the moral shortcomings of the characters, along with the more general pointlessness of their lives, rather than its celebration of them with a more positive upswing. This theory seems to be supported by many of the DVD commentaries for the show, where writers indicate surprise when people claim that the characters on the show were "like a family;" the writers' vision of the characters was always much more selfish, if not outright malicious. Even though the series finale was not well received, the show itself remains one of the best-known and most beloved sitcoms in television history. While Seinfeld has pursued other outlets for his comedy, the show is clearly what he will be remembered for by fans.

See also: David, Larry; Shepherd, Jean

Further Reading

Dalton, Mary, ed. *The Sitcom Reader: America Viewed and Skewed*. New York: State University of New York Press, 2005.

Irwin, William, ed. *Seinfeld and Philosophy: A Book about Everything and Nothing*. Chicago: Open Court, 1999.

Weiner, Jonah. "Jerry Seinfeld Intends to Die Standing up." *New York Times Magazine* (December 23, 2012): 24–31.

Zeke Jarvis

SHANDLING, GARRY (1949–)

Garry Shandling was born in Chicago, Illinois. While he was still a child, Shandling's family moved to Tucson, Arizona, where he was raised. Shandling's brother, Barry, died of cystic fibrosis when Gary was 10. After graduating from high school, Shandling attended the University of Arizona, where he studied subjects ranging from electrical engineering to marketing. Following his college graduation, he studied creative writing for a time.

In 1973, Shandling moved to Los Angeles to pursue his career. He continued working in marketing before have success in selling scripts to popular television programs like *Sanford and Son* and *Welcome Back, Kotter*. Frustrated with the limits of sitcoms, Shandling began exploring stand-up comedy. In 1977, he was in an auto accident, which he integrated into his stand-up routines. During the 1979 stand-up comedians strike, Shandling was one of the few comedians to cross the picket lines to continue performing.

Shandling's success in performing led to an opportunity to appear on *The Tonight Show* with Johnny Carson. His success in that venue ensured that he became a guest host on the show, alternating with Joan Rivers. Ultimately, Shandling landed his own television show, *It's Garry Shandling's Show*, which broke many sitcom rules. For example, it openly acknowledged that the incidents occurring on it were part of a television show. The show's writing staff included writers who would go on to work on both *The Simpsons* and *Seinfeld*, two other shows that would also rewrite many conventional rules for television comedies.

After the success of *It's Garry Shandling's Show*, Shandling starred in another hit show, *The Larry Sanders Show*, which examined the life of a fictional late-night talk show host. This premise allowed Shandling's host to have a number of prominent guest stars, typically playing themselves as guests on the fictional talk show.

Shandling continues to perform on stage and in television and film. Although he lived with former co-star and Playboy playmate Linda Doucett, Shandling has never been married, and he is generally averse to discussing his personal life.

Shandling's film and television style often revolves around a sense of awkwardness stemming from the characters he portrays. While slightly different, it is generally in keeping with his stage persona, which relies on a sense of anxiety and insecurity, with Shandling often discussing dating woes or other sources of personal discomfort. This approach to comedy is in keeping with Shandling's espoused desire to escape the formulaic strictures of most situational comedy for the more free and open realm of stand-up comedy performance. In his career choices, he has often tended toward projects that would give him a greater degree of artistic freedom. In one example, Shandling turned down an offer to take over the NBC late-night slot left vacant by David Letterman so as to pursue his work on *The Larry Sanders Show*. Shandling's work overlaps with other stand-up comedians' in various ways. For example, he grounds his work in real-life observation as Jerry Seinfeld does and expresses a sense of discomfort as Emo Philips and Jeremy Hotz do. Nevertheless, his combination of material and approach have established Shandling as a distinctive and memorable comedic performer.

Further Reading

Ajaye, Franklyn. *Comic Insights: The Art of Stand-up Comedy*. Los Angeles: Silman-James Press, 2001.

Hirschberg, Lynn. "Garry Shandling Goes Dark." *New York Times Magazine* 147, no. 51174 (May 31, 1998): 46.

O'Neill, Tom. "Garry Shandling." *US* 245 (June 1998): 104.

Zeke Jarvis

SILVERMAN, SARAH (1970–)

Sarah Silverman was born in Manchester, New Hampshire. While she was growing up, her parents divorced. Silverman began trying her hand at stand-up while still in high school and attending summer school in Boston. After graduating from high school, she attended New York University to study drama, though she eventually dropped out to begin her stand-up comedy career.

After performing stand-up comedy for a few years, Silverman got a position writing and sometimes appearing on *Saturday Night Live*. She was let go from the show, but then got a job working on David Cross's and Bob Odenkirk's show *Mr. Show*. Silverman continued to work in television as well as in film, steadily building a reputation. In 2001, she received some attention after telling a joke referencing stereotypes about Asian Americans on Conan O'Brien's program. Many comedians, including Bill Maher, stood by Silverman's humor, claiming that the joke was a satire of racism rather than racist.

Silverman began dating comedian Jimmy Kimmel in 2002. The two would date on and off for years, ultimately splitting for good, but remaining friends. Silverman has also dated comedians Dave Attell, Colin Quinn, and *Family Guy* writer Alec Sulikin.

Sarah Silverman has shown the ability to balance absurdity and daring. Her stand-up work has propelled her to a place of genuine cultural significance. (Carrienelson1/Dreamstime.com)

In 2005, Silverman's special *Jesus Is Magic* was released, garnering significant critical and commercial success. In 2007, *The Sarah Silverman Program* debuted on Comedy Central. It was canceled after three seasons, but developed a significant cult following and reunited Silverman with a number of performers from *Mr. Show*.

Silverman continues to write and perform on television, in film, and on stage. She released her autobiographical humorous book, *The Bedwetter: Stories of Courage, Redemption and Pee*, in 2010. She lives and often works in New York.

Silverman is known for her edgy work. Her work incorporates not only potentially offensive material, however, but also a clear sense of absurdity and self-ridicule. Not surprisingly, she lists both Lenny Bruce and Steve Martin as influences. While Silverman has received significant positive response from both critics and fans, she has received harsh criticism from multiple sources, including Asian American groups and Jewish leaders. Even so, she has been described as groundbreaking and as representing a new and exciting model for female comedians. Although Silverman is not as prominent as she once was, her combination of comedy and political activism keep her a significant and striking public figure.

See also: Kimmel, Jimmy; Posehn, Brian

Further Reading

Kohen, Yael. *We Killed: The Rise of Women in American Comedy*. New York: Sarah Crichton Books, 2012.

Silverman, Sarah. *The Bedwetter: Stories of Courage, Redemption and Pee*. New York: Harper, 2010.

Solomon, Deborah. "Funny Girl." *New York Times Magazine* (January 21, 2007): 19.

Zeke Jarvis

STERN, HOWARD (1954–)

Howard Stern was born in Queens, New York. While he was still an infant, his family moved to Long Island. Stern's interest in radio started early, when he saw voice artists like Wally Cox and Larry Storch work with his father, who co-owned a recording company. After graduating from high school, Stern attended Boston University, where he worked in the college radio station. While still attending school, Stern began professional work in Newton, Massachusetts. In 1976, he graduated from BU with a degree in communications.

Following his college graduation, Stern left radio to pursue a career in advertising. Quickly becoming dissatisfied with the work, he returned to radio, first as a temporary replacement and eventually getting a morning slot. In 1978, Stern married for the first time. He and his wife had three children, but divorced in 2001.

Stern moved to Michigan, working there for a time, but quickly moved to Washington, D.C., then to New York. During these years, Stern developed his edgy and striking approach to talk radio. He was sometimes fined and had segments cut for being potentially offensive. Nevertheless, he garnered national attention, even getting an appearance on David Letterman's show. In 1993, Stern released his book *Private Parts* to large critical success; it was later adapted into a film in which Stern played himself. Stern continued to host his radio show, also making multiple appearances on television. However, the FCC began to monitor and fine Stern aggressively, eventually leading him to jump to Sirius Satellite Radio, where he could be free of restrictions.

In 2008, Stern married for the second time. In 2011, he became a judge on a reality television competition show, *America's Got Talent*. Stern serves as a judge and continues to host his radio program.

Stern is best known for being provocative and edgy, frankly discussing sex, celebrity, art, and even his first wife's miscarriage. Stern's fans and critics make similar observations about his work—namely, that he neither withholds commentary nor seems concerned with boundaries. Even so, Stern is known for conducting effective interviews with rising comedians, helping to bring attention to Conan O'Brien and Gilbert Gottfried, among others. Stern also conducted perhaps the definitive interview with Bill Hicks after the controversy in which Hicks was cut from David Letterman's show. While many regard Stern as being too vulgar and offensive—leading to his labeling as a "shock jock"—his staying power helps to demonstrate his impact upon the American comedy scene.

See also: Gottfried, Gilbert; Hicks, Bill

Further Reading

"Howard Stern, American." *Esquire* 144, no. 1 (July 2005): 116–119.

Soley, Lawrence. "Sex and Shock Jocks: An Analysis of the Howard Stern and Bob & Tom Shows." *Journal of Promotion Management* 13, nos. 1/2 (2007): 75.

Stern, Howard. *Private Parts*. New York: Simon and Schuster, 1993.

Zeke Jarvis

SYKES, WANDA (1964–)

Wanda Sykes was born in Portsmouth, Virginia. Her father worked at the Pentagon, and her family lived in Washington, D.C., for her early life. After graduating from high school, Sykes attended Hampton University, where she received a degree in marketing. Following her graduation from college, Sykes got a job at the National Security Agency. Becoming bored with her work, she began pursuing stand-up comedy in 1987. Steadily gaining a mastery of her craft, she moved to New York in 1992.

In 1991, Sykes had married, though she would divorce in 1998. She got her first big break while opening for Chris Rock, which would eventually lead to her job as a writer for *The Chris Rock Show* in 1997. In 2003, Sykes had a short-lived show on Fox and also released her first stand-up special. In the meantime, she continued to consistently perform in stand-up venues.

In 2006, Sykes began appearing on *The New Adventures of Old Christine*. The show eventually used Sykes's sexuality as part of the plot, having her engage in a same-sex relationship with the title character. That same year, Sykes began regularly performing as a voice actor in animated films such as *Over the Hedge*. Also in 2006, Sykes married her wife, with whom she has two children. 2009 was a breakout year for Sykes, when she had her own talk show and became the first openly gay comic to host the White House Correspondents Dinner. Sykes continues to be an outspoken activist for the gay and lesbian community. She and her family currently live in California.

Sykes is known for her sassy, sarcastic persona in both her stand-up comedy and her acting career. This brash persona is a major driver of her success as a voice actor, too. As both a writer and a performer, Sykes explores the short-sightedness of people in issues of both race and sexuality. Her turn on *The New Adventures of Old Christine* established another lesbian character on mainstream television. Although Sykes does keep an eye turned toward political and social issues, she has consistently been willing to take part in lighter but more absurd fare, allowing her to appear on a wider variety of venues and perform for both large and small audiences. Sykes also has emerged as a strong female humorist without delving into some of the topics most often covered by female comics of an earlier generation. In this way, Sykes has been able to forge new paths without leaving behind rich comic traditions. The slim gap between her persona and her life makes Sykes an interesting and dynamic performer who has achieved real and sustained success.

See also: Rock, Chris

Further Reading

Ballard, Scotty. "Wanda Sykes, Wanda at Large." *Jet* 104, no. 16 (October 13, 2003): 58–62.
Stein, Joel. "Wanda Sykes Wants It All." *Time* 164, no. 19 (November 8, 2004): 76–78.
Sykes, Wanda. *Yeah, I Said It.* New York: Atria Books, 2004.

Zeke Jarvis

TITUS, CHRISTOPHER (1964–)

Christopher Titus was born in Castro Valley, California. While he was still a child, his parents divorced. Titus stayed with his father, despite the fact that his father was a heavy drinker and womanizer. The major factor that led to Titus not living with his mother was her mental issues. Titus would go on to joke about both his father's behavior and his mother's instability in his comedy. When Titus was four, he was removed from his father's home so that he could live with his maternal grandparents. Titus's father eventually regained custody, and Titus lived with him until he turned 12, at which point he briefly lived with his mother. Titus's mother took her own life in 1994. Prior to that, she had killed her then-husband (not Titus's father) in self-defense. Shortly after his mother's suicide, Titus had a nervous breakdown.

Like his father, Titus had many issues with substance abuse when he was young. He became and stayed sober after an incident in which he fell into a bonfire, badly burning his arms.

In 1991, Titus married Erin Carden. The two would have two children, but divorced in 2006. Largely as the result of his own childhood troubles, Titus founded the Insight Youth Project, an organization working to serve children from dysfunctional families. Titus currently lives and works in California, and he continues to perform stand-up.

Like Richard Pryor, Titus is known for being brutally honest about his personal life, frequently laughing at his own pain. This comes through in both his stand-up work and in his sitcom, *Titus*, which ran for three seasons on the Fox Network. Many of the incidents that made up the plots for *Titus*'s episodes were drawn from Titus's real life. The series also interspersed full scenes with commentary from Titus or other characters, as other shows, such as *The Office*, would go on to do. Typically, this was done to underscore the gap between what the characters were saying and what they were actually feeling. In addition to his sitcom, Titus has written for or appeared in a number of television projects, including *Twilight Zone*, *Yes Dear*, and *Lois & Clark: The New Adventures of Superman*.

In addition, Titus has performed in a number of stand-up comedy specials. While the specials cover different topics, they are generally tied closely to Titus's life, either discussing his childhood, as he does in *Norman Rockwell Is Bleeding*, or his divorce, as he does in *Love Is Evol*. He also delves into political territory at times, particularly on *Neverlution*, where he discusses generational change and political issues, generally leaning away from what he perceives as knee-jerk conservatism and politics grounded in ignorance. He has been an outspoken critic of Sarah Palin, the former governor of Alaska and Republican vice-presidential nominee. Still, his work tends to look inward, putting his own frailties and anxieties on display rather than going after other people. While Titus is not necessarily a household name, his honesty and the novel format of his sitcom have had a significant impact on the comedic landscape.

Further Reading

Staskiewicz, Keith. "Christopher Titus: Neverlution." *Entertainment Weekly* 1161 (July 1, 2011): 68.

Titus, Chris. *The God Complex*. New York: CreateSpace Publishing, 2011.

Zeke Jarvis

TOMPKINS, PAUL F. (1968–)

Paul Tompkins was born and raised in Philadelphia, Pennsylvania. At the age of 17, he performed at the Comedy Works, a club then located in Philadelphia. He attended Temple University for a time before dropping out and moving to Los Angeles to pursue a career in entertainment.

In Los Angeles, Tompkins was associated with a number of prominent comedic troupes, such as the Upright Citizens Brigade and *Mr. Show*, which launched the careers of Bob Odenkirk and David Cross, among many others. As he rose in prominence, Tompkins began to gain even more visibility, writing for *The Daily Show* and appearing on VH1's *Best Week Ever* and HBO's *Real Time with Bill Maher*. He also released two stand-up comedy albums. He has appeared in numerous critically acclaimed television shows and movies, including *Mr. Show*, *There Will Be Blood*, and *The Informant!*, which featured a number of comedians performing in serious roles. Tompkins currently lives and works in Los Angeles.

Tompkins has excelled in a variety of humorous ventures, appearing in sketch comedy, television shows, and stand-up comic performances. His presentation incorporates both a traditional look (his suit is one of the signature pieces of his performances) and a transgressive, cynical tone to his delivery. That said, not all of his performances are political. While he has done a good deal of political work, particularly on *Real Time*, he also has maintained the absurdist roots that he established on *Mr. Show*, such as in bits that deal with issues like smashed coins or the imagined debate over cake versus pie. Tompkins's "alternative" approach to comedy and his strange, striking combination of delivery and presentation have led him to seek out independent venues rather than established comedy clubs for his stand-up. Tompkins's alternative choices can be traced back to his colleagues and roots. The entire cast of *Mr. Show* regularly employed absurd concepts and deliveries, and Tompkins was no different. He continues to explore the fringes of comedy while keeping a clear presence in contemporary humor, making him a humorist to watch.

See also: Maher, Bill

Further Reading

Maxwell, Dominic. "Paul F. Tompkins." *The Times (London)* (April 9, 2013): 6.

Seabaugh, Jule, ed. *2012 Best of the Spit Take: A Compilation of Professional Comedy Criticism*. Bettendorf: Paradisiac, 2013.

Thompson, Ethan. *Parody and Postwar Taste in American Television Culture*. New York: Routledge, 2011.

Zeke Jarvis

WHITE, RON (1956–)

Ron White was born in Fritch, Texas. At age 17, White joined the Navy. After serving and being discharged, White sold windows in Arlington, Texas; he also lived in Mexico for a brief period. Though White held different jobs, he always had an eye toward performing.

In 1980, White married for the first time; the couple divorced in 1993. White has one son from that marriage.

Although White had some success with stand-up comedy, it was not until 2000, when he began touring with Jeff Foxworthy, Bill Engvall, and Larry the Cable Guy as part of the Blue Collar Comedy Tour, that he broke through into major fame. In 2003, a tape of the tour was released as a movie. Also in 2003, White released his first solo comedy CD, *Drunk in Public*.

In 2004, White married for the second time, this time divorcing his wife in 2008. Shortly after the divorce, White married again, and he remains married.

Although White has had some acting roles, the vast majority of his work remains his stand-up comedy. He has also written a number of books, all strongly rooted in his stand-up work and humorous anecdotes about his personal life. He continues to tour regularly.

White is known for his laidback style, often having a cigar and alcoholic beverage in hand during his stand-up routines. He generally mines his own life for comedy, looking at his troubled first marriage for jokes and laughing at both his own drinking and the politics of his home state of Texas for comedic value. While White has a strong following in the core audience for the Blue Collar Comedy Tour, he has extended his appeal further beyond that audience than some of the other members of the tour, with many people appreciating his laidback, story-based humor. While White has not necessarily gained the prominence of some other stand-up comics, his general eschewing of film and television roles in favor of stand-up comedy make him a striking figure.

See also: Foxworthy, Jeff

Further Reading

Hook, Chris. "The Climb to Fame Begins at Rock Bottom." *Daily Telegraph (Sydney)* (June 5, 2012): 48.

Seidell, Streeter. "College Humor Interview with Ron White." *CollegeHumor.com*, February 14, 2006.

Spong, John. "Ron White Gets Last Laugh." *Texas Monthly* 34, no. 12 (December 2006): 164–168.

Zeke Jarvis

WINTERS, JONATHAN (1925–2013)

Jonathan Winters was born in Bellbrook, Ohio. While his father was an investment banker and the descendent of Valentine Winters, who founded Winters National Bank, Winters describes him as an alcoholic who was unsuccessful. After the stock market crash that led to the Great Depression, his father's alcoholism worsened. When Winters was seven, his mother moved herself and Jonathan to her mother's home.

At 17, Winters dropped out of school to join the Marines and serve in World War II. After being discharged, he attended first Kenyon College and then the Dayton Art Institute, where he studied cartooning. It was at the Art Institute that he met his wife, Eileen. The two married in 1948.

Winters's performance career began when he won a talent contest, which then led to other opportunities on radio and television. Although Winters was successful in Ohio, when he requested a raise from the network, he was denied it. Angered, he moved his family to New York on very little money. Within a short time, Winters was regularly performing in clubs and getting bookings on a variety of television shows. During this time, he also suffered two nervous breakdowns, and voluntarily institutionalized himself. Winters would go on to make light of this experience in his act. His reputation as an eccentric was also enhanced by his performances. He often appeared on Jack Paar's show in character or doing an impression. On *The Tonight Show with Johnny Carson*, Winters would often remain in character throughout the interview, leaving Carson to ask questions of Winters's persona rather than speaking directly to Winters himself.

Winters also received a number of roles as an actor, perhaps most notably in *It's a Mad, Mad, Mad, Mad World*. He was a regular on *The Dean Martin Celebrity Roast* and *Mork and Mindy*, which starred Robin Williams. Winters's presence on the show was largely due to Williams's desire to have one of his stated idols on the show.

In his later years, Winters performed less frequently, but still had some prominent roles, such as doing the voice of Papa Smurf in the live-action movie version of *The Smurfs*. He also received a number of awards and recognitions. Winters had two children with his wife Eileen, who died in 2009. Winters died four years later, in 2013

Winters is known for his offbeat approach to humor. In one television performance, he was simply handed a stick and told to improvise with it, which he did in a variety of ways. He is also known for his many voices and characters, particularly the sharp-tongued Maude Frickett. His many characters and insistence on staying in character for appearances on television shows influenced later comics such as Robin Williams and Sacha Baron Cohen. Winters also used his size to comic effect, appearing as Williams's gargantuan child on *Mork and Mindy*. His strange, unpredictable behavior and solid comic timing have made him a distinctive humorist in the American canon.

See also: Williams, Robin

Further Reading

Smith, Jim. *Jonathan Winters: After the Beep*. New York: Perigree Trade, 1989.

Winters, Jonathan. *Mouse Breath, Conformity and Other Social Ills*. Indianapolis: Bobbs-Merrill, 1965.

Young, John. "Welcome Back Jonathan Winters." *Entertainment Weekly* 1151/1152 (April 22, 2011): 55.

Zeke Jarvis

WRIGHT, STEVEN (1955–)

Steven Alexander Wright was born in Cambridge, Massachusetts. One of the four children of Lucille and Alexander Wright, he was raised in a Catholic household. Wright grew up in Burlington, Massachusetts. He spent the beginning of his college years at Middlesex Community College and received his associate's degree there before transferring to Emerson College, where he graduated in 1978.

The year after his graduation, Wright performed stand-up comedy at the Comedy Connection, a Boston comedy club. Wright's break came when Peter Lassally, executive producer of *The Tonight Show,* came across Wright performing at the Ding Ho comedy club in Cambridge in 1982. Lassally booked Wright for *The Tonight Show*, and Wright impressed Johnny Carson and the studio audience to the point that he was invited back less than a week later. Wright's first comedy album, *I Have a Pony,* was released by Warner Bros. Records in 1985 and netted the comedian a Grammy nomination for Best Comedy Album. Due to the album's success, he was given a special on HBO, *A Steven Wright Special.* This performance has been one of HBO's longest-running (and most requested) comedy specials.

In 1989, Wright made the jump into filmmaking, putting out a 30-minute short film, *The Appointments of Dennis Jennings.* He, along with producer Dean Pariscot, won an Academy Award for the film. Wright cowrote the film and also starred in it. In addition to taking many small roles, he landed a recurring role on *Mad about You* and was in Quentin Tarantino's *Reservoir Dogs* as the voice of the radio DJ. Wright's next major performance was *Wicker Chairs and Gravity*, a comedy special that aired in 1990.

While he continued doing stand-up, Wright moved away from television in the 1990s. In 1999, he wrote and directed another 30-minute film, *One Soldier.* In 2006, he produced *Steven Wright: When the Leaves Blow Away* for Comedy Central and released a corresponding CD, *I Still Have a Pony*, which was nominated for Best Comedy Album at the Grammy Awards. Despite largely abandoning television, Wright continued to appear on late-night television talk shows, most specifically *The Late Late Show with Craig Ferguson.*

Wright's comedic style is defined by his gratuitous deadpan delivery coupled with his lethargic voice. He often uses surrealist humor—a brand of humor that focuses on creating illogical events and behavior, due in part to basing the comedy on bizarre, irrational situations. Wright is also known for his use of one-liners with little to no build-up or embellishment that often fit into his surrealist approach: "Friday I was in a bookstore. I started talking to this very French-looking girl. She was a bilingual illiterate—she couldn't read in two different languages." Wright has cited George Carlin and Salvador Dali as two of his primary influences.

In addition to winning an Oscar in 1989 for *The Appointments of Dennis Jennings,* Wright was the first inductee into the Boston Comedy Hall of Fame in 2008. A 2005 poll of fellow comedians put Wright in the top 50 comedy acts, while Comedy Central placed him at number 23 in its list of the 100 Greatest Stand-up Comics.

Further Reading

Bolles, Dan. *Seven Days*. "Chatting Up Comedian Steven Wright." http://www.sevendaysvt.com/vermont/chatting-up-comedian-steven-wright/Content?oid=2468280.

Boskin, Joseph, ed. *The Humor Prism in 20th Century America*. Detroit: Wayne State University Press, 1997.

McMurran, K. "TV Comic Steven Wright Starts off, Worriedly, on a Steep Ascent." *People* 31, no. 10 (March 13, 1989): 106.

Brian Davis

YANKOVIC, WEIRD AL (1959–)

Alfred Yankovic was born in Downey, California. Yankovic's music career began shortly before his sixth birthday, when he received accordion lessons. Although Yankovic continued to study the accordion, he also had a wide variety of other influences, including Elton John, Allen Sherman, Frank Zappa, and the Zucker Brothers. Yankovic excelled academically in school, starting kindergarten early and skipping the second grade. While this indicated success as a student, it led Yankovic to be a bit of a social outcast. He ultimately became valedictorian of his class.

After graduating from high school, Yankovic attended California Polytechnic State University, where he earned a degree in architecture. During this time, he appeared on the *Dr. Demento Show*, where he got his first real exposure with "Another One Rides the Bus," one of his early song parodies. Yankovic also had a single release of "My Bologna," a parody of the Knack's song "My Sharona." The band's lead singer was instrumental in the release, marking the first in a long series of musicians appreciating Yankovic's parodies. In 1981, Yankovic began touring In 1984, he released the album *"Weird Al" Yankovic in 3-D*, which contained the singles "Eat It" and "Like a Surgeon." These songs, along with their accompanying videos, helped to launch Yankovic into mainstream and widespread popularity. Yankovic continued to perform and release albums, also starring in the film *UHF*.

In 1998, Yankovic had corrective eye surgery, losing his glasses and generally changing his look. In 2001, he married; he and his wife have one daughter. Yankovic tours and continues to put out records as well as appear on episodes of *Tim and Eric Awesome Show, Great Job!* In 2014, Yankovic's album, *Mandatory Fun*, reached number one on the Billboard Chart, a feat that is extraordinarily rare for a comic performer.

Yankovic is known for his high-energy and inventive performances, using costumes, videos, and other methods to produce a wild stage show. He is also known as a kind person, working with charitable causes. He generally gets permission from the artists he parodies, although the rapper Coolio claims to not have been consulted before Yankovic released the song "Amish Paradise." Yankovic has carved out a unique space for himself, being at once a gifted musician and a genuinely funny entertainer. Few other performers have achieved this feat, leaving Yankovic an interesting and exciting performer to watch.

See also: Tim and Eric

Further Reading

Frizell, Sam. "Weird Al Yankovic Makes Fun of Your First World Problems." *Time.com* (July 22, 2014): 1.

Rothman, Lily. "The Al Yankovic Paradox: He Doesn't Seem That Weird Anymore." *Time.com* (July 3, 2014): 1.

Seabaugh, Jule, ed. *2012 Best of the Spit Take: A Compilation of Professional Comedy Criticism.* Bettendorf: Paradisiac, 2013.

Zeke Jarvis

Selected Bibliography

Anderson, Kyle. "An 80's Oddity Worth Watching." *Entertainment Weekly* 1271 (August 9, 2013): 67.

Beach, Christopher. *Class, Language and American Film Comedy*. Cambridge: Cambridge University Press, 2002.

Booth, William. "Shtick Shift: Stand-Up's Edge No Longer Cuts." *Washington Post*, April 24, 2005.

Brennan, Patricia. "Madcap Pioneer of Sketch Comedy." *Washington Post*, February 13, 2014.

Budd, Louis J., ed. *On Humor: The Best from American Literature*. Durham, NC: Duke University Press, 1992, x.

Clark, Leroy D. "The Second Coming of Amos 'N' Andy." *New Crisis* 107, no. 1 (January/February 2000): 34.

Cohen, Rich. "The Godfather of Studio 8H." *Rolling Stone* 1113 (September 16, 2010): 68–84.

Cohen, Sarah Blacher, ed. *Comic Relief: Humor in Contemporary American Literature*. Detroit: Wayne State University Press, 1992, xiii.

Cole, Ryan. "Sketch Comedy." *New Criterion* 32, no. 6 (February 2014): 73–75.

Collis, Clark. "Saturday Night's All Right." *Entertainment Weekly* 983 (March 21, 2008): 22–29.

Critchely, Simon. *On Humor: Thinking in Action*. London: Routledge, 2002.

Debruge, Peter. "Comedy Hatchlings." *Variety* 324, no. 16 (July 22, 2014): 49–51.

Dolan, Jon. "The New Queen of Shocking TV Comedy." *Rolling Stone* 1209 (May 22, 2014): 24.

Edwards, Savin. "*Key & Peele*: TV's Funniest Show." *Rolling Stone* 1194 (October 24, 2014): 24.

Farley, Christopher John, and Simon Robinson. "Dave Speaks." *Time* 165, no. 21 (May 23, 2005): 68–73.

Fauset, Jessie Redmon. *Comedy: American Style*. Dover: Dover Publishing, 2013.

Gruber, Eva Rochester. *Humor in Contemporary Native North American Literature: Reimagining Nativeness*. New York: Camden House, 2008.

Helem, Lisa. "Triumph the Dog." *Newsweek* 145, no. 1 (December 27, 2004): 34.

Horwitz, Simi. "Who's New, Pussycat?" *Back Stage East* 48, no. 8 (February 22, 2007): 9–10.

Kim, Serena. "But Seriously." *Vibe* 12, no. 4 (April 2004): 128–131.

Kohen, Yael. *We Killed: The Rise of Women in American Comedy*. New York: Picador, 2013.

Kois, Dan. "Unfrozen Cerebral Humorist." *New York Times Magazine*, July 21, 2013, 22–25.

Kraft, Robert N. "Humor in American Literature." *Metaphor & Symbolic Activity* 8, no. 2 (1993): 141.

Krichtafovitch, Igor. *Humor Theory: Formula of Laughter*. Parker: Outskirts Press, 2006.

LaMarre, Heather L., Kristen D. Landreville, Dannagal Young, and Nathan Gilkerson. "Humor Works in Funny Ways: Examining Satirical Tone as a Key Determinant in Political Humor Message Processing." *Mass Communication & Society* 17, no. 3 (2014): 400–423.

McDonald, Paul. " 'They're Trying to Kill Me': Jewish American Humor and the War against Pop Culture." *Studies in Popular Culture* 28, no. 3 (April 2006): 19–33.

McElroy, Steven. "Sketchfest NYC." *New York Times* 156, no. 53969 (June 8, 2007): E25.

Morreal, John. *Comic Relief: A Comprehensive Philosophy of Humor*. Hoboken: Wiley-Blackwell, 2009.

Nordlinger, Jay. "Rodney Rules." *National Review* 53, no. 11 (June 11, 2001): 60–61.

Peyser, Marc. "Prepare to Twitch." *Newsweek* 143, no. 26 (June 28, 2004): 13.

Pinsker, Sanford. "The Tall Tale, American Humor and America." *Midwest Quarterly* 41, no. 4 (Summer 2000): 448.

Poniewozik, James. "Slow Jamming the Laughs." *Time* 183, no. 7 (February 24, 2014): 51.

Salamon, Julie. "An Evolving Vision in Black and White." *New York Times* 151, no. 52016 (February 1, 2002): E1.

Smith, Greg. "Red Skelton, the Crack-Up and the Quick-Change." *Journal of Popular Culture* 45, no. 3 (June 2012): 592–610.

Steinberg, Don. "Another Comic Springs out of *The Daily Show*." *Wall Street Journal—Eastern Edition* 261, no. 97 (April 26, 2013): D6.

Stott, Andrew. *Comedy: The New Critical Idiom*. London: Routledge, 2004.

Tafoya, Eddie. *The Legacy of the Wisecrack: Stand-up Comedy as the Great American Literary Form*. New York: Brown Walker Press, 2009.

Trillin, Calvin. "Uncivil Liberties." *Nation* 241, no. 15 (November 9, 1985): 464.

Watkins, Mel. *On The Real Side: A History of African American Comedy*. Chicago: Chicago Review Press, 1999.

Weitz, Brian. "Can Roseanne Save Sketch Comedy?" *FADER* 65 (December 2009–January 2010): 82–85.

Weeks, Brigitte. "Good for a Laugh." *Washington Post News Feed* 118, no. 153 (May 7, 1995): 16.

Weitz, Brian. "The State." *FADER* 65 (December 2009–January 2010): 82–85.

Witchel, Alex. "Shades of Black Humor." *New York Times Magazine* 154, no. 53152 (March 13, 2005): 32–37.

Wright, Lavinia Jones. "He Who Laughs Last." *Billboard* 120, no. 39 (September 27, 2008): 48.

Zoglin, Richard. "The Laugh Factory." *Time* 176, no. 6 (August 9, 2010): 40–43.

Index

Note: Page numbers in **bold font** indicate main entries.

About the Editor and Contributors

The Editor

Zeke Jarvis, PhD, is an associate professor at Eureka College. His other works include *So Anyway . . .* and the forthcoming *In a Family Way*. Jarvis holds a doctorate in English from the University of Wisconsin at Milwaukee.

The Contributors

Brian Davis has a degree in English from Eureka College. His creative work has appeared in *Impressions*, and he has worked as head editorial assistant for ELM. He is a founding member of *A Metropolitan Guide*. His albums include *Pioneering* and *Lesser Tragedies*.

Kristen Franz has worked on the editorial staff of Impressions and ELM. Currently, she is pursuing a degree in writing.

Stephen Powers is an associate professor at Gordon State College. His works have appeared in *Shenandoah*, *Main Street Rag*, *Natural Bridge*, and *The Comstock Review*. His first book, *The Follower's Tale*, is a collection of bluegrass-inspired lyric and narrative poems about country music icon Dolly Parton and her theme park, Dollywood. It was published by Salmon Poetry in 2009. His second book, *Hello, Stephen*, was published by Salmon Poetry in 2014. He holds a PhD from the University of Wisconsin-Milwaukee.